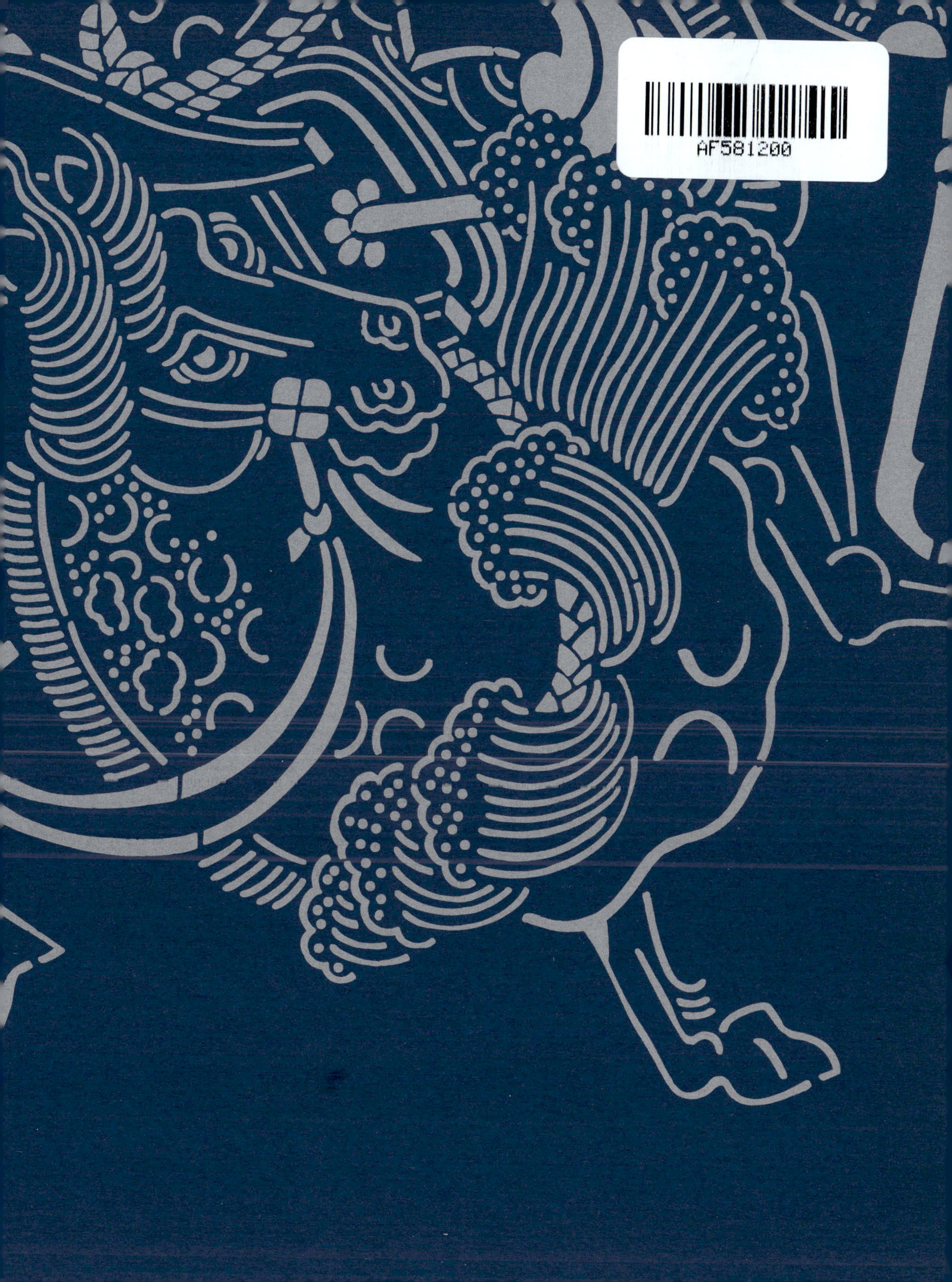

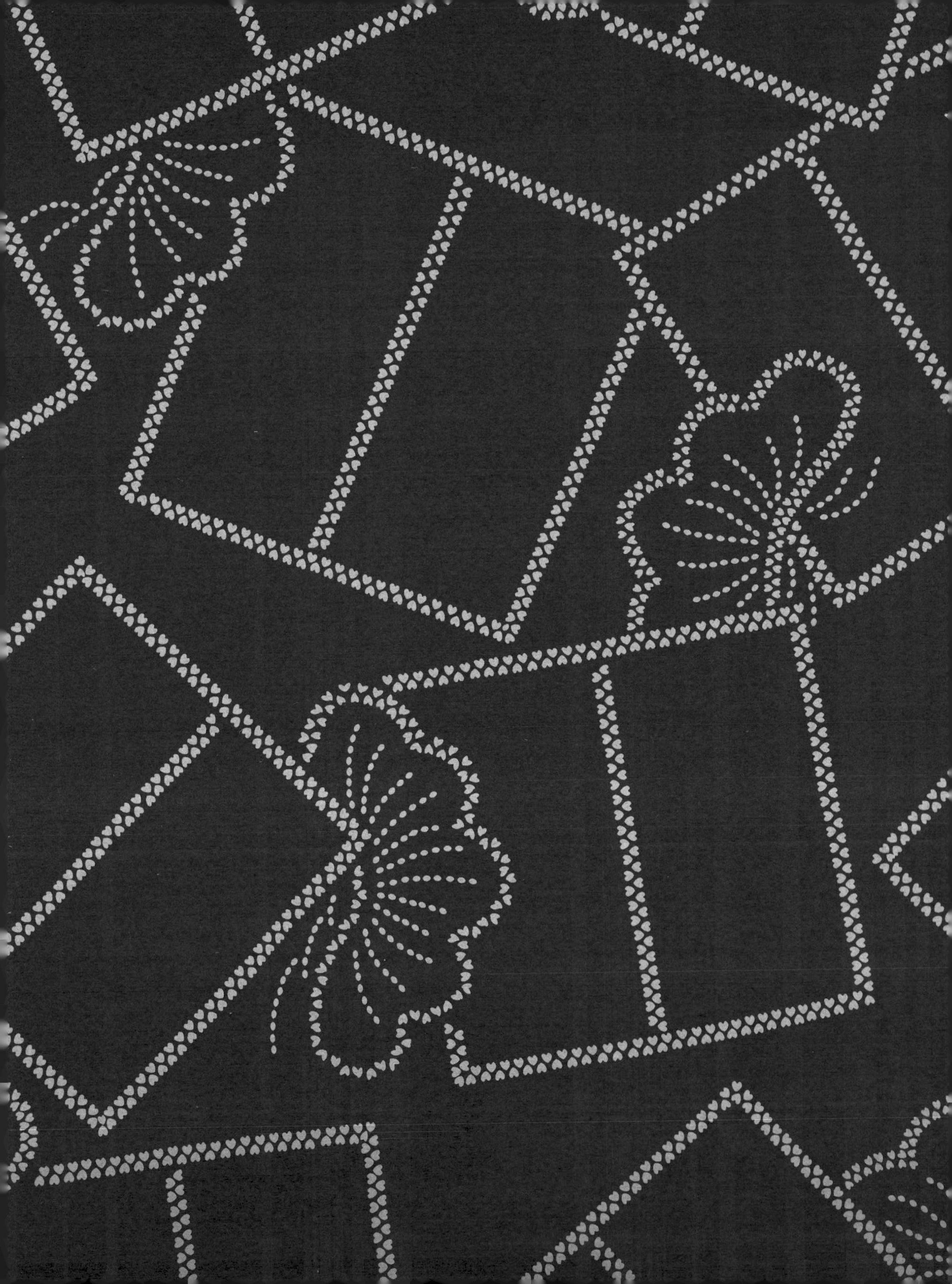

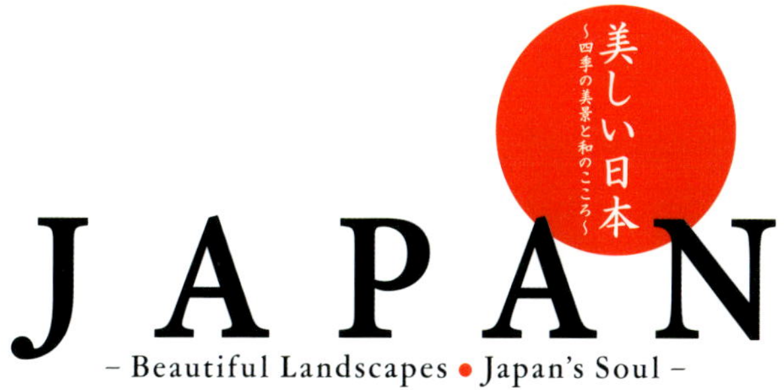

ナツメ社

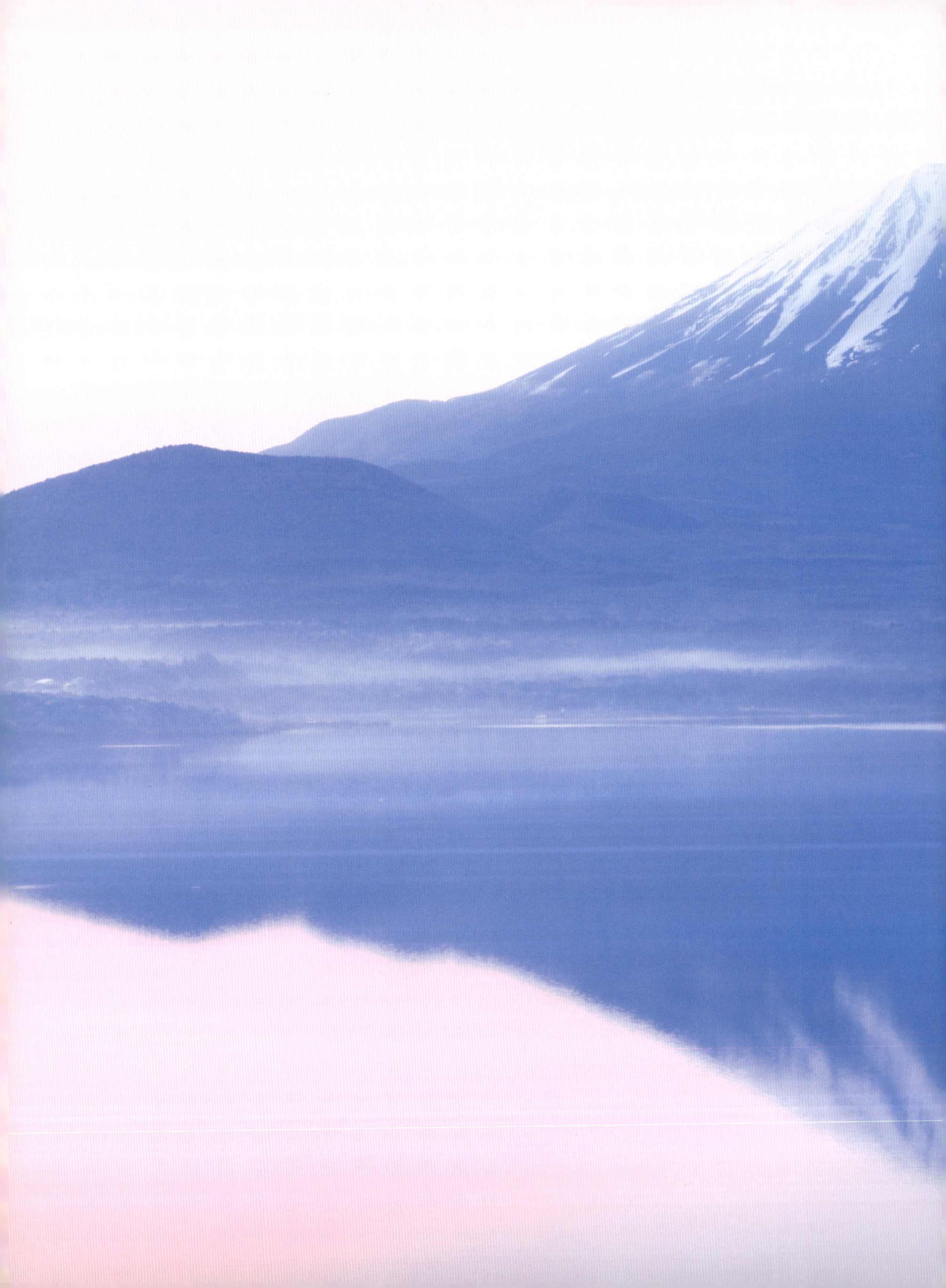

Imprint

Photographs by amanaimages
Text by Seino Hiroshi, Hori Masatoshi, Otaki Michiko, Hasebe Yuko
Translation by Bilingual Group Ltd.
Emendation by Sophie Knight
Design by Okamura Daisuke
DTP by Meisho-do

Published by Natsumesha CO., LTD.
Natsumesha Building. 3F, 1-52 Kanda-Jimbocho
Chiyoda-ku, Tokyo 101-0051
http://www.natsume.co.jp

First Edition 30 December 2014
ISBN 978-4-8163-5731-2
Printed in Japan

Contents

Introduction Section

The F●ur

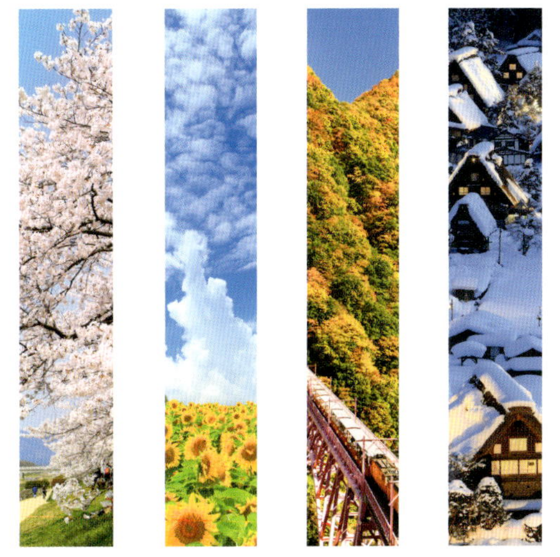

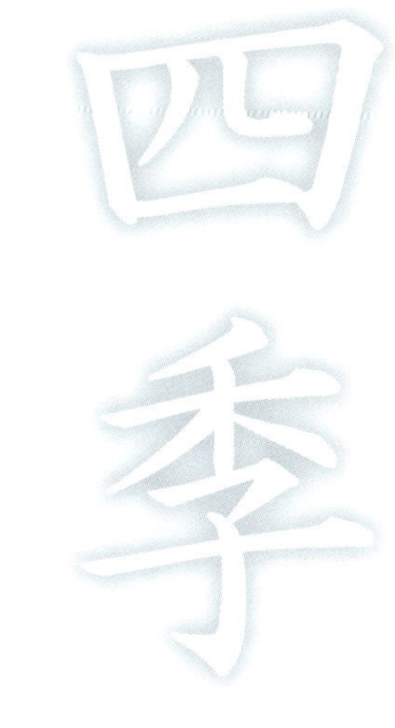

Seasons

Spring

春

In Japan people feel that spring has arrived when the plum trees and cherry trees bloom. Japan even has what is called a cherry-blossom 'front' when, from late March through April, the blossoming of the cherry trees starts in the south and gradually works its way north, up the Japanese archipelago, with cherry trees in different regions blooming slightly apart from each other. Koizumi Yakumo (Lafcadio Hearn), a British journalist who was born in Greece, wrote the following: *With us, a plum or cherry tree in flower is not an astonishing sight; but here it is a miracle of beauty...* (*Glimpses of Unfamiliar Japan*).

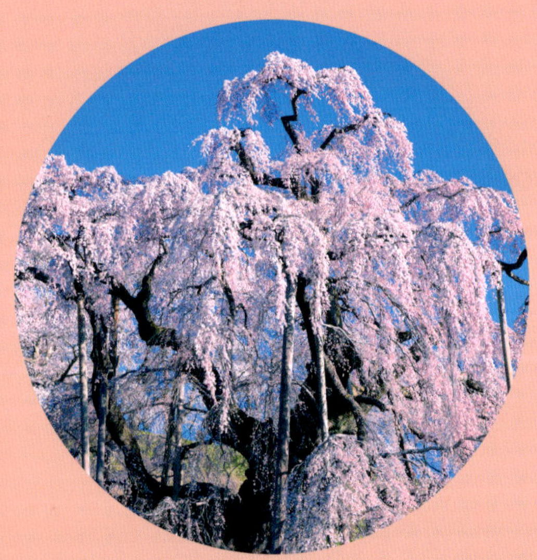

Miharu Takizakura / FUKUSHIMA

Miharu Takizakura (literally, *waterfall cherry tree of Miharu*) is one of the largest cherry trees in Japan, located in the town of Miharu, Fukushima Prefecture.
It is a weeping higan cherry (Prunus pendula *Pendula Rosea*) and is estimated to be over 1,000 years old. With a height of 13.5 meters and a circumference of 11.3 meters at its base, it has a formidable presence.
© TAKAHIRO MIYAMOTO

Somei-yoshino

Somei-yoshino (*Prunus x yedoensis*) is the national flower of Japan as well as the official metropolitan flower of Tokyo. Somei-yoshino was the species of cherry tree planted the most in Japan in the middle of Meiji Period (late 1800s) and is the most commonly seen at cherry blossom viewing parties nowadays. Before the leaves appear, pale-pink flowers completely cover the branches and the sight is breathtakingly beautiful. © daj

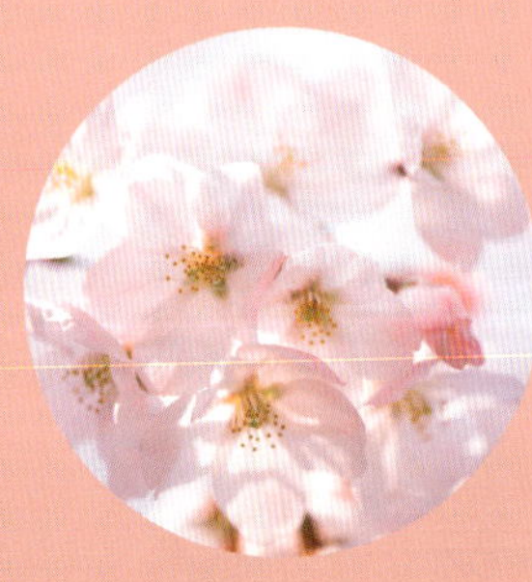

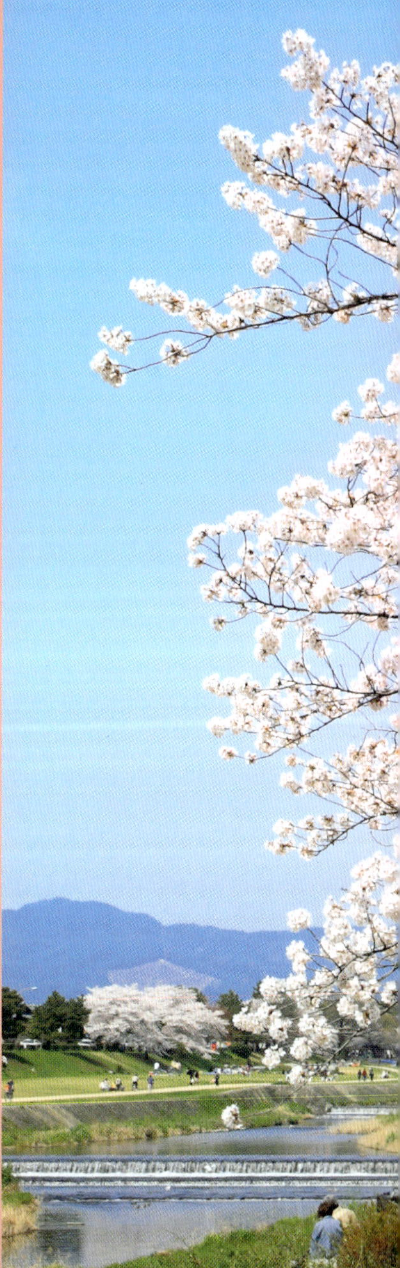

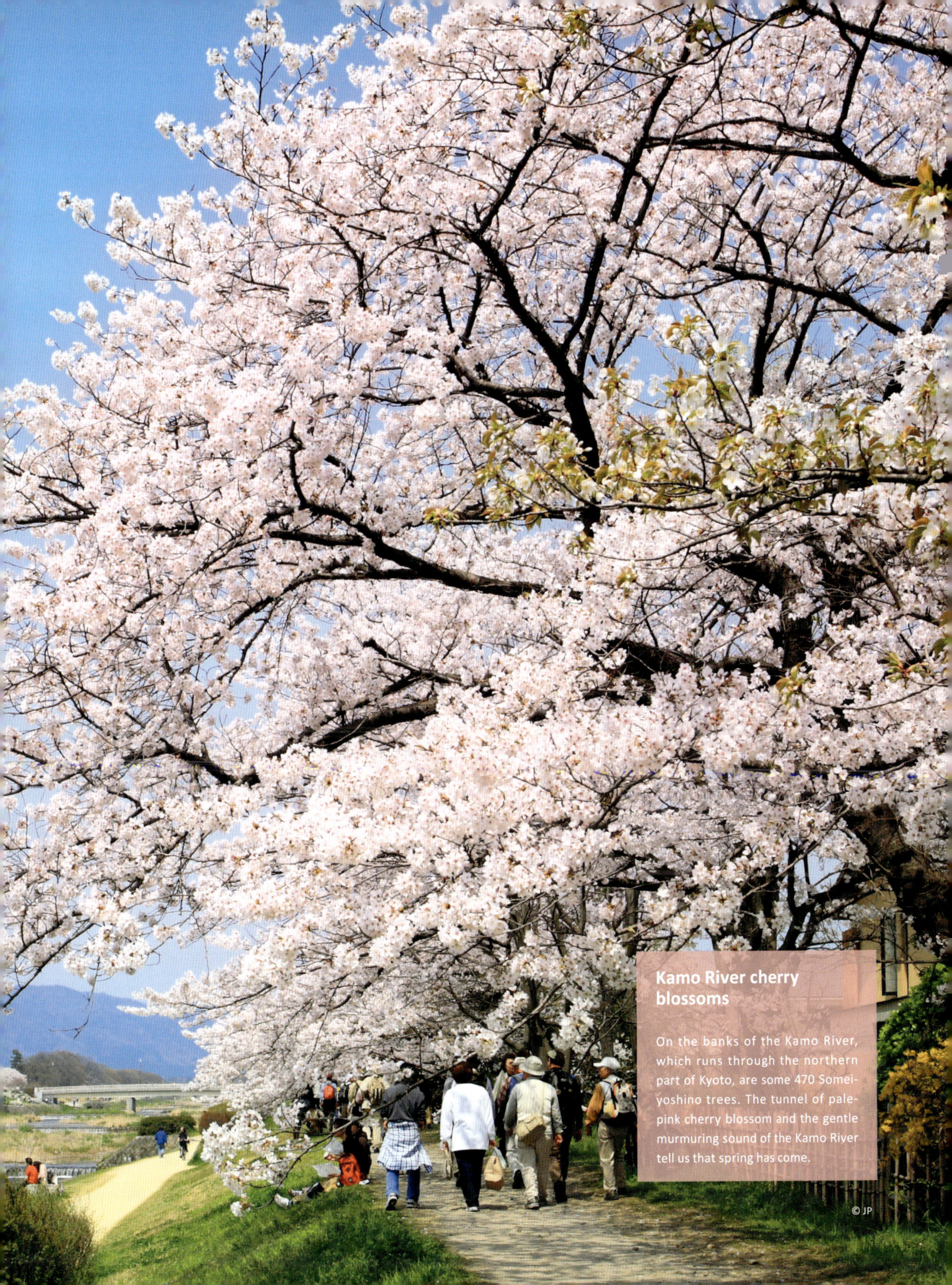

Kamo River cherry blossoms

On the banks of the Kamo River, which runs through the northern part of Kyoto, are some 470 Somei-yoshino trees. The tunnel of pale-pink cherry blossom and the gentle murmuring sound of the Kamo River tell us that spring has come.

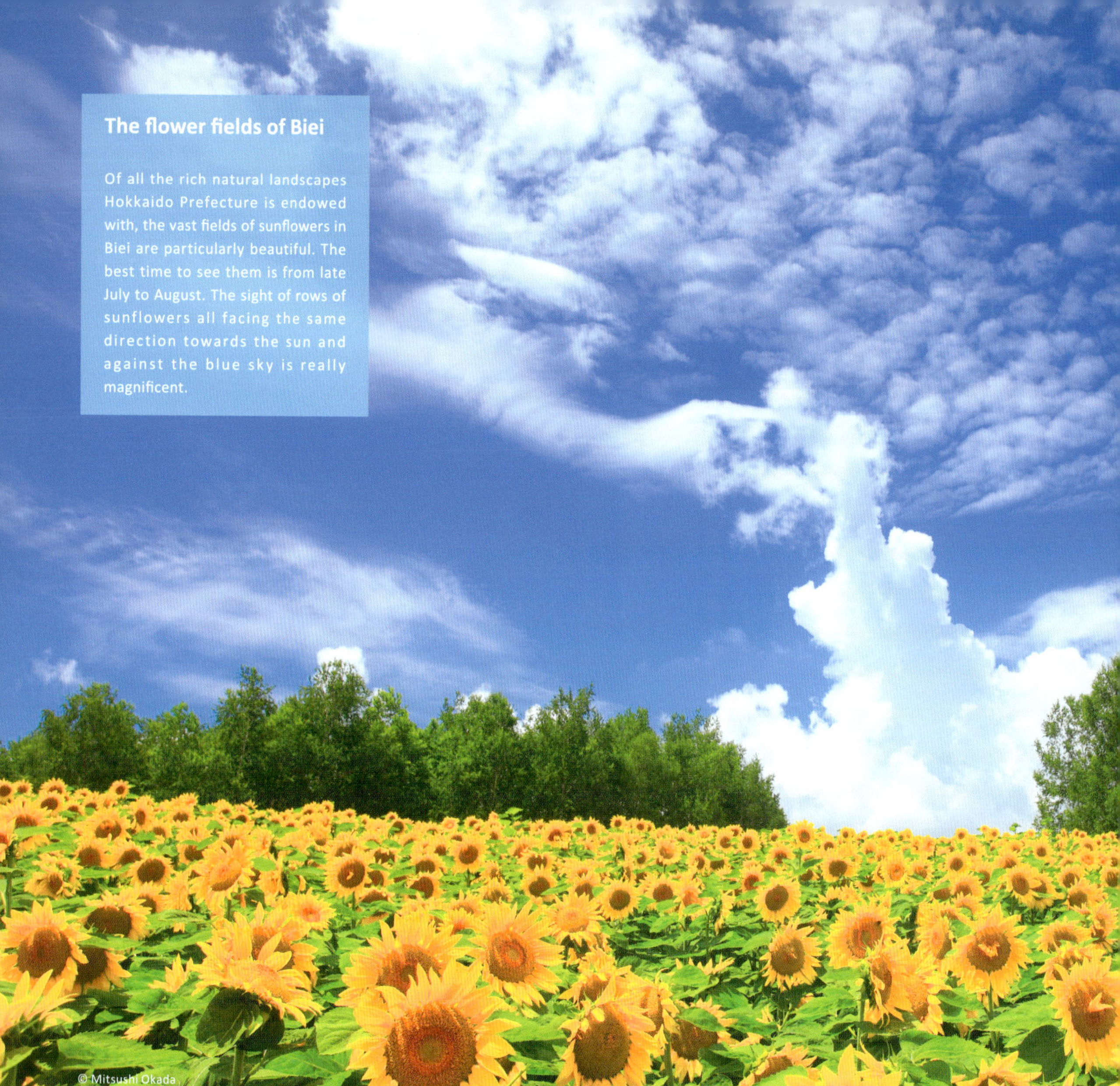

© Mitsushi Okada

The flower fields of Biei

Of all the rich natural landscapes Hokkaido Prefecture is endowed with, the vast fields of sunflowers in Biei are particularly beautiful. The best time to see them is from late July to August. The sight of rows of sunflowers all facing the same direction towards the sun and against the blue sky is really magnificent.

Summer

In *haiku*, the world's shortest fixed form of verse with 17 syllables, *kigo* are defined words or phrases that symbolize or imply the season of the poem. *Kigo* must be used at least once in a *haiku*. The phrase *natsu-kodachi* is a *kigo* representing summer. It refers to a grove of trees brimming with life in summer as their green leaves grow thick under the strong rays of the summer sun. From *natsu-kodachi* we can hear *semi-shigure* (a loud chorus of cicadas). *Semi-shigure*, also a summer *kigo*, likens the sound of many cicadas singing together to the sound of a shower of rain.
Japanese people feel summer to be at its zenith when they are resting in the summer shade of *natsu-kodachi* and listening to *semi-shigure*.

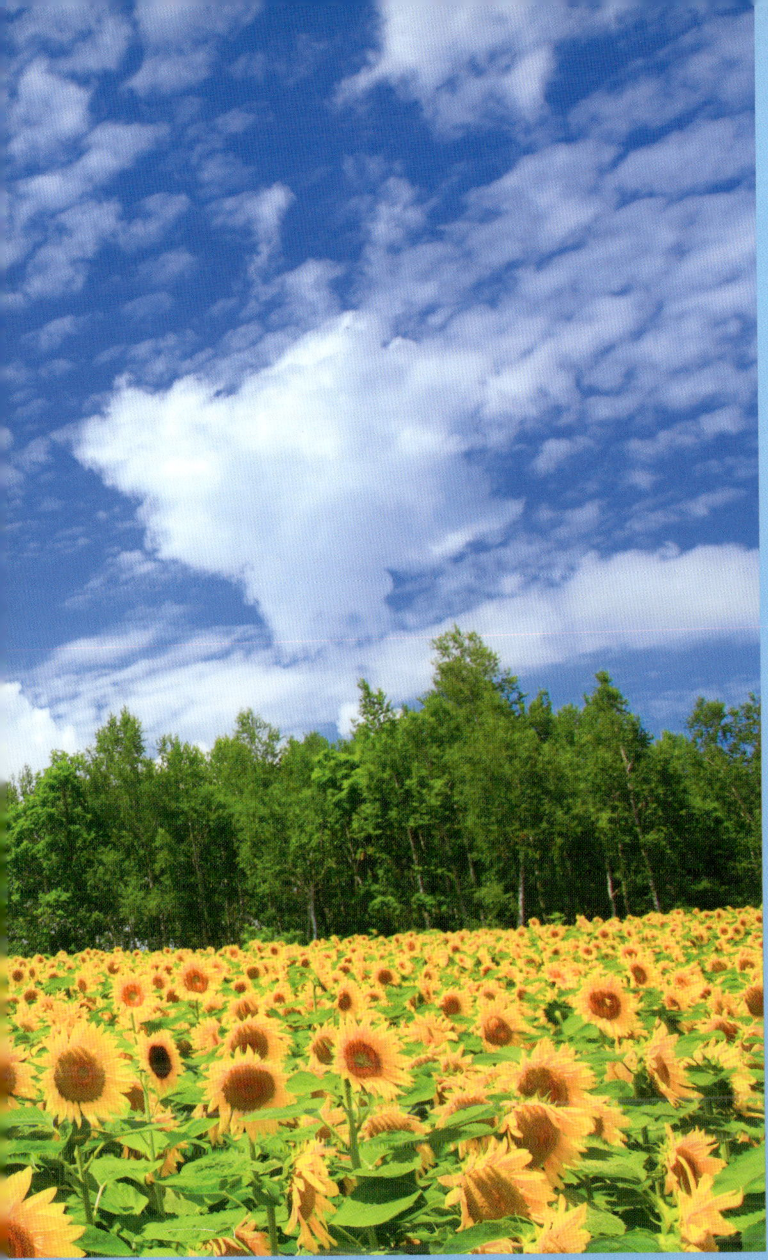

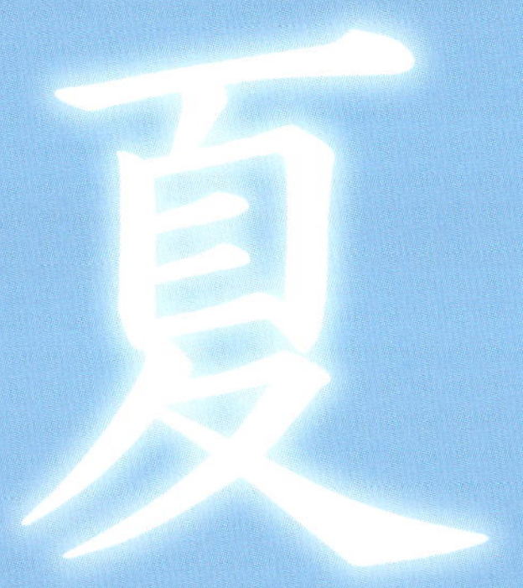

HANABI (fireworks)

Fireworks are a special attraction of summer in Japan. It is not an exaggeration to say that Japanese techniques for fireworks are the most sophisticated and splendid in the whole world. This is because of the traditional expertise that is passed on generation to generation by skilled fireworks experts.

© IWAO KATAOKA

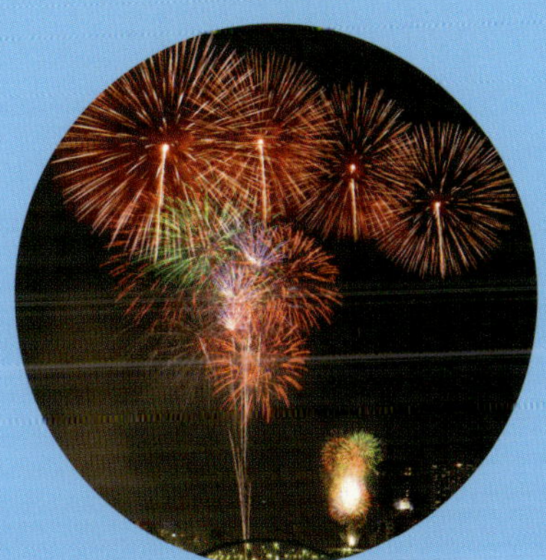

Yukata

Yukata are a kind of kimono but differ to regular kimono as *yukata* are worn directly over the skin, with no lining. People like *yukata* because they are more casual than kimono. Nowadays they are worn mostly to fireworks displays, summer festivals, *bon-odori* (dance) festivals and so on. *Yukata* are very easy to wear and are quite popular with foreign tourists, too.

© R. CREATION

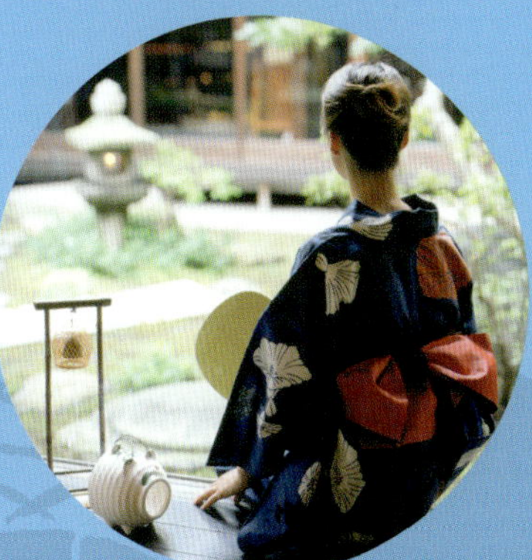

Autumn

The sun on the waterfall sparkled and in front of me, were trees with leaves of dazzling colors. Looking at these leaves with the sun shining on them, I really felt I would get dizzy from the sight of it.

In 1895, the wife of the Belgian envoy to Japan wrote this in her journal after visiting Lake Chuzenji in Nikko, where the autumn foliage is particularly beautiful. This lady was involved in creative activities and wrote poems and novels. It seems that when she saw for the first time leaves that were deep red, crimson, scarlet and bright yellow, colors not seen in autumn foliage in the West, she was so deeply impressed that it was difficult to find words to describe it.

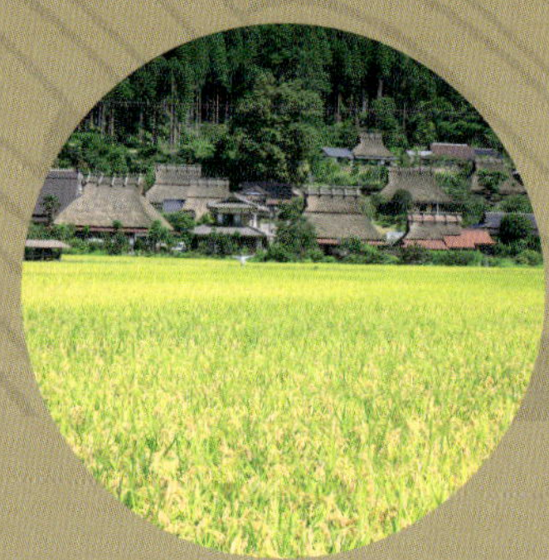

Rice fields

Golden ears of rice swaying in the breeze tell us that autumn has come. A countryside scene of rice fields is said to be the archetypal image of Japan and evokes a feeling of nostalgia.

秋

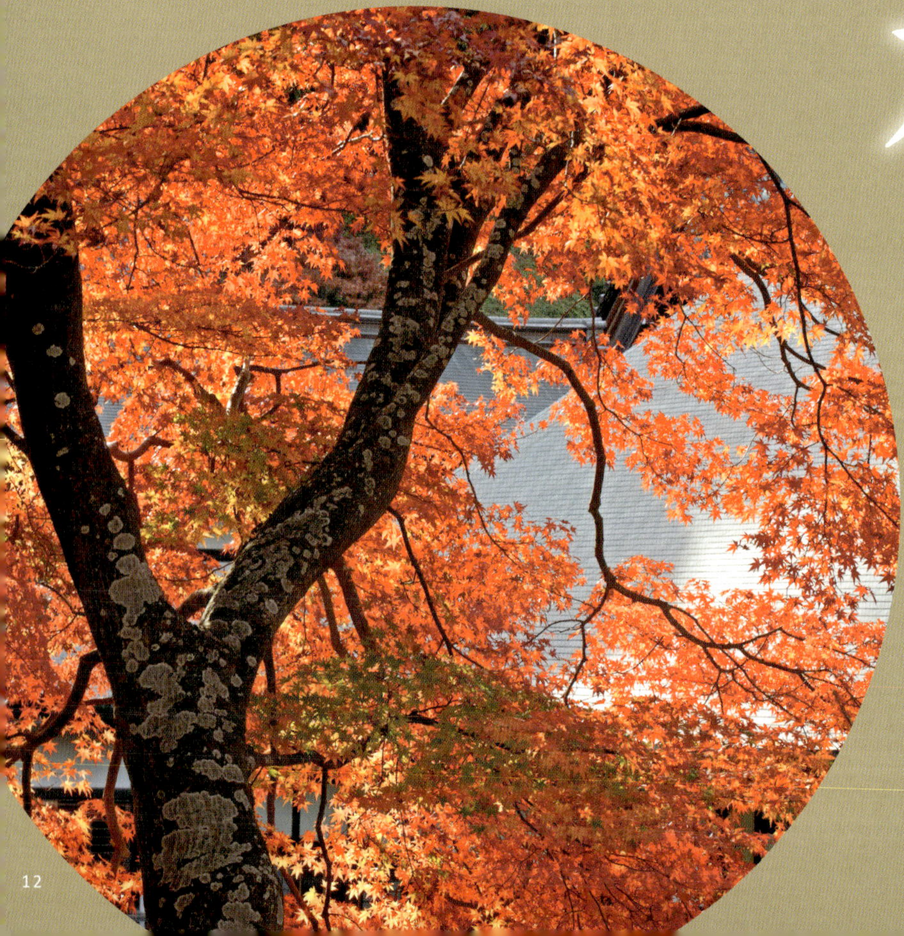

Kencho-ji (kencho Temple)

Kencho-ji, located in the city of Kamakura in Kanagawa Prefecture, is famous for being the oldest Zen training monastery in Japan. The sight of autumn leaves on the huge trees in the temple grounds, framed against the blue sky, is splendid. The best time for viewing the autumn colors is from mid-November to mid-December.

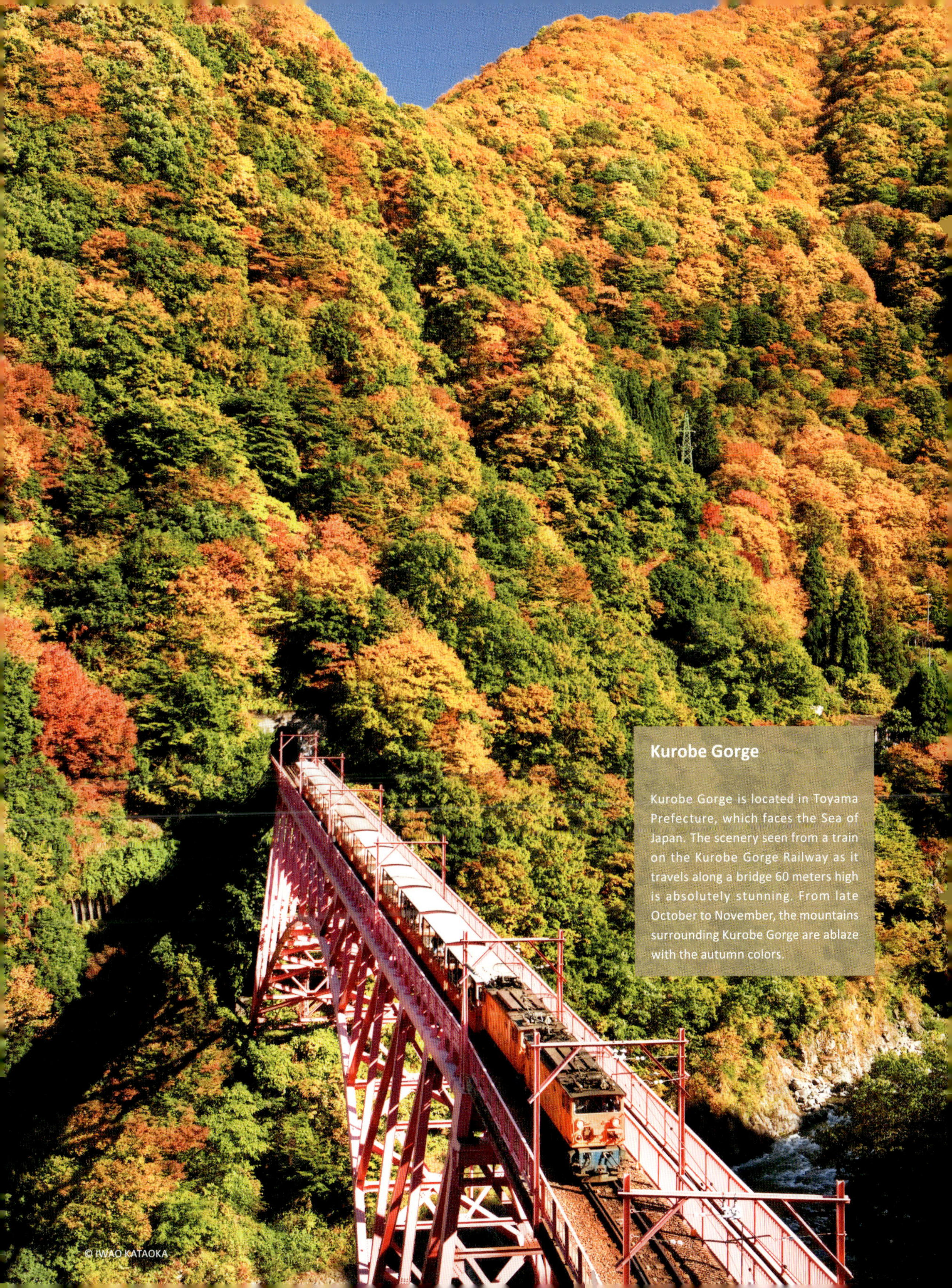

Kurobe Gorge

Kurobe Gorge is located in Toyama Prefecture, which faces the Sea of Japan. The scenery seen from a train on the Kurobe Gorge Railway as it travels along a bridge 60 meters high is absolutely stunning. From late October to November, the mountains surrounding Kurobe Gorge are ablaze with the autumn colors.

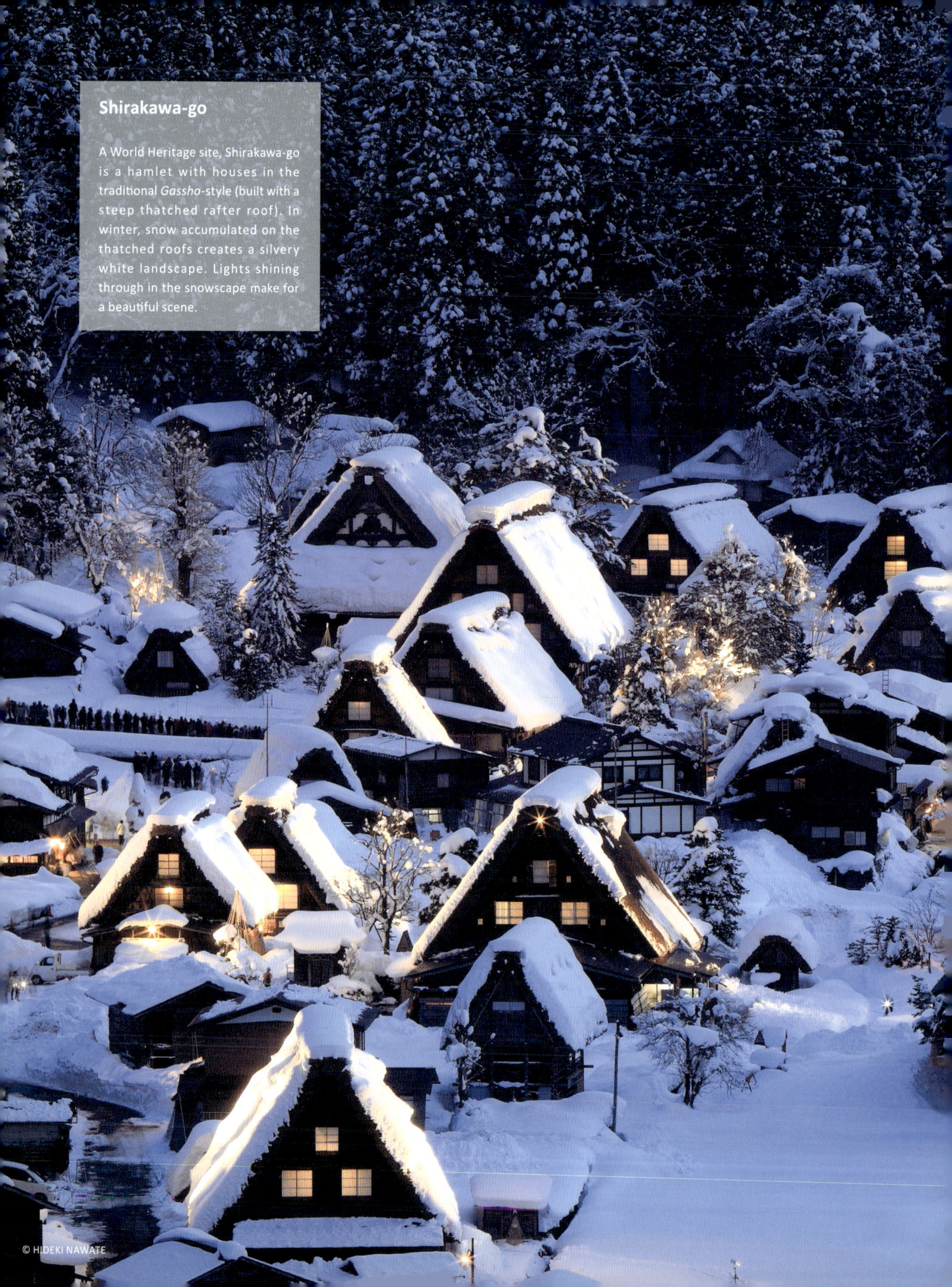

Shirakawa-go

A World Heritage site, Shirakawa-go is a hamlet with houses in the traditional *Gassho*-style (built with a steep thatched rafter roof). In winter, snow accumulated on the thatched roofs creates a silvery white landscape. Lights shining through in the snowscape make for a beautiful scene.

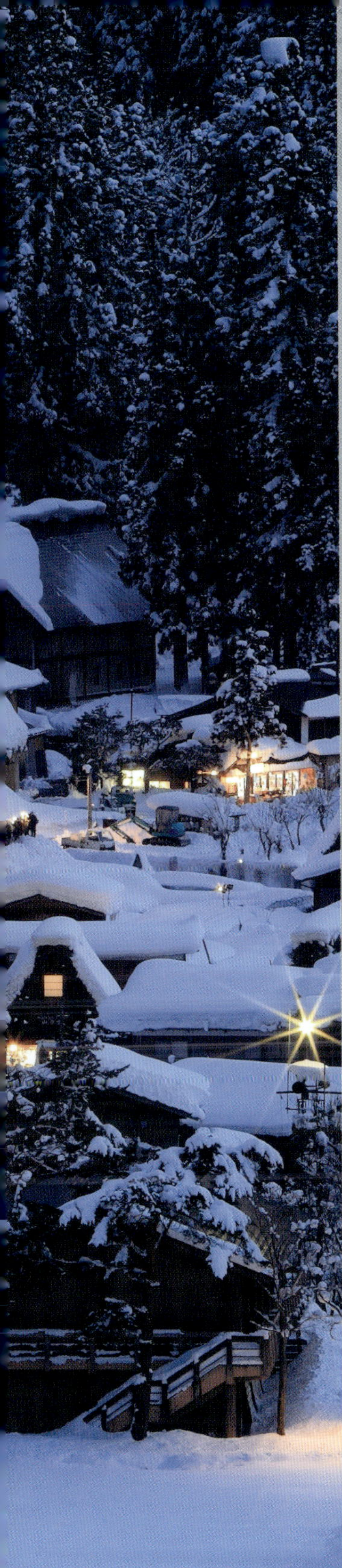

Winter 冬

Snow falls over a wide area of Japan in winter, although the amount of snow varies from place to place. Perhaps because of that, from ancient times the Japanese language has developed distinctive expressions for snow such as *konayuki* (powder snow), *zarameyuki* (granular snow), *awayuki* (light snow), *tamayuki* (ball-shaped snowflakes), and so on. Other Japanese expressions for snow liken it to *hana* (flowers) such as *yukihana* (snow decorating the plants and trees like blossoms), and *botanyuki* (large, fluffy snowflakes).

Beautiful Japanese expressions include *yukiakari* which refers to the faint light at night from snow accumulated on the ground; and *ginsekai* or 'silver world' which refers to a landscape mantled in snow. When the landscape takes on a pure white appearance as it is covered by a blanket of snow, it is called *yukigesho* in Japanese.

Mount Fuji

Mount Fuji is Japan's highest mountain and is not part of a mountain range. When snow covers Mount Fuji's summit, the mountain has a commanding presence.

From ancient times, Japanese people have worshipped various creations of nature as being precious. Mount Fuji has long been an object of worship.

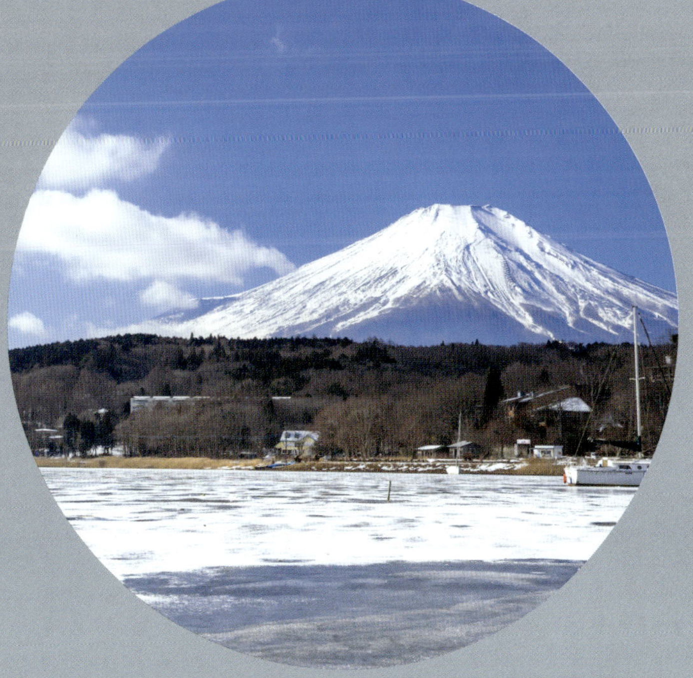

Chapter1

Scenery of Japan

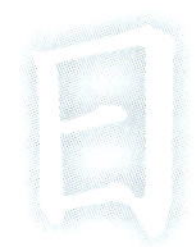

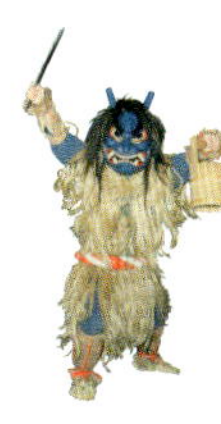

HOKKAIDO • TOHOKU Region

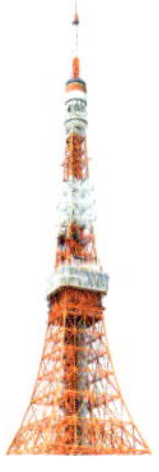

KANTO • CHUBU Region

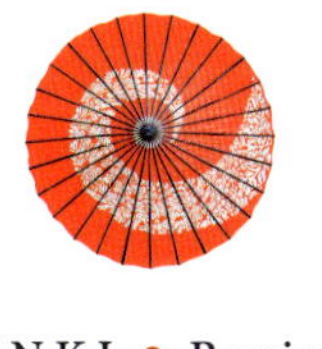

KINKI • Region

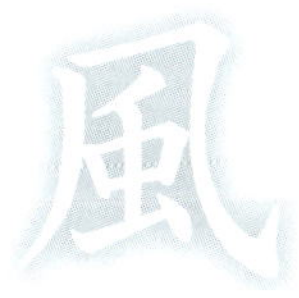

CHUGOKU • SHIKOKU Region

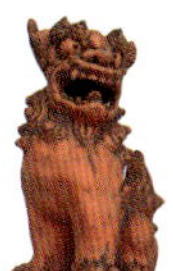

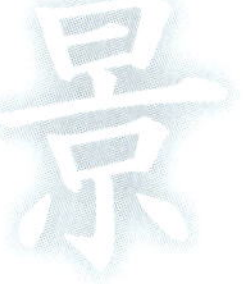

KYUSHU • OKINAWA Region

北海道・東北地方

HOKKAIDO/ TOHOKU Region

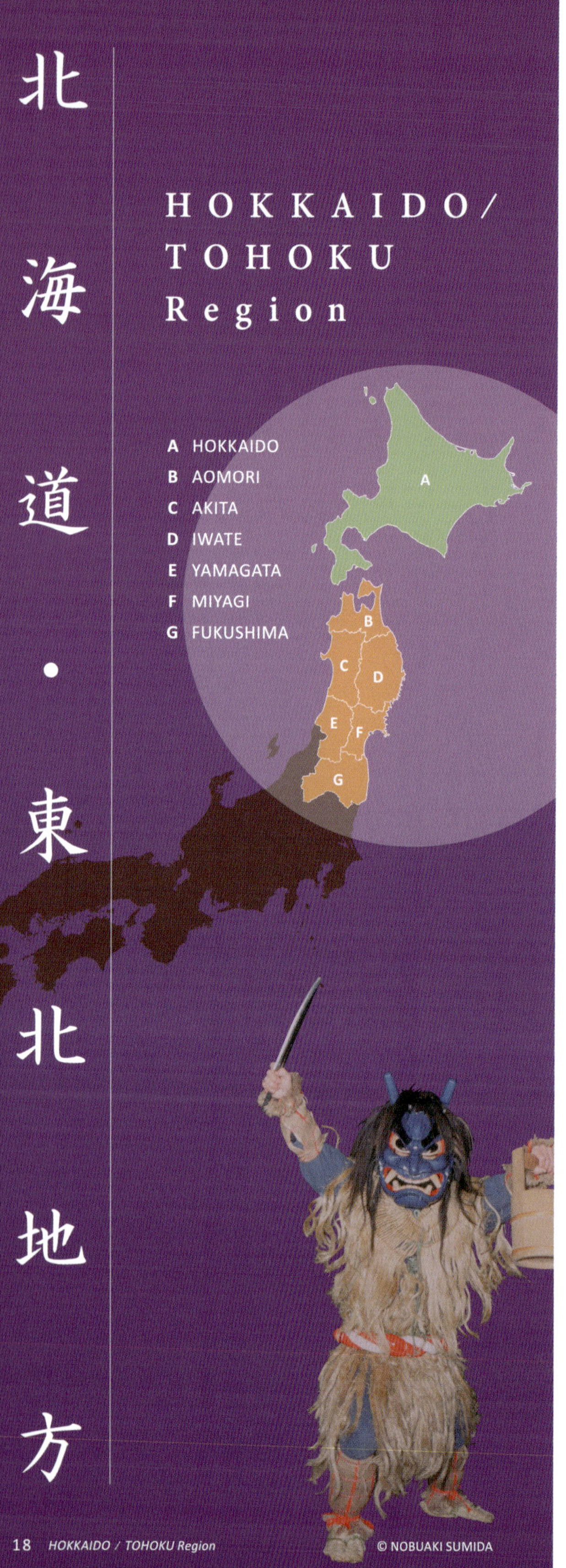

© NOBUAKI SUMIDA

Area located in Northern Japan. Scenes of expansive natural beauty, with the broad horizon against the blue sky.

Hokkaido Prefecture and the six prefectures of Aomori, Akita, Iwate, Yamagata, Miyagi, and Fukushima that comprise the Tohoku region, have a harsh environment and experience heavy snow throughout, with the exception of the Pacific coastal areas of some of the prefectures. At the same time, however, the abundant scenic rural areas, with tall mountains, national parks, and areas such as Shiretoko and the Shirakami-Sanchi, which are also World Natural Heritage sites, are also a distinctive characteristic of the region.

Hokkaido and the Tohoku region are also famous for the abundance of foods and other natural products found in their oceans and their mountains, which draws large numbers of tourists.

The area has long been predominantly rural, as well, and visitors are likely to feel the warmth of the people living there.

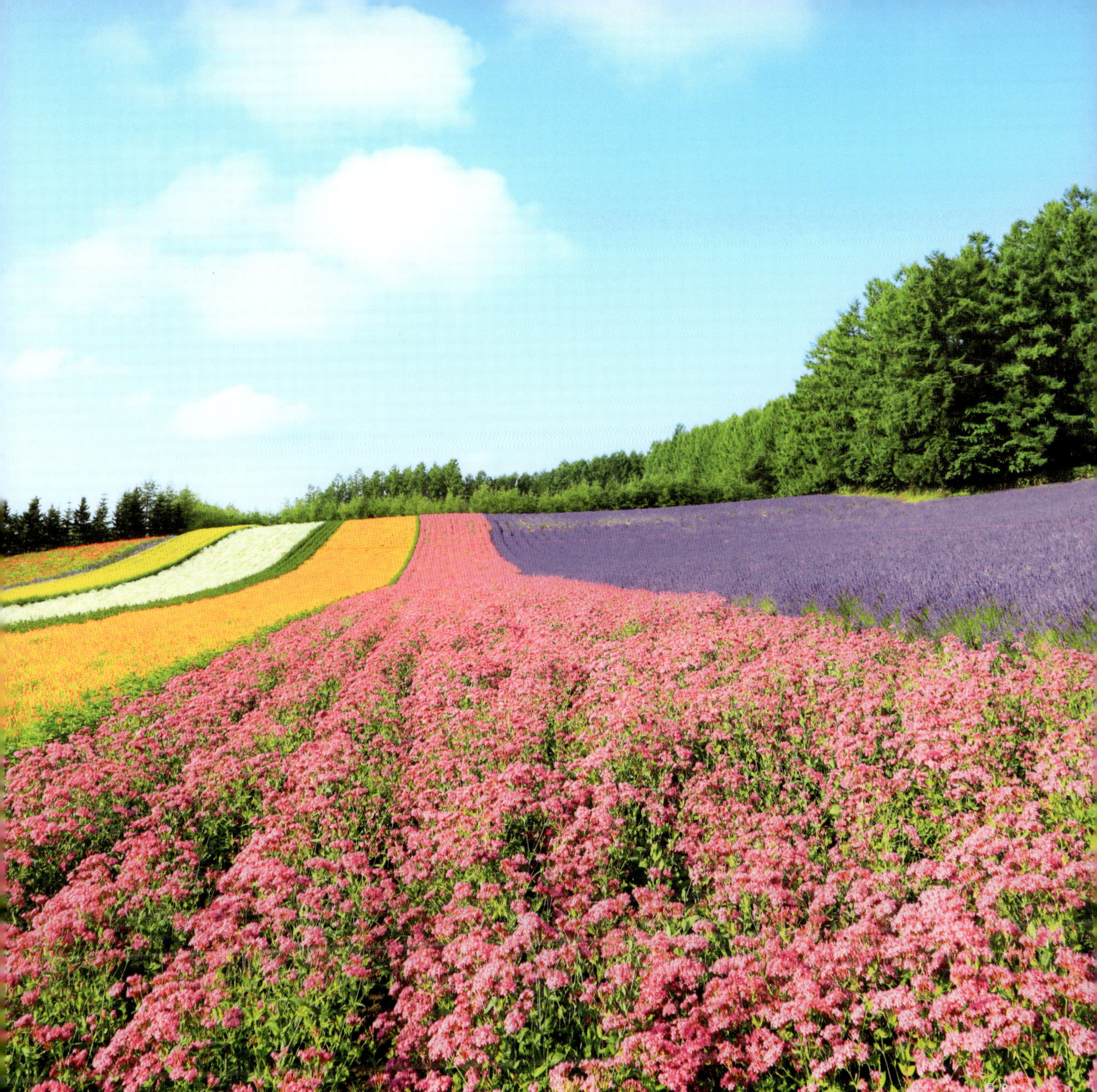

撮影地：ファーム富田

The flower fields of Furano ■ HOKKAIDO

Hokkaido Prefecture experiences extremely cold winters but in July, the lavender fields in Furano bloom profusely telling us that a warmer season has arrived. Lavender's elegant purple flowers and its rich fragrance blowing in the pleasant breeze charm visitors to the fields in Furano.

At the tourist farm, poppies, cosmos, marigolds, salvias and lupines all compete with each other for space on the gentle slope where they bloom. The magnificent scene, together with the Tokachi mountain range in the background, makes those who view it feel at peace.

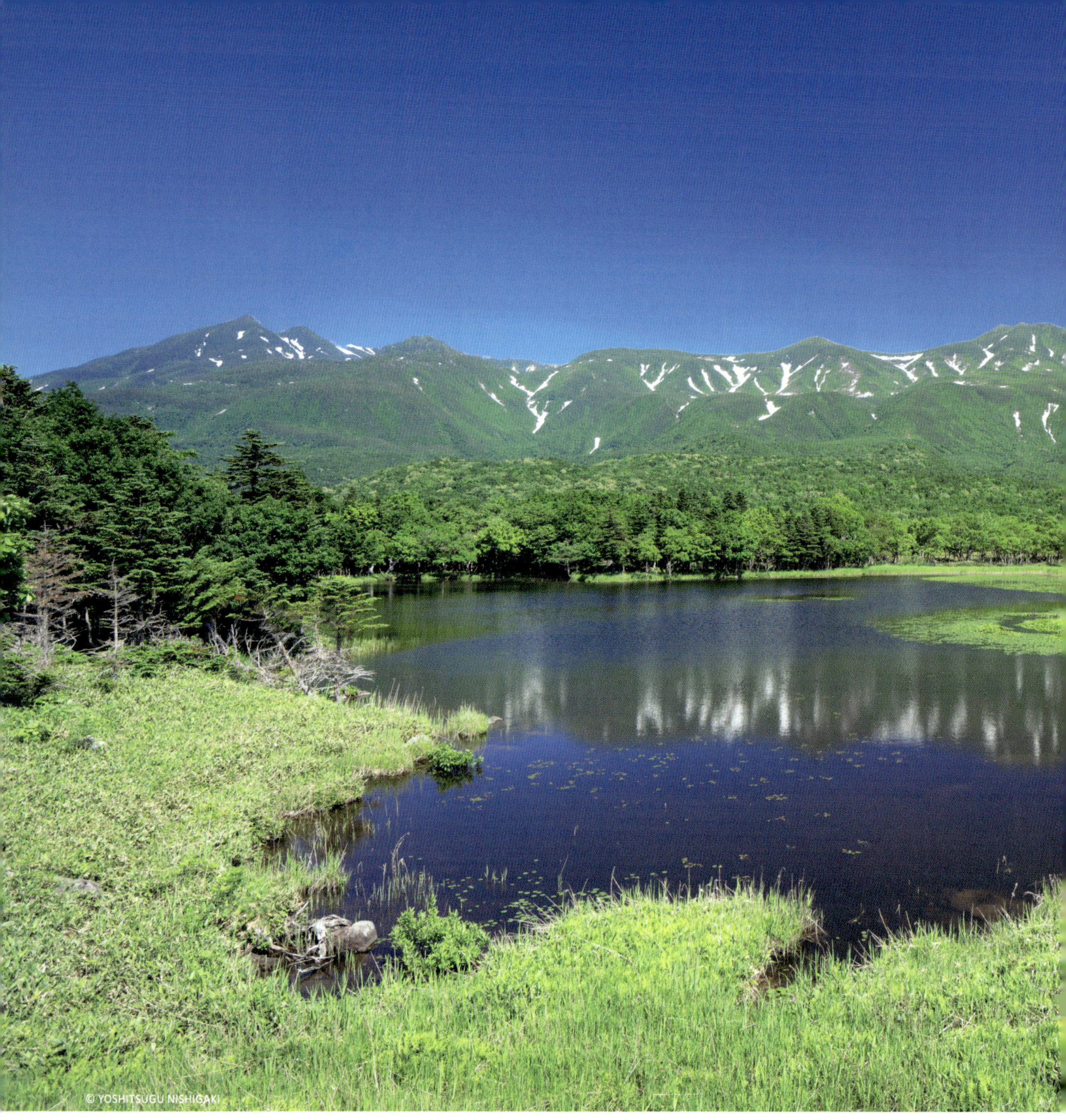

Shiretoko
■ HOKKAIDO

The rich ecosystem of Shiretoko has been preserved mainly because of its complex terrain encompassing both sea and land areas. In 2005, Shiretoko was added to the World Heritage list. As well as being a habitat for larger mammals including brown bears, Hokkaido shika deer, Steller sea lions and seals, Shiretoko is also a breeding ground for internationally rare species such as Blakiston's fish owls, Steller sea eagles and white-tailed sea eagles. Shiretoko has many scenic spots including Shiretoko Five Lakes with the Shiretoko mountain range reflected on their lake surface; Furepe Falls, also known as *Otome-no-namida* (Maiden's Tears); and Oronoko Rock, a massive rock 60 meters high that stands out near the port of Utoro.

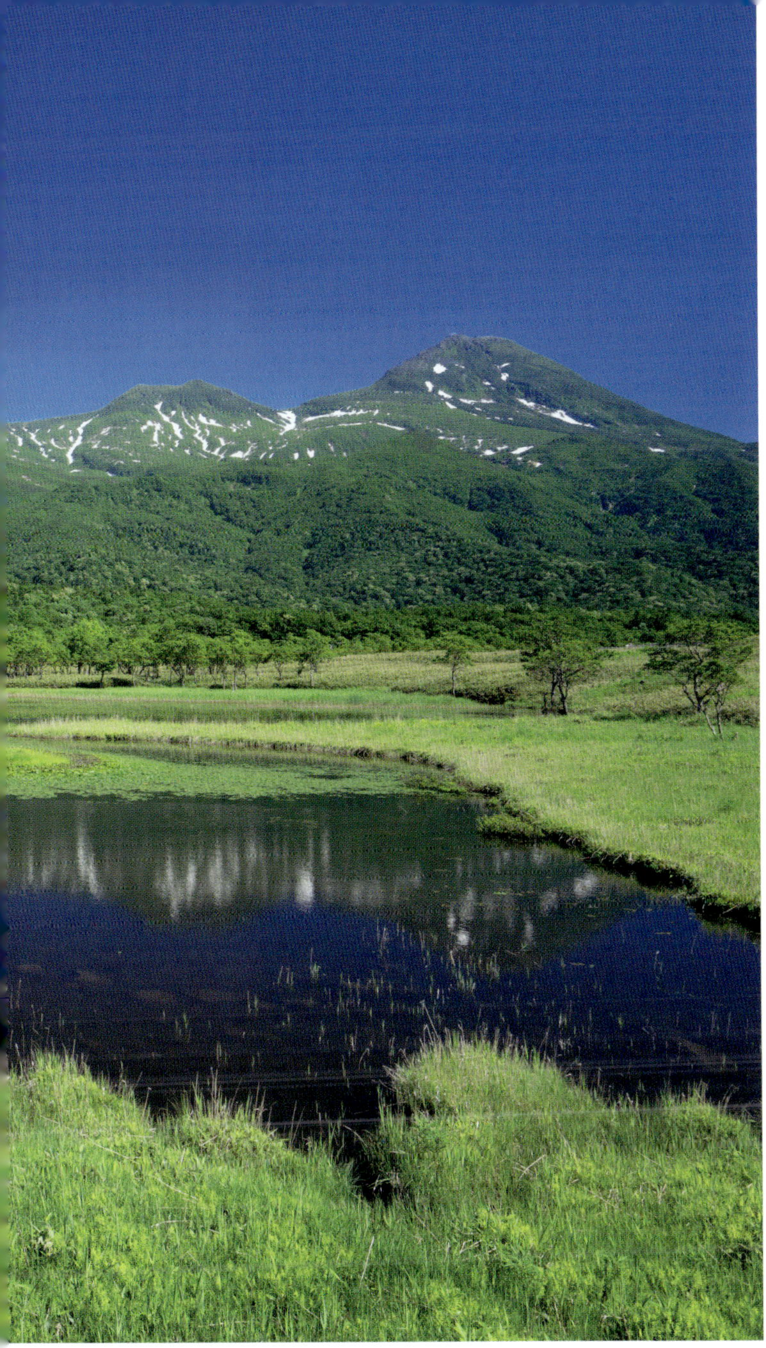

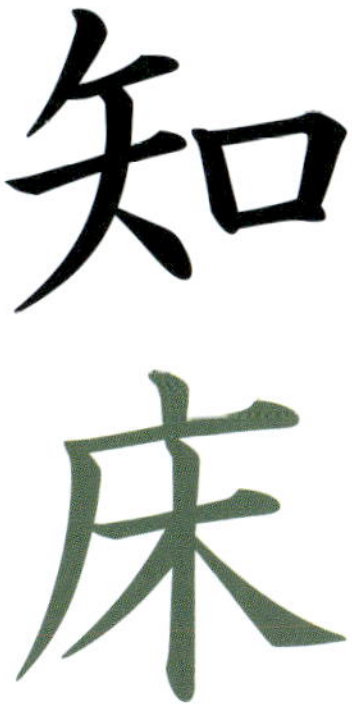

知床

Shiretoko drift ice

In January, floes of ice come floating down from the Amur River in Russia to the Shiretoko Peninsula. Gradually the Sea of Okhotsk becomes completely white from the pack ice formed by the compacted drift ice. The sheer cliffs of the Shiretoko coastline are a natural sculpture carved out the erosive action of the ice. The beautiful pattern woven by the blue ocean and the white ice signals the end of the harsh Shiretoko winter.

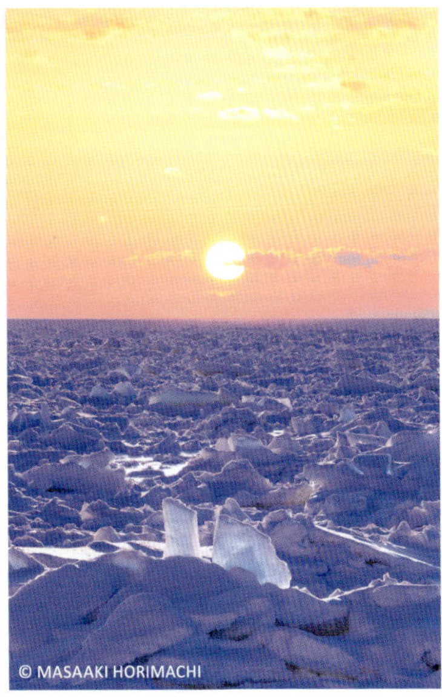

© MASAAKI HORIMACHI

Hakodate ▪ HOKKAIDO

函館

Mount Hakodate has an elevation of 334 meters and it takes just 3 minutes to reach the peak by the ropeway. The night view from the peak of the lights twinkling in the city and port areas is exceptional — it ranks along with Hong Kong and Naples as one of the three best night views in the world.

Sandwiched between the Tsugaru Straits and the port of Hakodate, the glittering city area on the narrow neck of land and the darkness of the ocean surrounding it create a stunning contrast. Moreover, looking down at an angle of 10° gives the effect of being able to reach out and touch the city lights sparkling like jewels in a jewel box, making the nightscape even more dramatic.

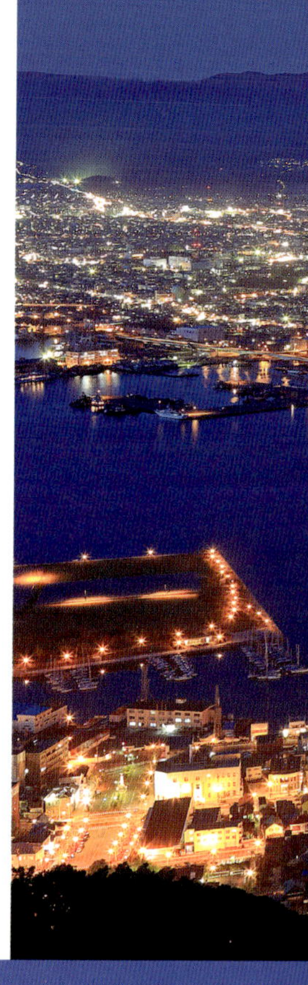

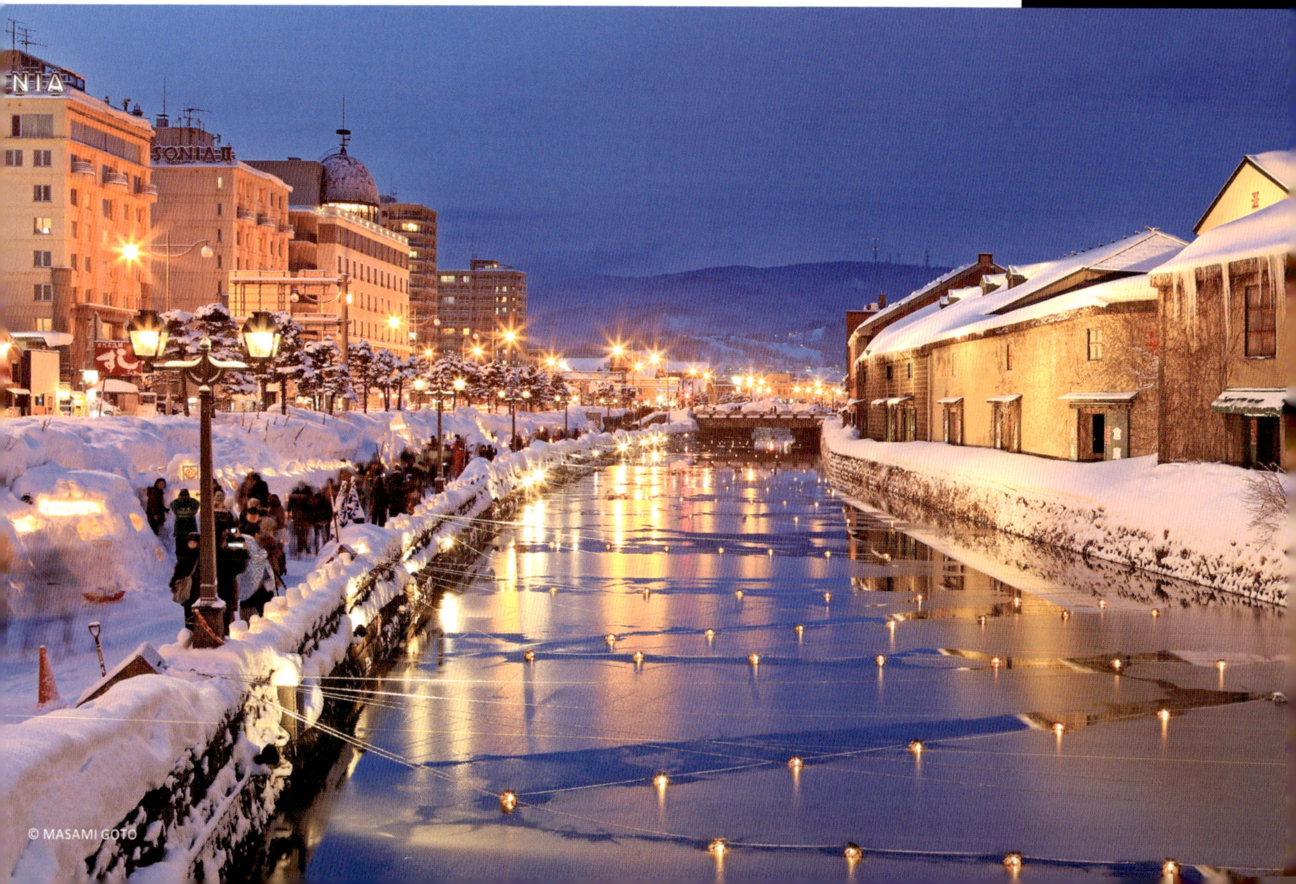

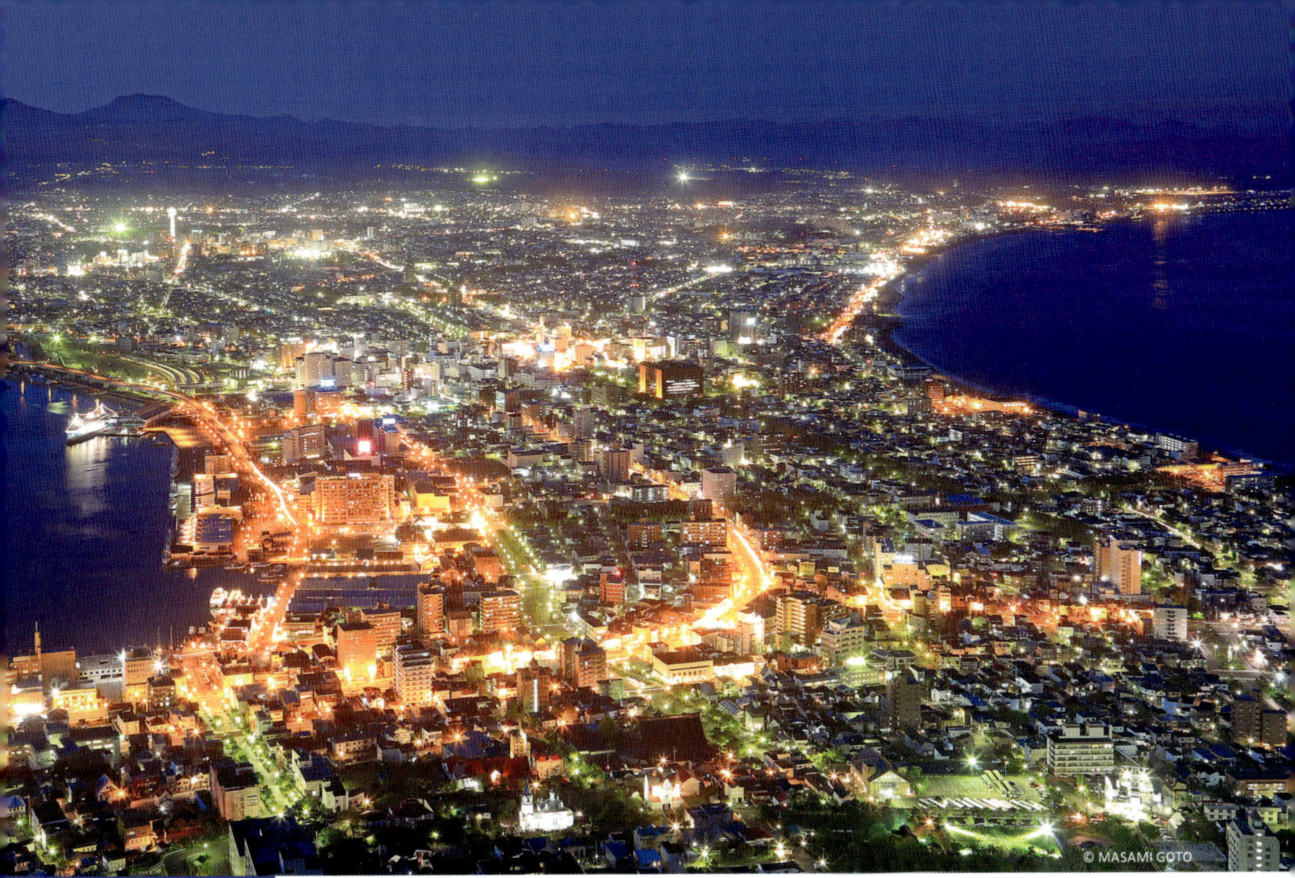

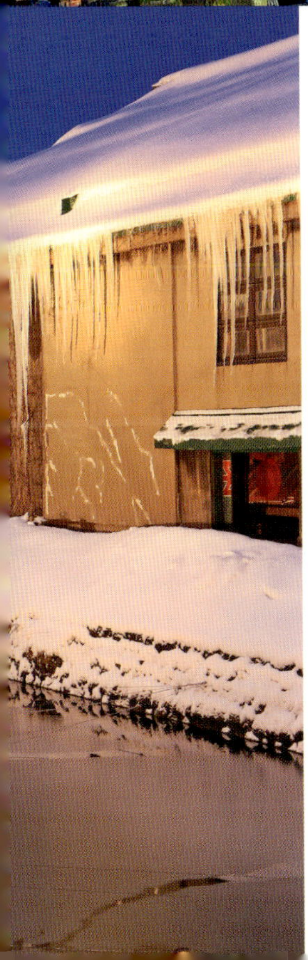

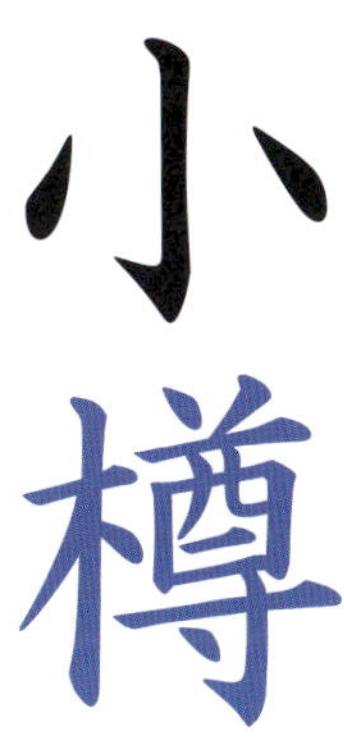

Otaru Canal ▪ HOKKAIDO

After the first railroad in Hokkaido Prefecture linked Otaru and Sapporo in 1880, Otaru became a shipping port for coal, timber, agricultural produce, etc. The canal was part of the town's development. However, times changed and since the canal's role became obsolete, it has been a popular tourist destination. Walking along the stone-paved promenade beside the canal, you can see the stone warehouses on the opposite bank reminding us of bygone times.

At dusk the old-fashion gas lamps are lit and their warm light shining on the old warehouses makes for a romantic atmosphere.

Goryokaku ■ HOKKAIDO

五稜郭

Goryokaku was built towards the end of the Edo Period (1864), in Hakodate, a frequent port of call for foreign ships. The reason Goryokaku is shaped like a star was to strengthen its defensive capacity as a fortress and it imitates the European style of castle construction. When Japan entered the Meiji Period in 1868, Goryokaku was the base of the Tokugawa shogunate army. It became the site of fierce fighting during the Battle of Hakodate which lasted for seven months.

Later Goryokaku became a park where the city's residents can relax and enjoy themselves. It has been designated as a Special Historical Site. A Japanese Red Pine tree planted when the fortress was built and estimated to be 150 years old, together with approximately 1,600 cherry trees make a pleasant sight for visitors to Goryokaku.

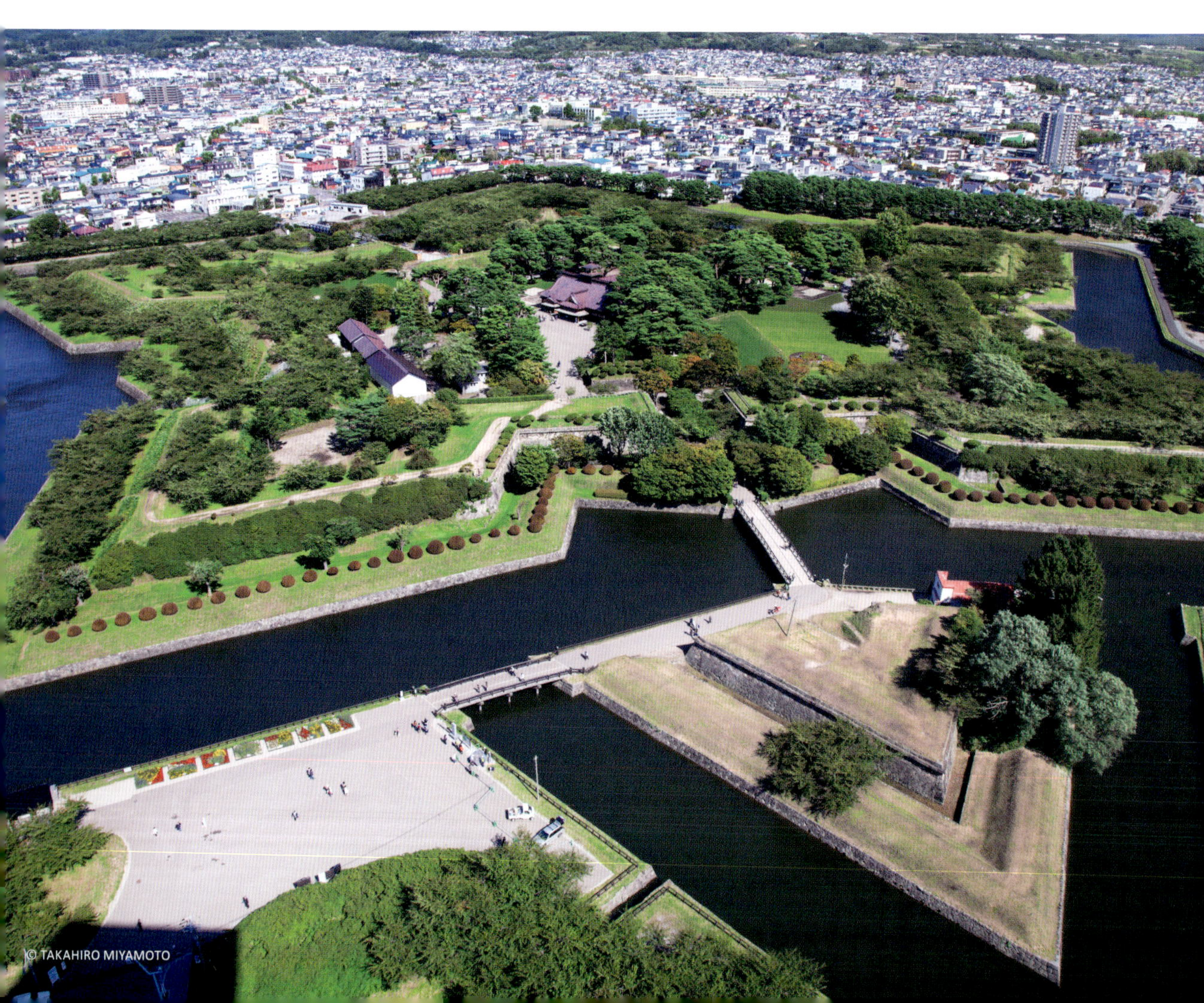

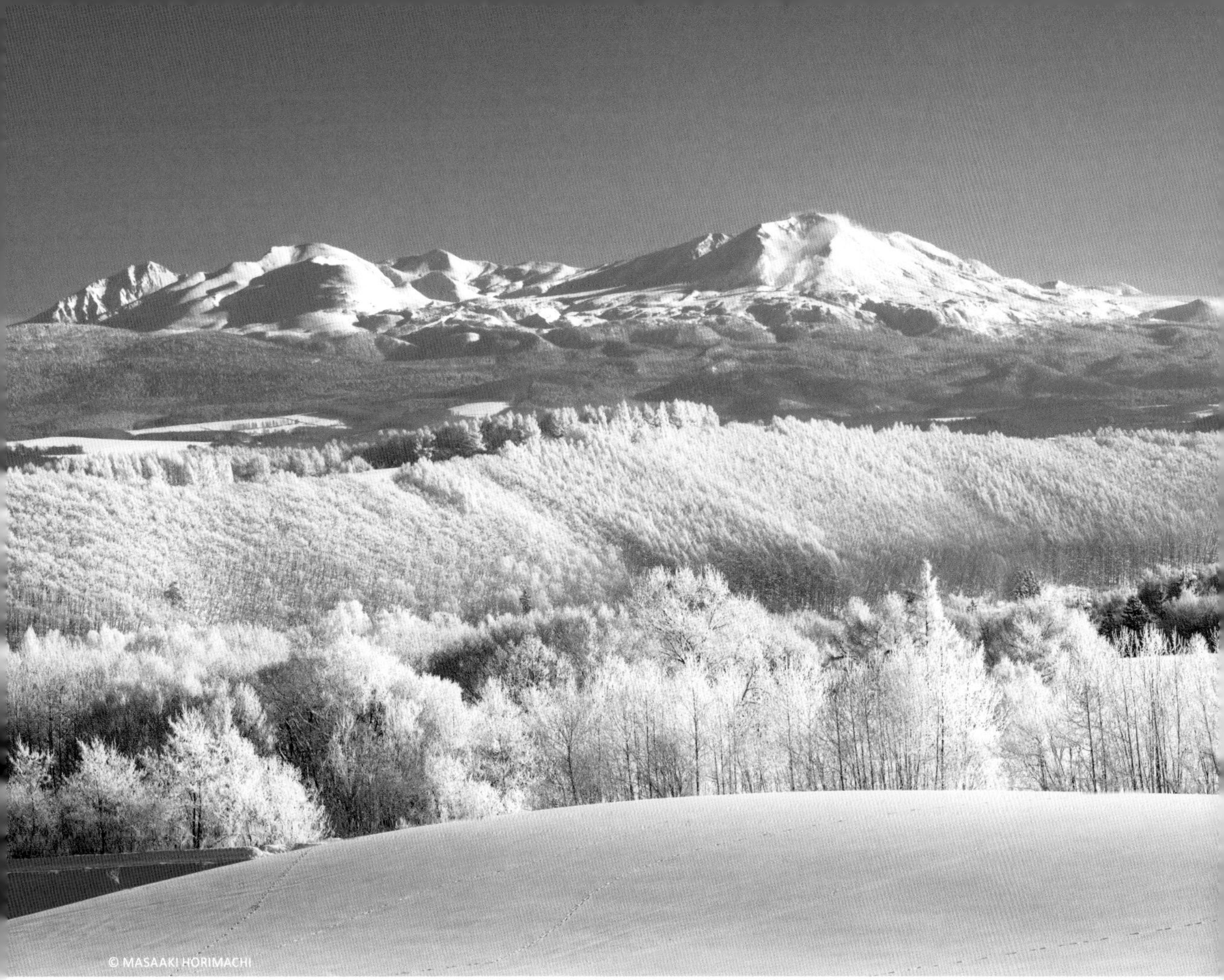

Daisctsuzan mountain range
■ HOKKAIDO

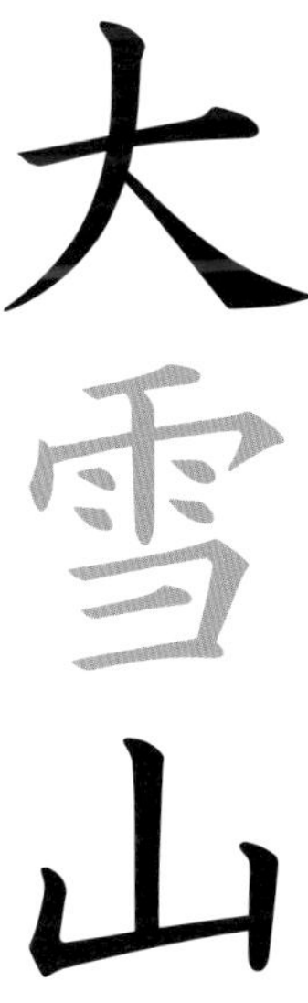

Daisetsuzan refers to not just a single mountain but a mountain range which includes the highest mountain in Hokkaido Prefecture, Mount Asahi. The mountain range lends its name to Daisetsuzan National Park which is the largest national park in Japan covering an area close to 230,000 hectares. Snow often remains on Daisetsuzan until early July while the first snow falls in mid-September, thus making it snow-bound for about eight months of the year.

A subarctic coniferous forest, made up of Yeddo spruce and Todo fir, covers the area at the foot of the mountains. The distinguishing features of this national park are its rural beauty rich in forest scenery, and various kinds of unusual fauna including the Japanese pika, alpine butterflies and rare species of birds.

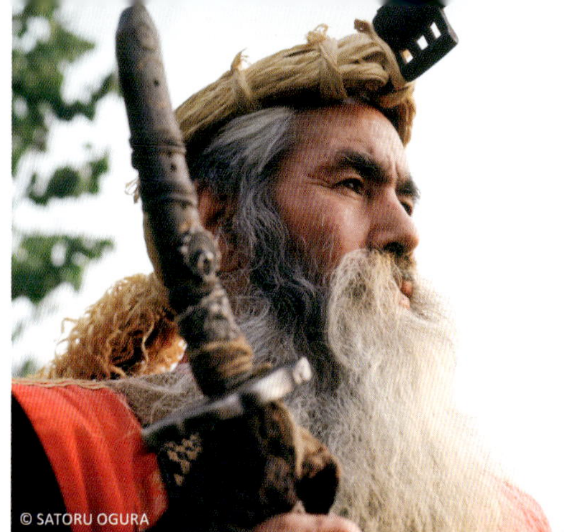

© SATORU OGURA

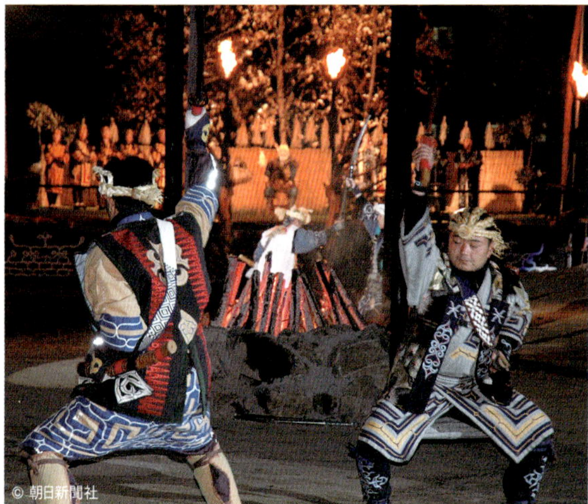

© 朝日新聞社

松島

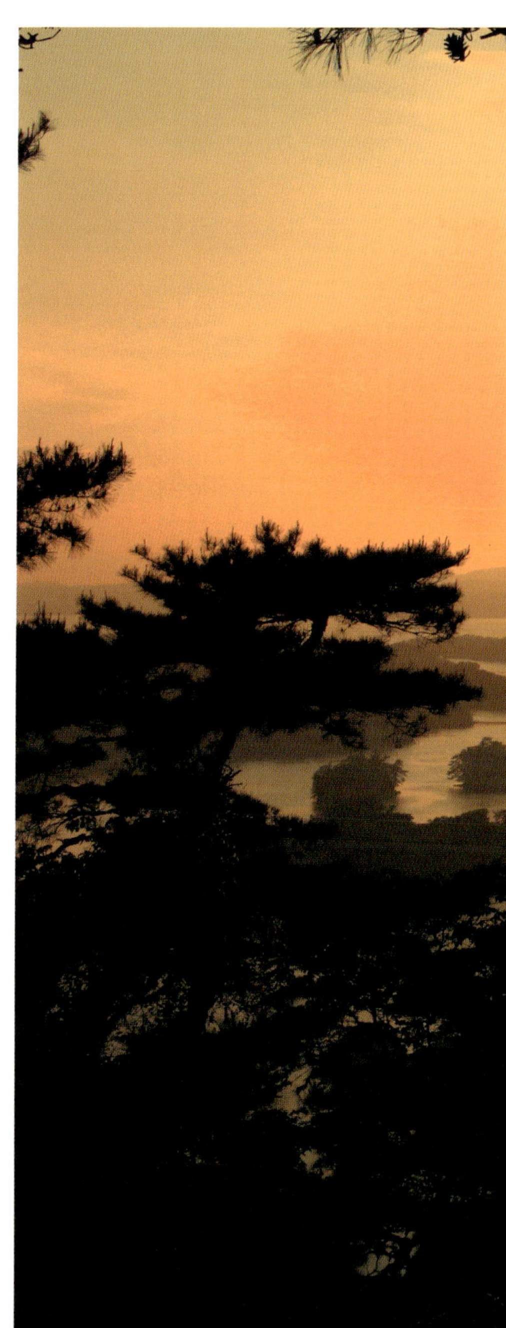

The Ainu people
▪ HOKKAIDO

Ainu are the indigenous people of Hokkaido Prefecture and the surrounding regions. Until the Meiji Period (1868-1912), when the Japanese government encouraged the opening up of Hokkaido on a large scale, Ainu people had preserved their unique culture and language through a way of life based on hunting, fishing and gathering, as they worshipped the natural world.

This includes *Kamui* (gods or spiritual beings), both physical and immaterial entities that provide many benefits to humans and possess abilities superior to those of humans. The photo is of *Iomante*, a characteristic Ainu religious ritual. The ceremony includes prayers for hunting and is held to send the spirit of the bear back to the world of the gods.

Matsushima Islands ▪ MIYAGI

Made up of some 260 islands in Matsushima Bay, Matsushima is famed as one of the three best views in Japan along with Amanohashidate in Kyoto Prefecture and Miyajima in Hiroshima Prefecture. Each is famous for its beautiful blue ocean and green pine trees, and these scenic spots touch the hearts of visitors.

Matsushima was one of the areas affected by the Great East Japan Earthquake in 2011 but because the many islands served as a buffer against the tsunami, damage was comparatively small compared to other coastal areas.

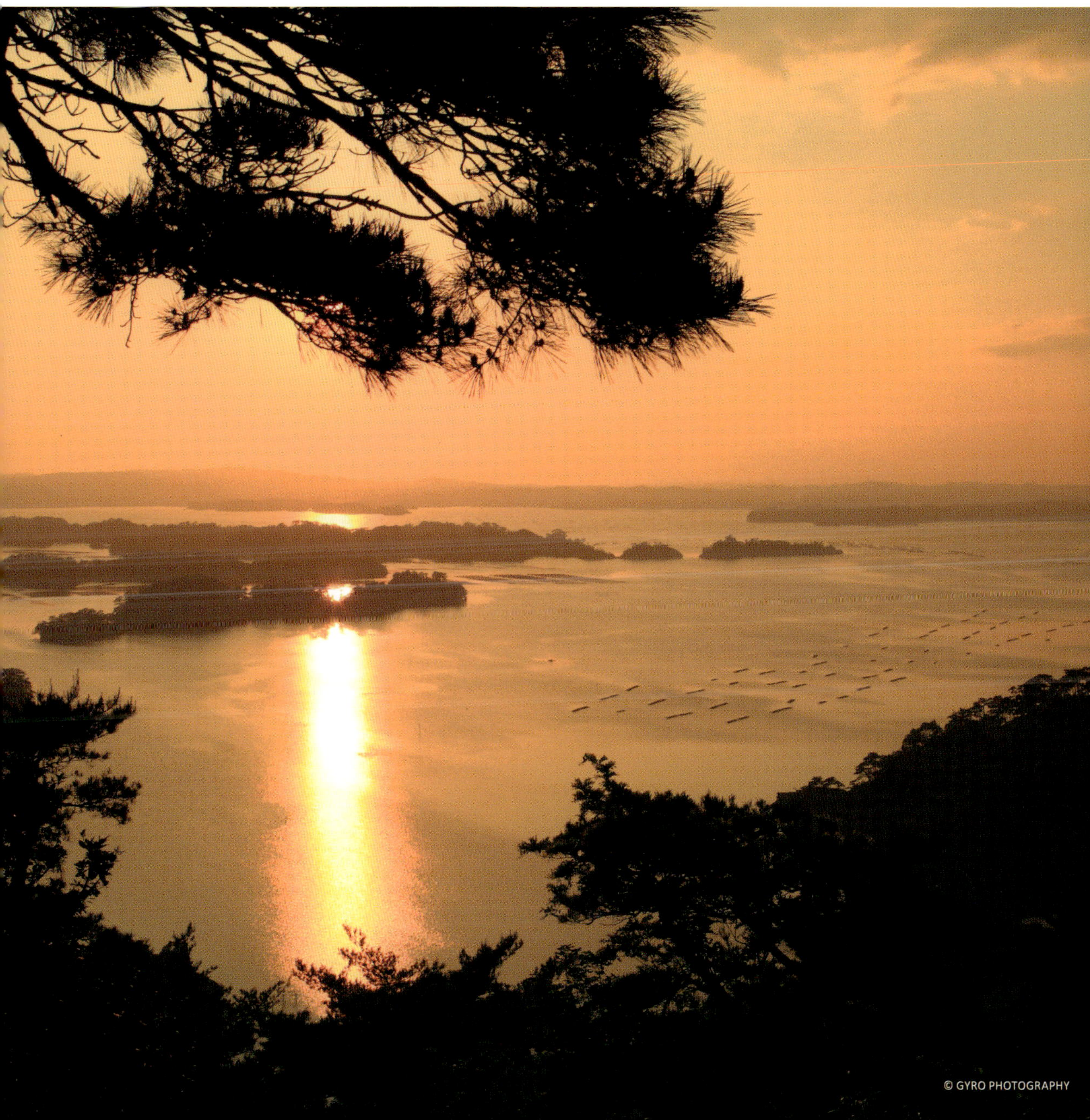

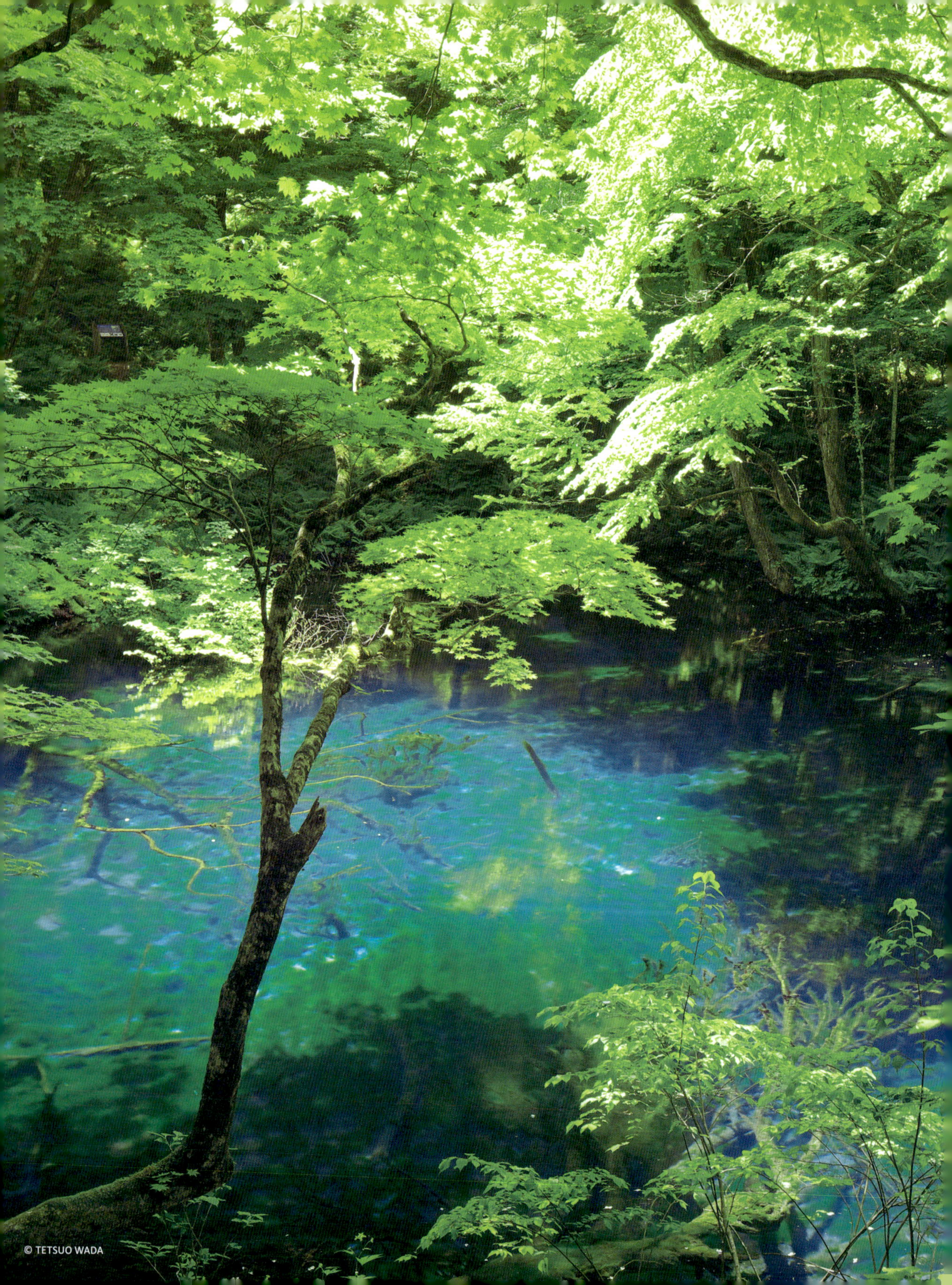

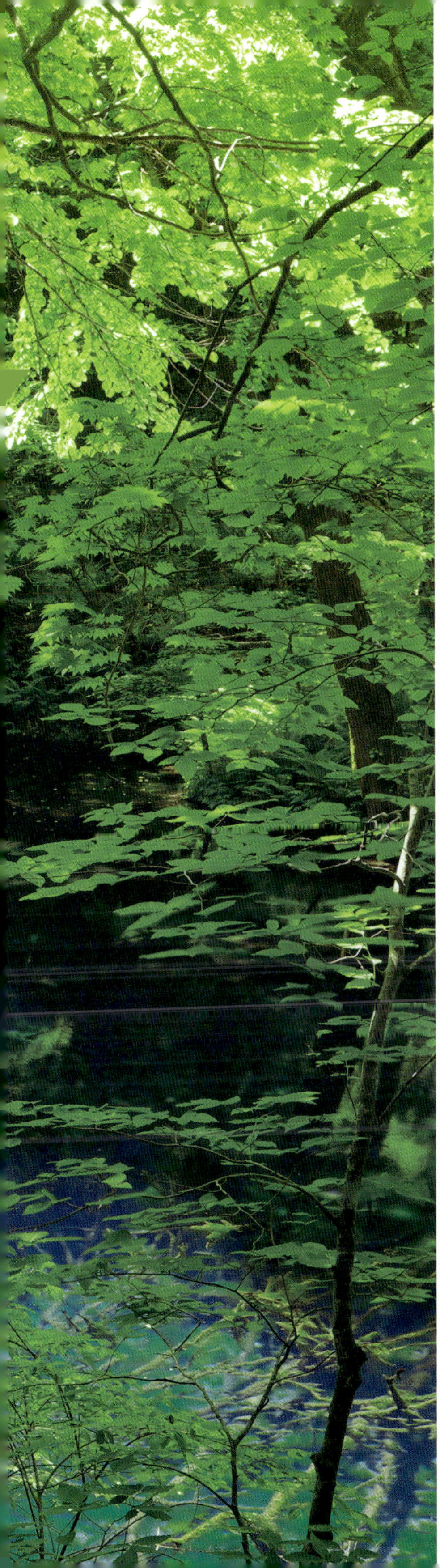

Shirakami-Sanchi

AOMORI

Situated in north-west Honshu, Shirakami-Sanchi is a mountainous area ranging in altitude from 200-1250 meters. In the Shirakami-Sanchi, Japanese beech and other trees make up a forestry ecosystem in which various flora and fauna coexist together, including unusual species such as black woodpeckers, Japanese serow and golden eagles. Due to the steep terrain, the area has not undergone much logging and is practically all virgin forest, heightening the mystical atmosphere of the area.

Shirakami-Sanchi was used for the image of the village where the main character of the aminated movie *Princess Mononoke* lives. The movie was directed by Miyazaki Hayao who is world-famous as an animator and movie director.

Primeval beech forest

The Shirakami-Sanchi area has one of the world's largest tracts of primeval beech forest. Plans were drawn up for a forestry road but a conservation movement put an end to the plans. As a result, the precious value of the abundant beech forest and the ecosystem with its diverse flora and fauna was recognized, and the Shirakami-Sanchi area was added to the World Heritage List.

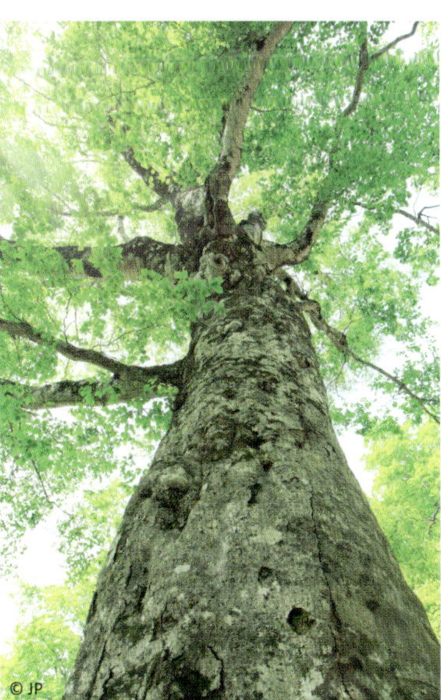
© JP

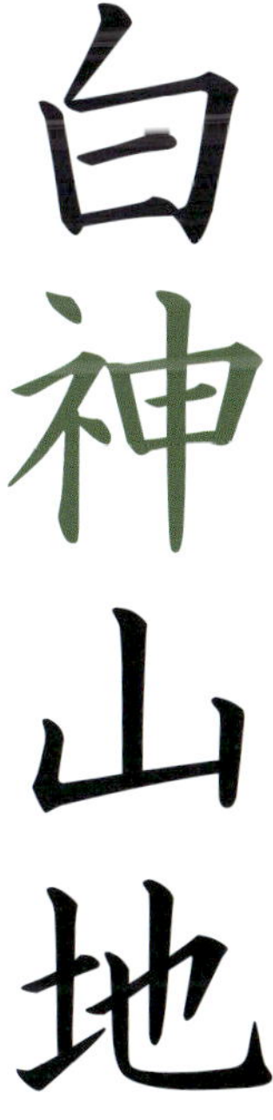

Hiraizumi ▪ IWATE

Hiraizumi was developed independently by the Oshu Fujiwara family, at the zenith of their rule, as their political and administrative base in northern Japan for approximately 100 years during the latter part of the Heian Period (794-1185). Chuson Temple still contains many cultural treasures such as Konjiki-do (*do* meaning hall), a wooden building covered entirely with gold leaf.

Konjiki-do is made with a Buddhist temple architectural style that represents the Buddhist Pure Land and is a mausoleum containing the remains or severed heads of the four rulers of the Oshu Fujiwara family. It is well known that Marco Polo, in his book *The Travels of Marco Polo*, introduced Japan as the golden country *Zipangu*. This is thought to refer to Konjiki-do in Chuson Temple.

Hiraizumi – Temples, Gardens and Archeological Sites Representing the Buddhist Pure Land was listed as a World Heritage site in 2011 and so is visited by many tourists.

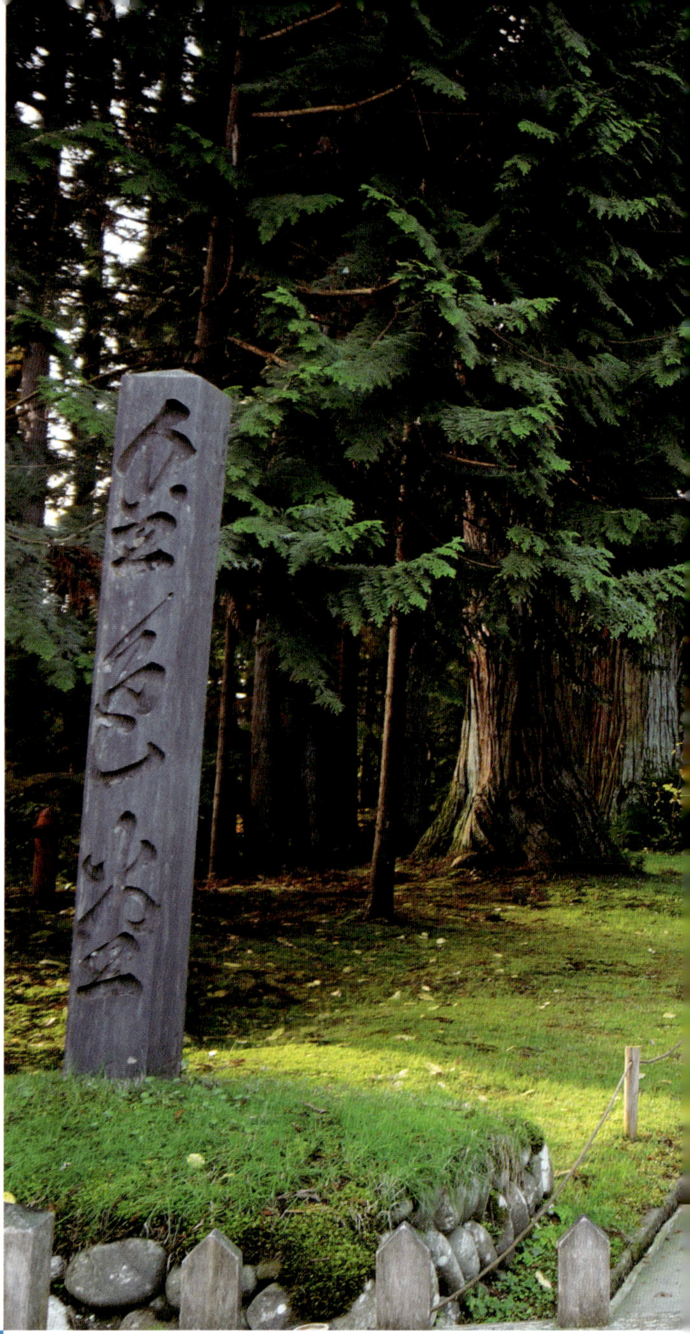

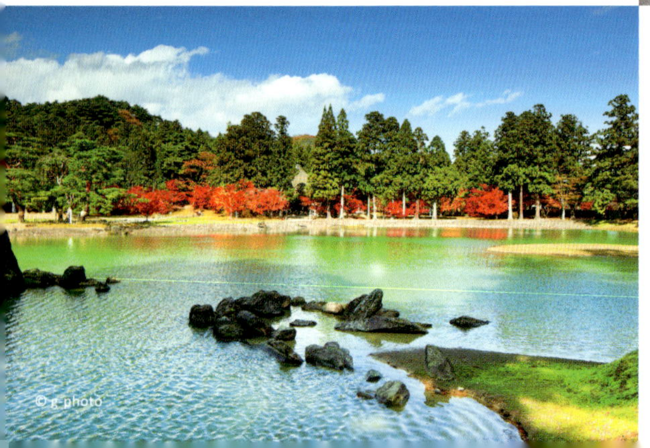

Motsu-ji (Motsu Temple)

Motsu-ji has a Jodo Garden which is a type of Japanese-style garden recreating the world of Pure Land. *Sakuteiki* (literally Records of Garden Making) is the oldest published Japanese text on garden making. The Jodo Garden at Motsu-ji was created based on *Sakuteiki* and is therefore extremely valuable academically, too. Even though the Jodo Garden is more than 800 years old, we can still view its beautiful form that has remained unchanged over the years.

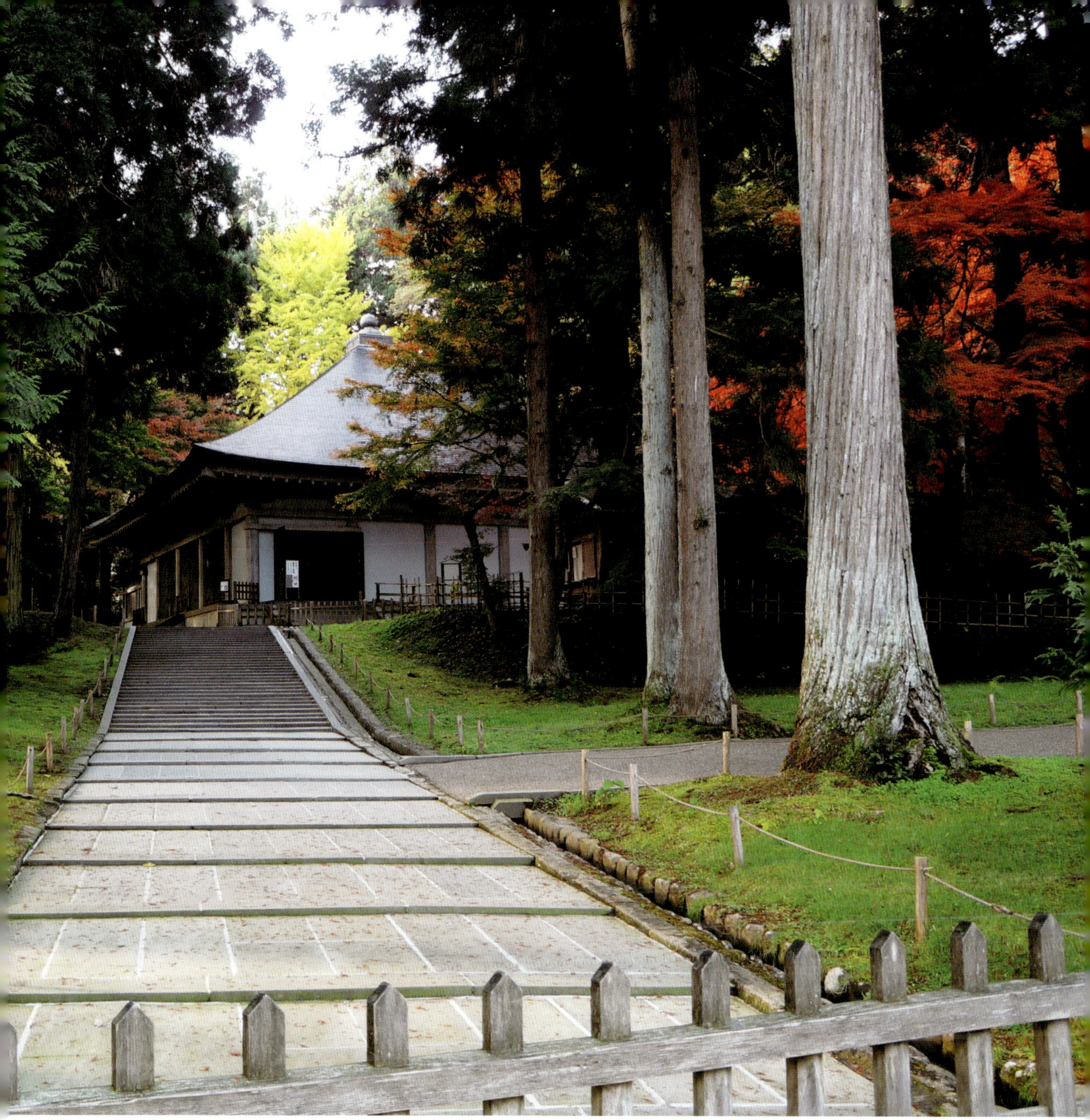

中尊寺所蔵

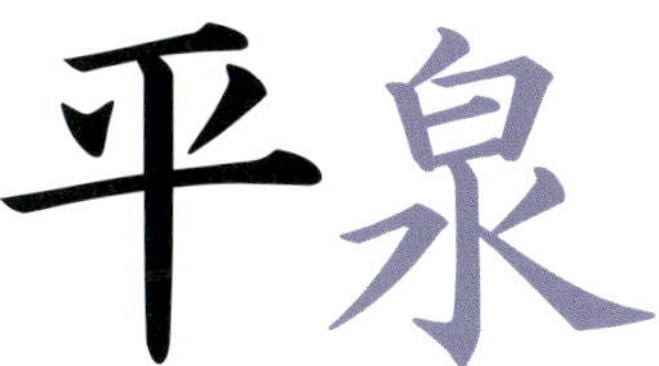

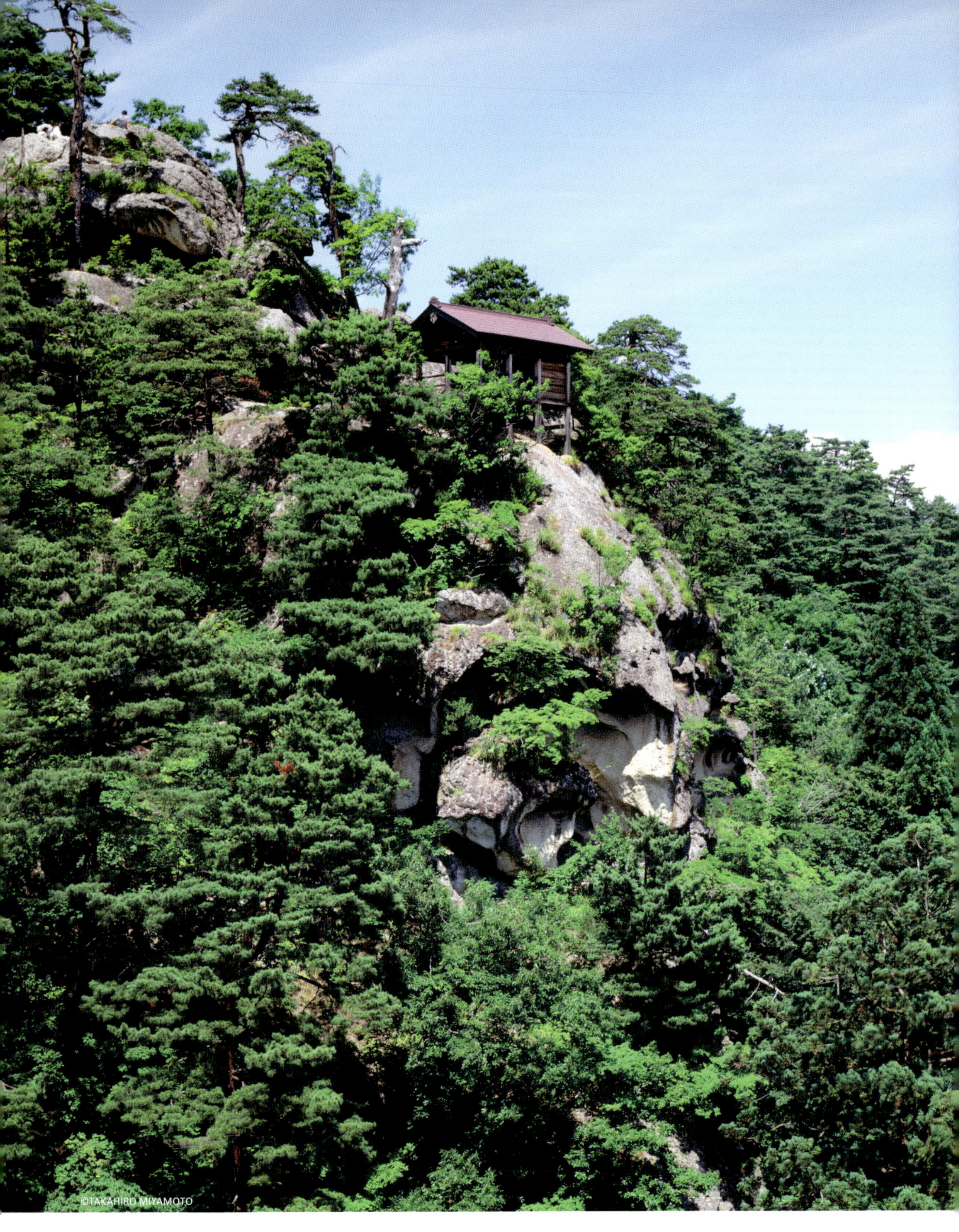
©TAKAHIRO MIYAMOTO

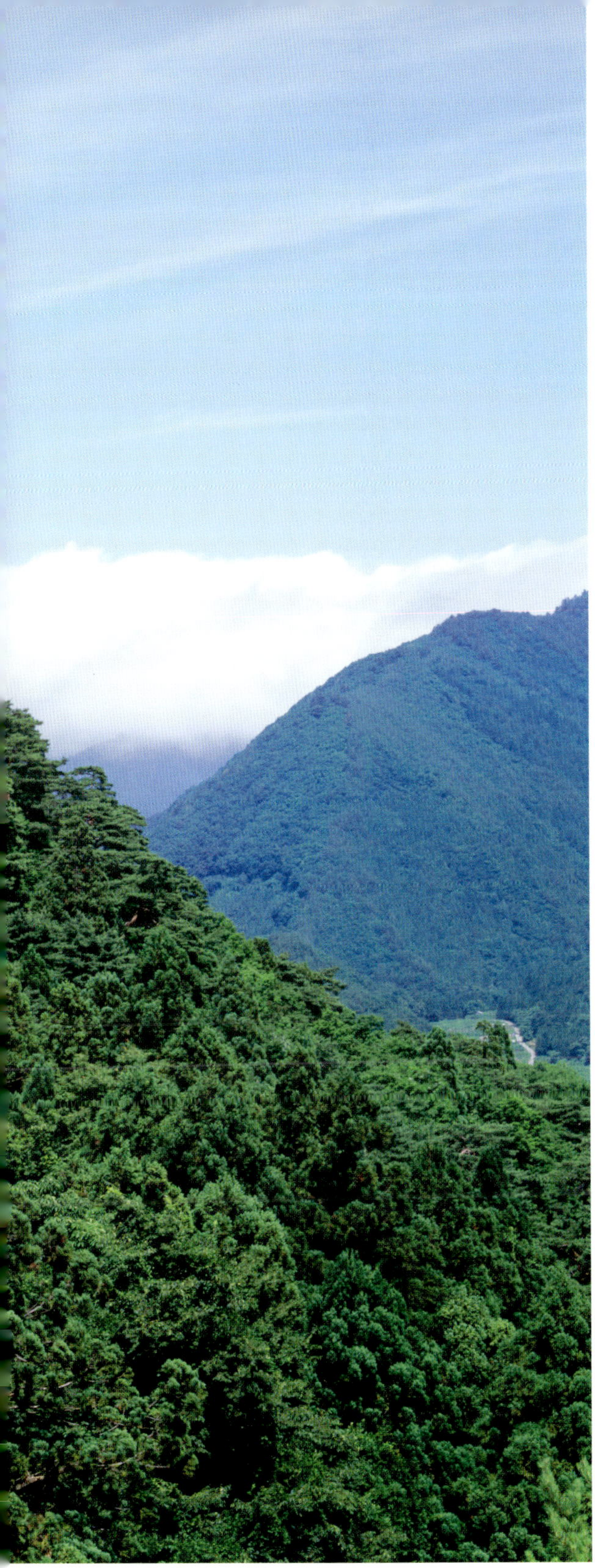

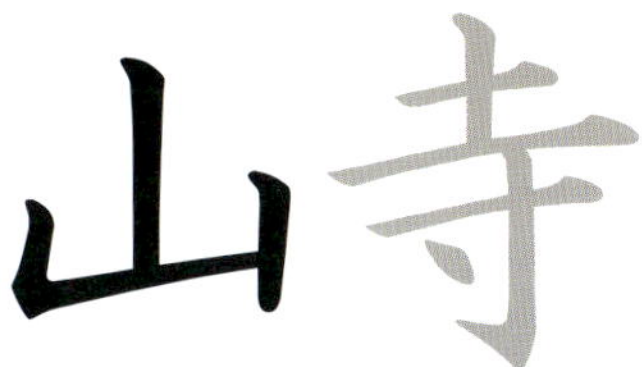

Risshaku-ji
(Risshaku Temple)
■ YAMAGATA

This temple is located on the outskirts of Yamagata city. In the middle of the 9th century, with Risshaku-ji as its official name, it was built as a branch temple of Enryaku-ji on Mount Hiei by the imperial decree of Emperor Seiwa. The temple is built on a mountain of volcanic rock and as the temple buildings are scattered from the foot to the top of the mountain, people know it by its common name, Yama-dera (Mountain Temple). From Konpon-chudo Hall at the bottom, there are about 800 steps up to Okunoin.

The beautiful scenery created throughout the seasons by the unusually shaped rock and nature is very impressive.

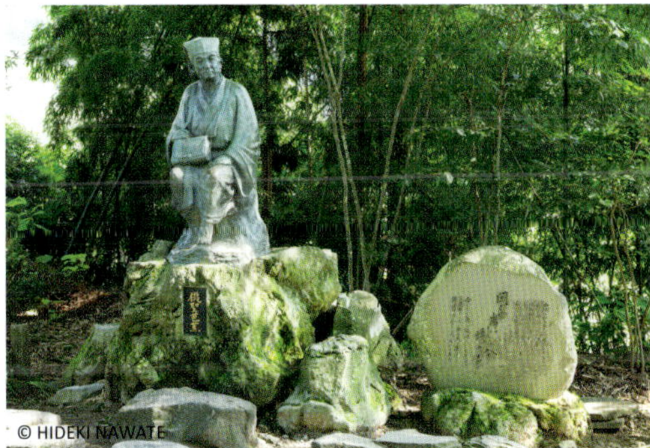
© HIDEKI NAWATE

Oku no Hosomichi
(The Narrow Road to the Deep North)

Matsuo Basho visited Yama-dera in 1689 on his travels narrated in *Oku no Hosomichi* (*The Narrow Road to the Deep North*). Later on, at this temple, his apprentice's *haikai* (linked verse poetry) friends buried a piece of paper with Matsuo's poem written on it and erected a stone monument. The words *The venerable Matsuo Basho* were engraved on the front while on the side is Matsuo's famous poem about cicadas.

Shizukasaya, iwa ni shimiiru, semi no koe (Ah, tranquility! Penetrating the very rock, a cicada's voice.)

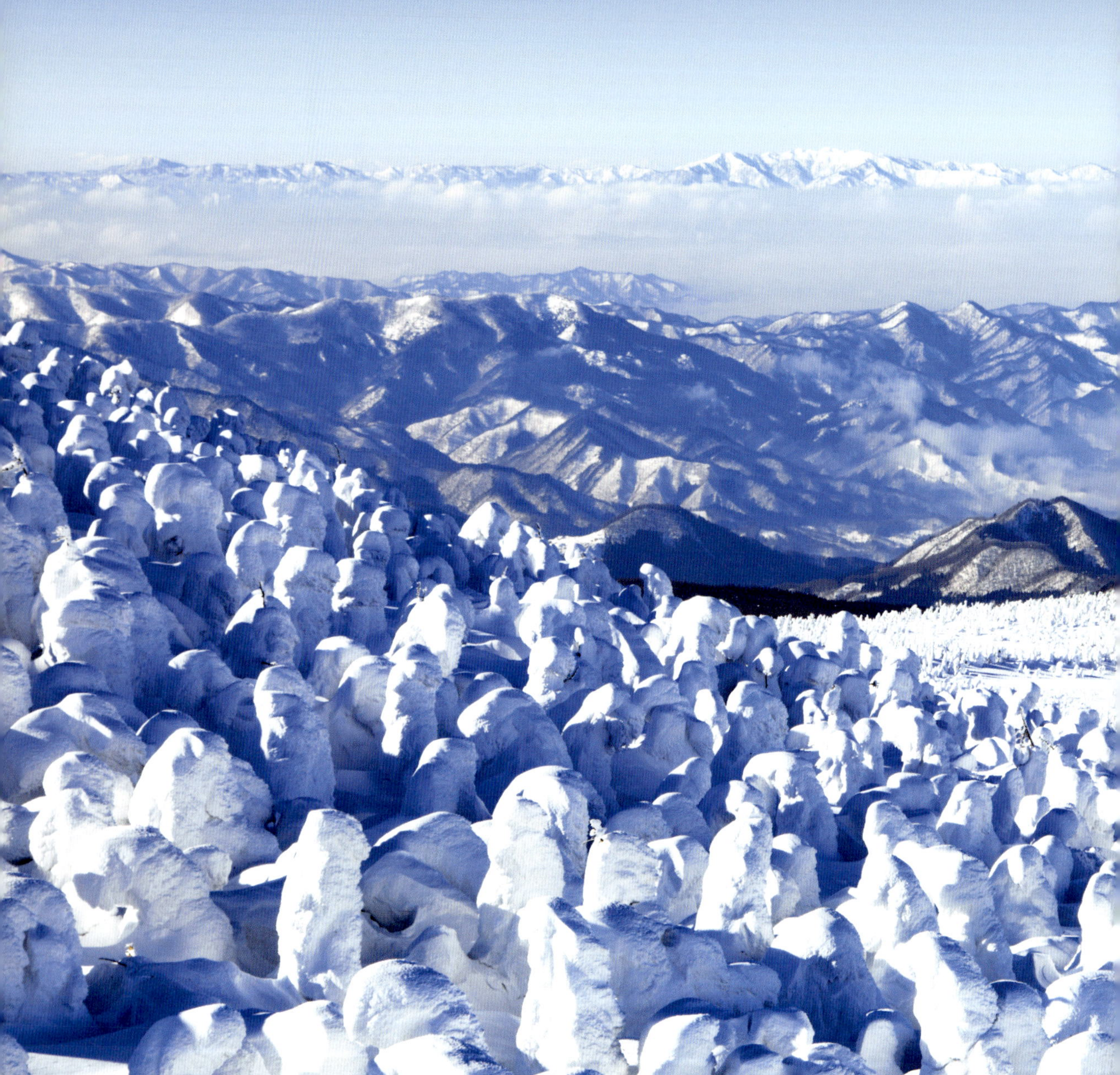

Ice monsters of Zao ▪ YAMAGATA

Ice monsters, or trees covered in ice, are a work of art created by Mother Nature. The phenomenon happens when moisture in the air forms droplets of water that then freeze onto trees. Ice monsters can only be seen in some parts of the Ou mountain range such as Zao mountain range, Mount Hakkoda and Hachimandaira. This phenomenon only occurs when certain conditions are fulfilled such as the trees being evergreens conifer (which are easily covered by ice), certain weather conditions, and a certain amount of snowfall.

Based on their appearance, the ice-covered trees are sometimes called *prawn's tails*.

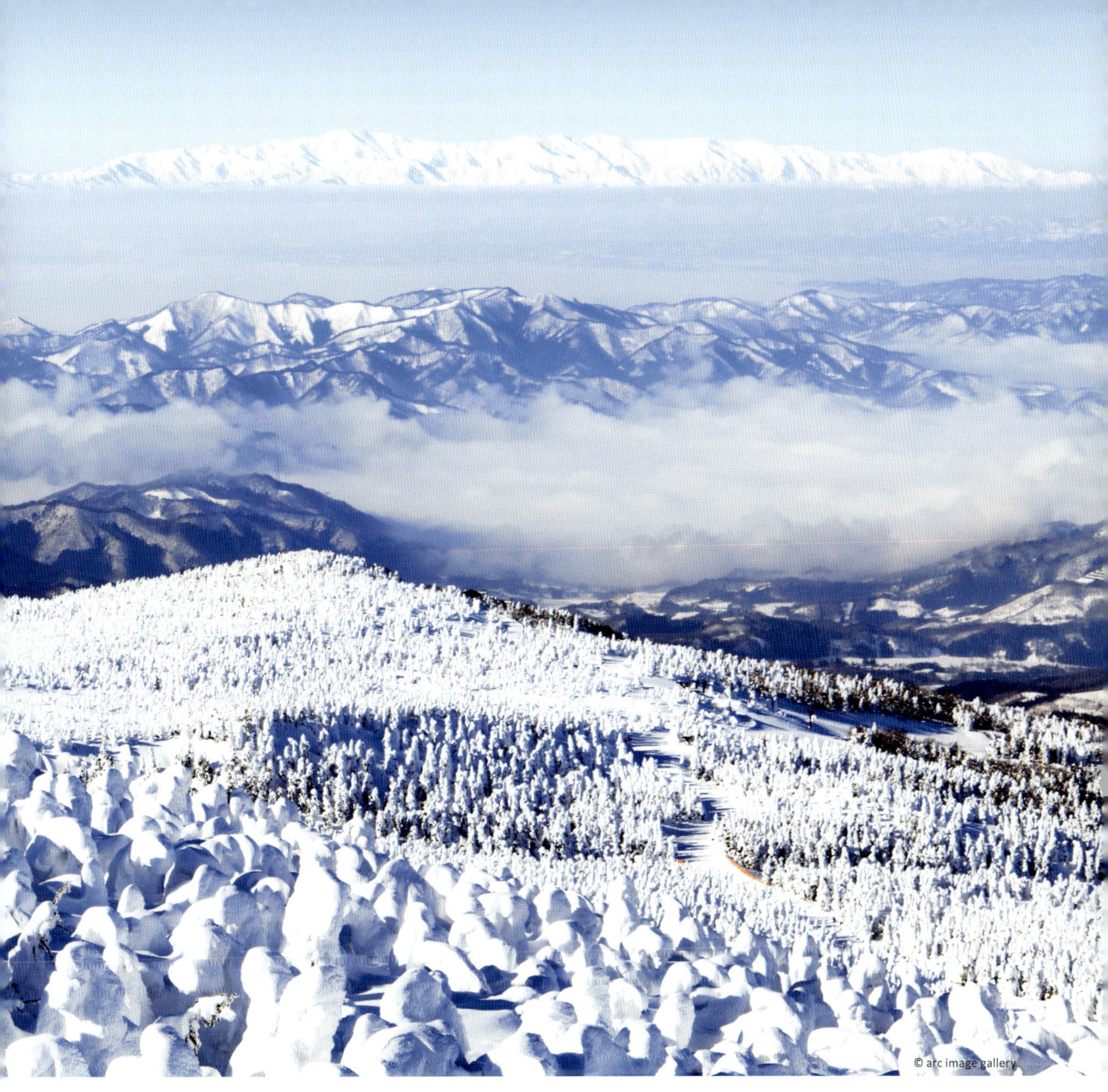

蔵王

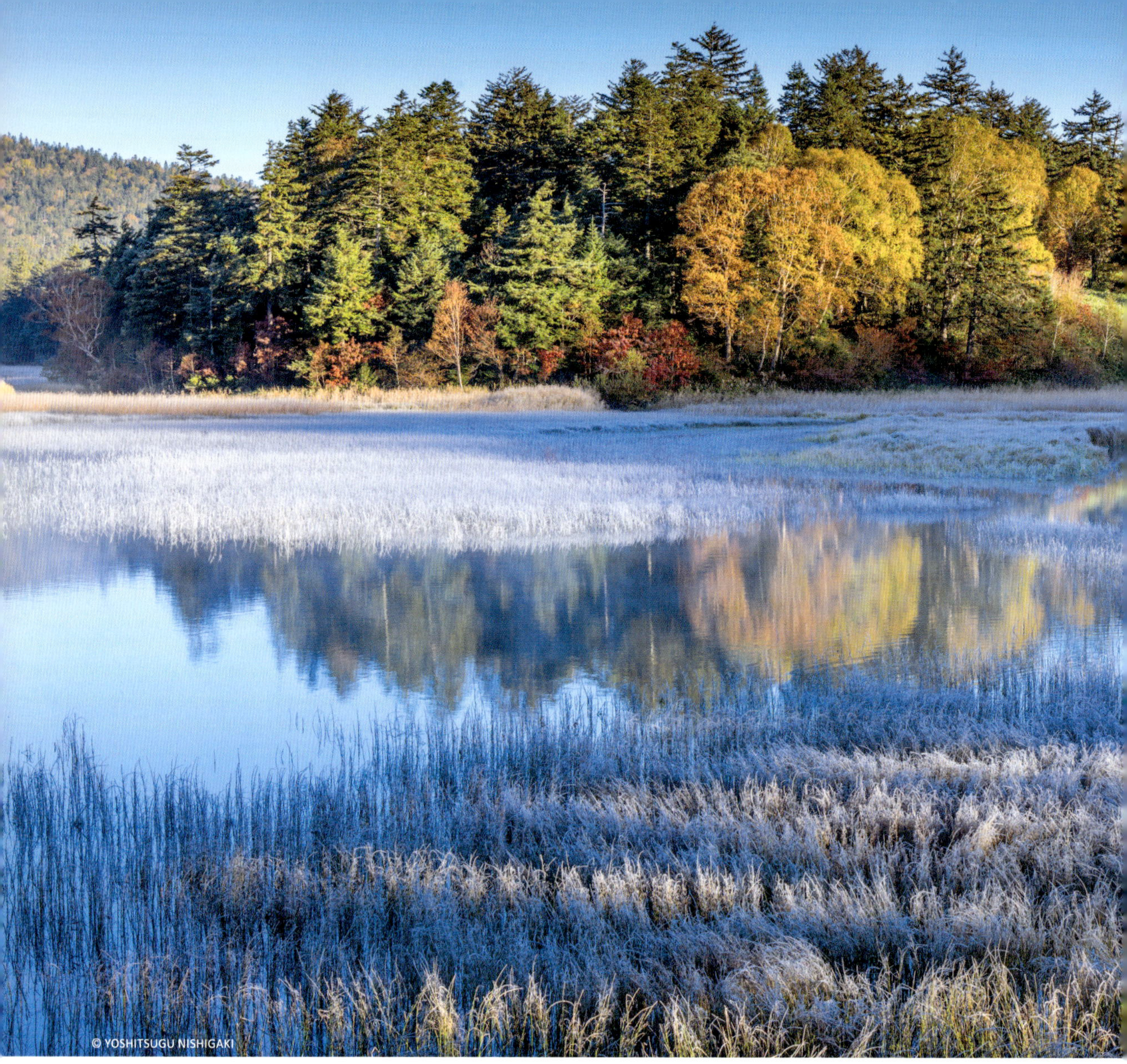

Oze Marshland ■ FUKUSHIMA

尾瀬沼

Oze National Park is the largest marshland on Japan's main island of Honshu and straddles three prefectures – Gunma, Niigata and Fukushima. Centered around Oze marsh and Ozegahara, there are many scenic places such as the marshland, lakes and marshes, forests and mountains where nature frequently changes its appearance. These scenic places are very popular with visitors to the park. Between May and October, more than 900 species of plants flower and then seed, including skunk cabbage, day lilies and scarlet-tinged grasses in autumn.

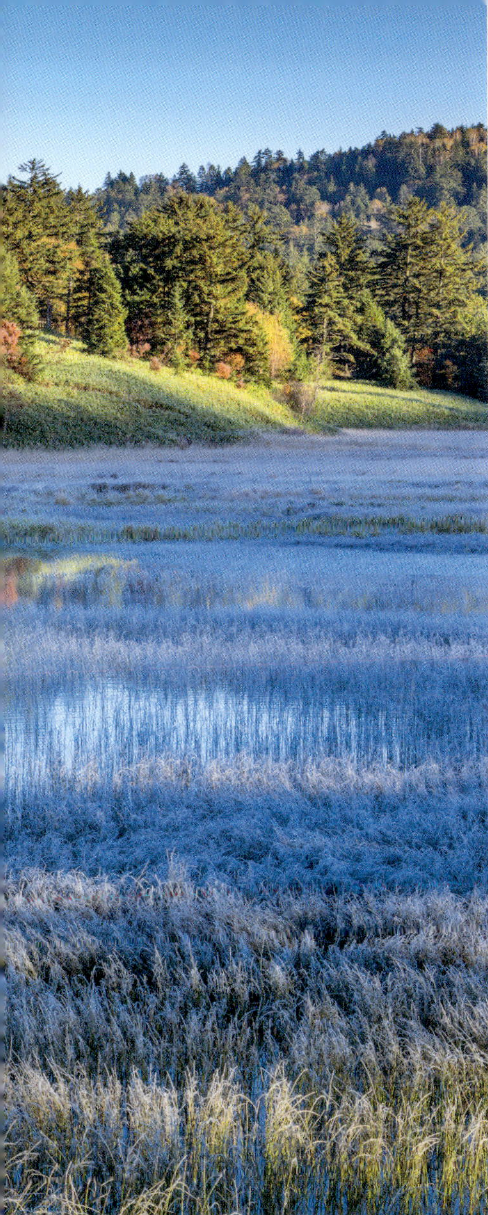

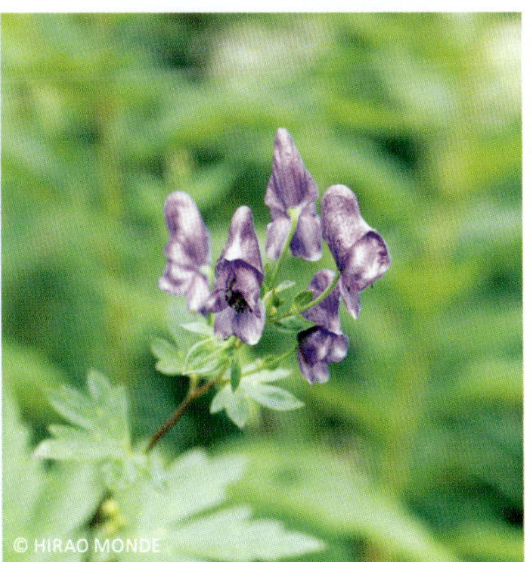

© HIRAO MONDE

The miracle pine tree ▪ IWATE

奇跡の一本松

On March 11 2011, an enormous earthquake and tsunami struck and damaged a wide area of East Japan, making it the most disastrous earthquake and tsunami on record.

In Iwate Prefecture's Rikuzentakata City, the pine grove of some seventy thousand pine trees in Takata-matsubara, which has protected the town from tsunami repeatedly in the past, were swept away in the tsunami. Just one pine tree, however, survived and was given the name of miracle pine tree. As a symbol for recovery, the tree gained international media attention.

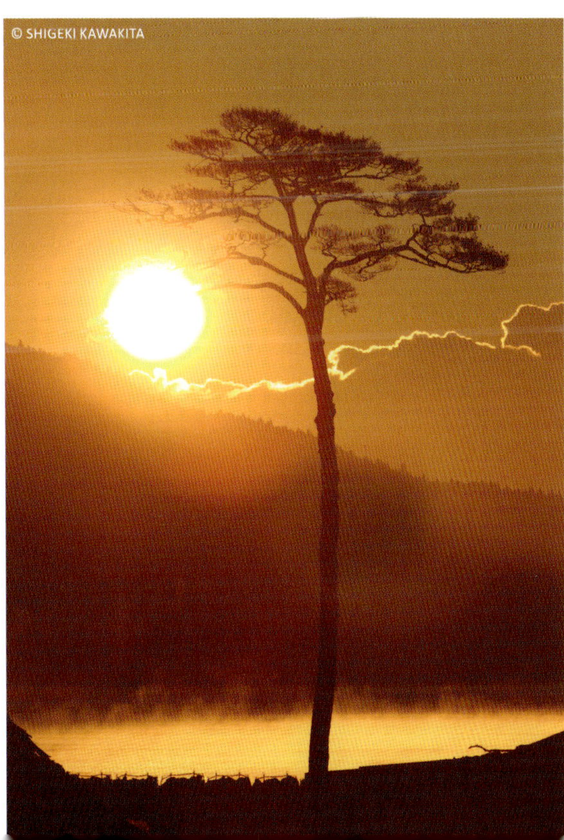

© SHIGEKI KAWAKITA

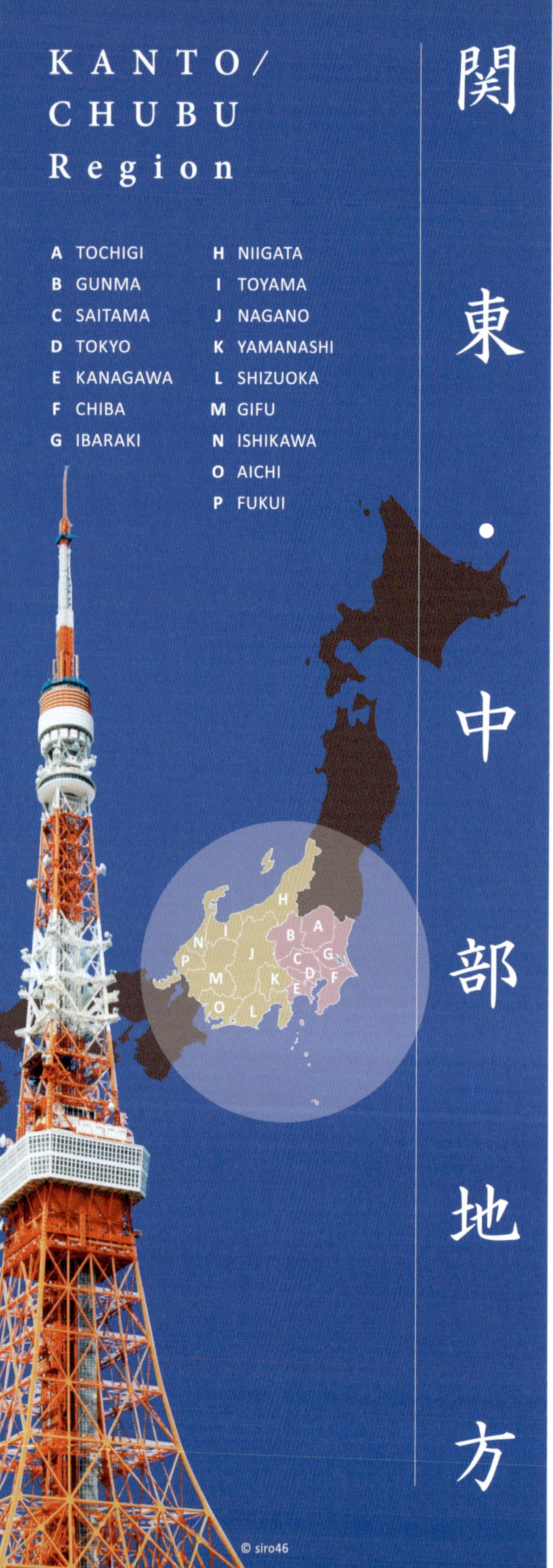

Japan's central region, with the Tokyo metropolitan area at its core.

The Kanto region encompasses the Tokyo Metropolitan area and the six prefectures of Ibaraki, Tochigi, Gunma, Saitama, Chiba, and Kanagawa. The Chubu region includes the nine prefectures of Niigata, Toyama, Ishikawa, Nagano, Yamanashi, Shizuoka, Gifu, Aichi, and Fukui. The Kanto region, in particular, is the political and economic center of Japan, and one-third of Japan's total population is concentrated there.

The Kanto region has a comparatively mild climate that makes all four seasons relatively comfortable. Nagano Prefecture, however, which is enclosed by mountains, and Niigata, Toyama, and Ishikawa Prefectures, which are on the Sea of Japan side, are snow country. There visitors can experience the distinctive pleasures of snow country, such as the beautiful silver landscapes of winter and the warmth of the hot springs.

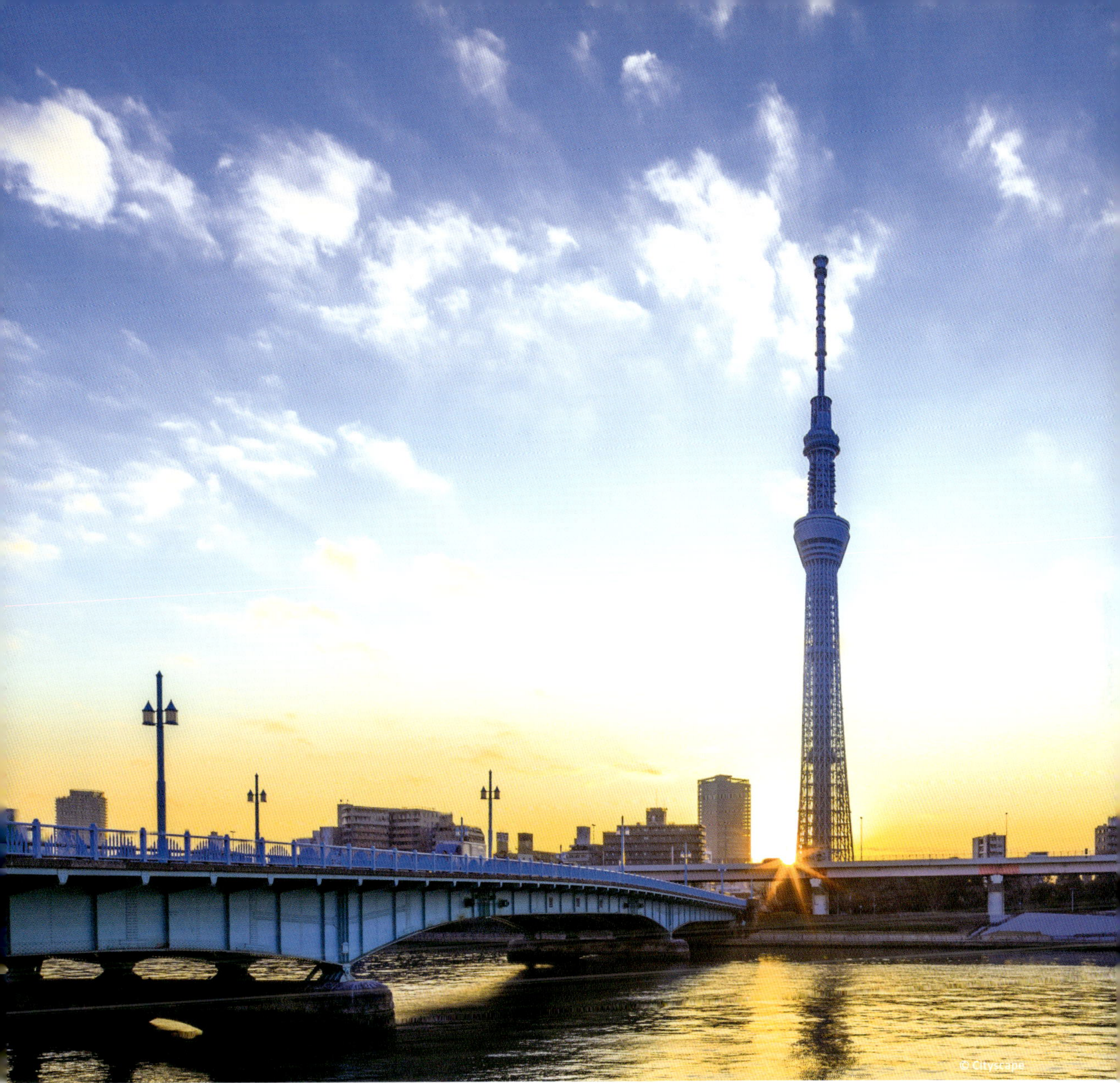

Tokyo Skytree ▪ TOKYO

Tokyo Skytree began service as a broadcasting tower in 2012, becoming a new Tokyo landmark. Tokyo Skytree holds the *Guinness Book of Records* title for the world's highest self-supporting broadcasting tower at a height of 634 meters. The number 634, which can also be read as *mu-sa-shi* in Japanese, is also a play on words for the old name for the Kanto area (including Tokyo) of Musashi Province. This is why the height of the tower is 634 meters. From either of the observations decks at a height of 350 meters and 450 meters, visitors can command a complete view of the flat landscape of Kanto area. The tower is beautifully lit up at night, with the lights changing depending on the time of the year.

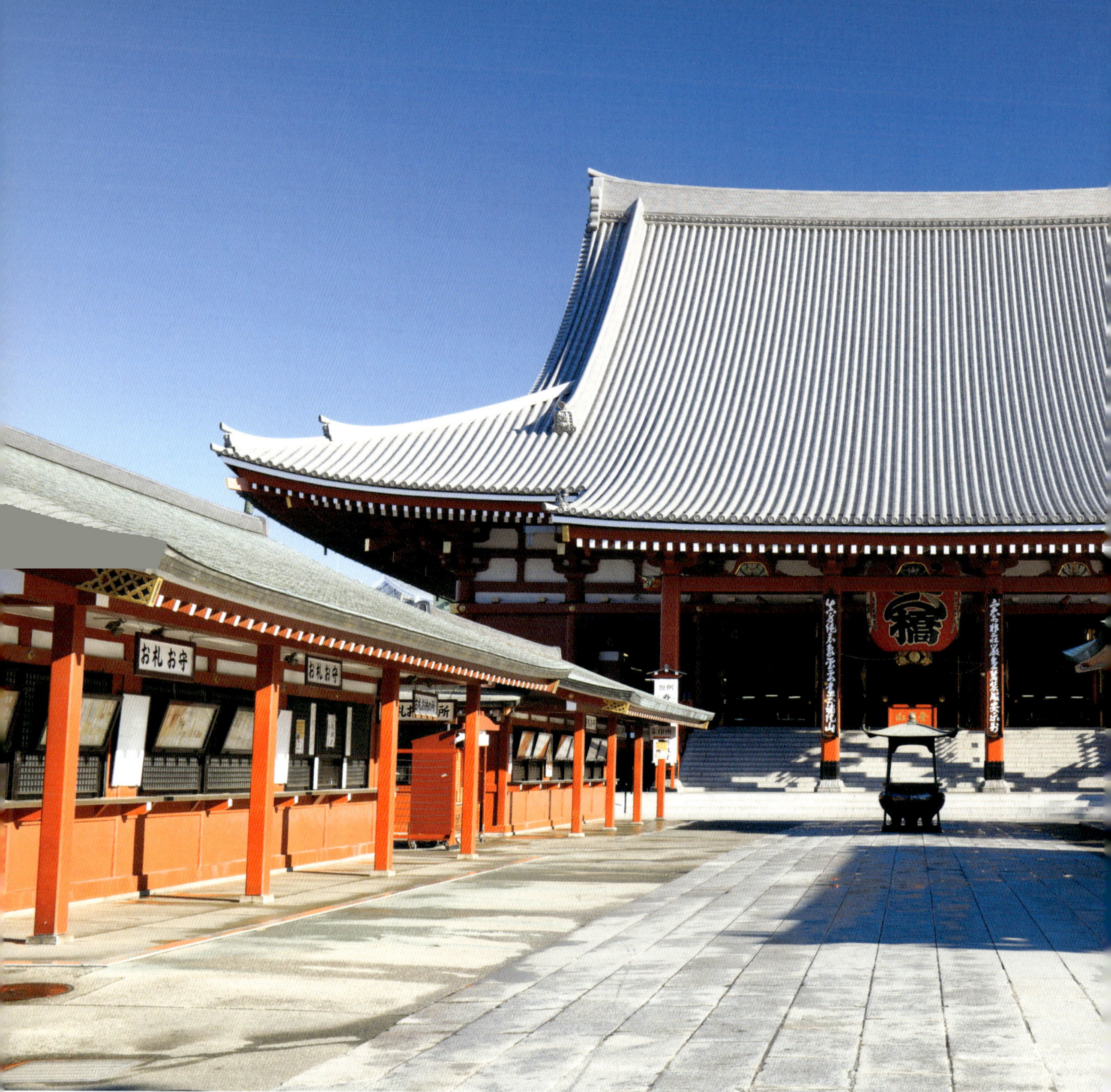

Senso-ji (Senso Temple) ▪ TOKYO

Senso-ji, built in the middle of the 7th century, is located in Asakusa, Taito Ward, Tokyo. When the Tokugawa Shogunate set up government in Edo (former name of Tokyo) Senso-ji was designated as the official temple of the Tokugawa family and Senso-ji became one of the most important temples in Edo. Senso-ji also attracted many worshippers from the common people and was a popular place to visit.

The Asakusa Shrine is located in the precincts of Senso-ji and honors the three men who founded the temple. The Sanja Festival is held there for three days in May and it ranks as one of three major festivals of Tokyo.

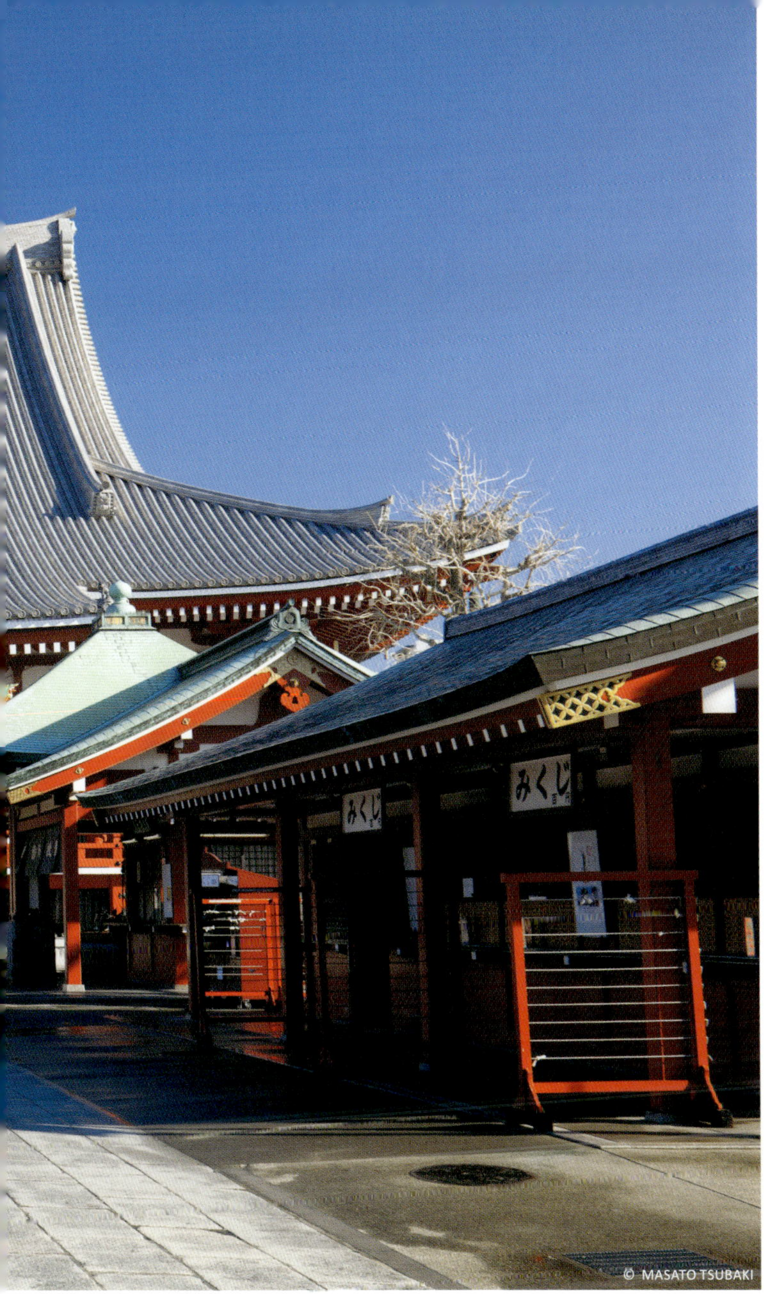

© MASATO TSUBAKI

浅草寺

Kaminarimon (Thunder Gate)

Kaminarimon, the gate to Senso-ji, was built in the middle of the 17th century to honor Fujin (the Wind God) and Raijin (the Thunder God) and to protect the people of Edo from storm and flood damage as well as fires. Facing the front of the gate, Fujin is enshrined on the right and Raijin on the left side. The giant lantern hanging in the center of the gate weighs 700 kilograms and is replaced once every ten years.

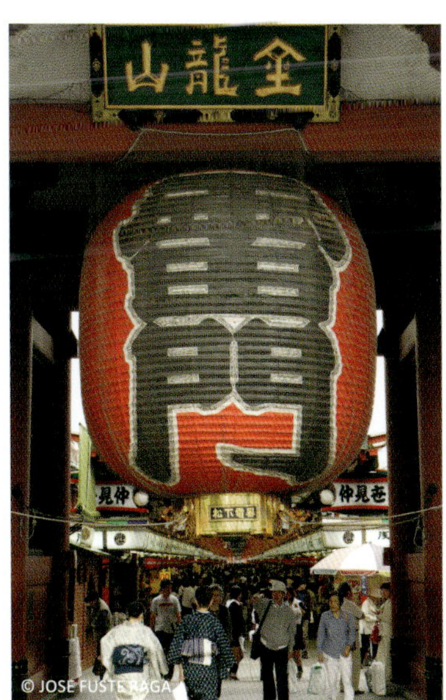

© JOSE FUSTE RAGA

Shinjuku skyscraper district ▪ TOKYO

Shinjuku in Tokyo is home to a major train station terminal and the number of passengers passing through the station average approximately 3.26 million per day (as of 2011), making it the world's busiest station. On the west side of the station is a business district where Japan's tallest skyscrapers can be found, including the Tokyo Metropolitan Government Building.

Videos taken by foreigners of Shinjuku skyscrapers and shared on Internet sites have received comments from people all over the world such as *Very impressive, You could never find another place like this in the whole universe – amazing!*

What do you think of the Shinjuku skyscraper district?

©AOI YOSHIHARU

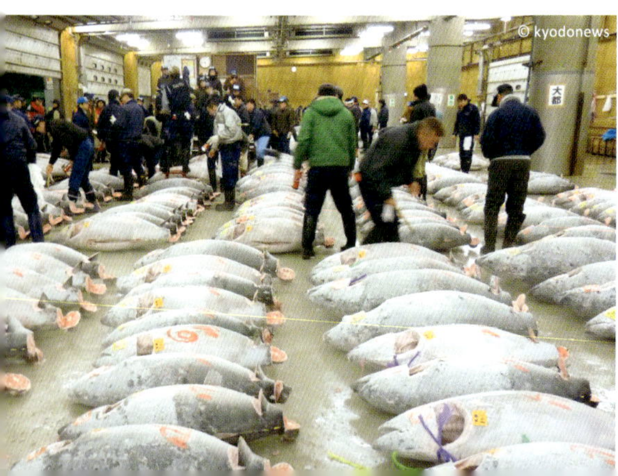

© kyodonews

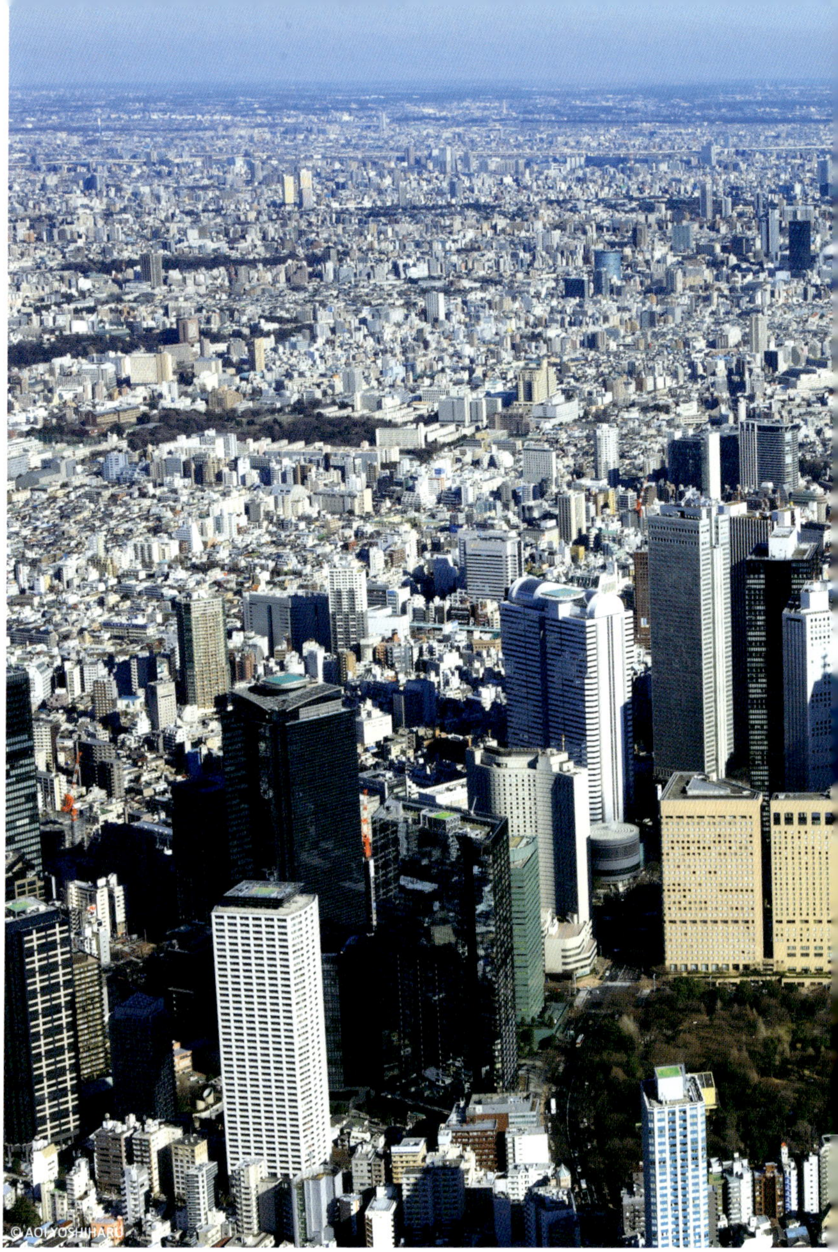

Tsukiji Fish Market ▪ TOKYO

Tsukiji Market in Tokyo handles the largest amount of seafood in Japan. From a global perspective, Tsukiji ranks as one of the world's largest fish markets with an area covering 23 hectares and a turnover of more than 2,000 tons of seafood per day. Particularly impressive is the auctioning of huge frozen tuna. Visitors are allowed to enter the wholesale market to observe the auction where buyers skillfully bid for the tuna one after another. Recently guided tours have been set up for foreign tourists and after observing the market, tourists can even be taught by a professional how to make sushi with their own hands.

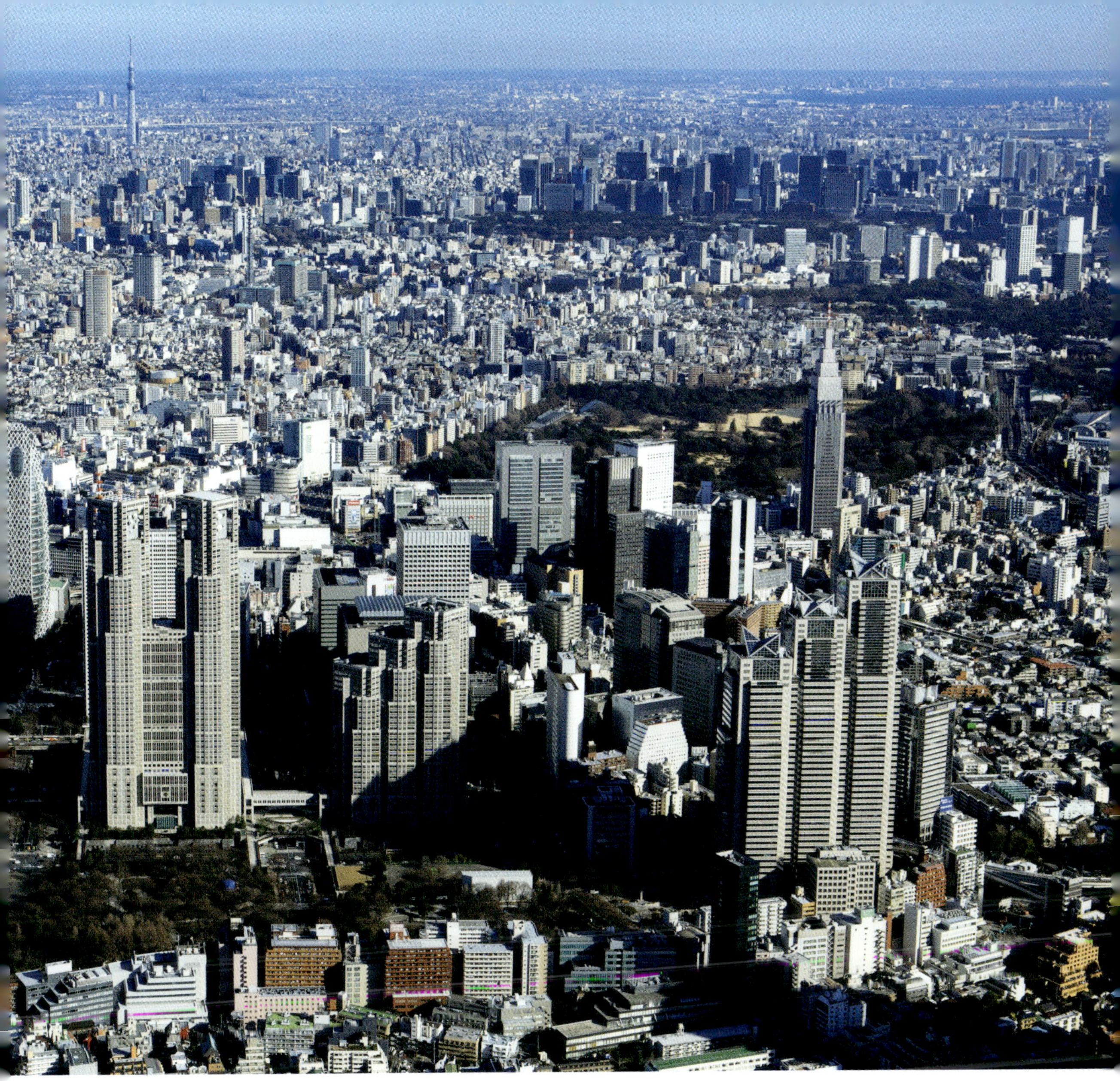

N.B. A project is underway to relocate the Tsukiji Market to the Toyosu area, also in Tokyo.

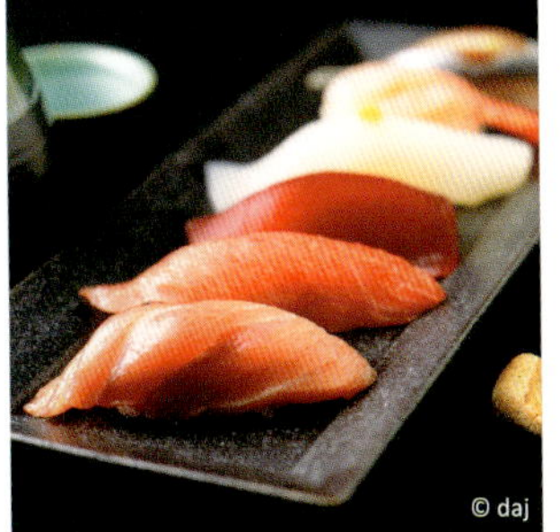

Sushi

Many shops in the Tsukiji Market offer sushi made from seafood freshly bought that day at the market, so it's a good idea to visit Tsukiji when you come to Japan.

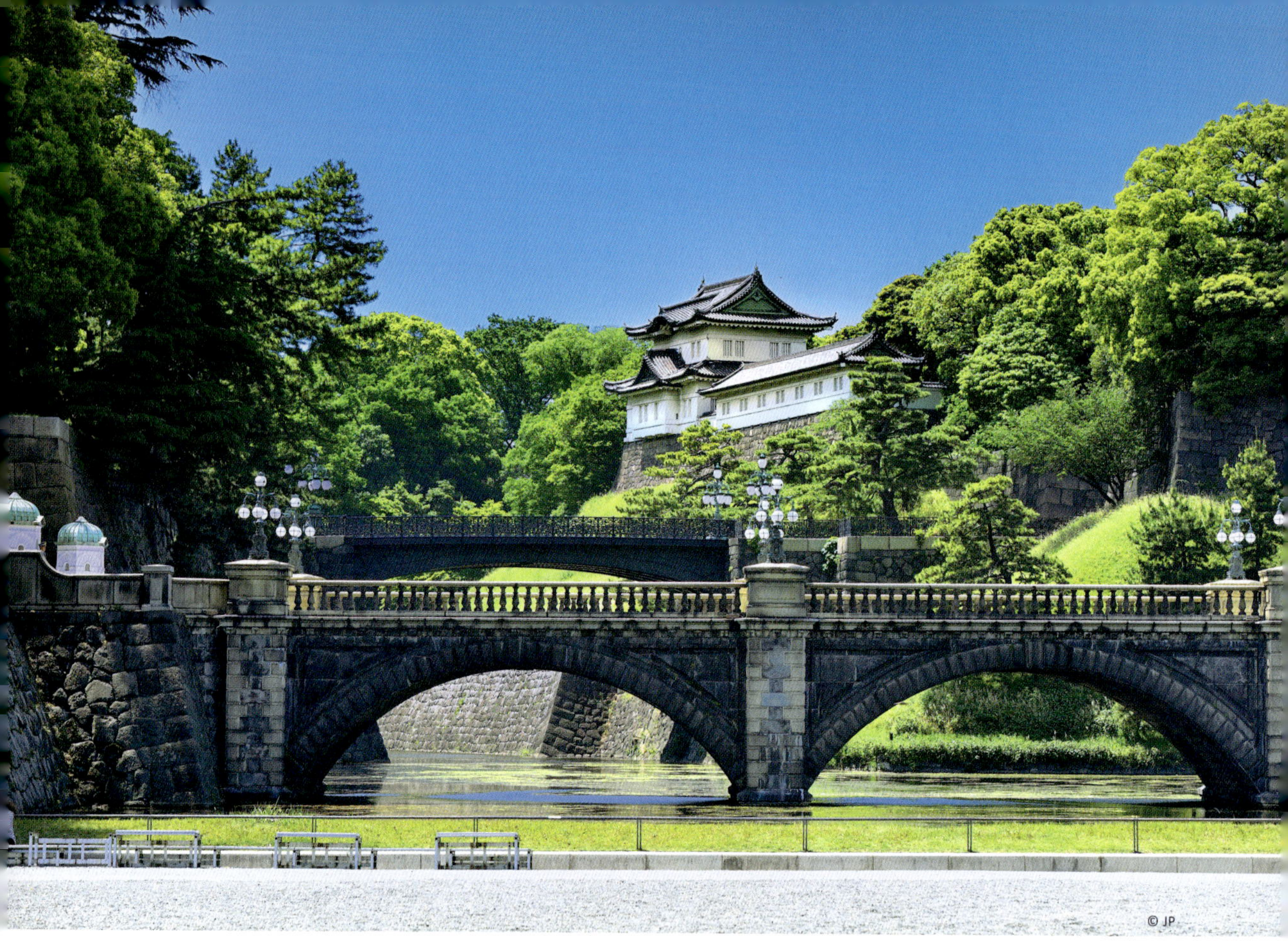

© JP

東京タワー
皇居

The Tokyo Imperial Palace ▪ TOKYO

The Tokyo Imperial Palace is located on the site of the old Edo Castle, the residence of the shogun and the location of the Tokugawa Shogunate. When it was completed approximately 400 years ago, Edo Castle was the biggest wooden building in Japan at a height of 60 meters. When Japan entered the Meiji Period in 1868, the old Edo Castle became the Tokyo Imperial Palace. It is the residence of the emperor and empress as well as the main palace hall where ceremonies are held. Nowadays, a portion of the grounds are made open to the general public.

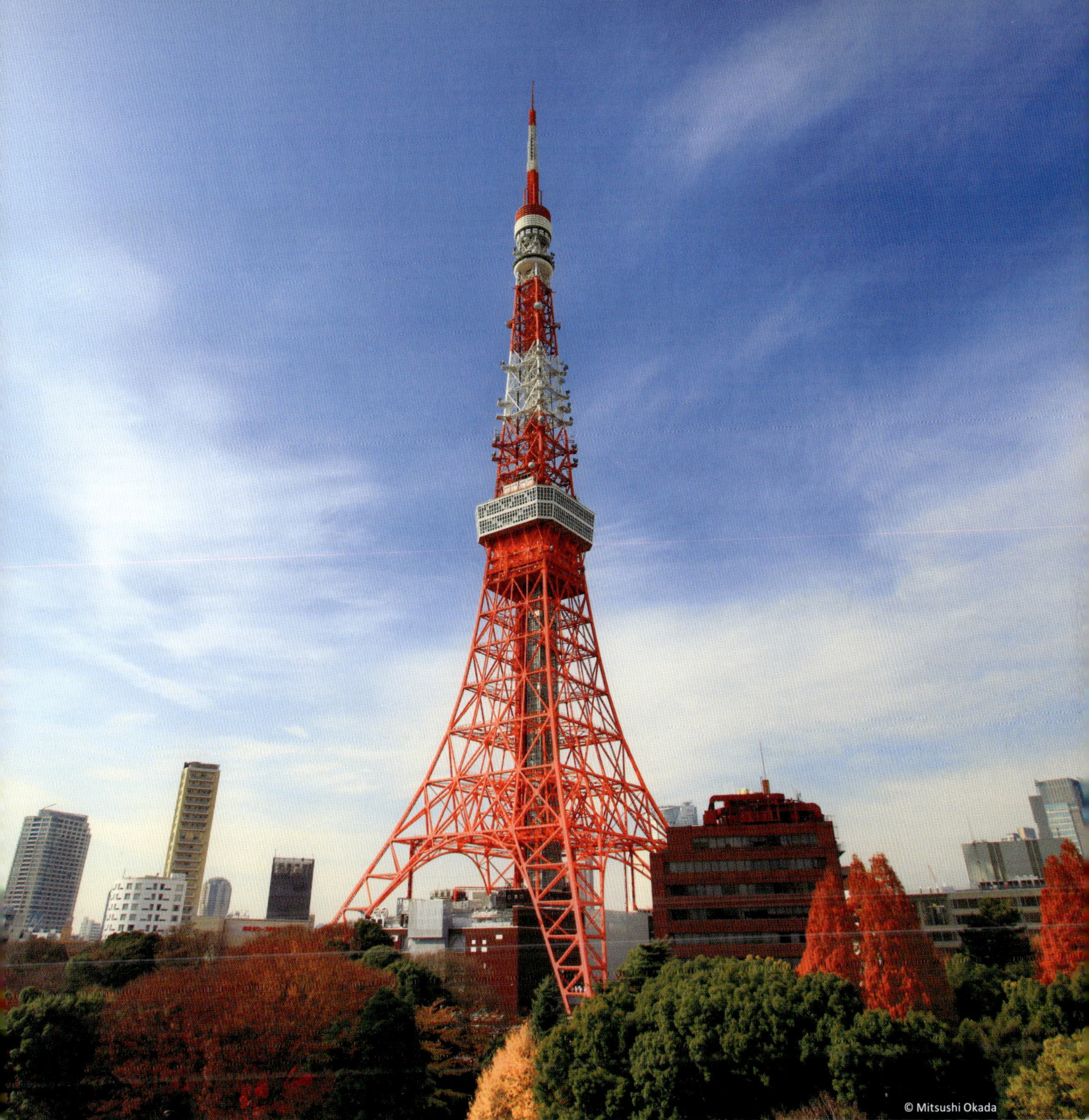
© Mitsushi Okada

Tokyo Tower ▪ TOKYO

Tokyo Tower came into operation in 1958. At the time, a tower 333 meters high was necessary in the middle of Tokyo to broadcast television signals all around the Kanto area and so Tokyo Tower, which surpasses the 324 meter high Eiffel Tower, was built. Ever since, Tokyo Tower has been a symbol of Tokyo and a tourist spot popular with visitors.

At the observatory 120 meters aboveground, part of the floor is made from strengthened glass, through which visitors can see straight down to the ground.

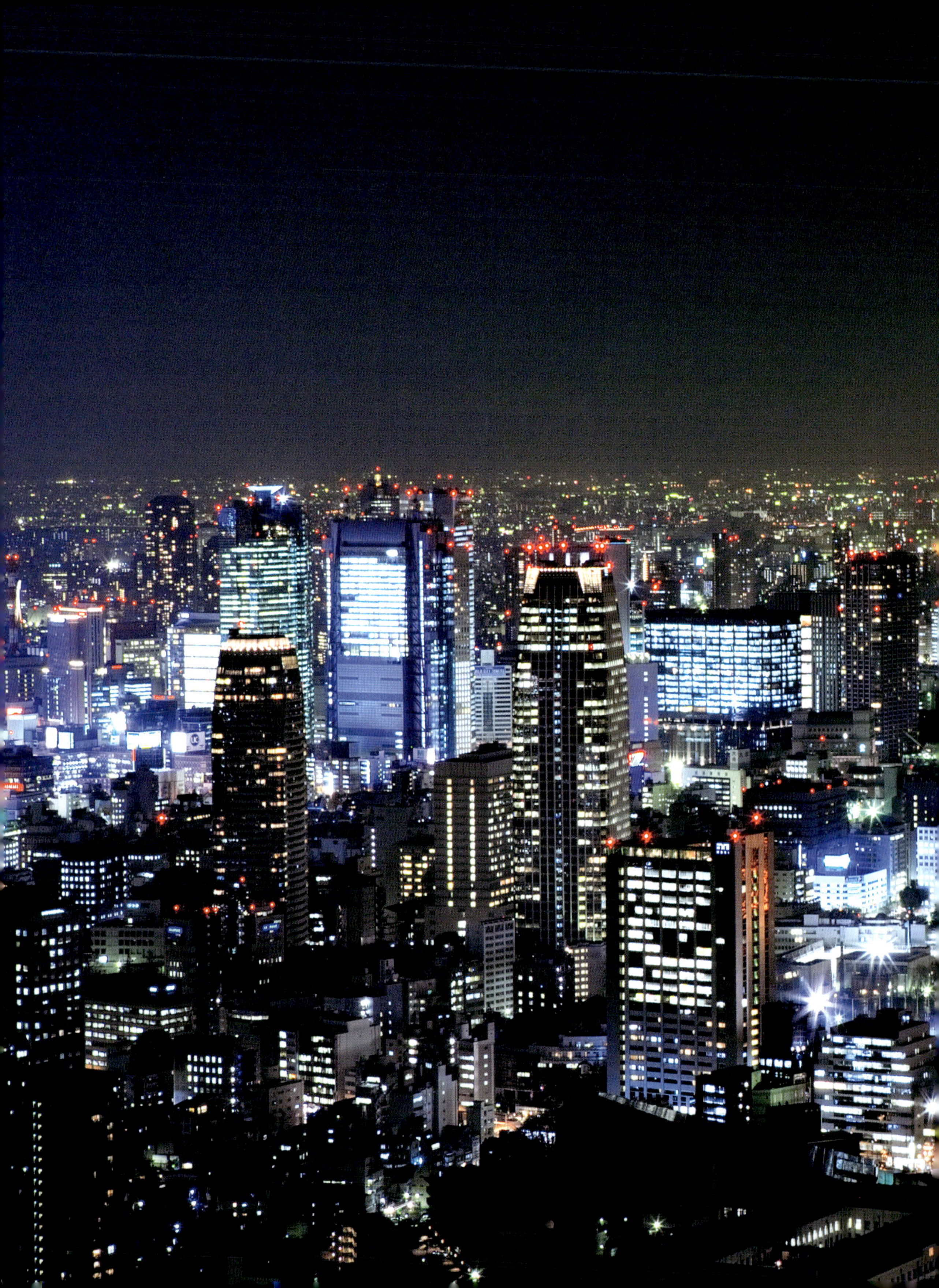

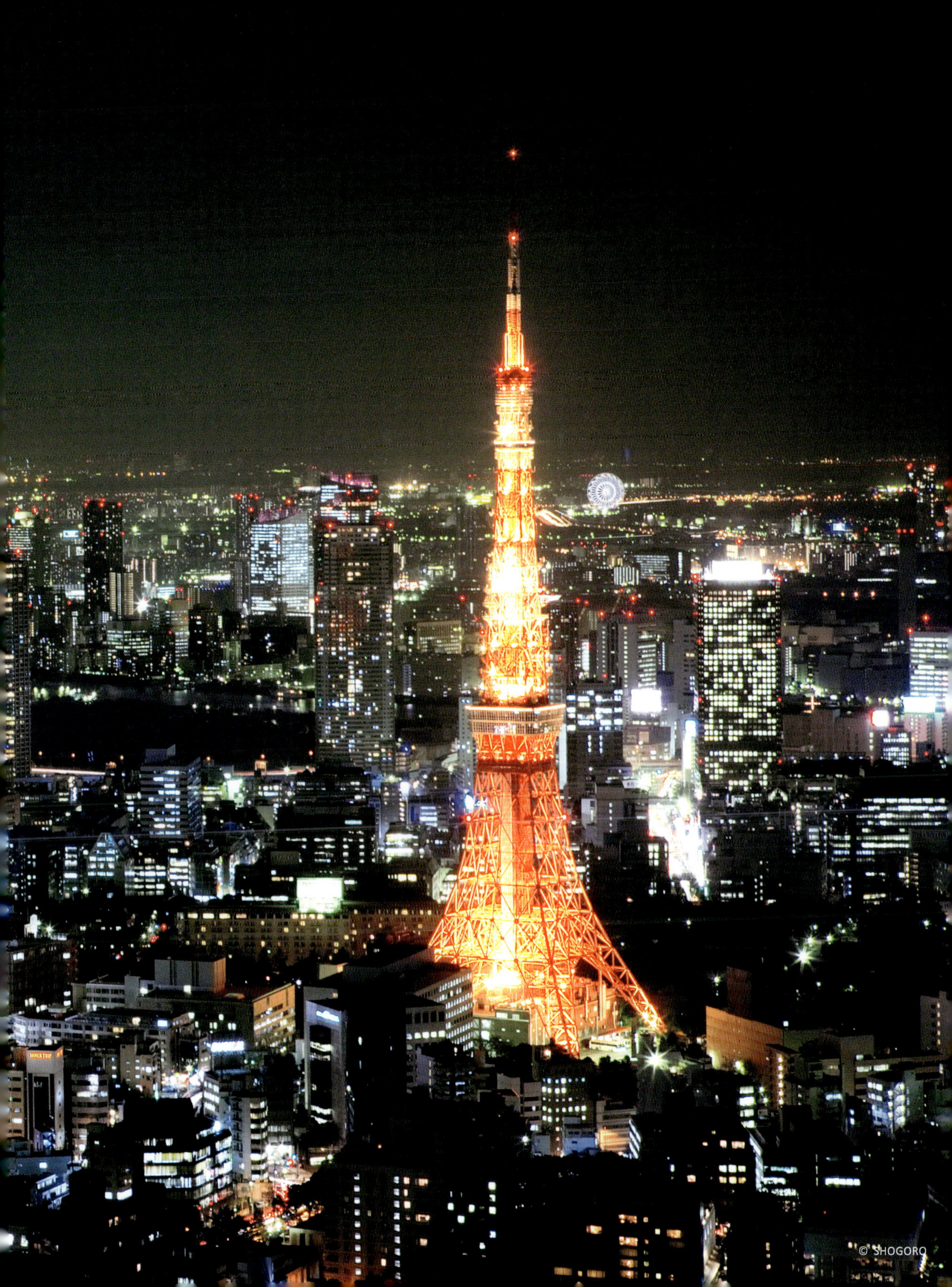

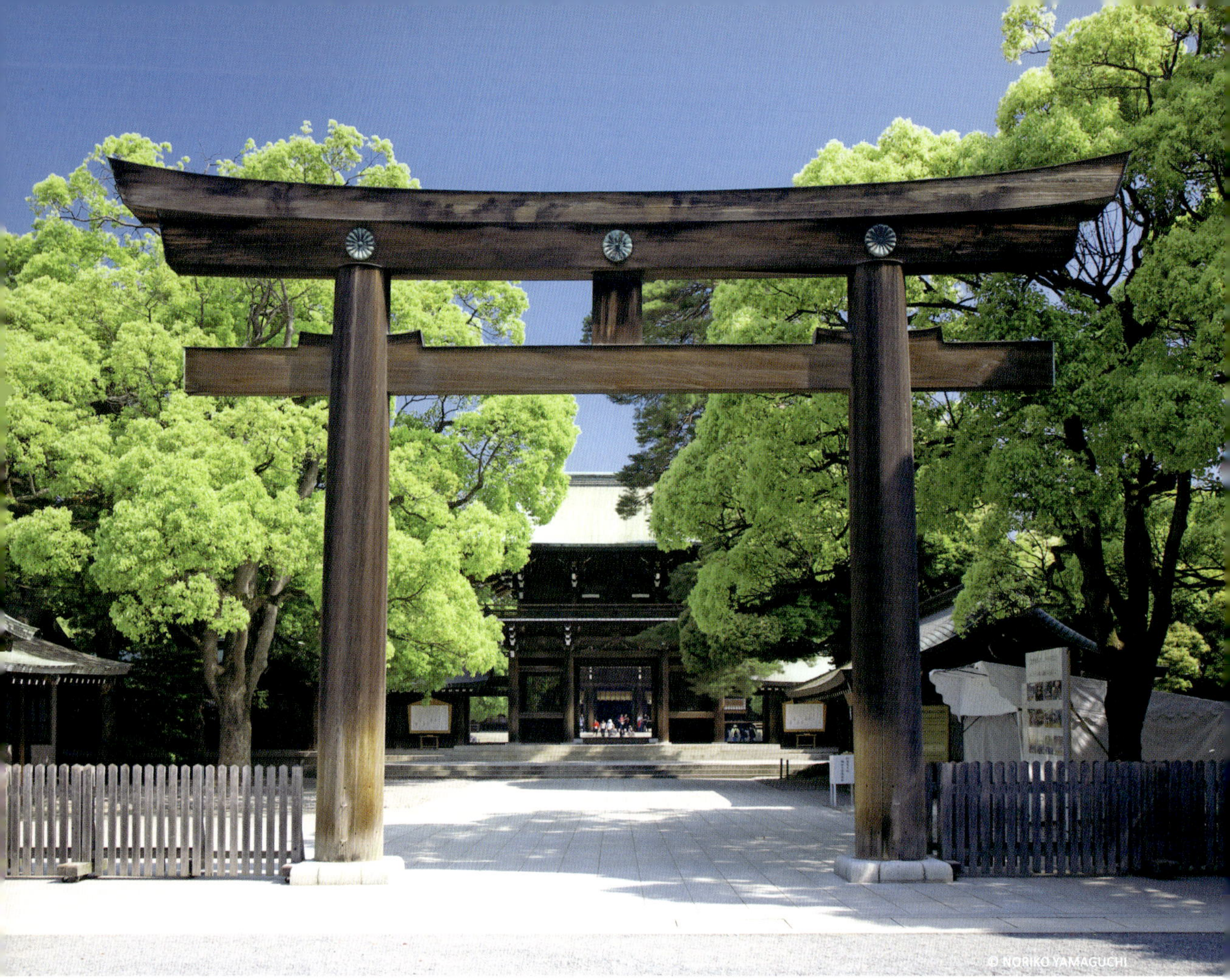

© NORIKO YAMAGUCHI

明治神宮

Meiji-jingu (Meiji Shrine) ■ TOKYO

Meiji-jingu was built in 1920 and is dedicated to the deified spirits of Emperor Meiji and his wife, Empress Shoken.
The shrine's grounds cover 700,000 hectares and members of the national youth organization volunteered their labor in laying out the grounds and the trees in the grounds of the shrine were donated from all over Japan. Meiji-jingu has the largest turnout of all shrines and temples in Japan of people visiting to celebrate the New Year (the first three of January).

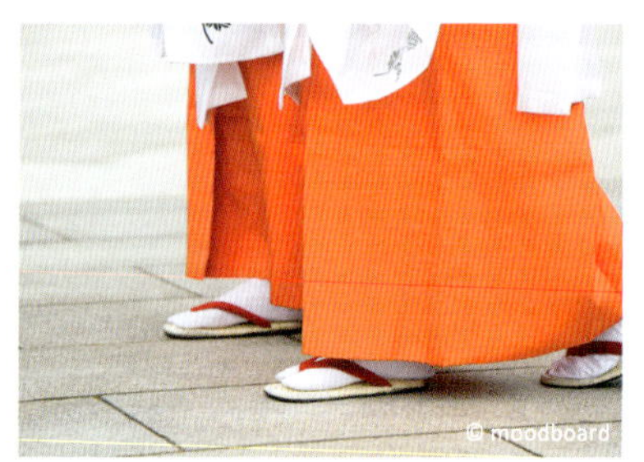

© moodboard

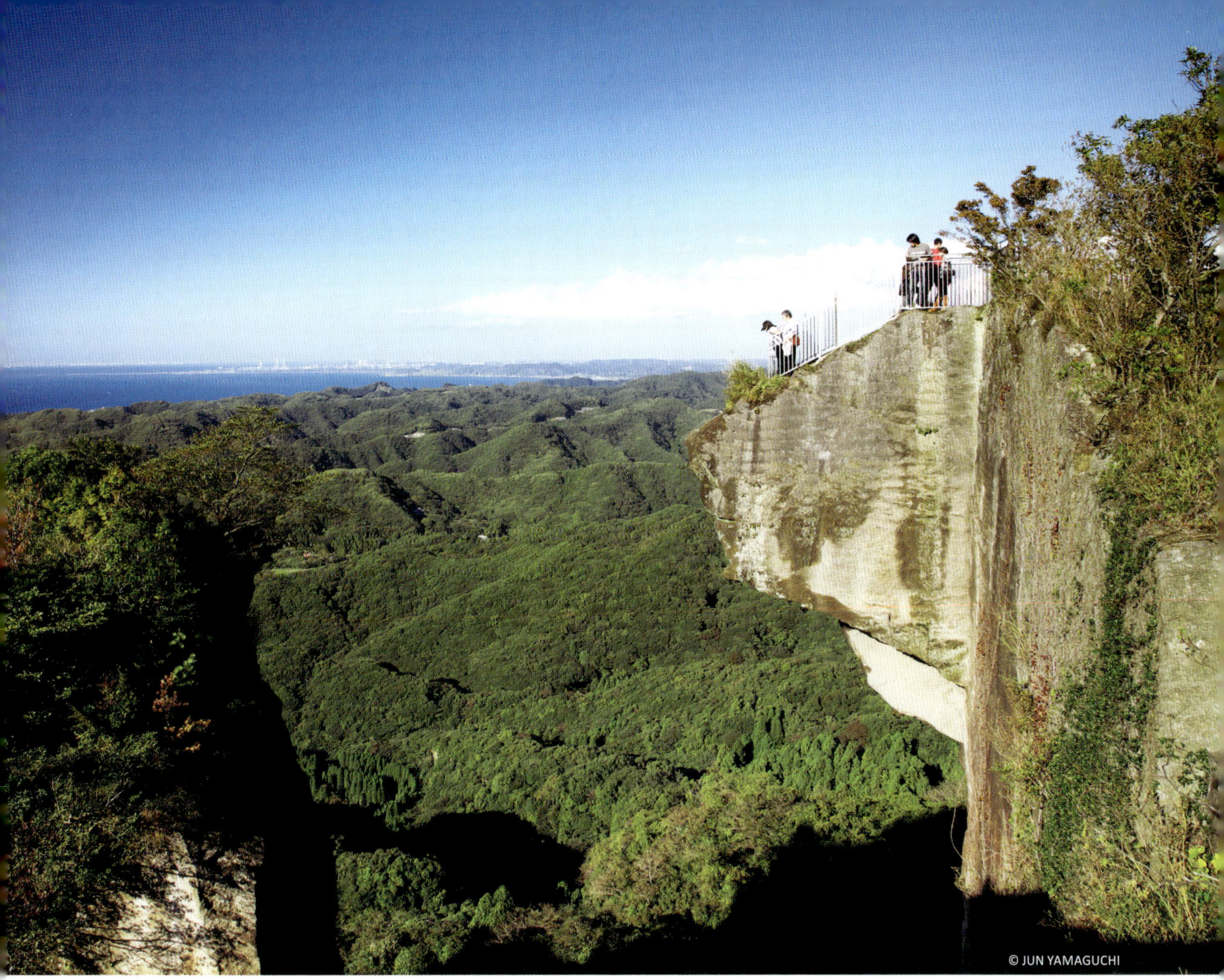

鋸山

Mount Nokogiri ▪ CHIBA

The mountain has a characteristic saw-toothed ridgeline and its name derives from this. Because stone used to be quarried there, steep cliffs are to be found all over the mountain.

On the mountain's upper slopes is the Nihon-ji temple, founded 1,300 years ago. At the peak is an overhanging cliff called *Jigoku-nozoki* ("peering into hell") and the observation deck there provides a panorama of Tokyo Bay, the Boso Peninsula and Mount Fuji. Hyaku-shaku Kannon is a 10.3 meters carving of the Buddhist deity of mercy in a stone wall on the mountain. Visitors pray to the Hyaku-shaku Kannon, the temple's main object of worship, for safety when travelling on land, sea and in the air.

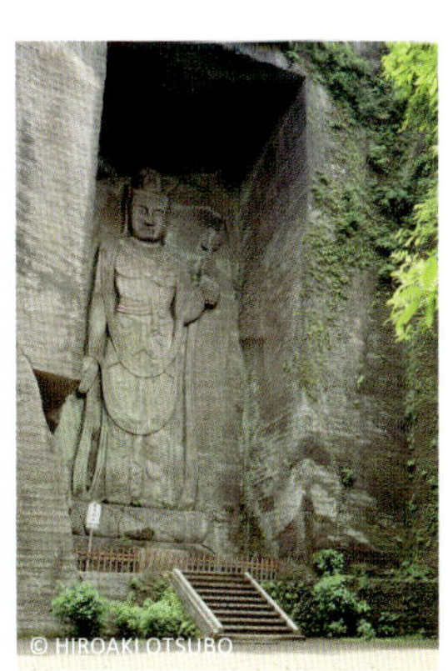

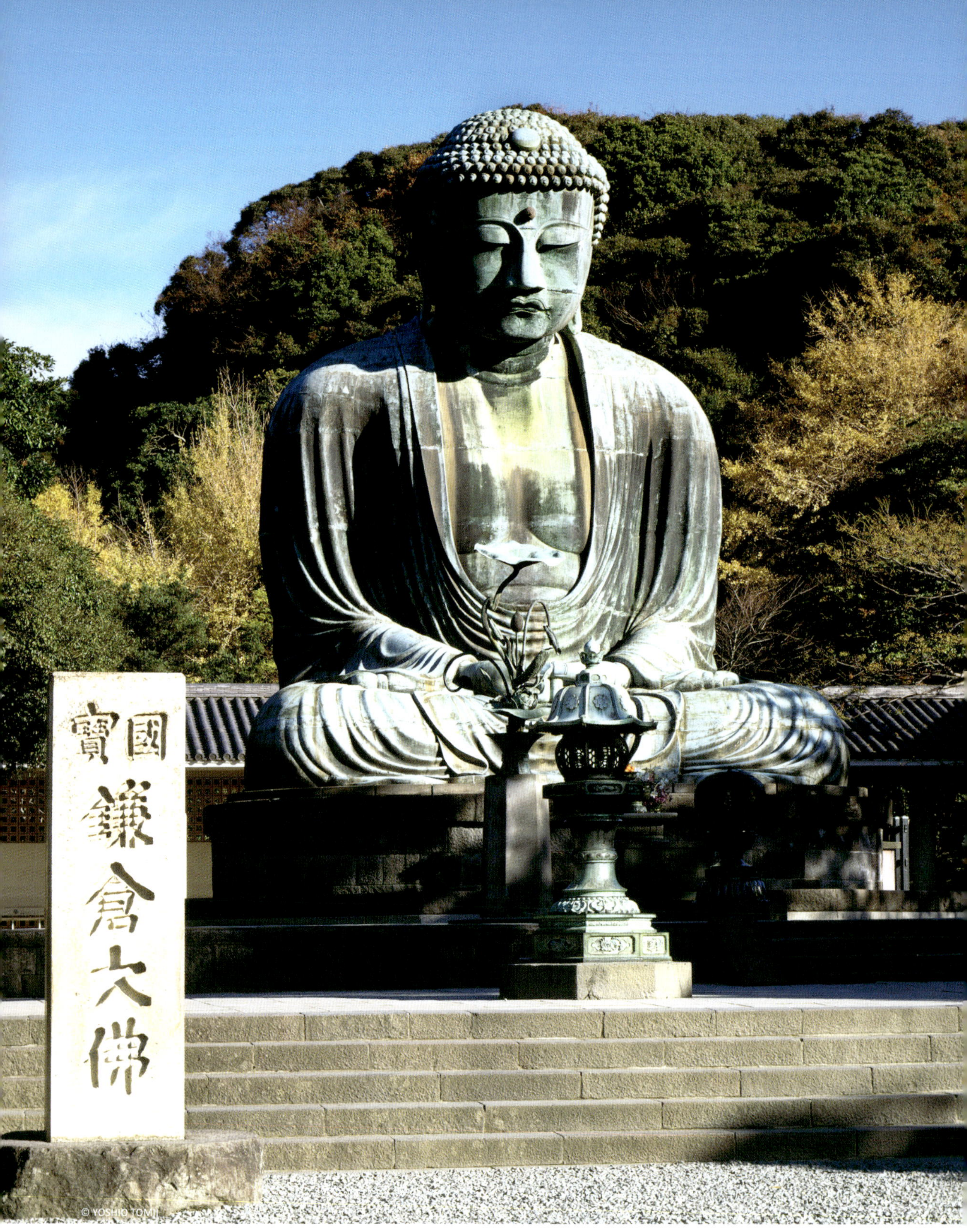

© YOSHIO TOMII

The Great Buddha ▪ KANAGAWA

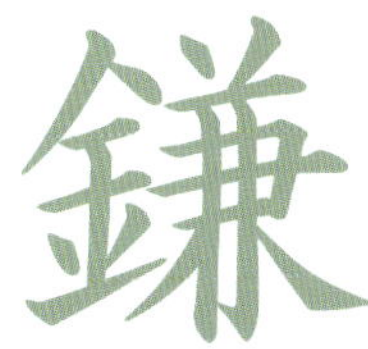

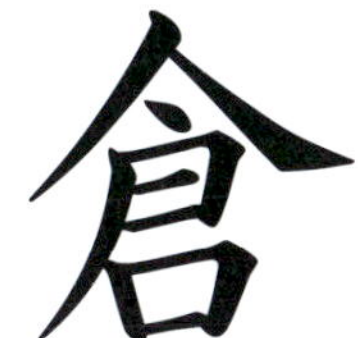

This giant bronze statue of a seated Buddha is 11.3 meters tall and weighs 121 tons. Known as the Kamakura Daibutsu (Great Buddha) or the Hase Daibutsu, it is the main object of worship at Kotoku-in, a Buddhist temple in Hase, in Kamakura City. The Nara Daibutsu and the Kamakura Daibutsu are the two biggest seated Buddha statues in Japan. The first Kamakura Daibutsu was completed in 1243. It was made of wood and sat inside a hall. However, in the late 15th century, records have the Kamakura Daibutsu as being out in the open air. It was resurrected in the 18th century and a ceremony was held in 1739 to consecrate the repaired statue of the Kamakura Daibutsu, as we know it today. Of all the statues of Buddha in Kamakura, it is the only one designated as a National Treasure.

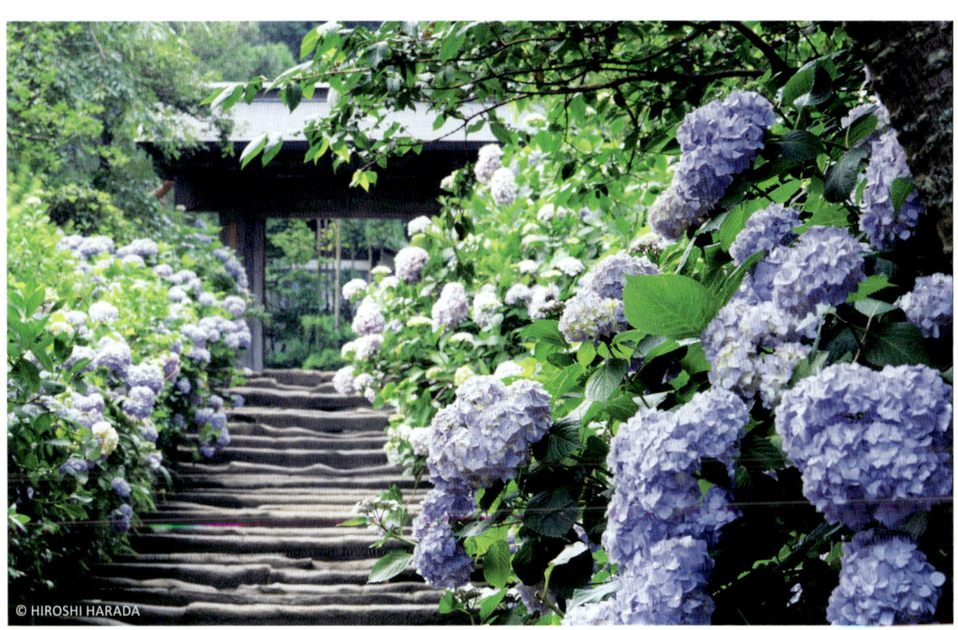
© HIROSHI HARADA

Meigetsu-in (Meigetsu Temple) ▪ KANAGAWA

Hydrangeas were planted in the temple grounds in the post-war period and they grew profusely in what was an ideal climate for them. By the 1960s hydrangeas covered the sides of the stones step entranceway to the temple and throughout the grounds. People began talking of it as a place famous for hydrangeas and it became popular with tourists giving rise to the name Ajisai-dera (Temple of Hydrangeas).
In June, the season for hydrangeas, large numbers of visitors to the temple can be seen getting off at Kita-Kamakura, the station closest to the temple.

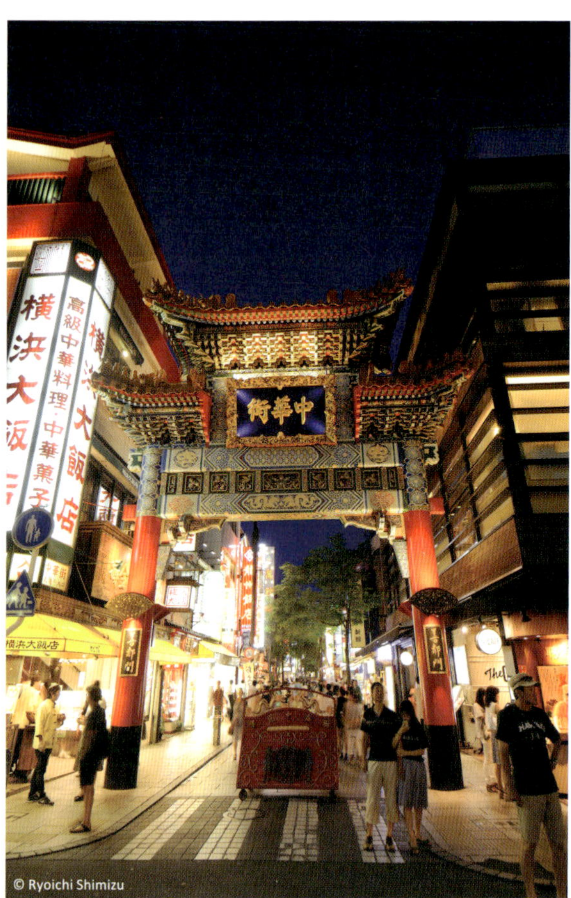

© Ryoichi Shimizu

横浜

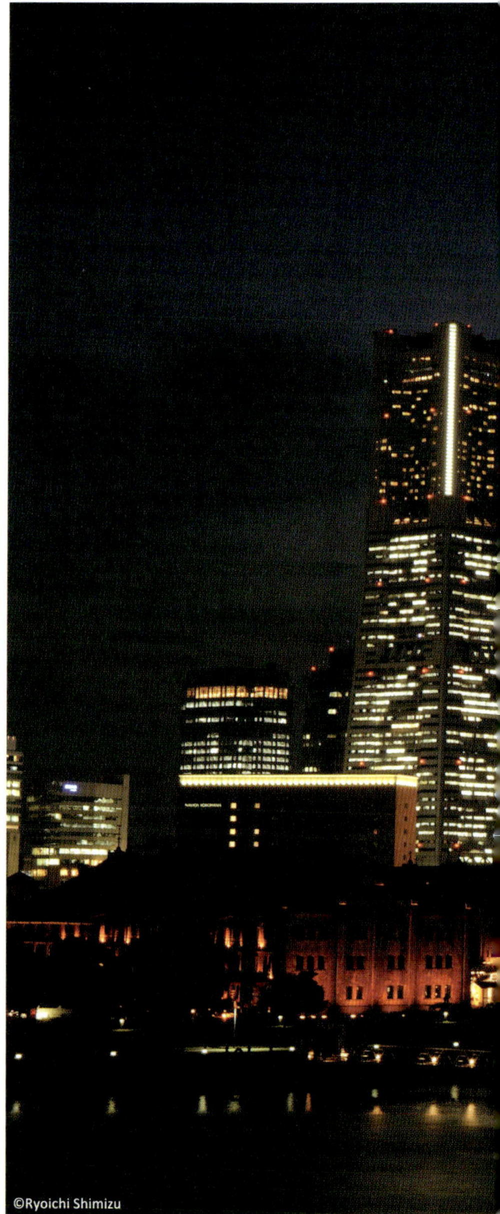
©Ryoichi Shimizu

Yokohama Chinatown
▪ KANAGAWA

There are more than 500 shops within the 200 square meters that make up this area, making it the largest Chinatown in East Asia.

The four main styles of Chinese cuisine from the Canton area, Shanghai, Beijing and the Sichuan province, can all be found in Yokohama Chinatown's small area. Four colorful gates mark the entrance to Chinatown on the east south, west and north sides. The shrine devoted to General Guan Yu, one of the characters in the Records of the Three Kingdoms, is said to be the most powerful spot of Yokohama Chinatown.

Yokohama Minato Mirai ▪ KANAGAWA

Facing the port of Yokohama, the Minato Mirai area is home to many attractions. Landmark Tower has an observatory on its 70th floor called Sky Garden which offers sweeping views of Yokohama. The Yokohama Red Brick Warehouse complex has historical buildings from the early Meiji Period. After the sun has gone down, visitors can enjoy the fantastic and beautiful illuminations from the giant Ferris wheel at the Cosmo World Amusement Park. The Minato Mirai area also boasts various shops, theatres and museums so visitors can spend the whole day here without getting bored.

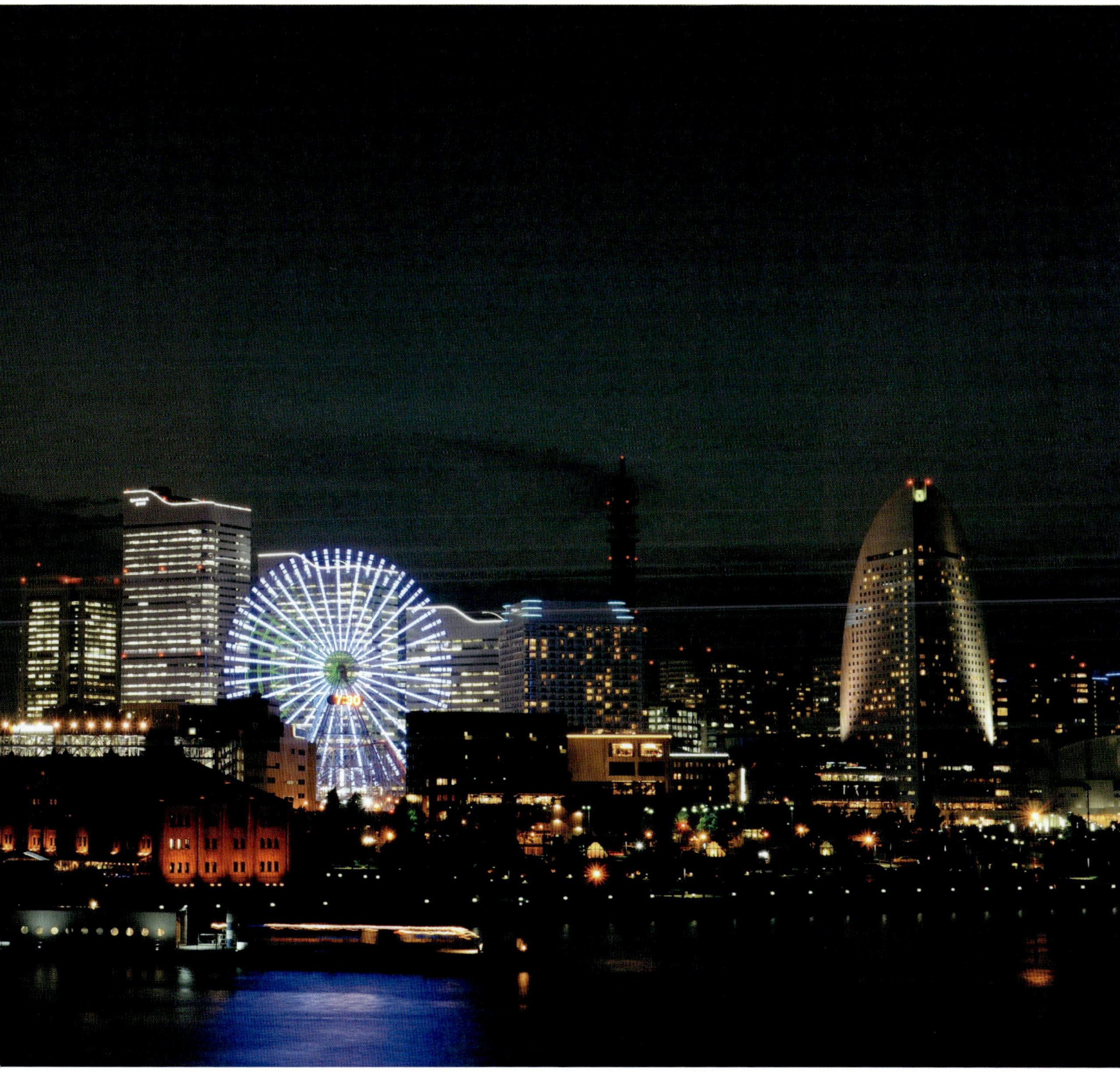

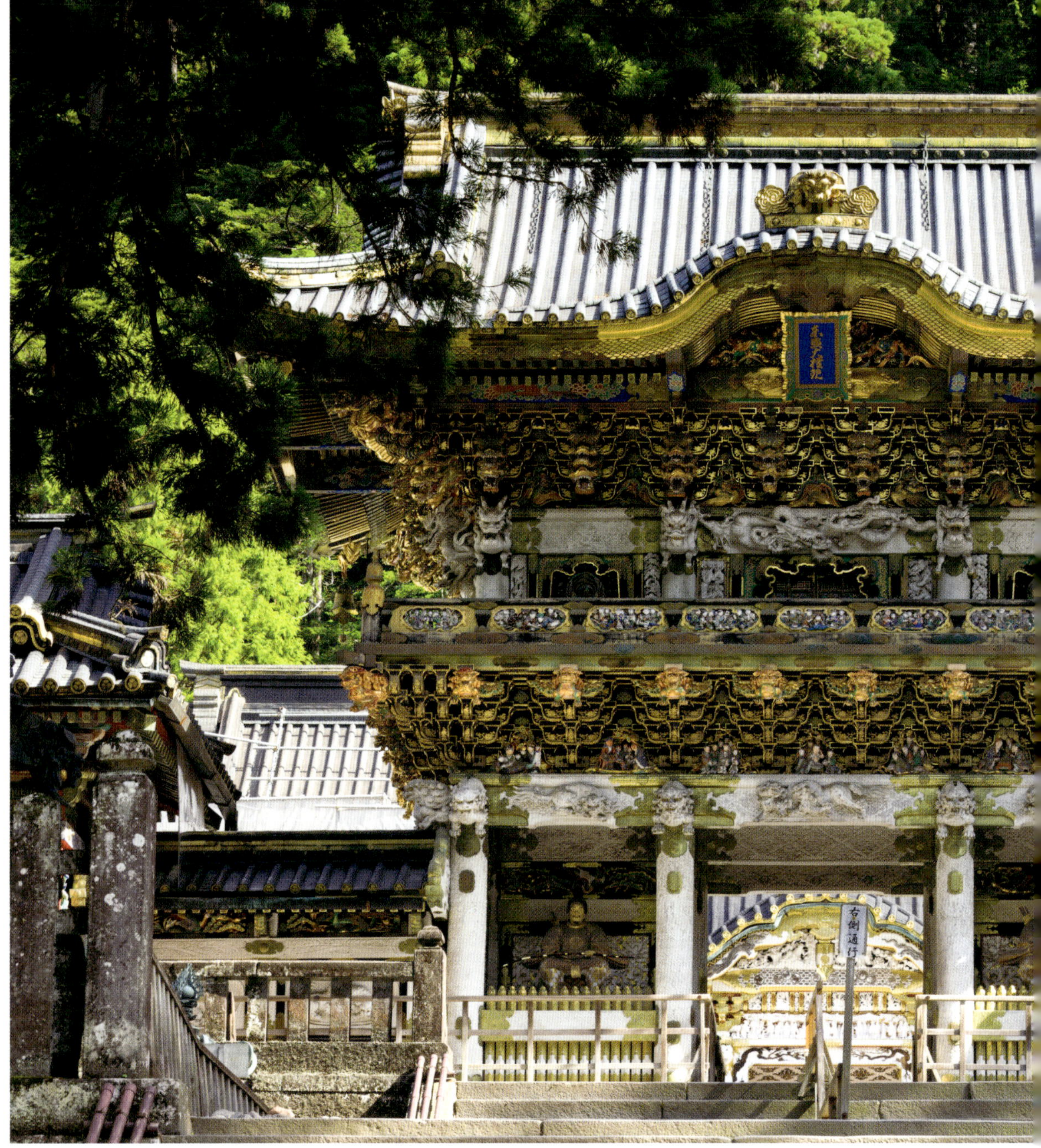

Nikko Toshogu Shrine ▪ TOCHIGI

Two Shinto shrines and one Buddhist temple in Nikko are inscribed on the World Heritage List as Temples and Shrines of Nikko. The most famous of these is Nikko Toshogu which is the mausoleum of Tokugawa Ieyasu. Nikko Toshogu is composed of a group of luxurious and splendid shrine buildings. The Yomeimon two-storied gate is characteristic of the Nikko architecture style. The gate is so splendid that it said to have used all the decorative techniques available at the time in Edo and has numerous carved decorations on it.

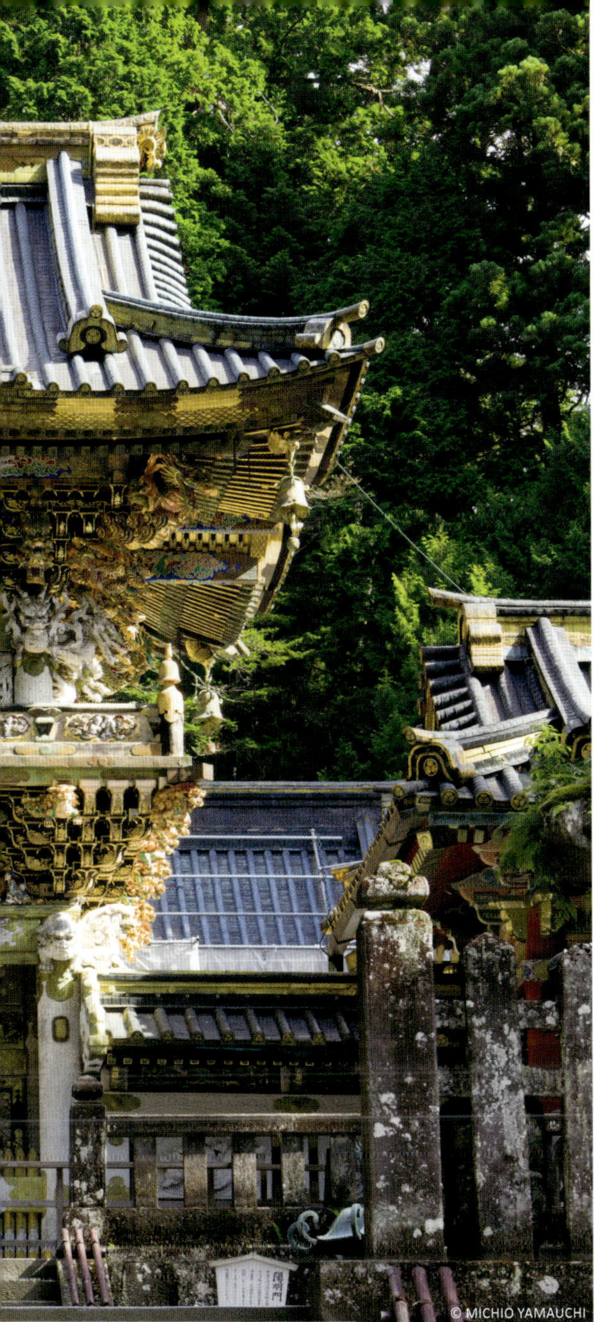
© MICHIO YAMAUCHI

日光東照宮

The Three Wise Monkeys

The carving of the Three Wise Monkeys is on the Stable of the Sacred Horse. Eight sections of carvings with monkeys are used to symbolize a person's life. One of those sections is the Three Wise Monkeys – *Mizaru* (see no evil), *Iwazaru* (speak no evil) and *Kikazaru* (hear no evil). *Zaru* is a play on words meaning "Do not..." and is a different pronunciation of *saru*, which means monkey. The Three Wise Monkeys, famous worldwide and seen in India and other countries, represent this teaching.

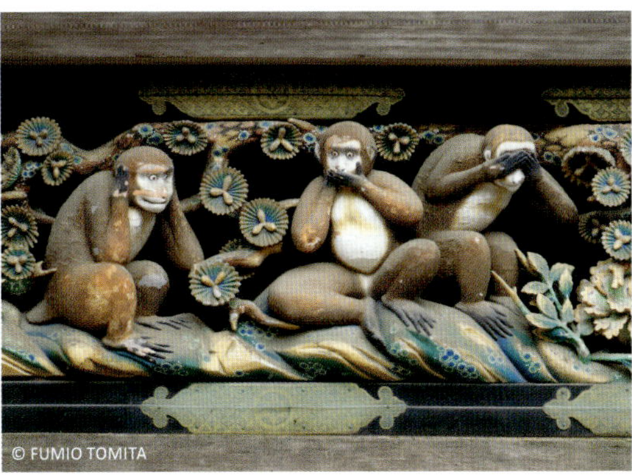
© FUMIO TOMITA

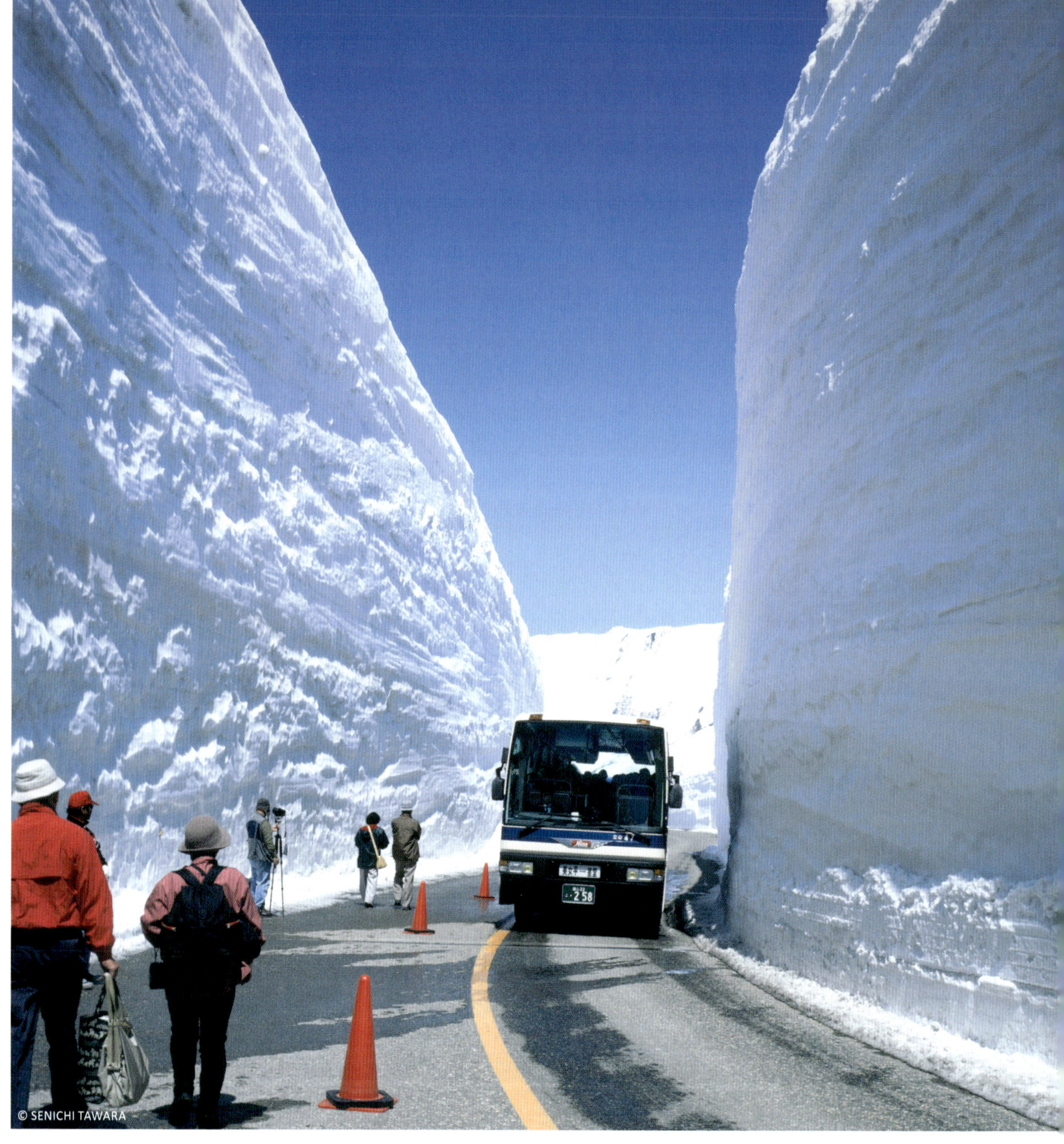

Otani walk in the snow ▪ TOYAMA

Murodo-daira, at an altitude of 2450 meters in the Tateyama district of Toyama Prefecture, is an area with one of the heaviest snowfalls in the world. Otani, in particular, boasts a high snowfall and when the snow is cleared from the roads, giant walls of snow on either side of the road are formed. The walls can sometimes be more than 20 meters high and continue for nearly 500 meters on both sides of the road.

From April to June every year, half of the road is shut off from cars so that people can walk along it and many tourists come to experience it. The area buzzes with activity as some people carve messages into the snow wall.

松本城

立山

Matsumoto Castle

▪ NAGANO

This castle with five levels and six stories in the keep is located in Matsumoto City in Nagano Prefecture, and is designated as a National Treasure. Of Japan's castles with keeps, this castle is the third oldest after Inuyama Castle in Aichi Prefecture and Maruoka Castle in Fukui Prefecture.

In 1868, when Japan entered the Meiji Period, the keep was auctioned and the castle was in danger of being torn down, but it was saved after protests by the local conservation society and subsequently renovated as a project to preserve national treasures since 1950. The sight of the keep with the Japanese Alps in the background is splendid.

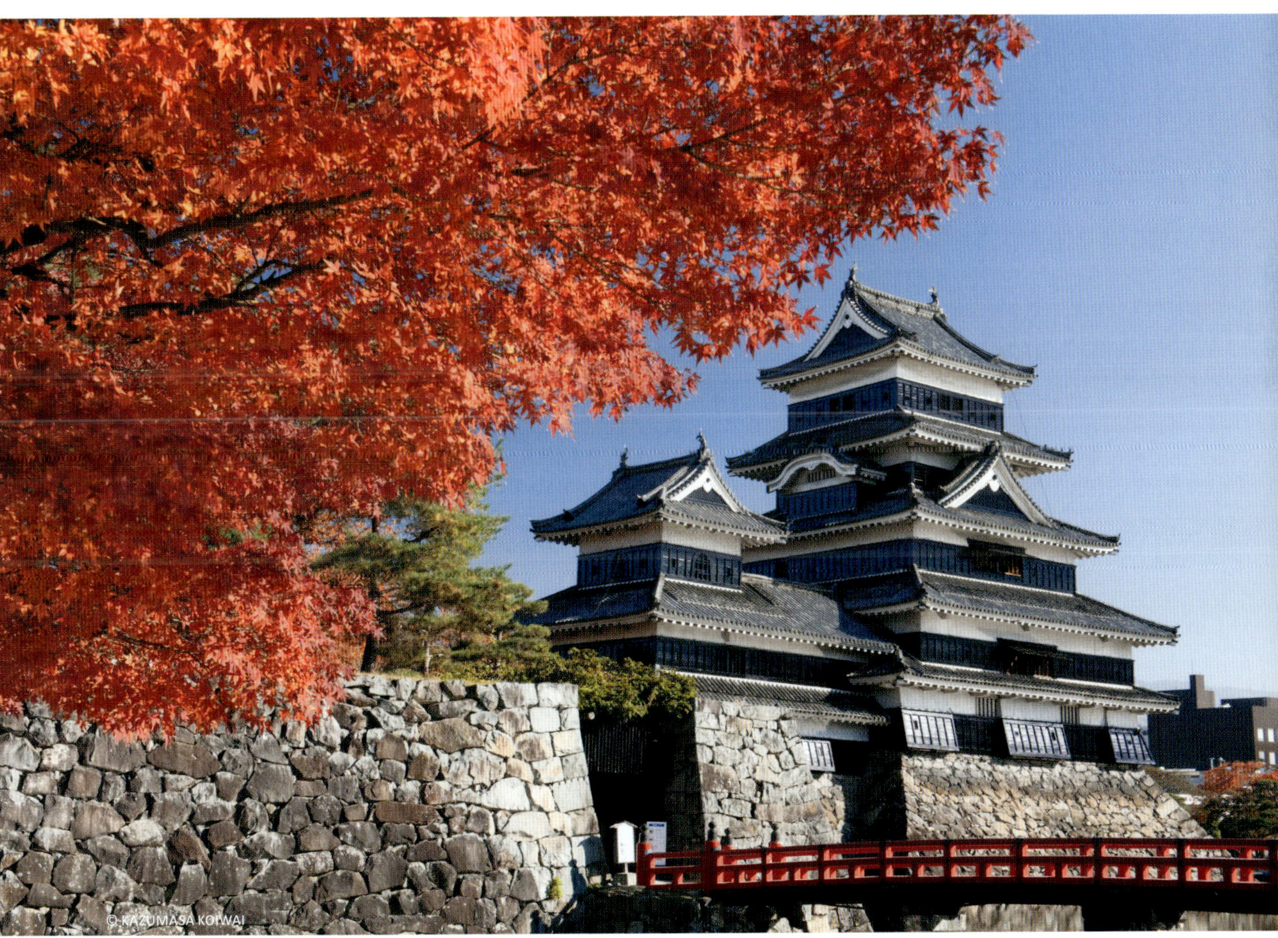

© KAZUMASA KOIWAI

Kusatsu Onsen (hot spring)

▪ GUNMA

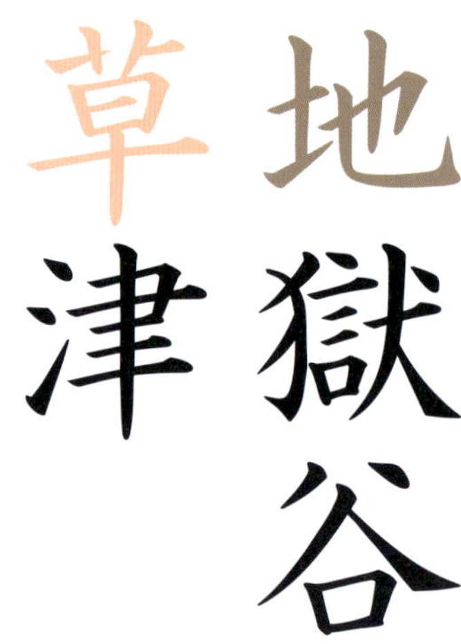

Kusatsu Onsen boasts the largest volume of natural flowing hot water in Japan at a rate of more than 32,300 liters per minute. Kusatsu has been well known for its hot springs from long ago and more than 2,700,000 people visit this famous and popular hot spring annually. Yubatake, in the middle of the cluster of Kusatsu's hot springs, is a symbol of Kusatsu as its largest spring. Yubatake always has clouds of steam billowing up from the hot water that gushes out. The promenade is paved with roof tiles and the area is imbued with a typical hot spring atmosphere.

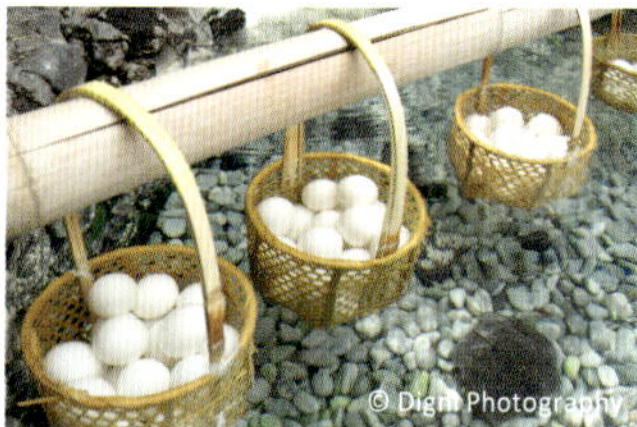

Onsen-Tamago (Hot spring eggs)

Onsen-tamago are made by using the steam or hot water from the hot springs to boil or steam eggs. A certain shop selling glasswork in Kusatsu has a small hot spring outside its premises especially for making *onsen-tamago*. The eggs look very cute when put into a basket and submerged into the hot spring.

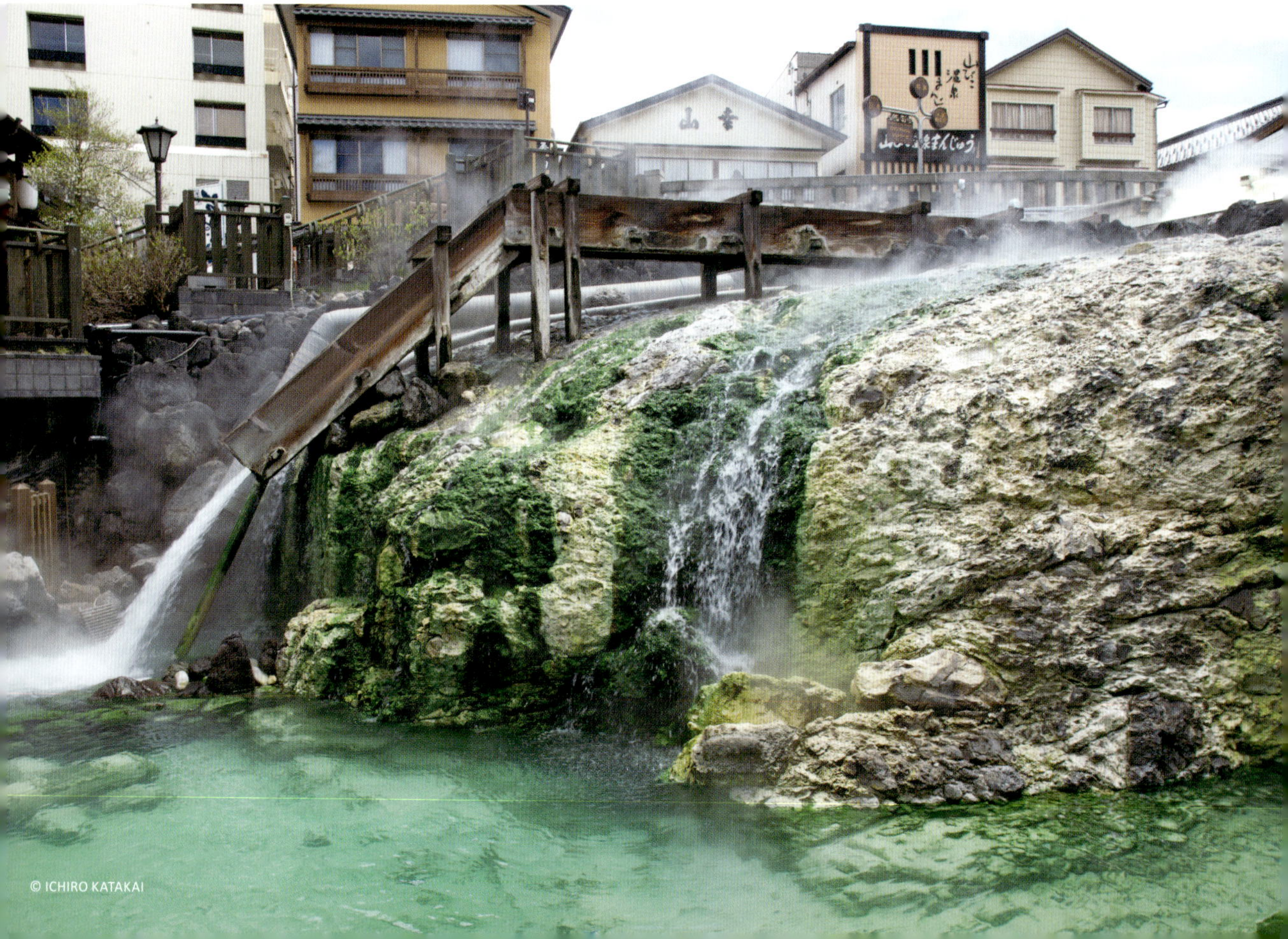

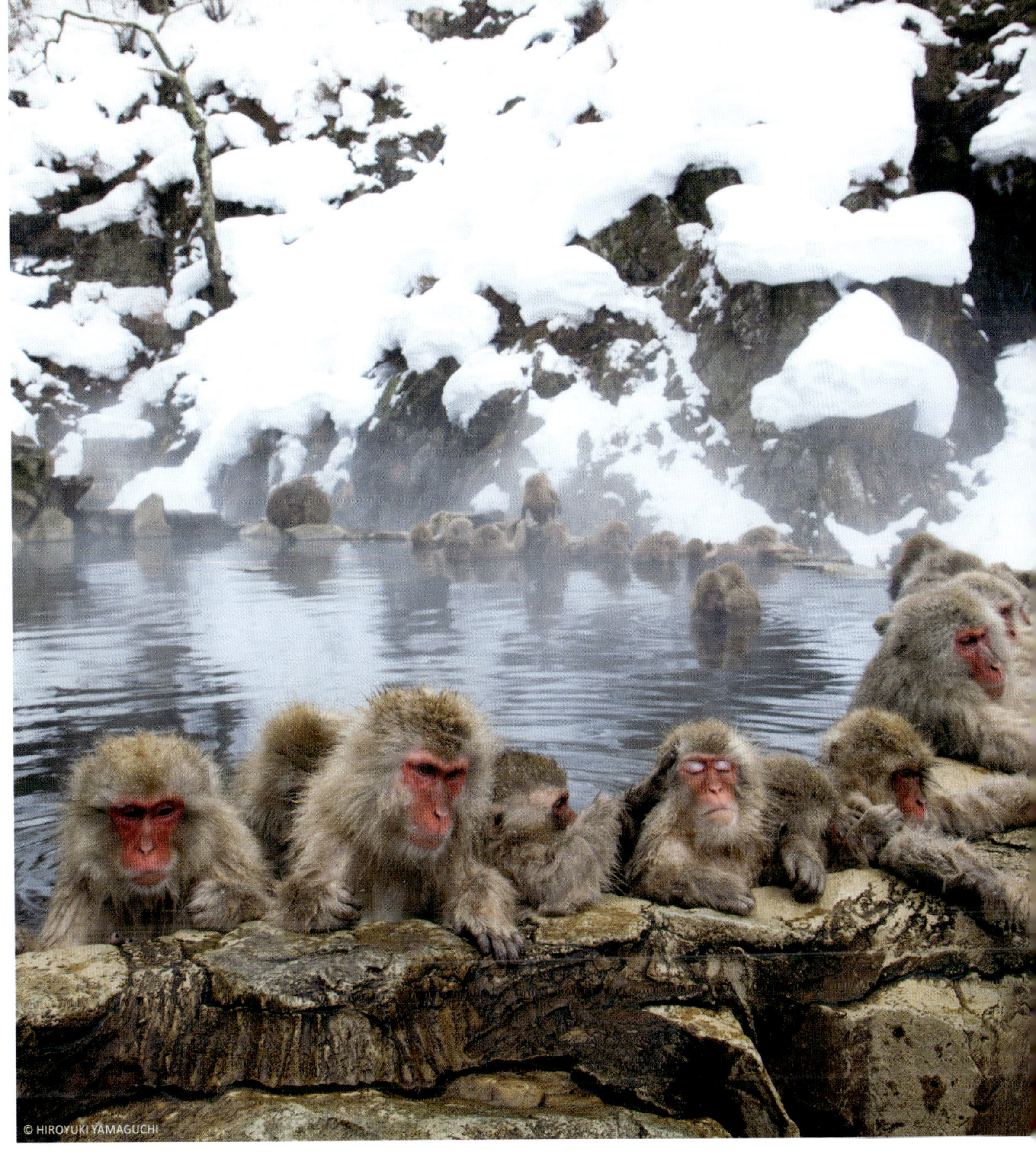
© HIROYUKI YAMAGUCHI

Jigokudani Monkey Park ▪ NAGANO

This Monkey Park in Nagano Prefecture was set up to protect Japanese monkeys and provide a place where they can be observed. Surrounded by very steep cliffs, and with the hot spring fountain always emitting steam, it was given the name Jigokudani (Hell Valley). The area experiences severe cold and deep snow in winter. The wild monkeys who inhabit this area starting coming to the Monkey Park to escape from the bitter cold by bathing in the hot spring. The Japanese monkeys of Jigokudani were featured on the cover of the U.S. magazine *LIFE* in 1970, and the Japanese monkeys who bathe in hot springs seem to be quite famous overseas.

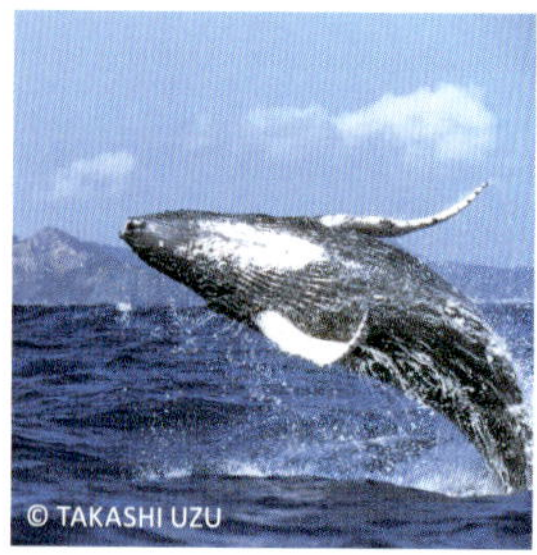
© TAKASHI UZU

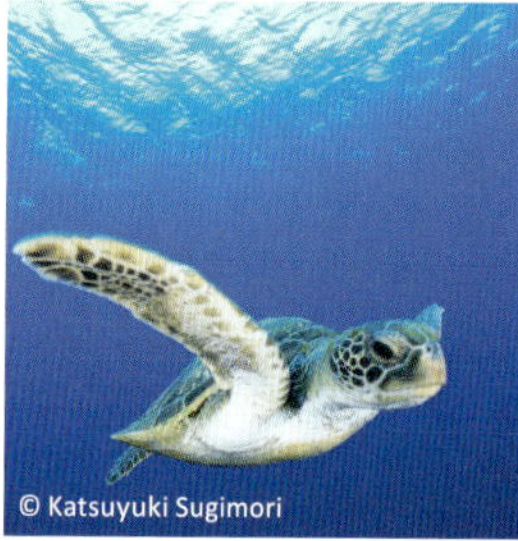
© Katsuyuki Sugimori

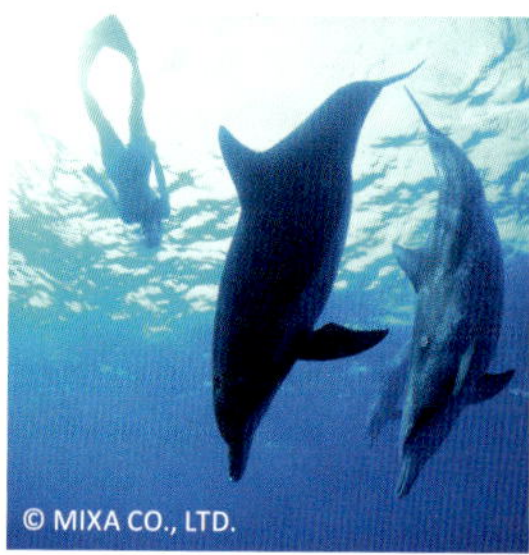
© MIXA CO., LTD.

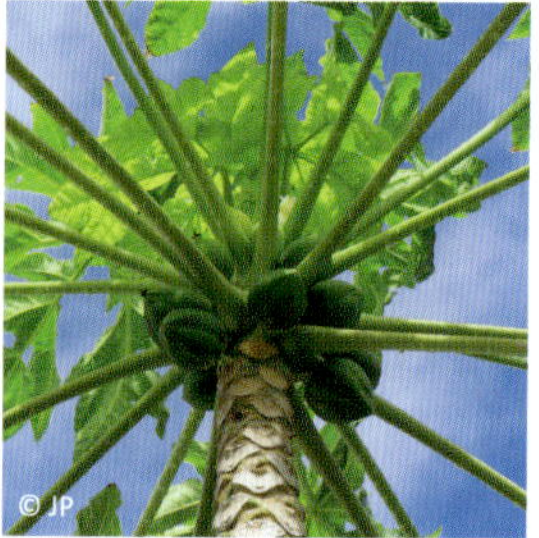
© JP

小笠原諸島

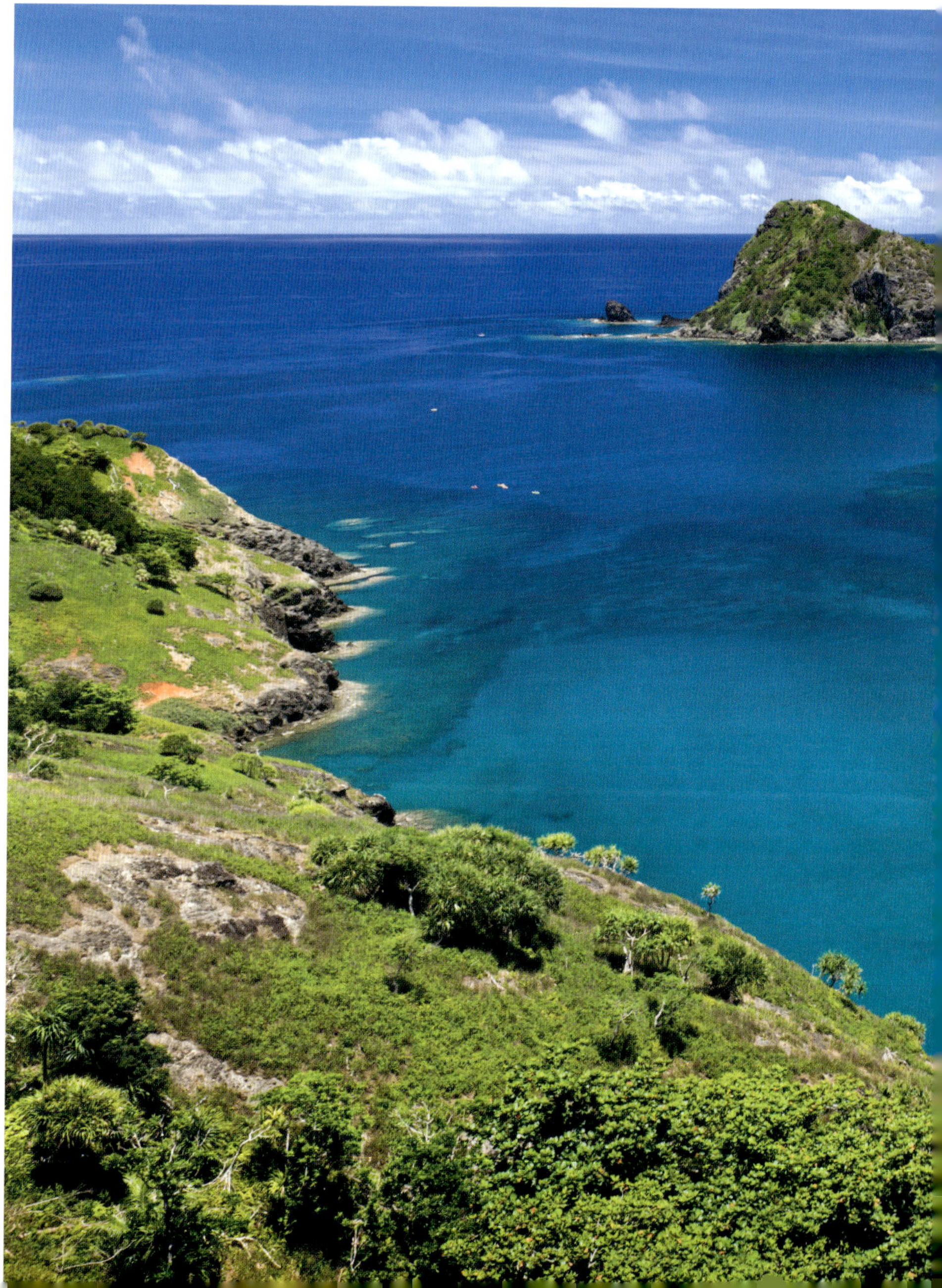

Ogasawara Islands ▪ TOKYO

Located 1,000 kilometers south of Tokyo, the Ogasawara Islands stretch for approximately 400 kilometers from north to south and are a group of 30 large and small islands. About 550 kilometers away from the Mariana Islands, none of the Ogasawara Islands has ever been connected to a continent. Because of that, they have a unique ecosystem which is a treasure trove of species endemic to the islands. The rarity of their ecosystem was appraised and in 2011, the Ogasawara Islands were listed as a World Heritage site. The only way of getting to the islands is by a liner service which runs just once every six days. Each year, 17,000 people visit the islands to enjoy whale-watching and scuba-diving.

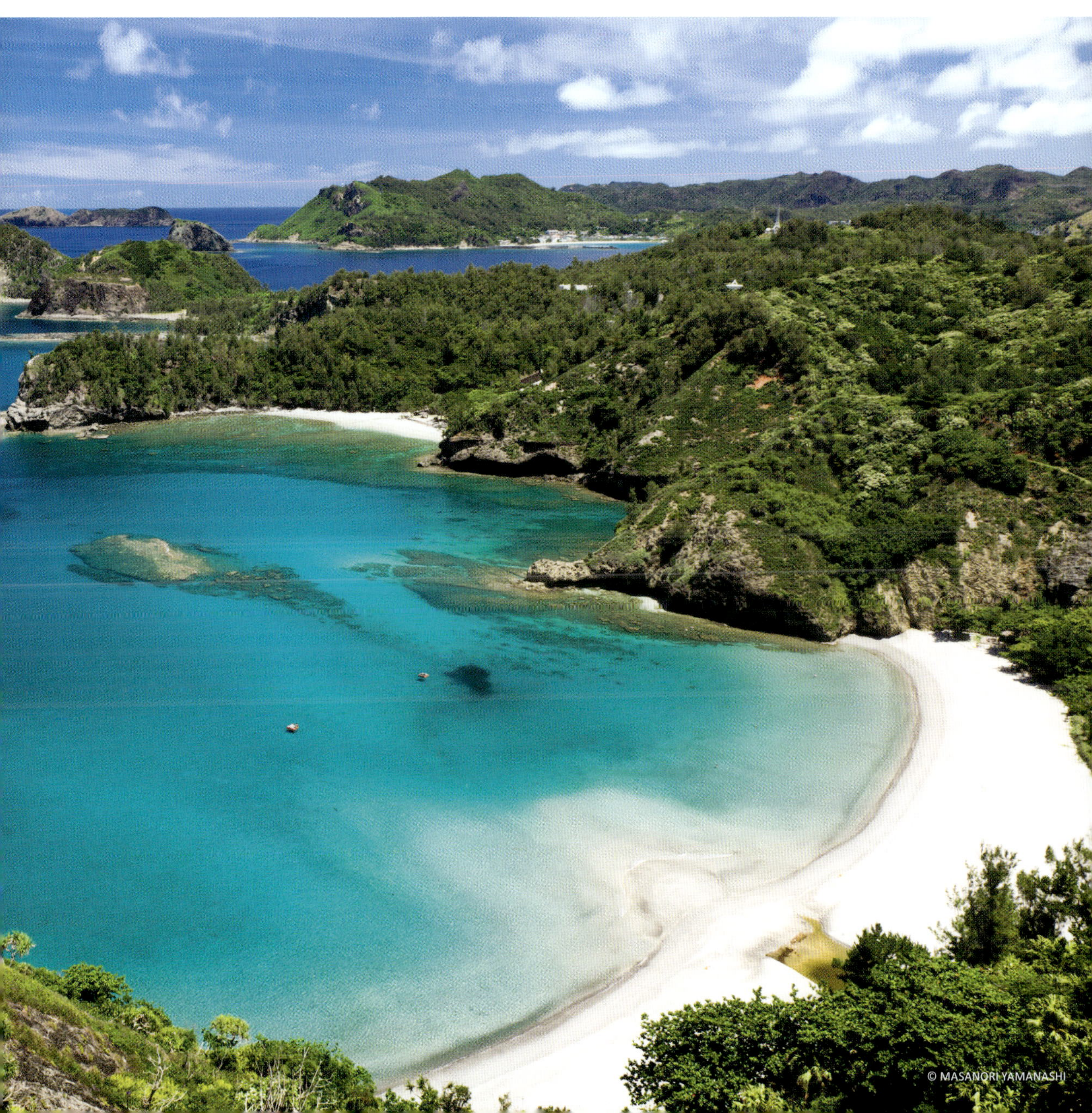

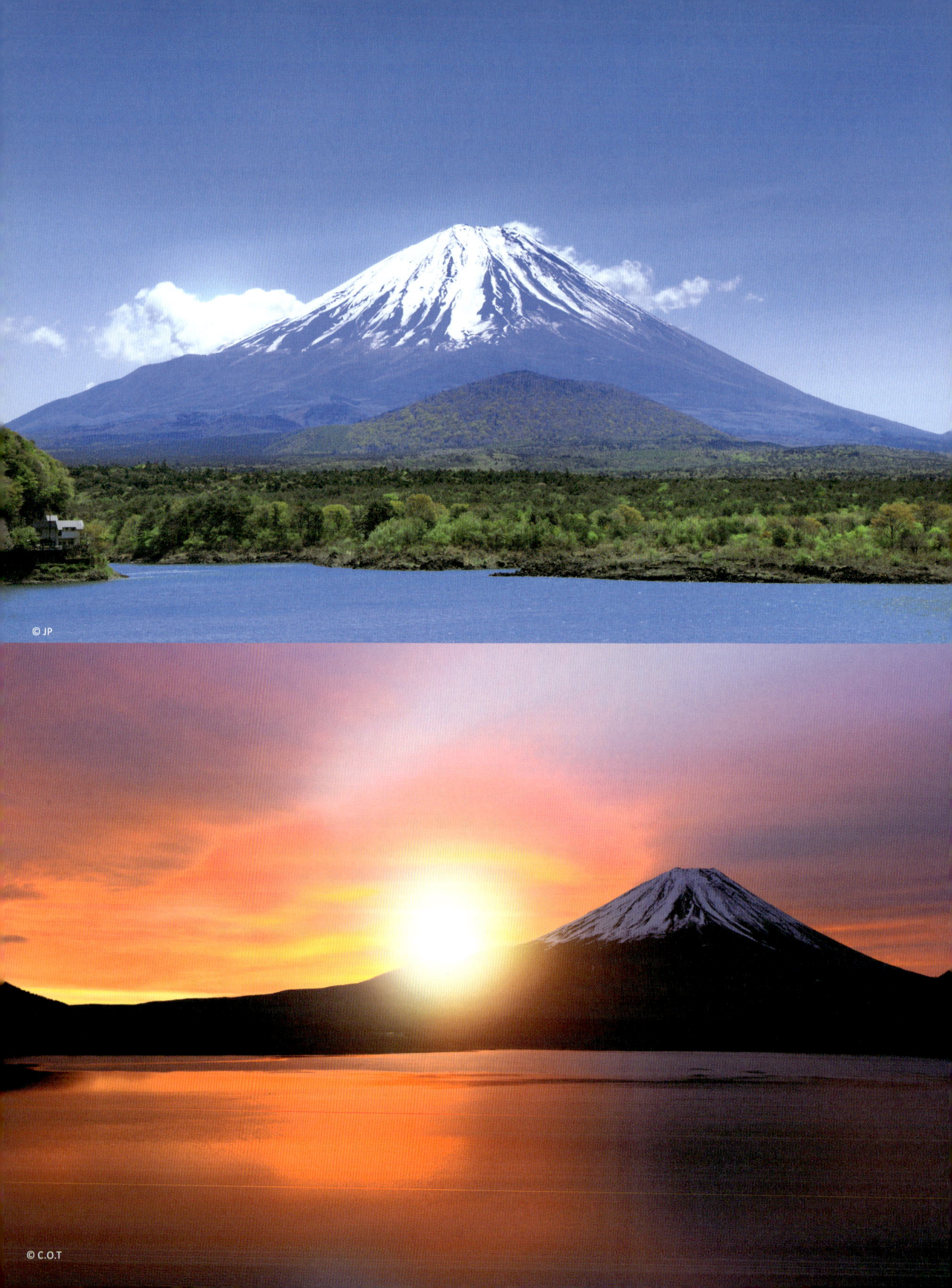

Mount Fuji ▪ SHIZUOKA

富士山

The highest mountain in Japan at a height of 3776 meters, Mount Fuji is the most famous Japanese mountain. Mount Fuji is a solitary mountain with no other big mountains close by. Mountains with a similar shape are often called given "Fuji" as a the suffix and can be found all over Japan. In other words, Mount Fuji is that special to the Japanese people. It is an object of worship and from long ago, Mount Fuji has been depicted by many artists.

The climbing season at Mount Fuji is from July 1 to August 31 and every year about 300,000 people climb the mountain during this period. Mount Fuji was listed as a World Heritage site in 2013.

Diamond Fuji

One of the more famous scenes created by Mount Fuji is the phenomenon known as Diamond Fuji. This refers to when the sun rises from the top of Mount Fuji or when it sinks down behind the peak at sunset. Because it appears bright and glittering like a diamond, this phenomenon is called Diamond Fuji.

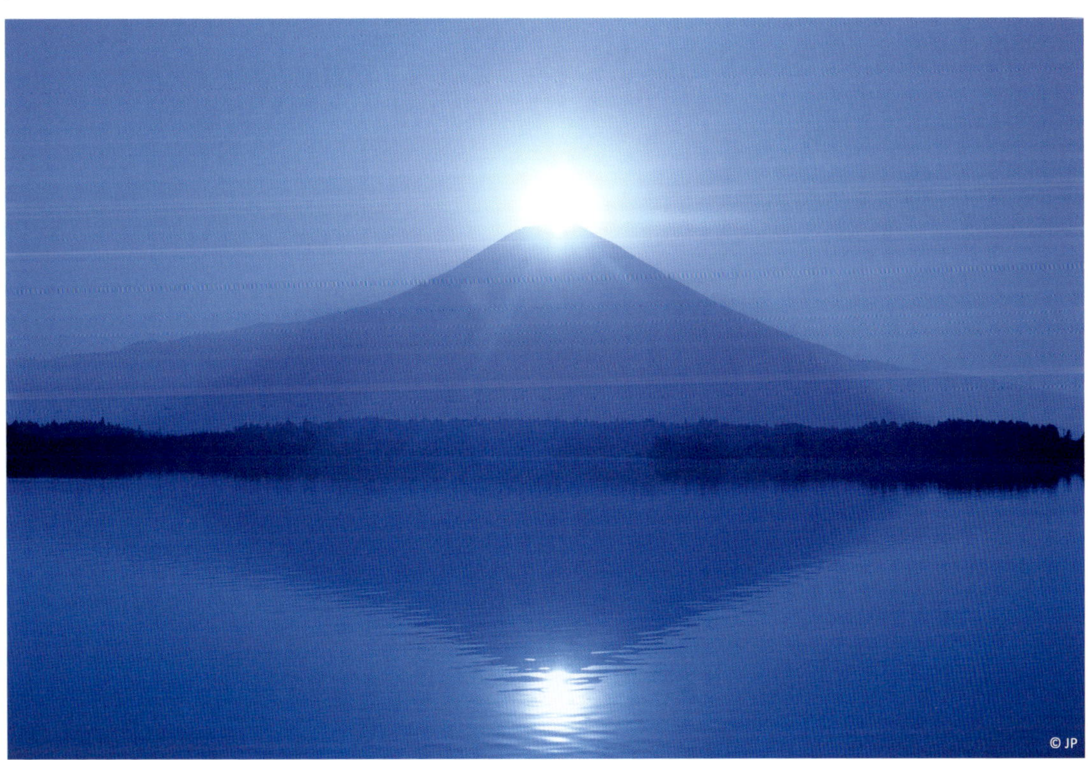

© JP

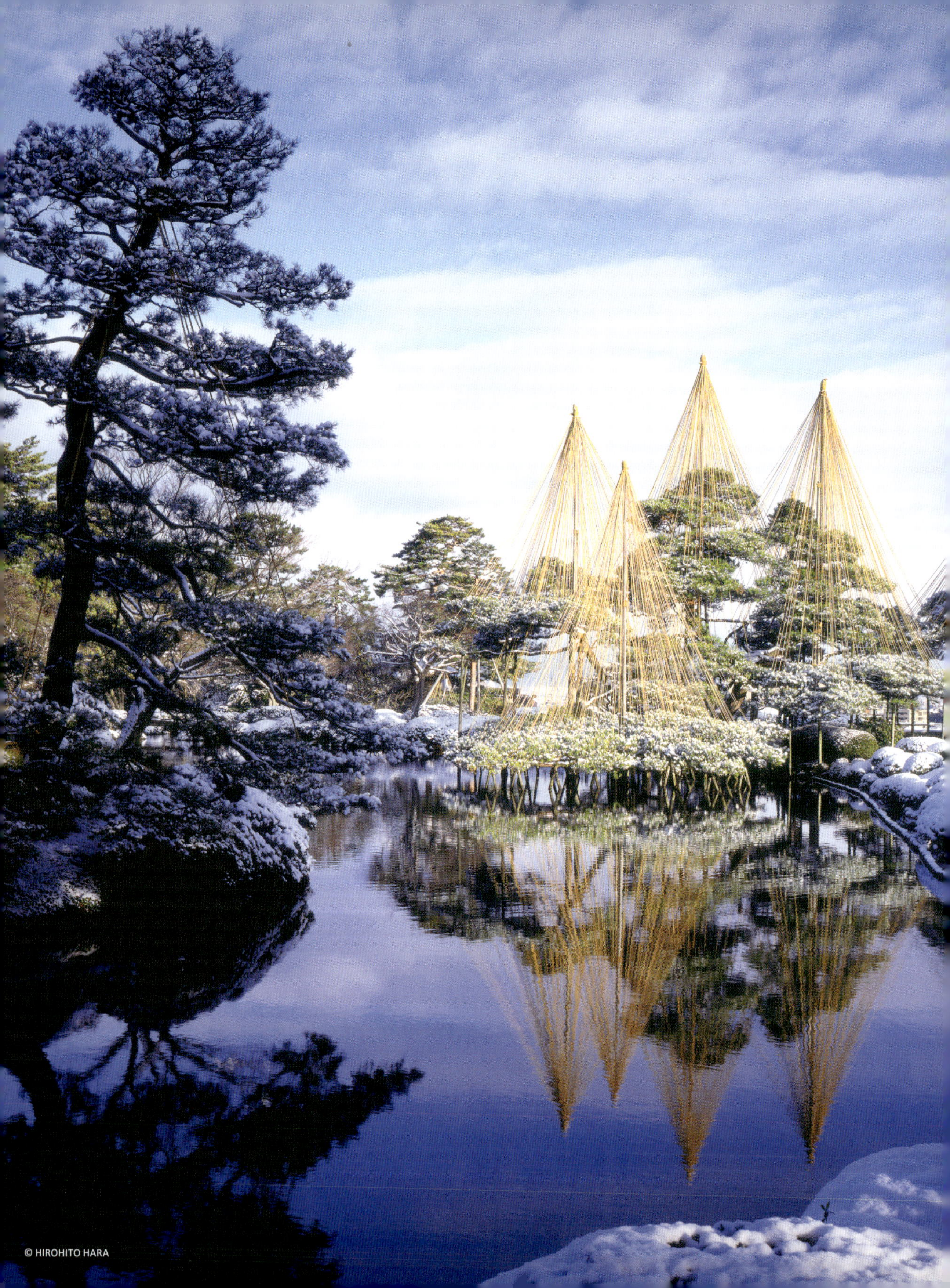

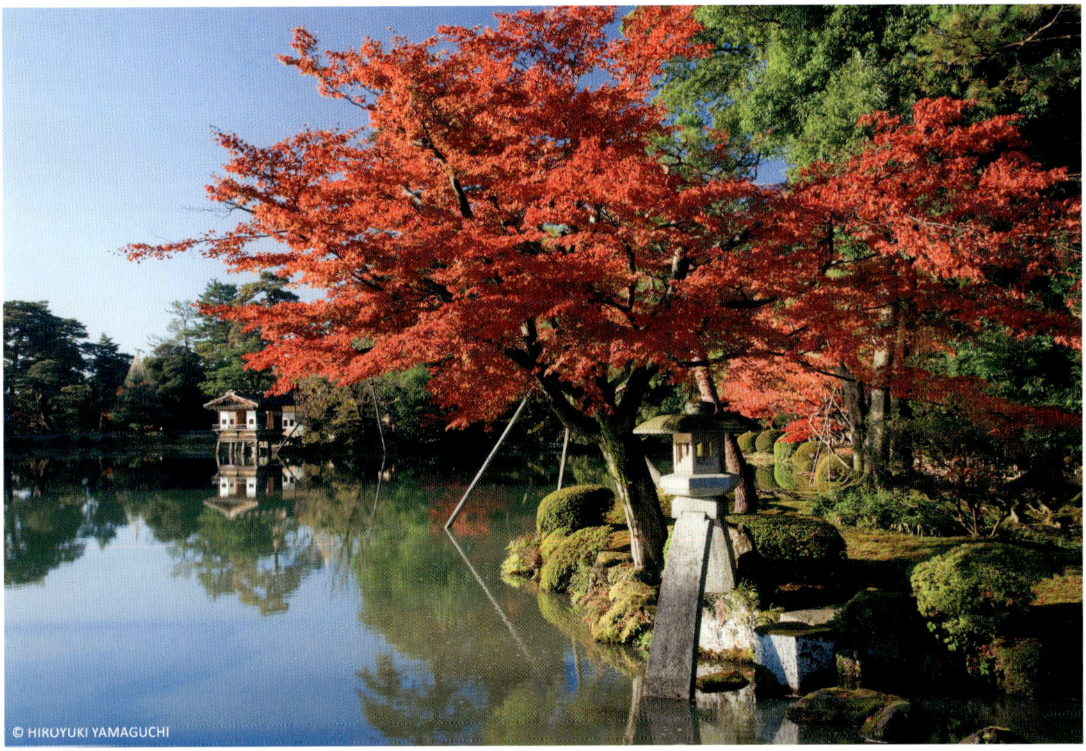

Kenroku-en (Kenroku garden)

▪ ISHIKAWA

Kenroku-en, situated in the heart of Kanazawa City, Ishikawa Prefecture, is a strolling-style landscape garden. Along with Kairaku-en in Ibaraki Prefecture and Koraku-en in Okayama Prefecture, Kenroku-en is one of Japan's three greatest gardens. It was Kaga's feudal rulers who developed Kenroku-en over centuries. They built ponds and a mountain over a large tract of land. Visitors may promenade through the garden by strolling between its multiple tea houses.

Kenroku (whose characters mean "concurrent" and "six") is so named because it combines six distinct landscapes. Following autumn leaves, pine branches are suspended from the tree top by rope, so as to support them against the weight of snow. This unique practice is famed as Kenroku-en's signature imagery for winter.

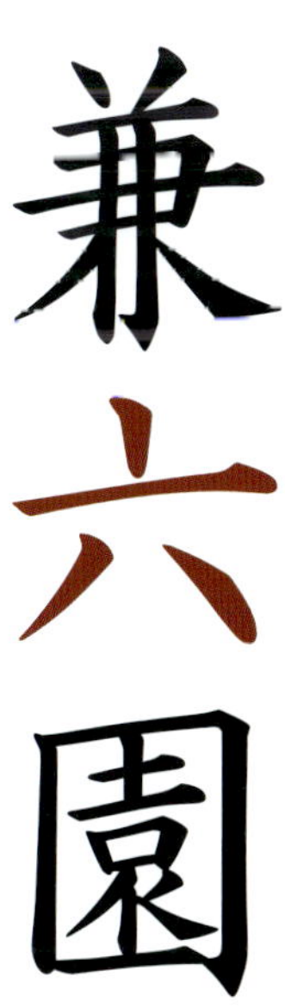

白米千枚田

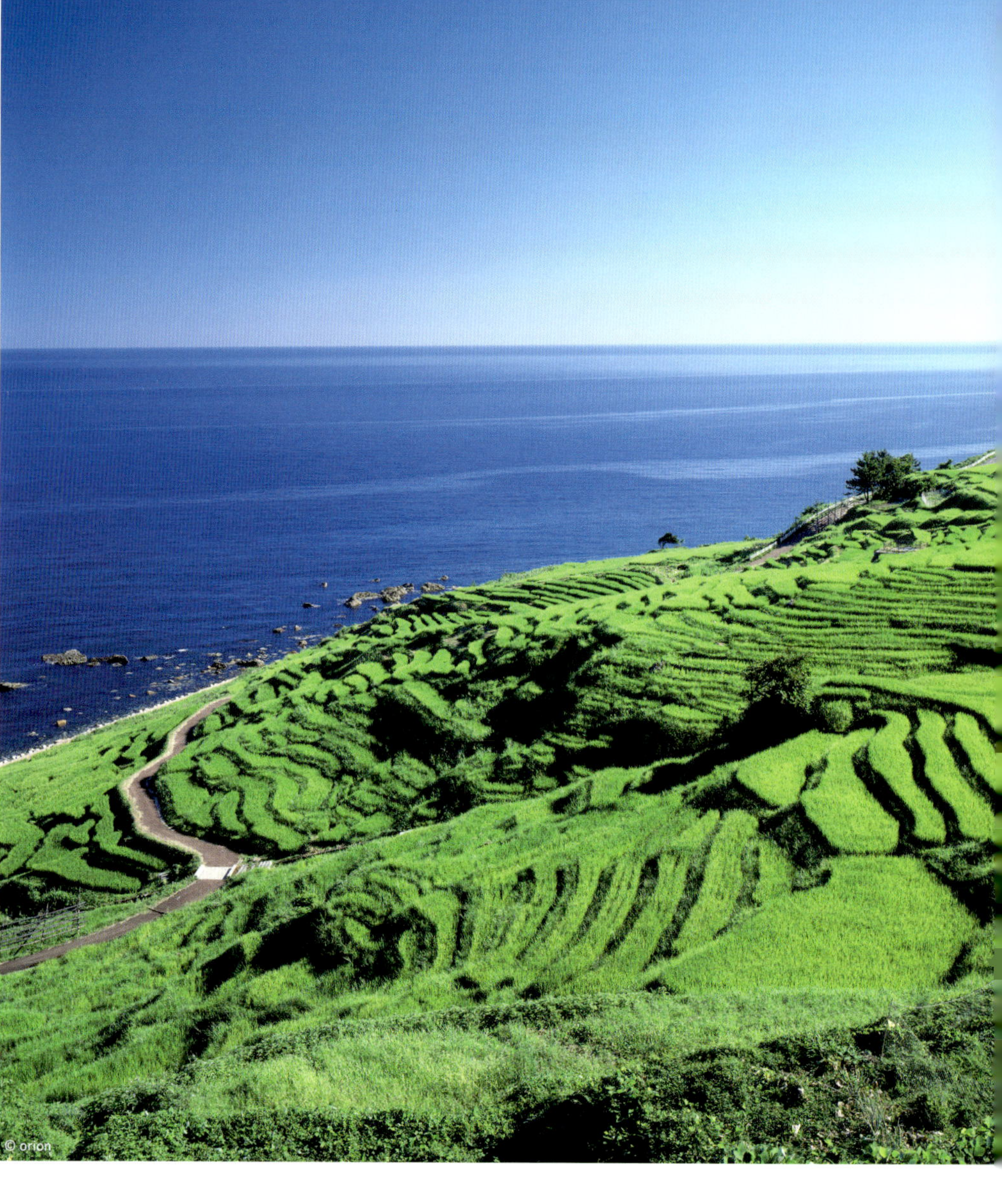

Shiroyone Senmaida (rice terraces) ▪ ISHIKAWA

1,004 small rice terraces on a mountainside overlooking the Sea of Japan in the Shiroyone district in Wajima City, Ishikawa Prefecture, are known as Shiroyone Senmaida (one thousand rice terraces). Each terrace is compact and only as wide as three tatami mats (about 1.8m by 2.7m). These terraces form characteristic geometrical patterns on the slope falling into the sea. Rice stalks, grown with care and rich in grains, are seen swaying in the wind from the Sea of Japan. In autumn, the rice is harvested manually. In 1999, Shiroyone's Senmaida were ranked among Japan's best hundred rice terrace landscapes and, in 2001, were designated by the country to be cultural property scenery.

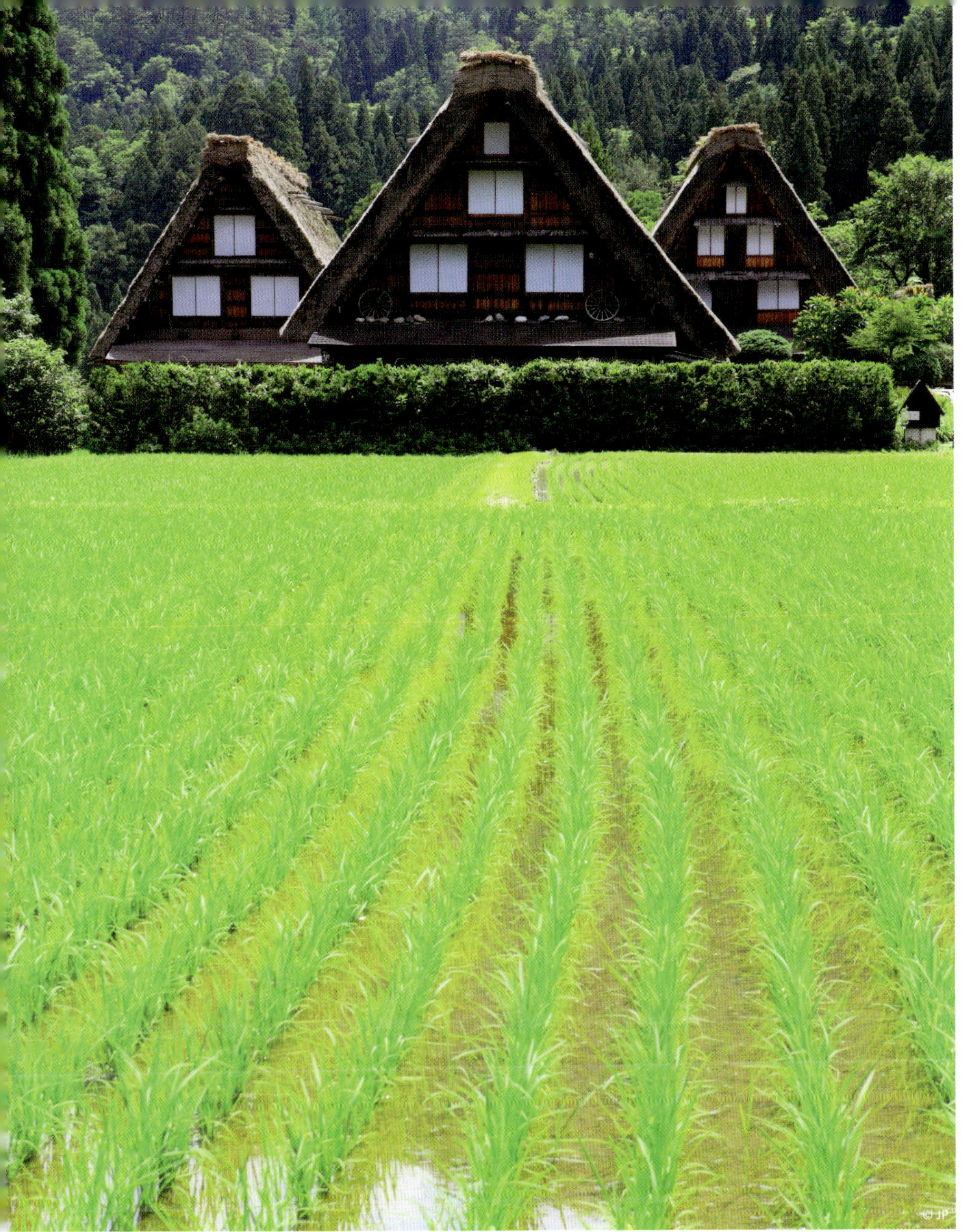

白川郷

Shirakawa-go ▪ GIFU

These communities are famed for so-called *gassho-zukuri* houses that look like hands held together in prayer. Without easy access and isolated in winter in very deep snow, Shirakawa-go used to be practically forbidden to outsiders. Because it has had few visitors, some see in it Japan's archetypal landscape in purest form. One characteristic of *gassho-zukuri* architecture is sharply steep thatched roofs. These are believed to be a local invention designed for easy snow clearing and drainage. The roofs are rethatched jointly by the community every 30-40 years. Shirakawa-go is committed to preserving thatched *kirizuma*-style *gassho-zukuri* houses. In 1995, it was listed as a World Heritage site.

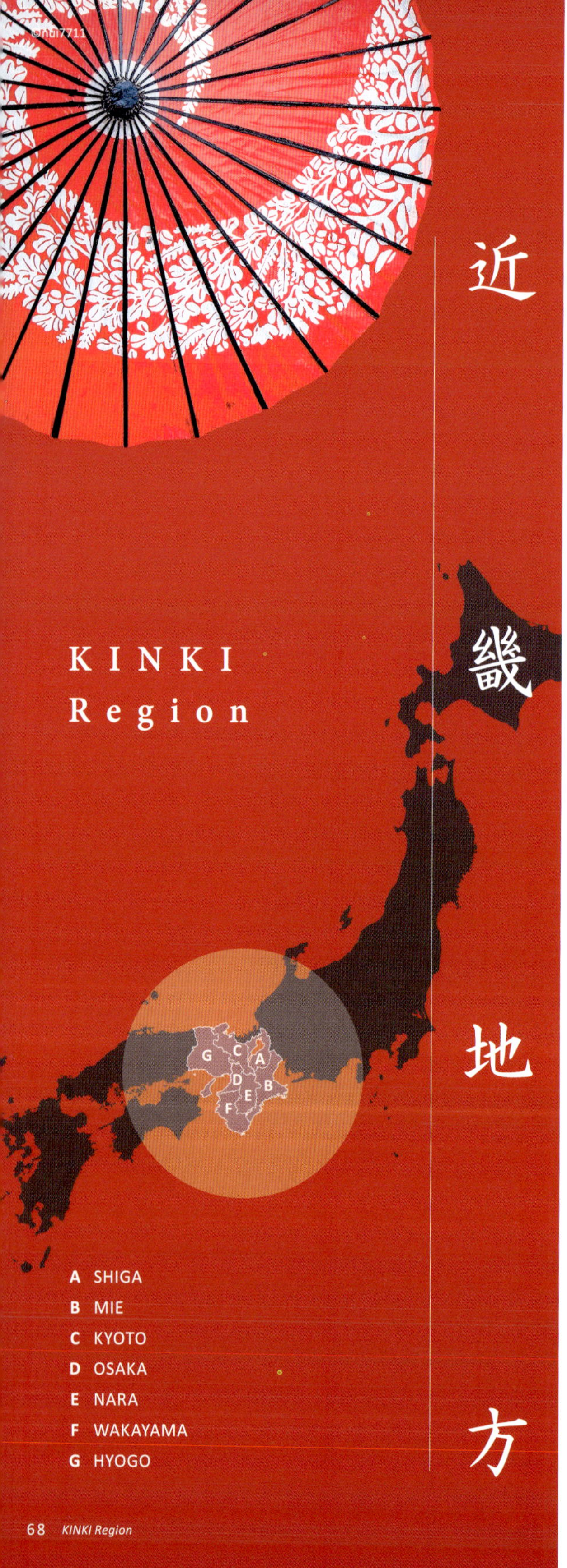

Japan's history started here. The traditions of old Japan are alive in the Kinki region.

The Kinki region encompasses the two urban prefectures of Osaka and Kyoto and the five prefectures of Hyogo, Nara, Mie, Shiga, and Wakayama. This ranks as the second key urban center of Japan, following the Kanto region.

Centered on Kyoto and Nara, this is the land of Japan's historical imperial palaces from the time of the Asuka Period (starting in 592) to the Heian Period (ending in 1180). Up to 1869, the residences of Japan's emperors and empresses were almost all to be found in the Kinki region.

The area attracts large numbers of tourist who visit the old capital cities to see the many temples and shrines, castle remains, cityscapes, and other historical sites and structures that are still to be found there today. This is an area where visitors can actually see temples and traditional city residences that many people from other countries imagine when they think of Japan.

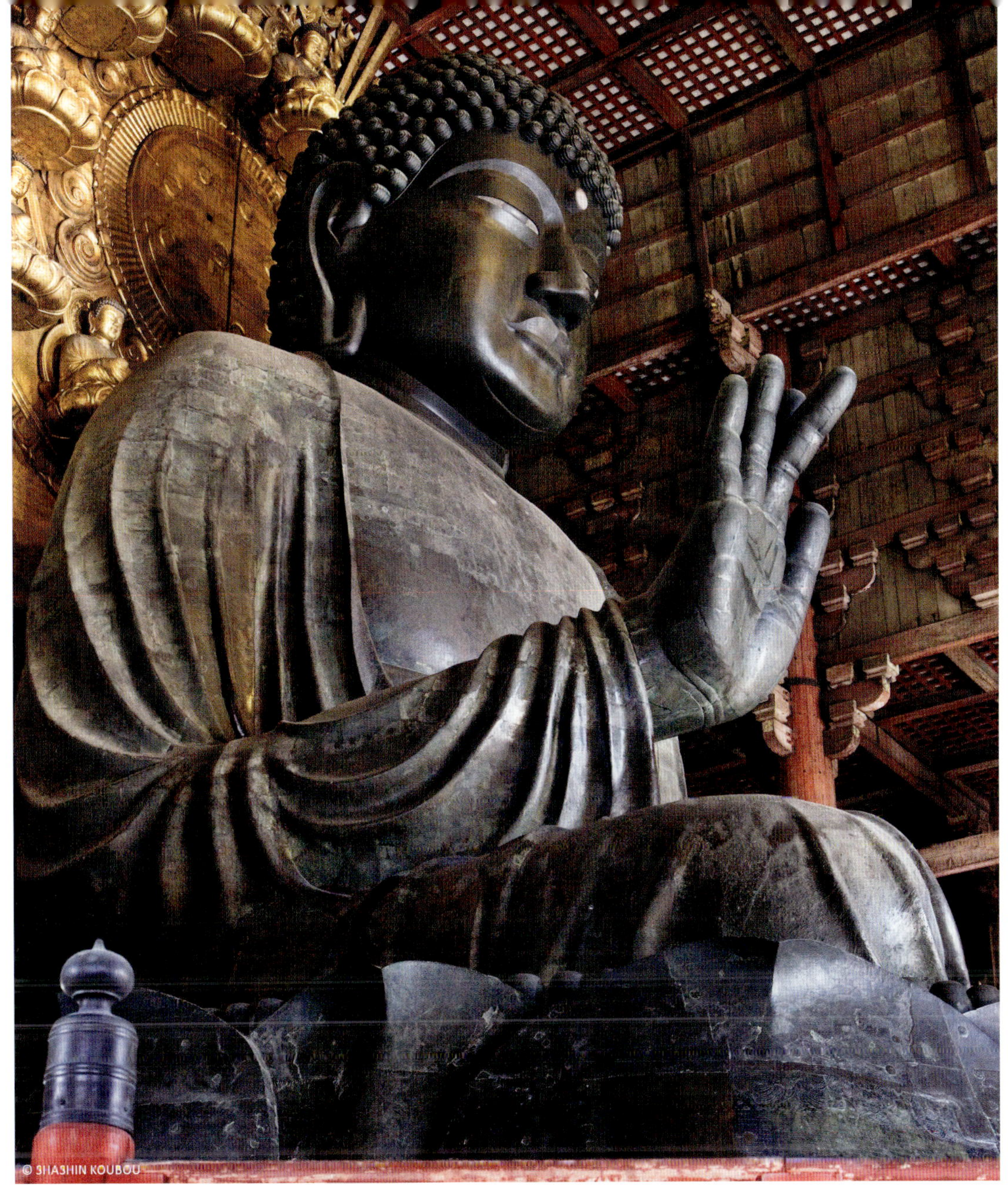

The Great Buddha at Todai-ji (Todai Temple)

▪ NARA

Todai-ji was the center of the Kokubun-ji temples located throughout Japan in the Nara Period, and was also known as Soukokubun-ji. The Daibutsu is the largest statue of Buddha in Japan, with a height of 14.98 meters, and when it was first erected it was a glittering gold color. Todai-ji was constructed with the main image of Buddha at its center, located in the Great Buddha Hall. The hall was reconstructed during the Edo Period (1603-1868), and is one of the world's largest wooden structures with a height of 52 meters and a length of 57 meters. Todai-ji was listed as a World Heritage site in 1998.

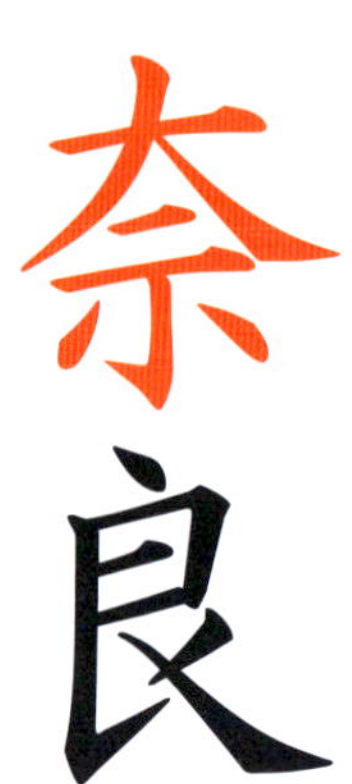

Kasuga Taisha (Kasuga Shrine) lanterns ■ NARA

The main building of Kasuga Taisha and the road approaching it are lined with a remarkable number of lanterns. All the lanterns were donated as gifts of worship, some of them said to be as old as the Heian Period (794-1185) when they were given in the 11th century by Fujiwara no Yorimichi, a court nobleman. Most of the lanterns were, however, donated by ordinary members of the public, and their number is said to total 3,000.

Nowadays the lanterns are lit in February on the last day of winter and during the Obon festival on August 14th and 15th. The glowing lanterns create an elegant and almost magical vista.

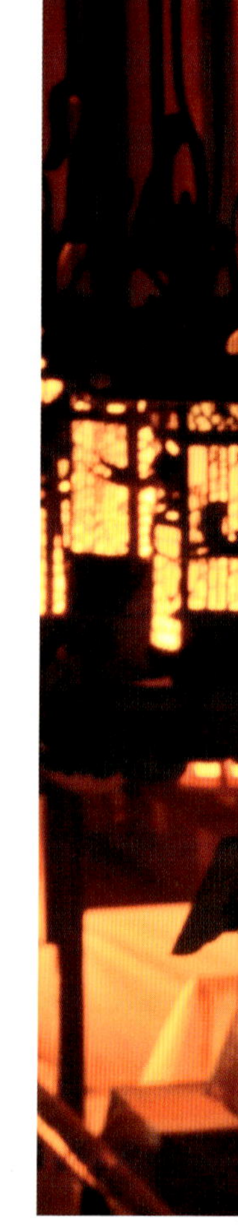

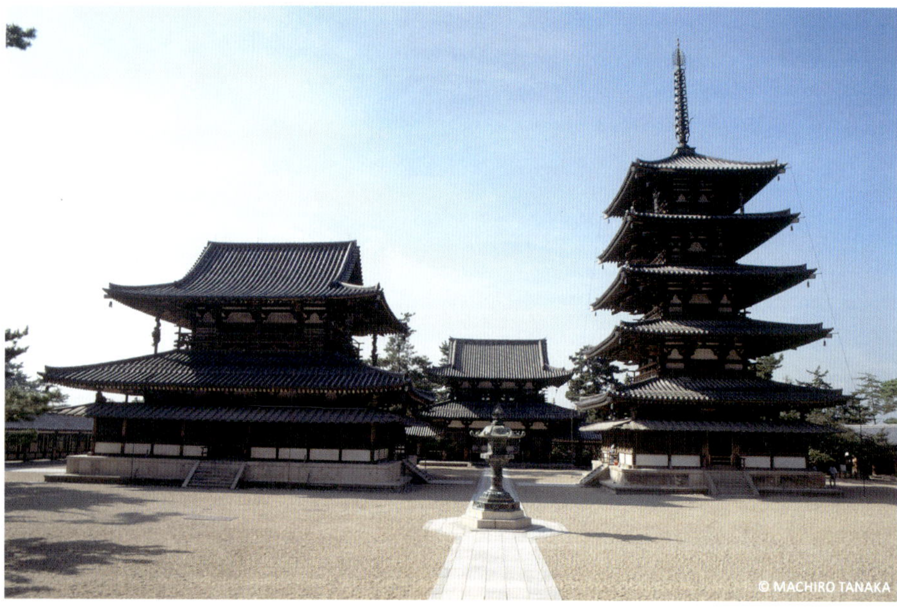
© MACHIRO TANAKA

Horyu-ji (Horyu Temple) ■ NARA

Houryu-ji's origins lie in the erection of the statue of Yakusi Nyorai (Bhaisajya-guru) at the behest of Empress Suiko and Prince Shotoku in 607. However, the temple was burnt to the ground when it was struck by lightning in 670, and the present Houryu-ji is a reconstruction of the temple that was completed in the early 8th century. The oldest grouping of wooden buildings in the world, the temple complex was listed as a World Heritage site in 1993.

Houryu-ji consists of two areas of the Sai-in Garan in the west and the To-in Garan in the east. The western area features the five-story pagoda, the oldest in Japan, Nandaimon (Great South Gate), Kondo Hall and Daikoudo Hall. The eastern area contains the Yumedono Hall ("Hall of Dreams"), which is famed for its octagonal shape.

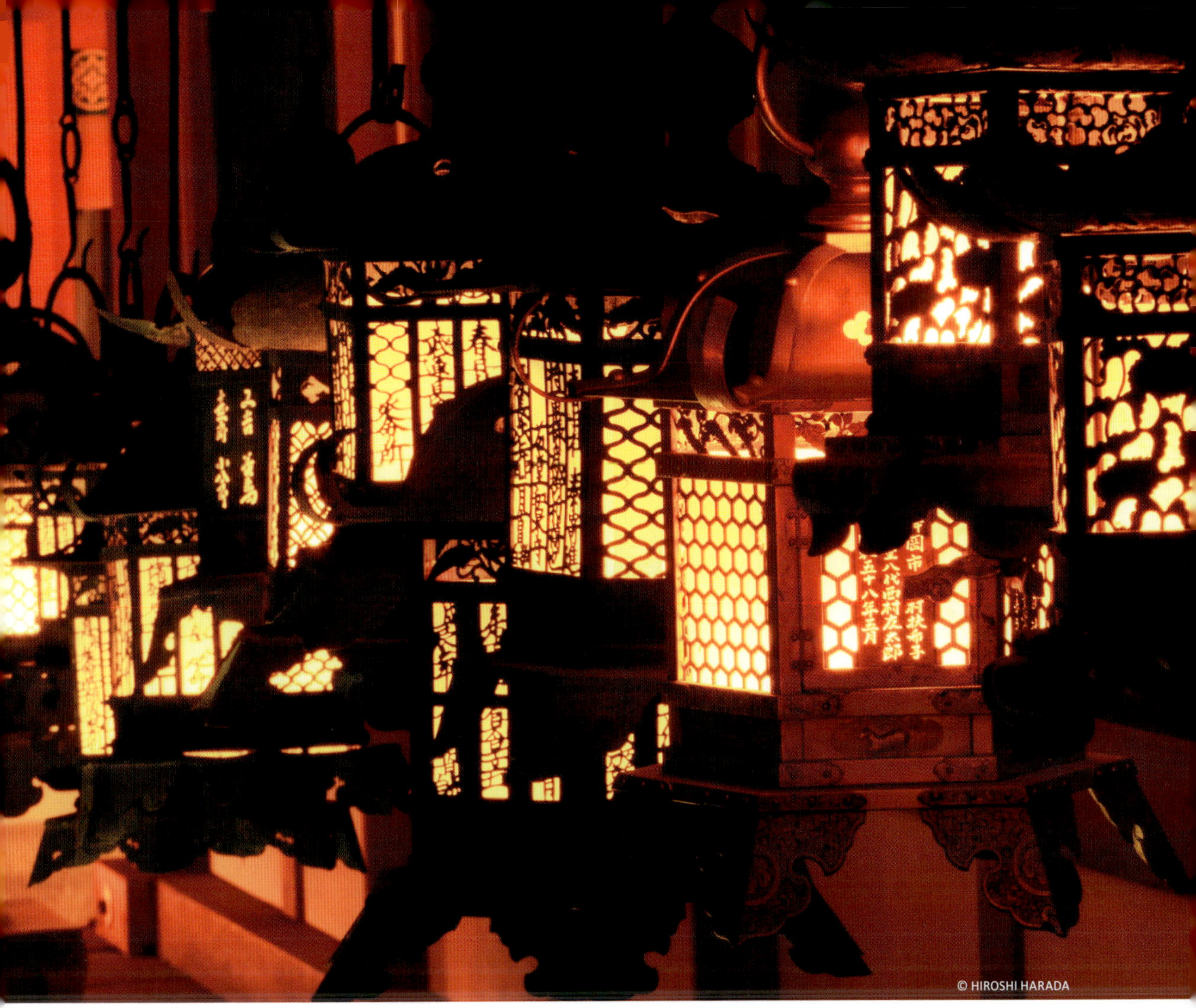

© HIROSHI HARADA

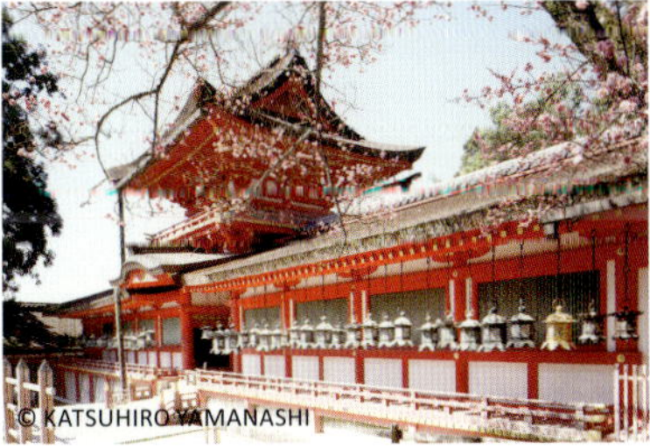
© KATSUHIRO YAMANASHI

Kasuga Taisha (Kasuga Shrine)

Japan's very first Kasuga Taisha dates back by about 1,300 years, when the national capital was moved to Nara. Since then, on Mount Kasuga, there have always been those red columns, white walls and roofs made of Japanese cypress. The structures look fresh because they are repainted every 20 years, a traditional renovation practice observed over the centuries.
In 1998, the original shrine and Kasugayama's primeval forest were listed as World Heritage sites.

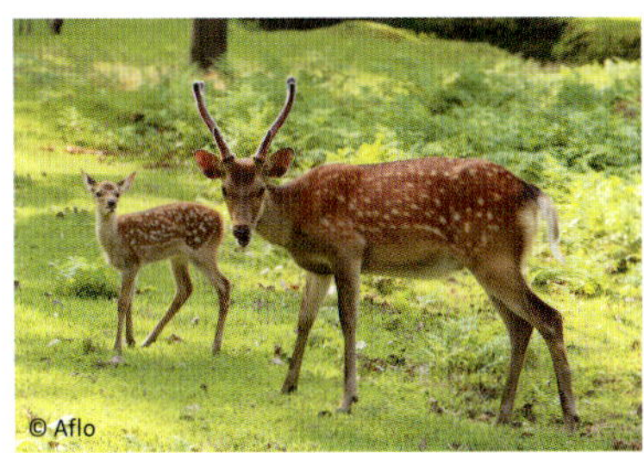
© Aflo

Deer of Nara Park

Nara Park where Todai-ji and Kasuga Taisha are located spreads across a large area and is an historical park, where wild deer, designated as a natural treasure, also live. The deer are regarded as the messengers of the god of Kasuga Taisha and have been carefully protected since ancient days.

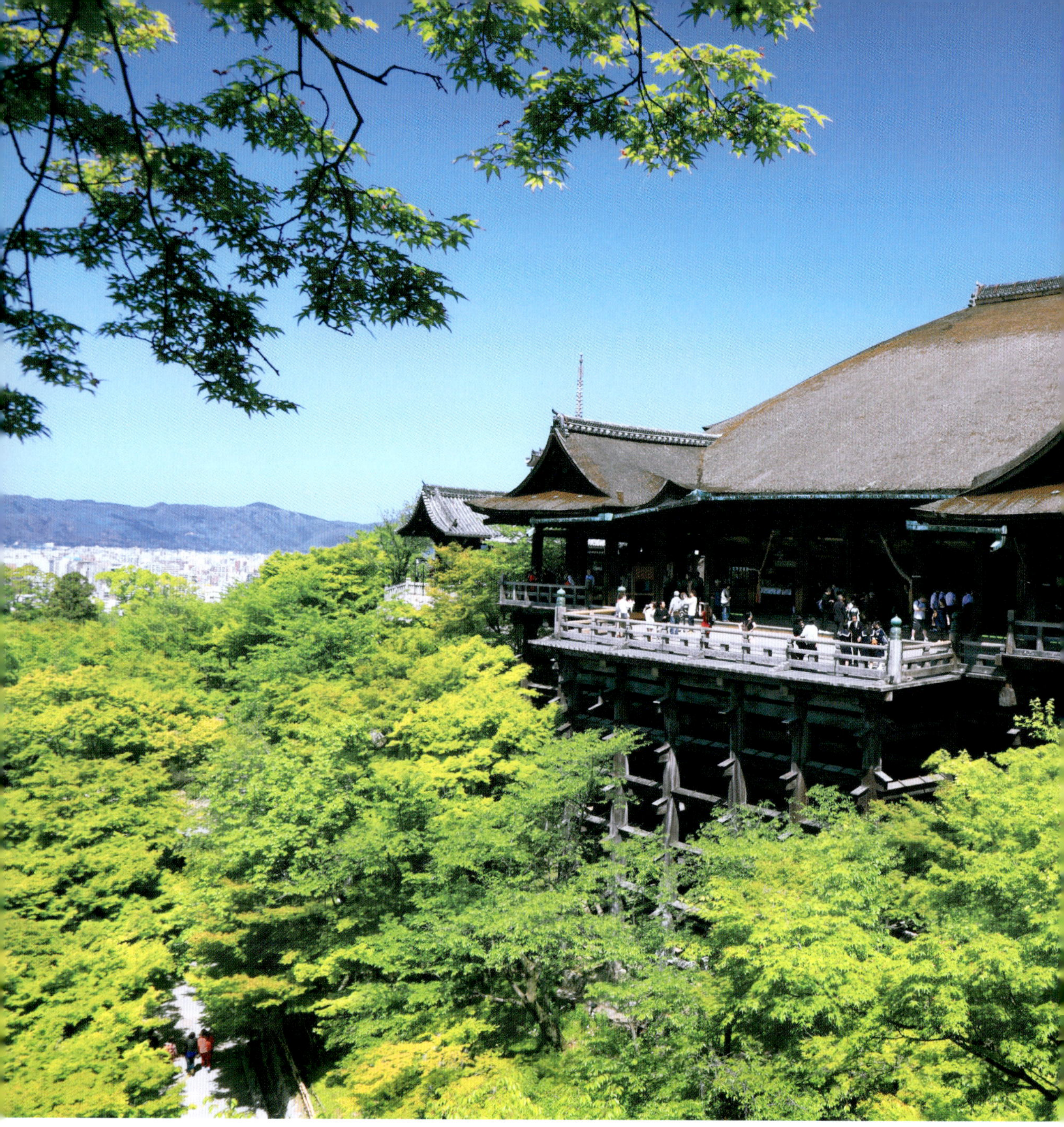

Kiyomizu-dera
(Kiyomizu Temple)

▪ KYOTO

Kiyomizu-dera is a World Heritage site situated in the Higashiyama Ward of Kyoto City, and is famed as the temple of the *Kiyomizu no Butai*, a veranda that hangs over the mountainside. After being rebuilt several times, the current Hondo, or main hall, which is designated as a national treasure was constructed by Tokugawa Iemitsu, the third shogun of the Tokugawa dynasty in 1633, and the veranda atop the

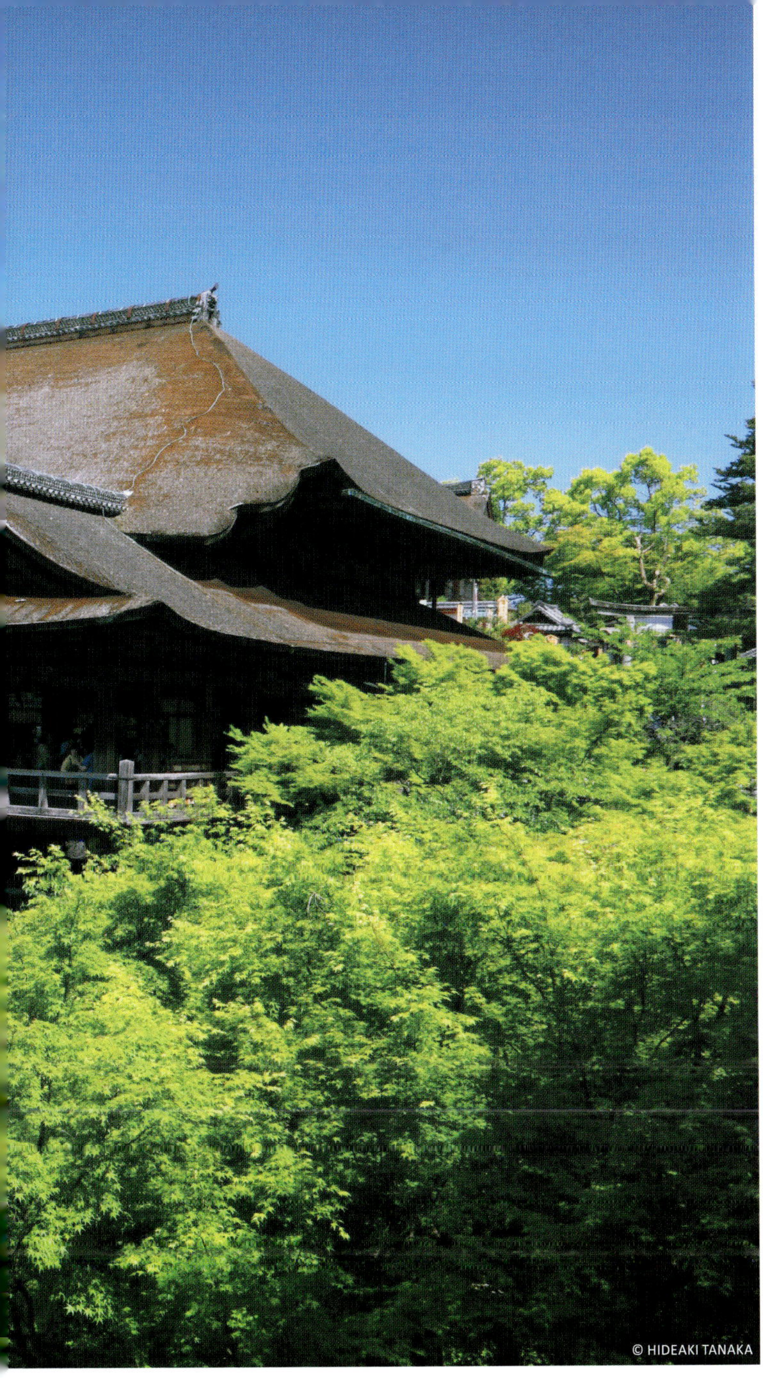

© HIDEAKI TANAKA

many-pillared structure hugging the mountainside is a famous location. The veranda is 13 meters high, 18 meters wide and has a depth of 10 meters; its floor is constructed from planks of cypress wood. It offers a panoramic view across the whole of Kyoto City, and beautiful scenery can be enjoyed in each of the four seasons. The building is lit up at night during the spring and autumn.

清水寺

The three-storied pagoda

The three-storied pagoda is called the *Gojunoto* Pagoda, and was constructed in the 9th century. The present tower, which is designated as a national important cultural property, is the largest in Japan and was rebuilt in 1632. The floors are about 5.5 meters square and it is 30 meters in height. The horizontal beams on each story are decorated in brilliant colors in the Momoyama style, with gilding and lacquer.

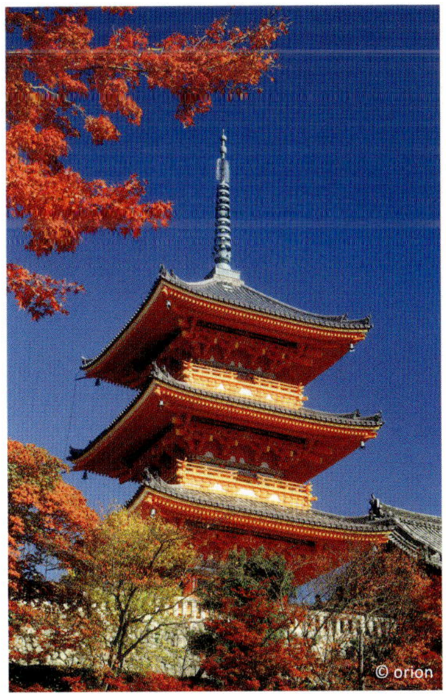

© orion

金閣寺

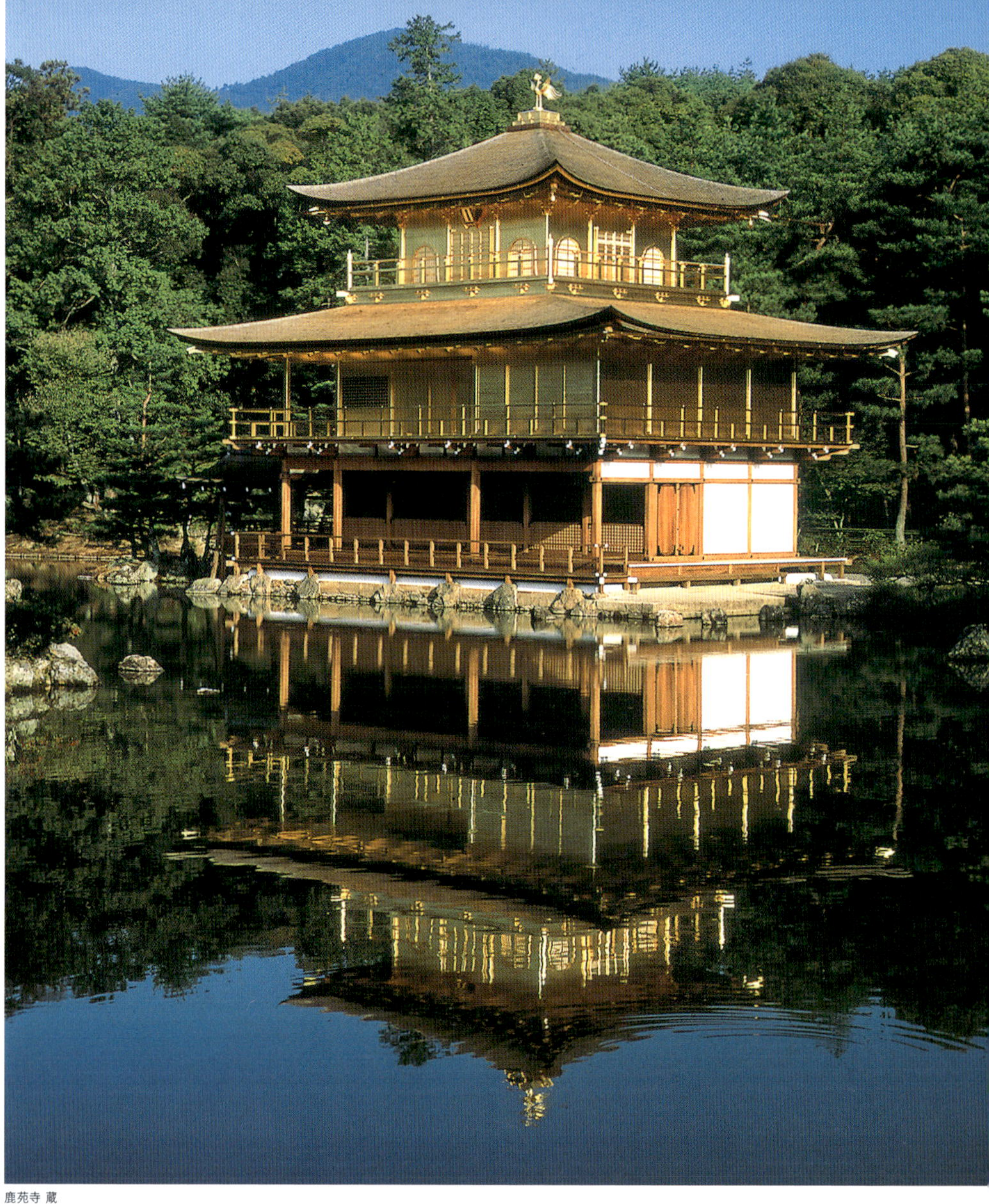

鹿苑寺 蔵

Kinkaku-ji (Kinkaku Temple) ■ KYOTO

Although its official name is Rokuon Temple, the Kinkaku (Golden Pavilion) building containing ashes of the Buddha is so famous the temple is usually just called Kinkaku-ji, or the Golden Temple. Centered around the Kinkaku the gardens and buildings became to be called a place of heavenly delight on earth, and the complex continued to expand.

Designated as a national treasure in 1929, Kinkaku and its Buddhist statues were lost when an arsonist burnt the building to the ground in 1950. It was rebuilt in 1955, and from 1986 to 1987 the great Showa Period restoration was carried out, creating the building you can see now, glittering in its thick coat of gold leaf. Kinkaku-ji was listed as a World Heritage site in 1994.

Ginkaku-ji (Ginkaku Temple) ▪ KYOTO

Ginkaku-ji (literally "Silver Pavilion" and officially named Higashiyama Jishou-ji temple), like Kinkaku-ji, is another sub-temple of Shoukoku-ji Temple, located at the foot of mountains. While its scale is smaller than that of Kinkaku-ji it is a representative work of Higashiyama culture, and perfectly expresses the tea-ceremony-like mentality of its builder Ashikaga Yoshimasa, a man who was said to have been earnest in his pursuit of beauty. Ginkaku is not decorated with silver leaf as was originally planned. The roof is re-thatched every 30 years, and major restoration work was undertaken between 2008 and 2010. Ginkaku-ji was listed as a World Heritage site in 1994.

提供 慈照寺

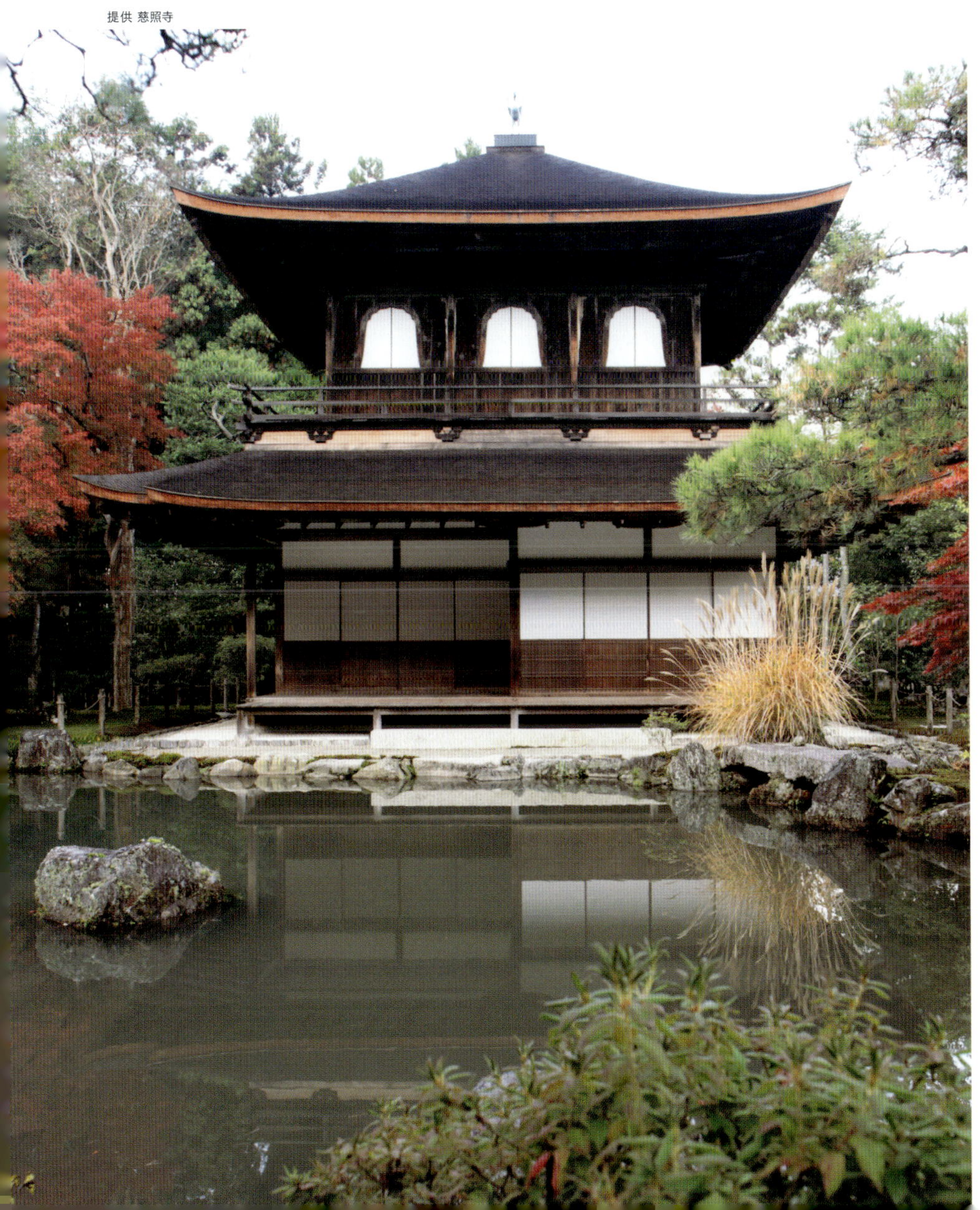

銀閣寺

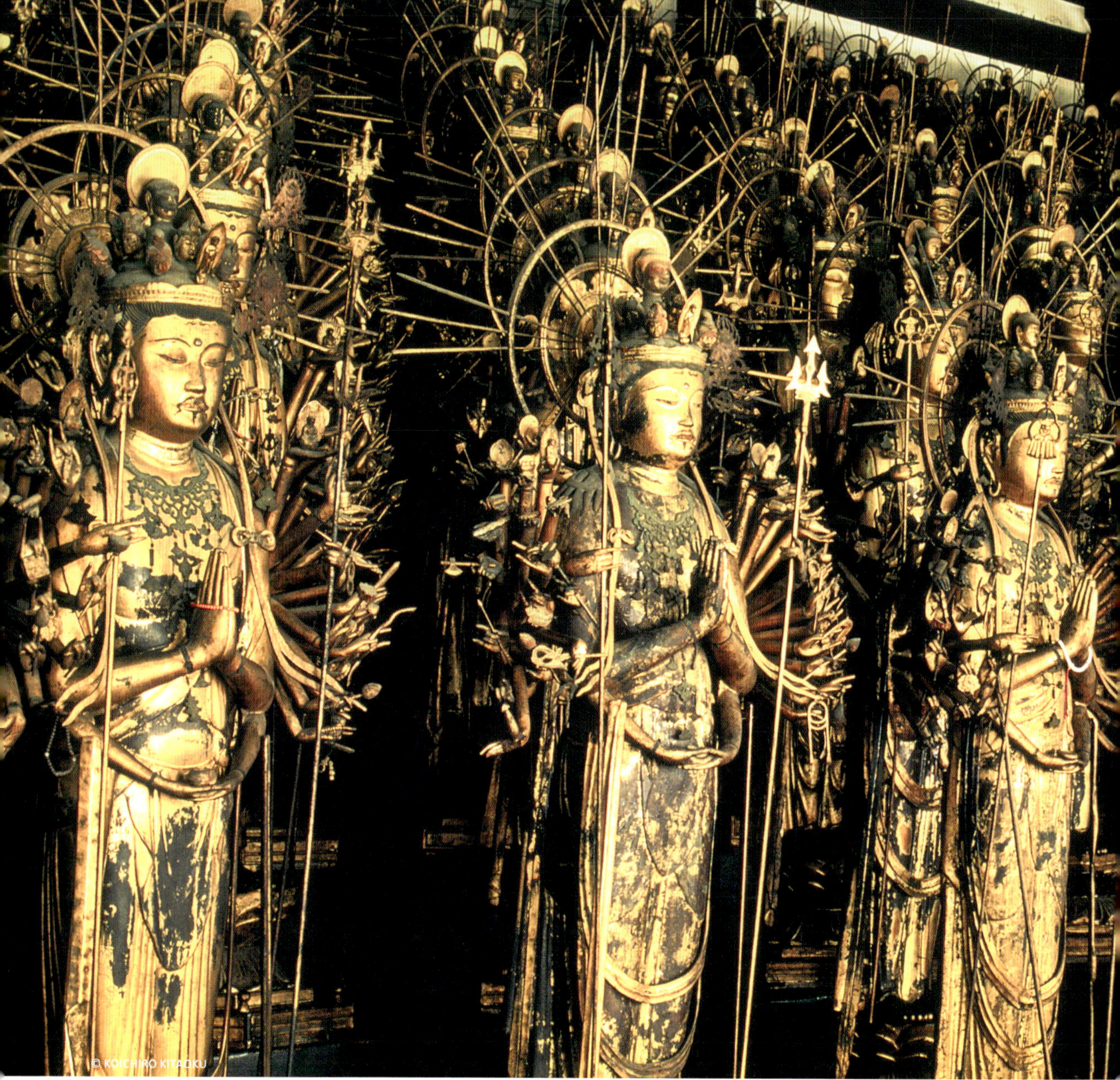
© KOICHIRO KITAOKU

Sanjusangen-do ▪ KYOTO

The vast tiled hall at Rengeo-in houses 1,000 statues of Senju Kannon (the Thousand-armed Buddhist Goddess of Mercy), and is generally known as Sanjusangen-do because it has thirty-three bays (*san-ju-san* is thirty-three, while *gen* means bay) created by the pillars that hold up the building running for from north to south for around 120 meters. The view straight down the massive hall , sharpening to a single transparent point in the distance, stirs the heart. Inside the hall, 1,000 statues of Senju Kannon are arranged in rows on ten tiers, providing a breathtaking prospect. Each of the statues has a further 11 heads on its head, and 40 arms on both sides. A great many of them were lost to a fire in the latter half of the 13th century, but they have all been restored.

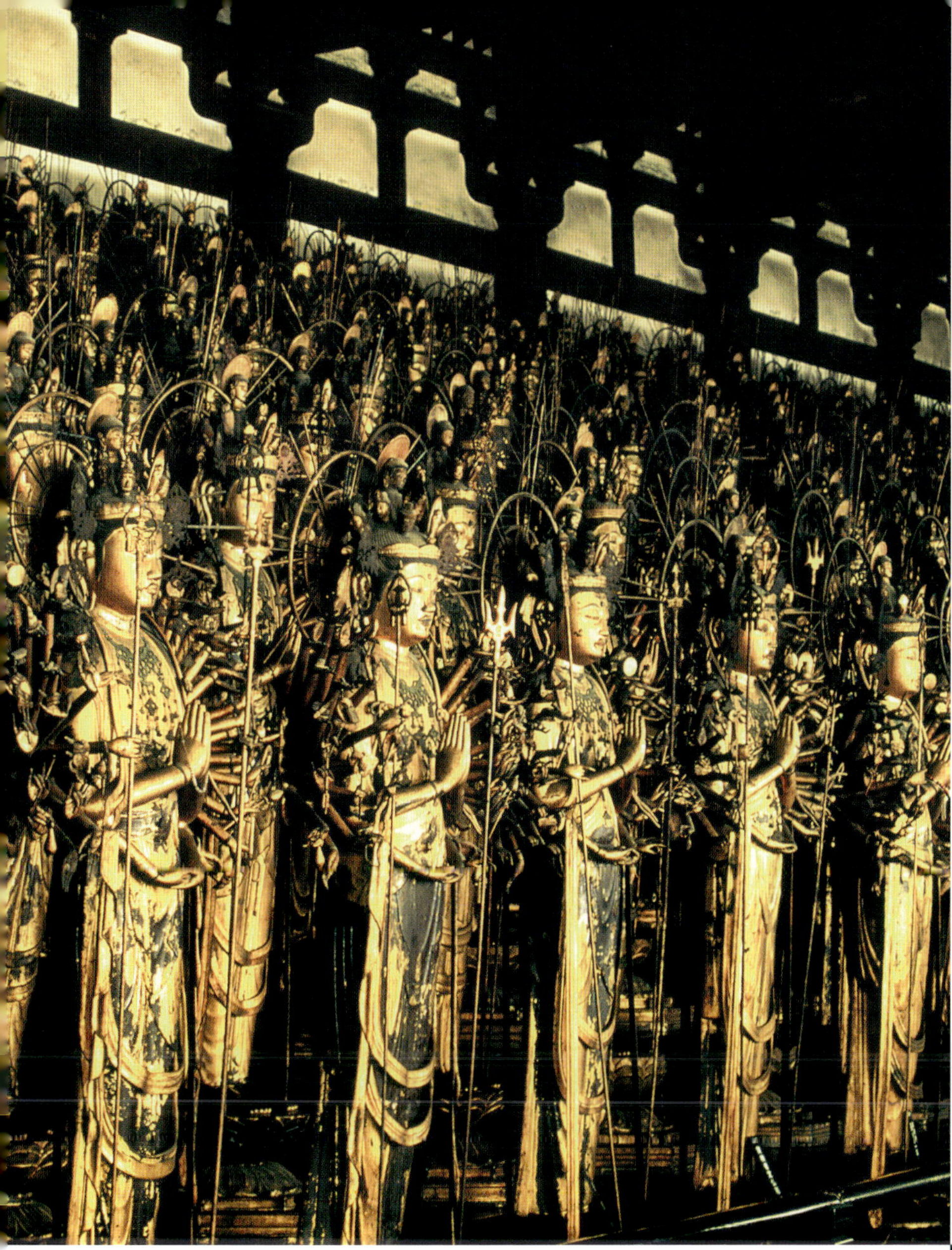

三十三間堂

Sanjusangen-do archery contest

On January 15, Sanjusangen-do is the site of the *Toshiya* (arrow firing) ceremony, which is famed as a time-honored custom. The current archery tournament derives from a practice of the Edo Period, and draws around 2,000 participants each year. In the *Toshiya* ceremony the contestants fire their arrows for a distance of 120 meters from the south end to the north end along the west side of the hall, competing to see who can hit the target the most.

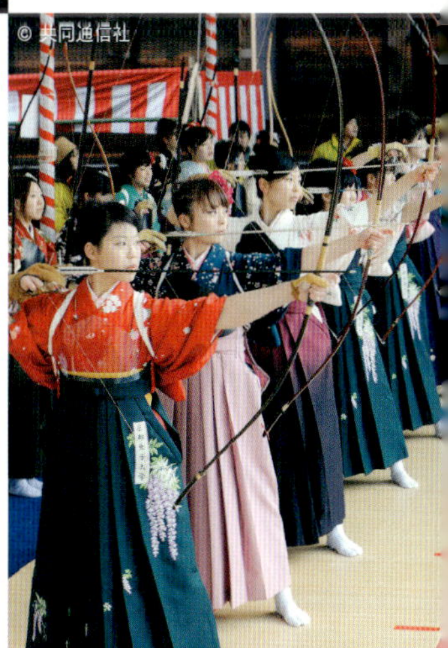

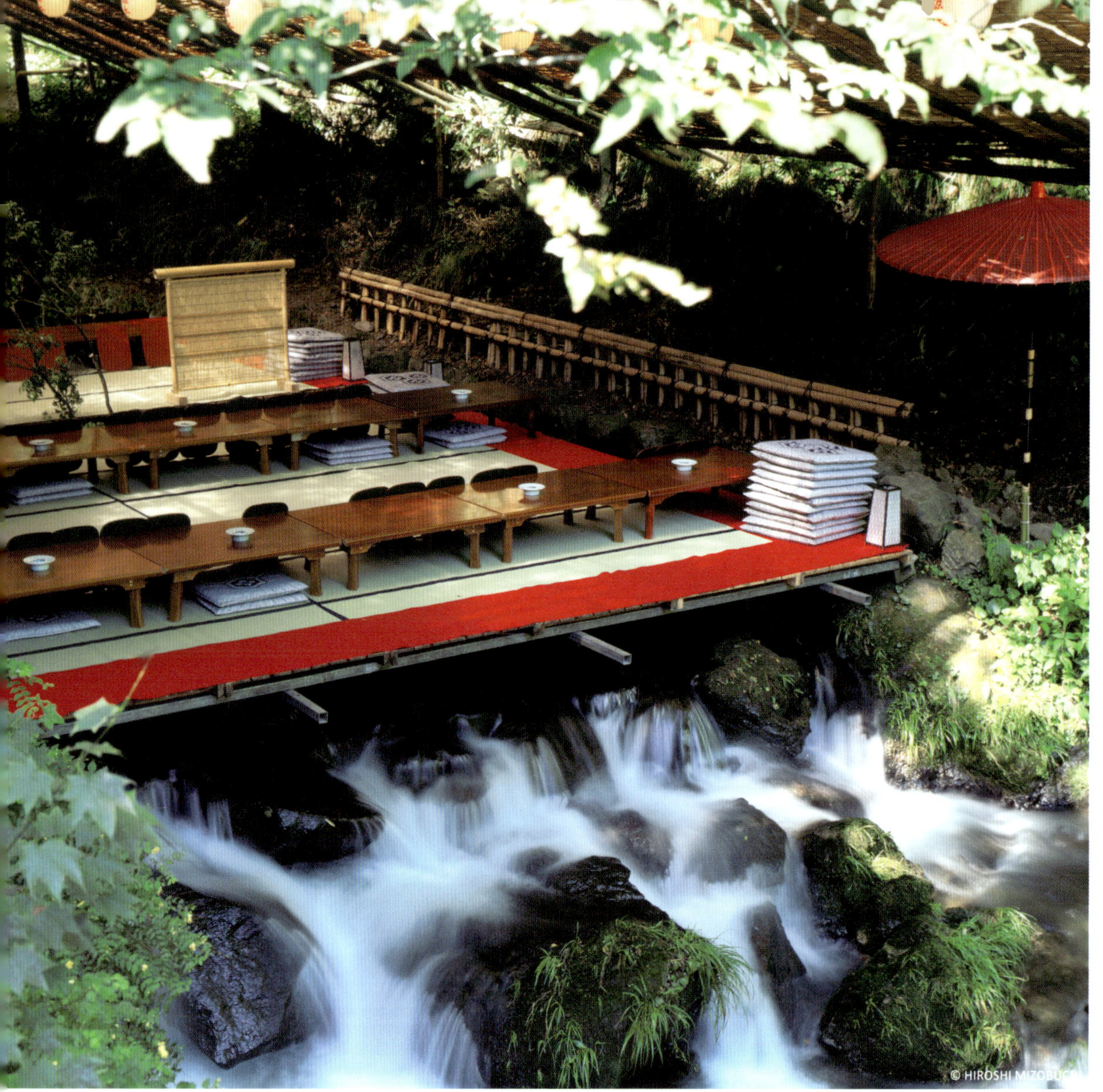

Kibune no kawadoko (Kibune riverbed platforms)

▪ KYOTO

One of the seasonal activities of summer in Kyoto, which becomes very hot as it is encircled mountains, is sitting on a raised platform over a cool running stream. Eating and drinking establishments build raised platforms over river beds where they provide meals to guests sitting on cushions on the platform. Kifune-jinja, a shrine in the foothills of Mount Kibune, is known as a place of the water gods. The nearby river is lined with about 20 eating places, and one can eat suspended just above the flow of the river. The Kibune riverbed platforms use natural materials such as bamboo and rush screens, and are just several dozen centimeters above the water surface. People can forget the summer heat for a while as they enjoy their meals with a view of the cool running water.

Bamboo walk of Sagano ▪ KYOTO

The Sagano district of Kyoto was the scene of hunting outings and other games by the nobility since the Heian Period (794-1185), and they built their summer villas and residences here. It is also the site of famous temples such as Tenryu-ji and Daikaku-ji. Although Sagano was said to be a place where the nature of old Kyoto still survived, the waves of urbanization have encroached upon it and the green areas are shrinking.

One of the representative views of what is left of the typical Sagano landscape are of the bamboo groves. The environs of Nonomiya Shrine are immaculately kept as a path for strolling through the bamboos. The fragrance of bamboo, the way the light shines in shafts between the trees, the gentle rustling of the leaves are all the most pleasant of sensations.

In autumn the bamboo groves are lit up at night, providing a novel landscape.

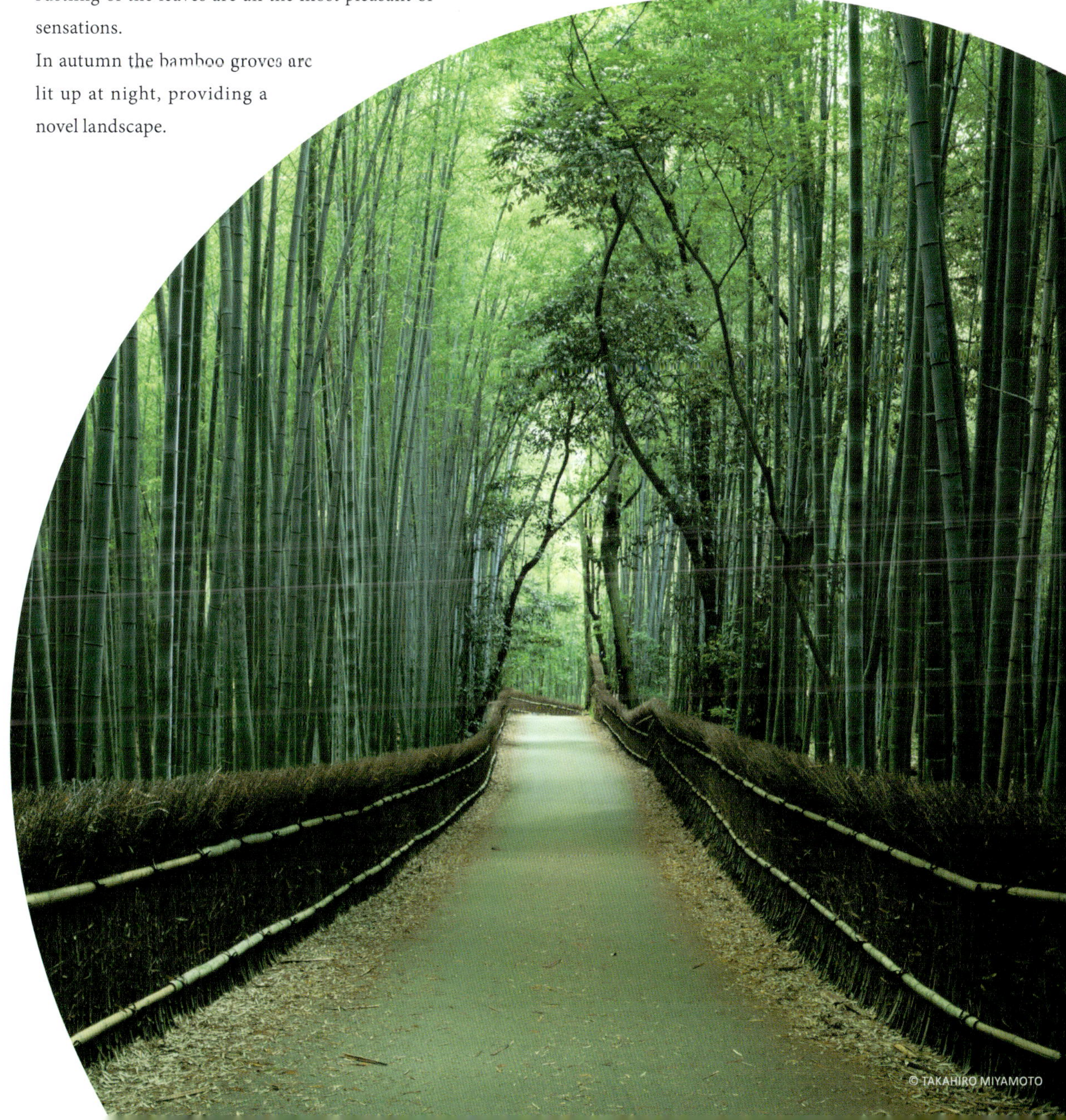

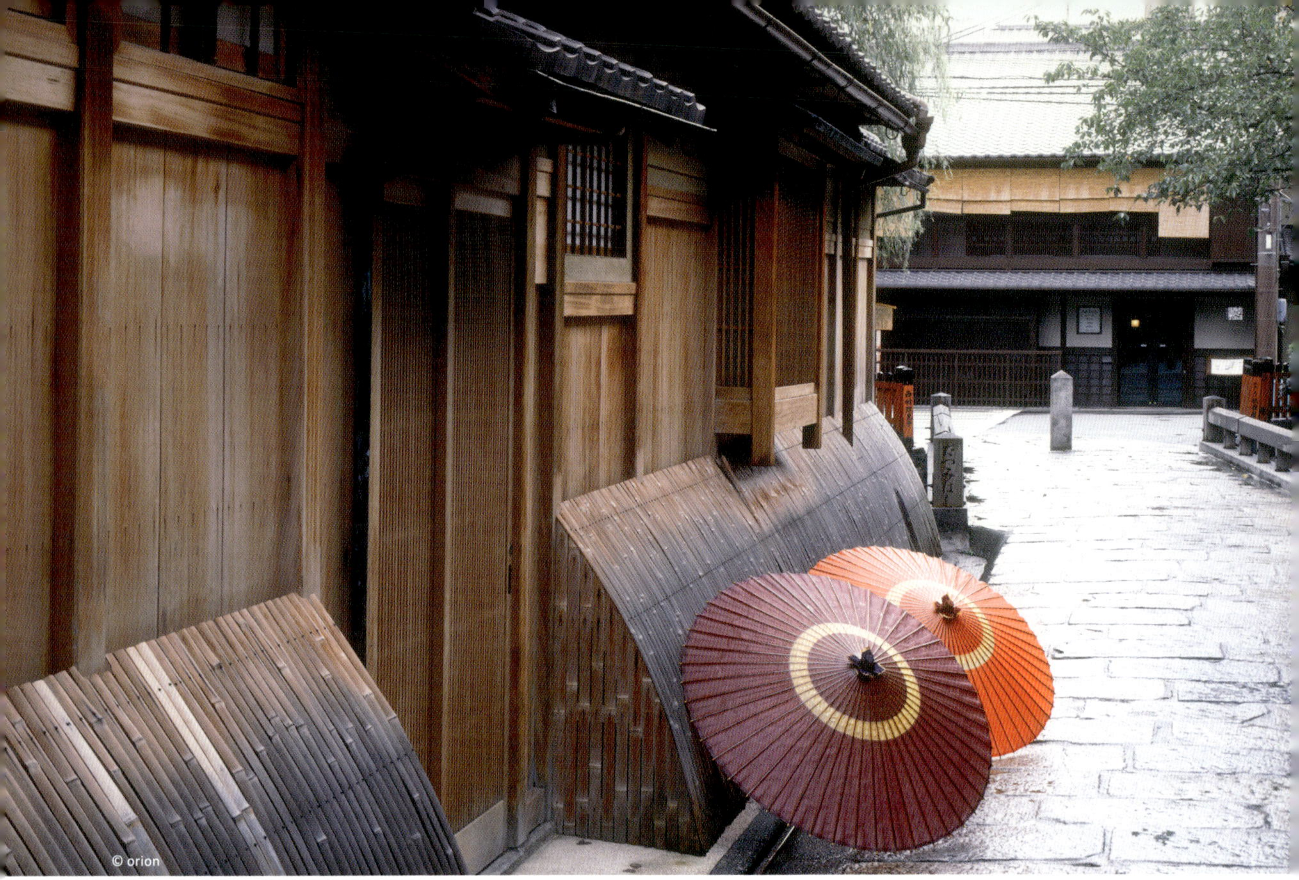

© orion

Gion ▪ KYOTO

The central area of Kyoto, centering on Yasaka Shrine, is called Gion. In the early days of the Edo Period the town was shaped by the teahouses that provided refreshments to thirsty pilgrims making the trip to Yasaka Shrine and Kiyomizu-dera, and this was the start of the present day *hanamachi* of Gion. Nowadays, the teahouses and restaurants that have survived since the old days have been joined by numerous drinking bars. While the vestiges of the old days are few and far between, the rows of houses with latticed windows still remind the visitor of the elegance and refinement of the past, and the sound of shamisen (Japanese three-stringed lutes) can still be heard on these streets.

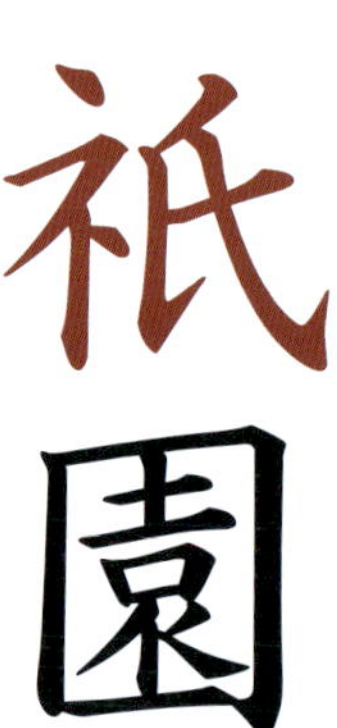

舞妓

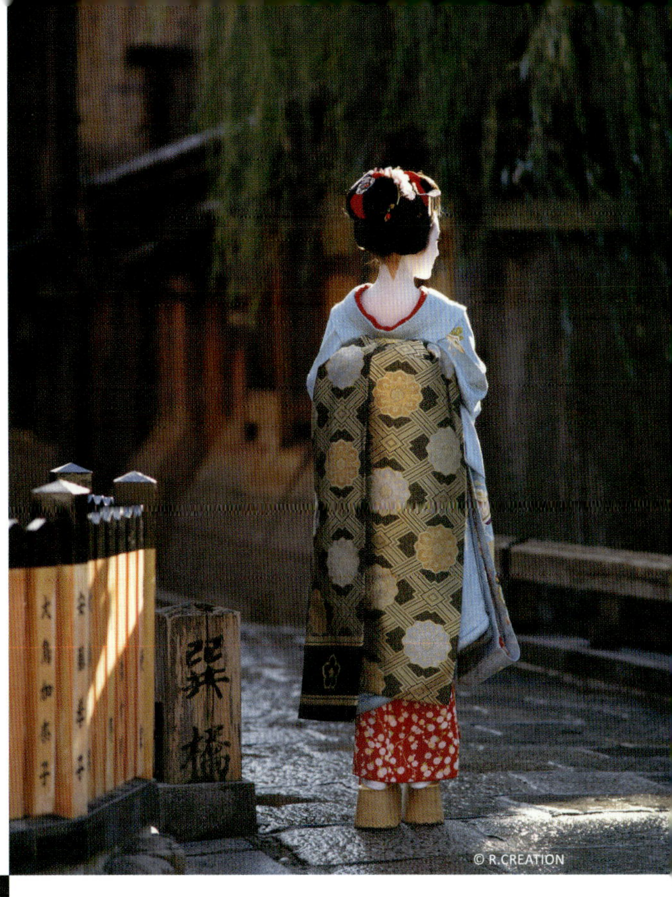

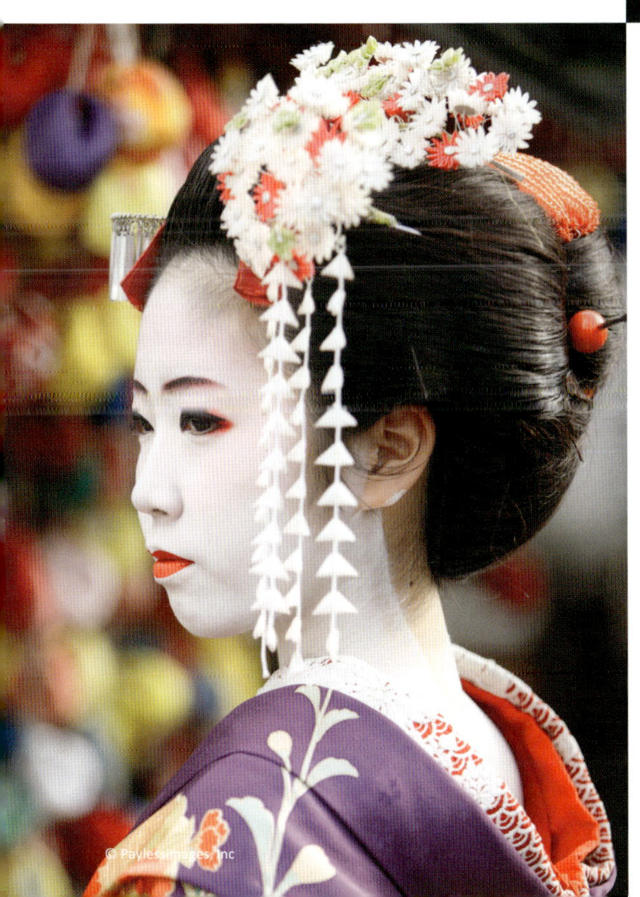

Maiko and *Geigi*

A *maiko* is an apprentice *geigi* who entertains guests at banquets, mainly in the *hanamachi* of Gion, with songs, dance and the shamisen. The terms *maiko* and *geigi* are peculiar to Kyoto, the *geigi* generally being known as geisha elsewhere. The name *geigi* expresses the meaning that the woman is a sophisticated female who excels in both the arts and cultivation. Rather than merely providing one-off entertainment, the *geigi* devote their energies to polishing their art and character so that people will repeatedly come to watch them. The *maiko* learn from the *geigi* art, the tea ceremony and flower arranging.

伏見稲荷大社

Fushimi Inari Taisha

(Fushimi Inari Shrine) ▪ **KYOTO**

Fushimi Inari Taisha located at the south end of Kyoto's Higashiyama district, in the foothills of Mount Inari, and is the head shrine of the 30,000 or so Inari shrines dotted across Japan. Inari was originally the god of harvests, but in the Heian Period when Kukai (known as Kobo-Daishi, a monk who led the propagation of Sino-esoteric Buddhism) was put in charge of overseeing the building of To-ji (To Temple), Inari became a tutelary deity. Ever since then, Inari has become the god of new industry, commerce and households.

The grounds of the shrine house over 10,000 torii gateways donated by the faithful, which are assembled tightly together in a tunnel-like form and known as the *Senbon Torii* (one thousand gateways). All the torii are painted a vivid red, and walking through the *tunnel* is to enter a beautiful and strange world.

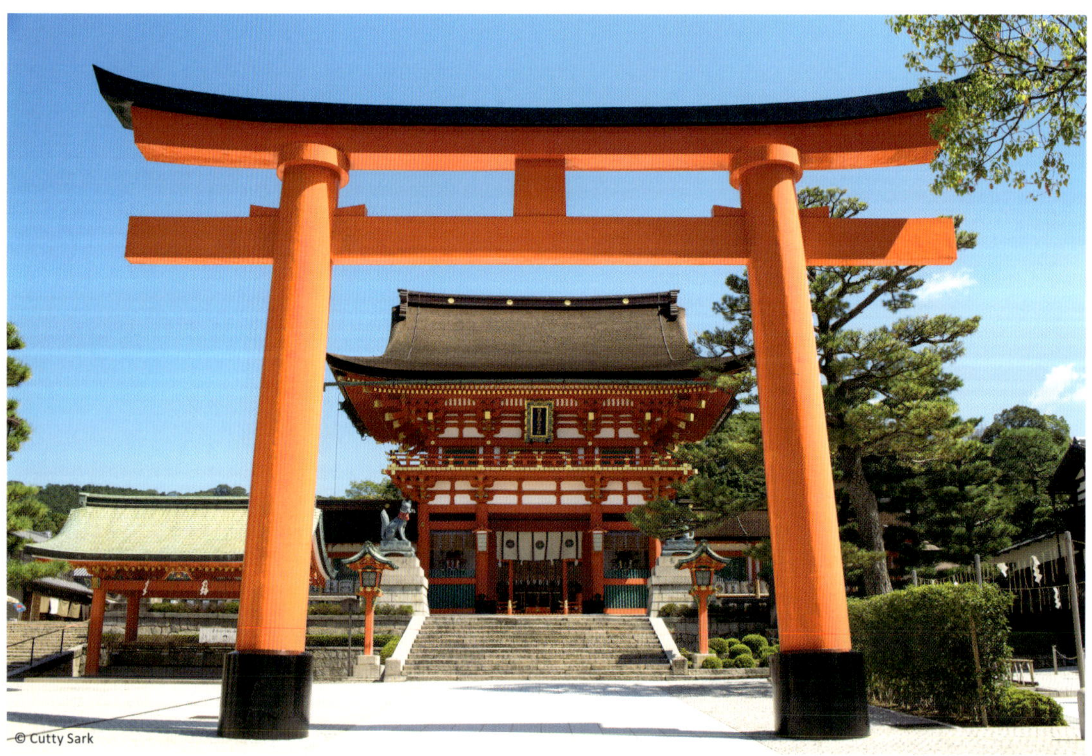

© Cutty Sark

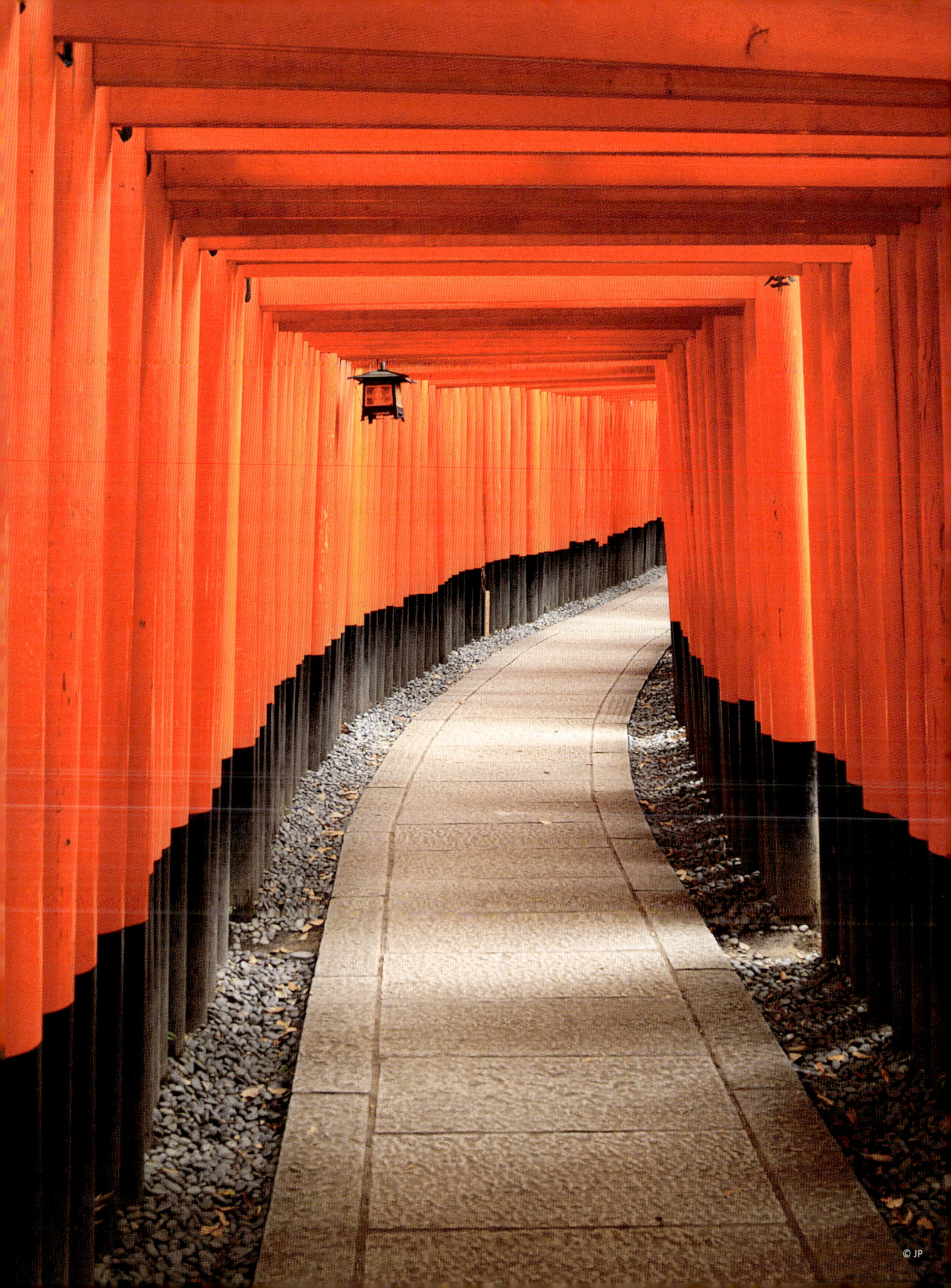

Byodoin (The Phoenix Hall) ■ KYOTO

Fujiwara no Michinaga, an influential courtier in the Heian Period (794-1185), purchased a villa in Uji, which his son Yorimichi converted to a Buddhist temple, Byodoin, in 1052. In those days the concept of *Jodo-shinko* (the Pure Land faith) was popular amongst the nobility and priests.

Byodoin was built under the principles of *Jodo-shinko*. The Amida-do Hall (Phoenix Hall) located on the west bank of the Uji River is positioned to give a panorama over the *Gokuraku-jodo* (The West Pure Land), which the hall's beautiful proportions are said to represent. Built around 960 years ago the building still houses an image of Buddha, and was determined a World Heritage site in 1994.

平等院

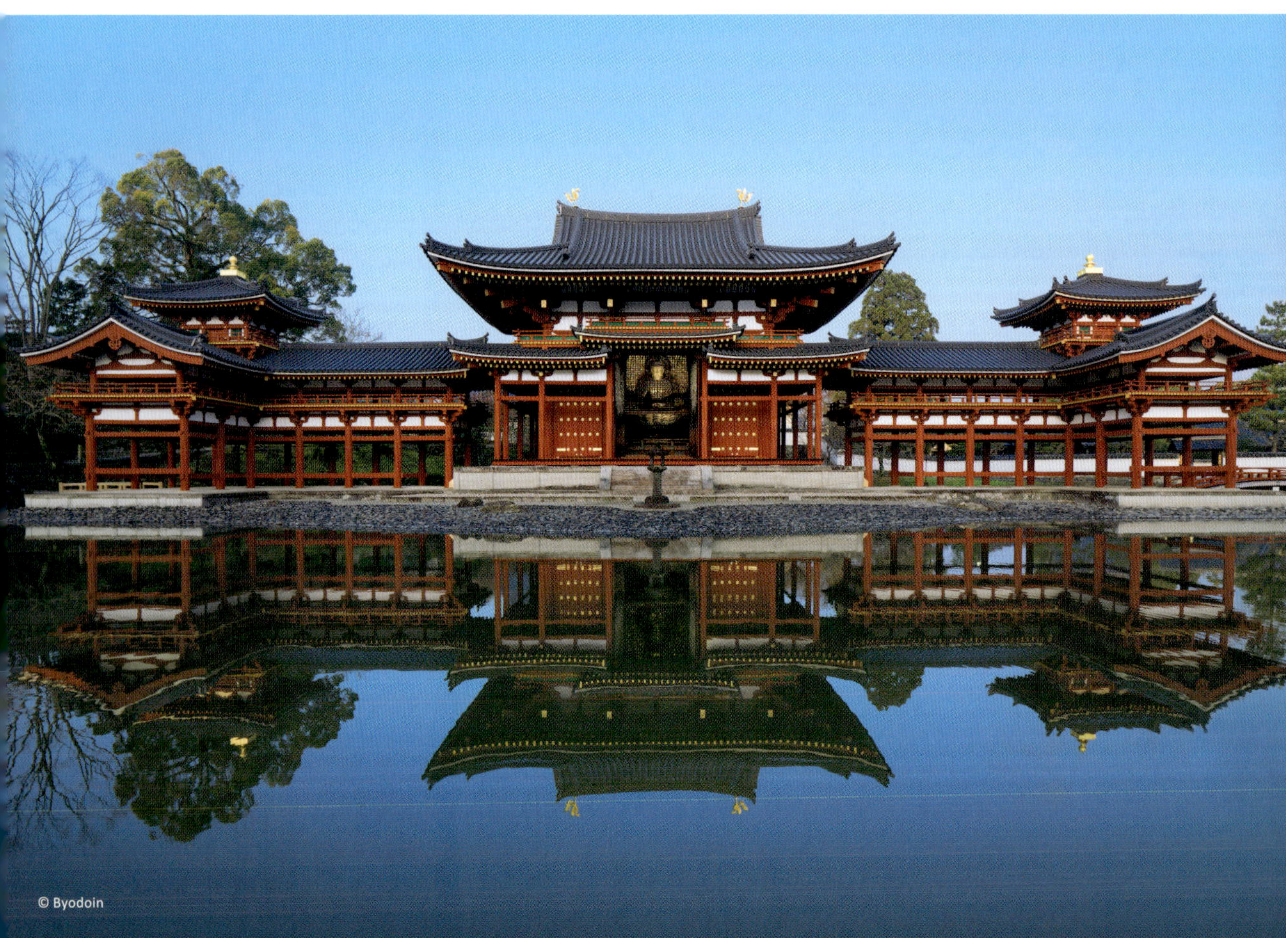

天橋立

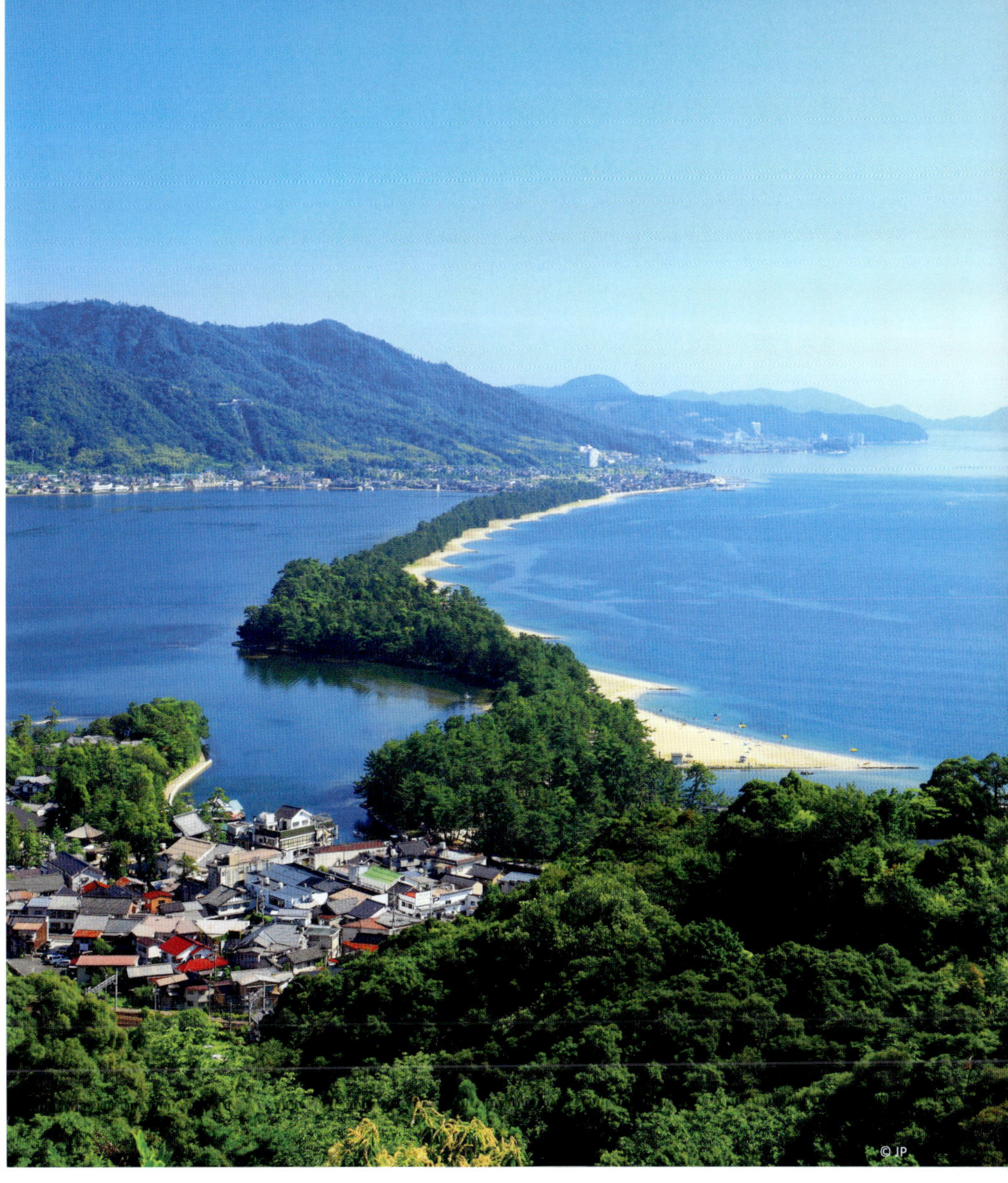
© JP

Amanohashidate ■ KYOTO

Amanohashidate is a sandbar that stretches from the northern part of Kyoto in a southerly direction, with Miyazu Bay on its eastern side and the inner sea of the Aso Sea on its western flank. The sandbar is 3.6 kilometers in length and has been planted with a pine forest of around 8,000 trees. Along with Matsushima in Miyagi Prefecture and Miyajima in Hiroshima Prefecture, it is famed as one of the "best views in Japan".

The shape and atmosphere of the sandbar differ depending upon from where you look at it, but one of the popular ways to view it upside down through your legs. Earth and sky are reversed, and the long line of the pine forest looks as though it is stretching up towards the sky.

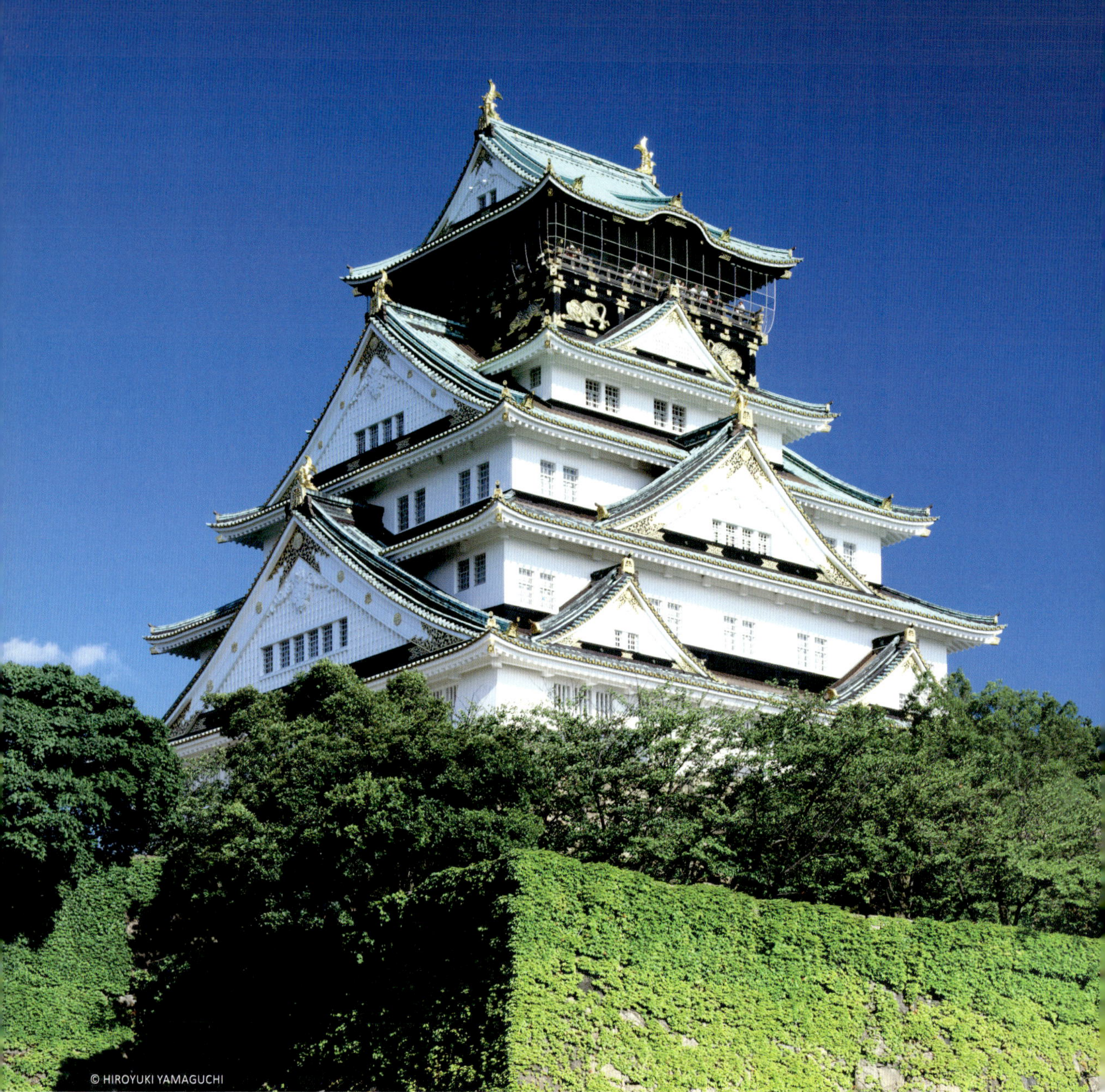
© HIROYUKI YAMAGUCHI

Osaka Castle ▪ OSAKA

Osaka Castle was built by Toyotomi Hideyoshi as a symbol of the unification of Japan. He mobilized several thousand laborers from over 30 different districts, completing the building in 1585. The castle has five levels and eight stories. The castle fell to Tokugawa Ieyasu's forces in the Summer War of Osaka in 1615 , the castle was burnt down and the Toyotomi clan wiped out. The present day castle keep is a 1931 reconstruction of how it would have looked in Toyotomi's days, and is well-loved by the citizens of Osaka as a symbol of their city. The keep, restored after 266 years, is decorated all over in dazzling gold.

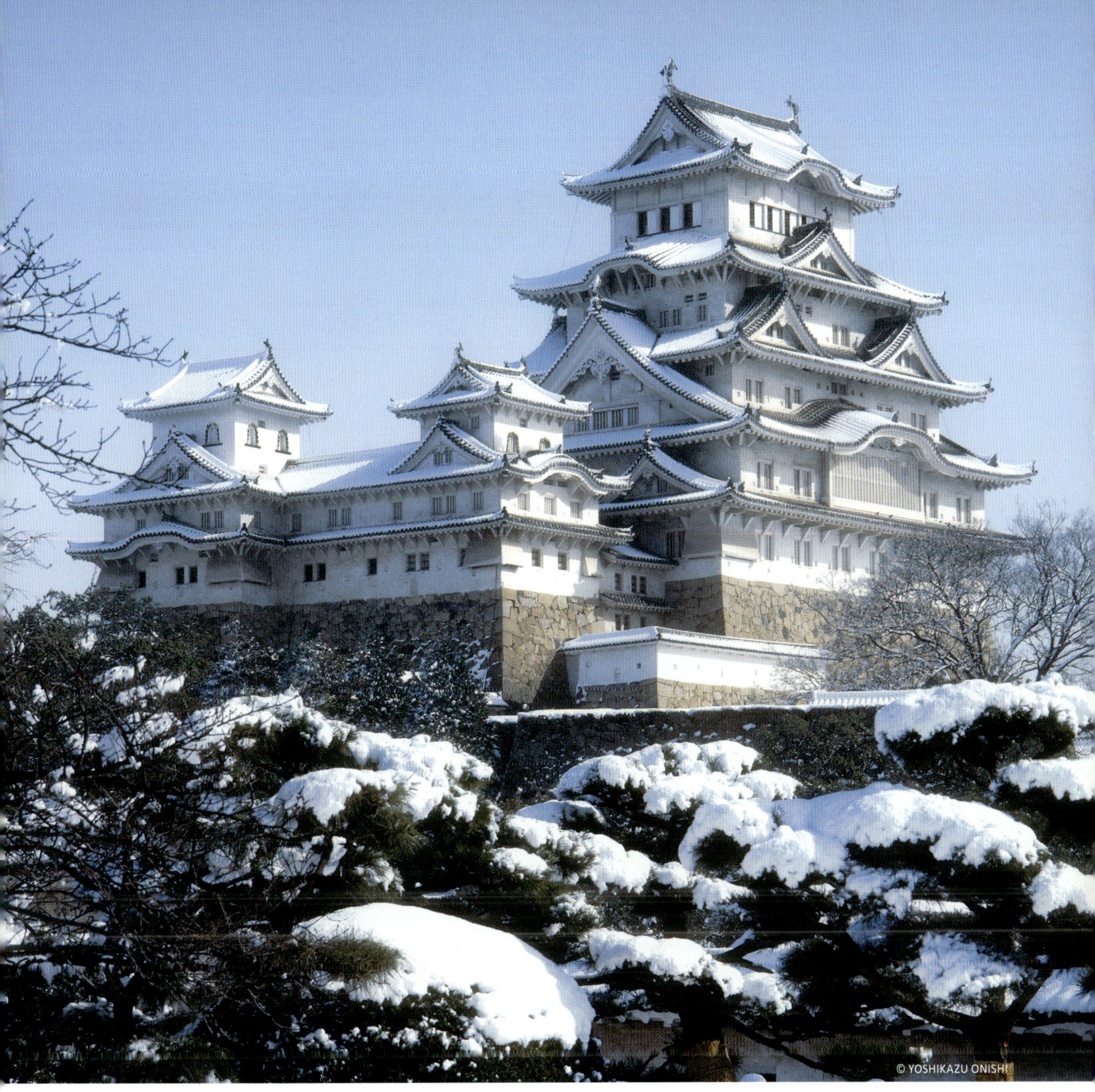
© YOSHIKAZU ONISHI

Himeji Castle ▪ HYOGO

Himeji Castle became Japan's first ever World Heritage site in the year 1993, and is still the only castle in Japan ever to have made the list. The castle keep, turrets and gates and so on are more or less in their original state despite being 400 years old. The keep consists of four large structures and four smaller ones, the present-day keep being the largest in Japan. With its unique architectural structure, and exterior coating of white lime plaster, the castle is known as the "white egret" castle for its beautiful shape. As a fortress too, it was built with elaborate design and ingenuity, earning it a worldwide reputation.

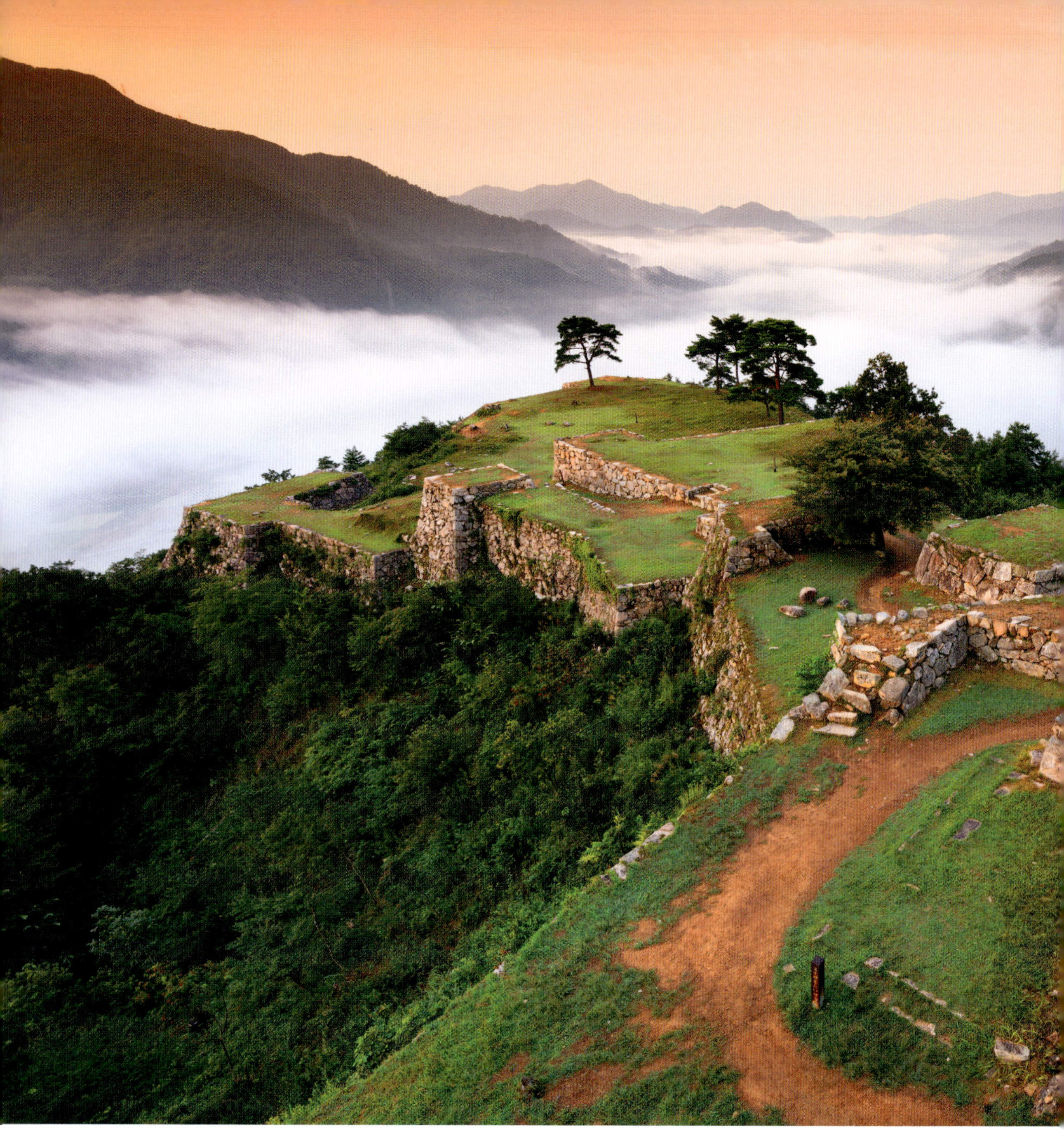

Takeda Castle ▪ HYOGO

Takeda Castle, in Asago City's Kojozan (formerly Takeda-machi), is unique because the structures remain almost fully intact from their original state. Its main keep stands on top of a mountain peak at an altitude of 354m. Constructed by the local Lord of Yamana in the middle of the 15th century, the castle fell to Toyotomi Hideyoshi in the late 16th century.

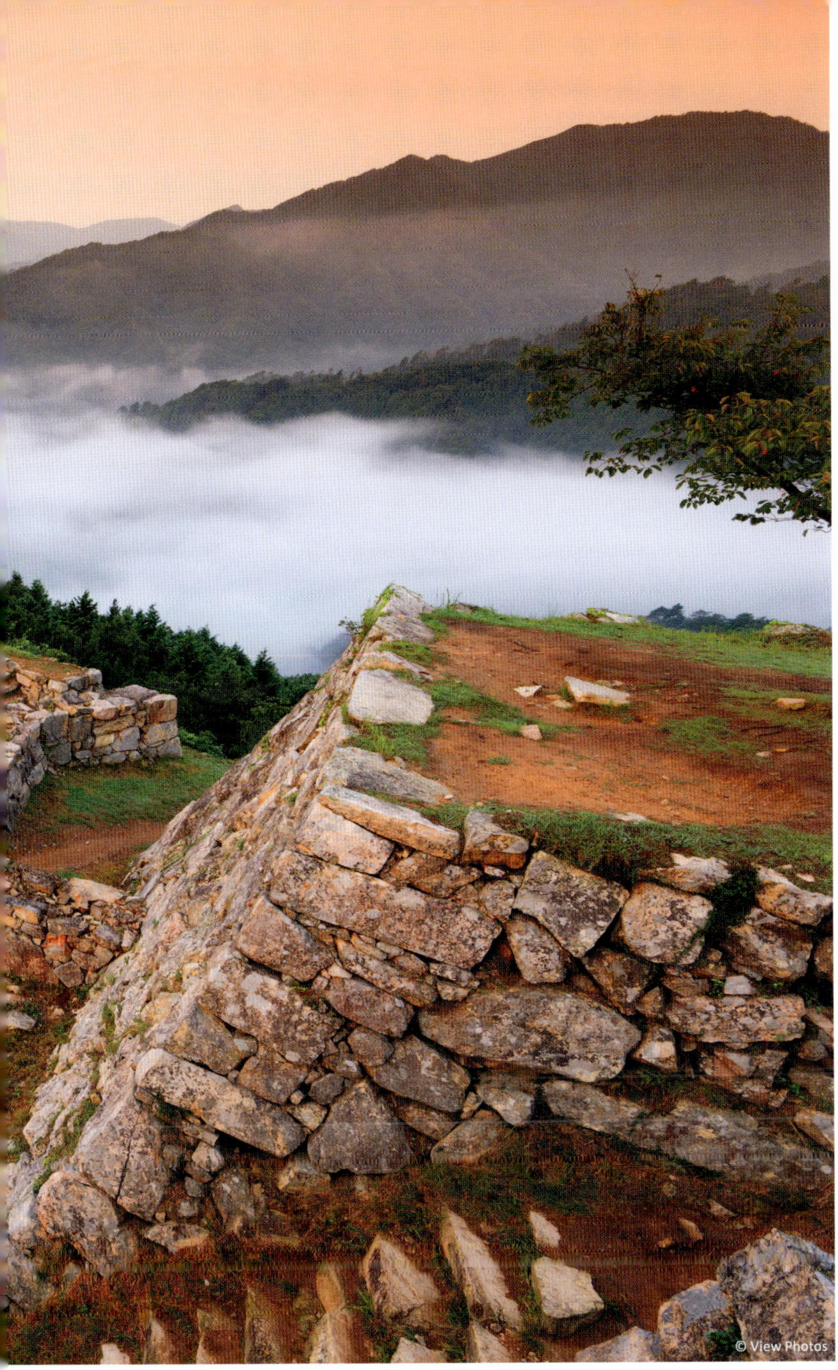

竹田城跡

© View Photos

Unkai (Ocean of clouds)

Between late September and early April, Takeda Castle is wrapped in mist early in the morning and is often called "a castle in the air", with visitors overwhelmed by its beauty. Lately, the scenery has also become known as Japan's Machu Picchu. Tourists come to Takeda to see the mysterious castle towering over the clouds.

Later, around 1600, Akamatsu Hirohide, the last lord of Takeda Castle, built outer stone fortifications, in the same engineering method as Himeji Castle's. The castle circles the central keep evenly, measuring 400m from north to south and 100m from east to west. Takeda Castle has been a national historic site.

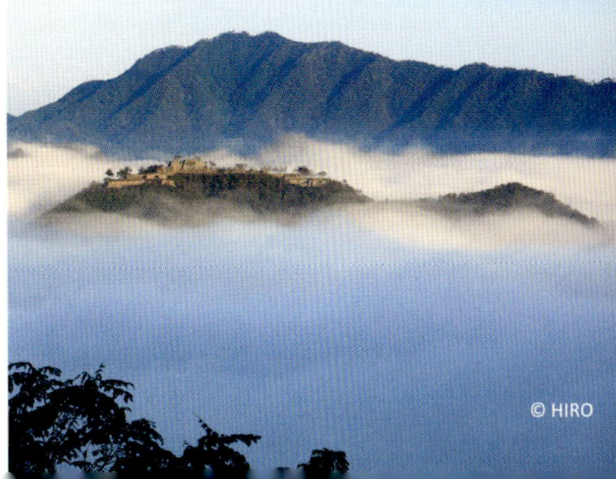

© HIRO

伊勢神宮

Ise-jingu ▪ MIE

Ise-jingu is popularly called by its nickname, *Oise-san*, but its exalted stature is special among Japan's shrines. Jingu consists of the Naiku and Geku, respectively called Kotai-jingu and Toyouke-daijingu, with Kotai-jingu being the main shrine of the complex. The deity enshrined in Kotai-jingu is Amaterasu-omikami, mythic ancestor of Japan's imperial household. Japan's imperial rulers throughout the ages have been worshipped there.

Visitors crossing the Uji bashi Bridge across the Isuzu gawa River enter the Naiku's sacred zone. Within this inner compound, the zone around the shrine building is called *Shin-iki* (an especially sacred one).

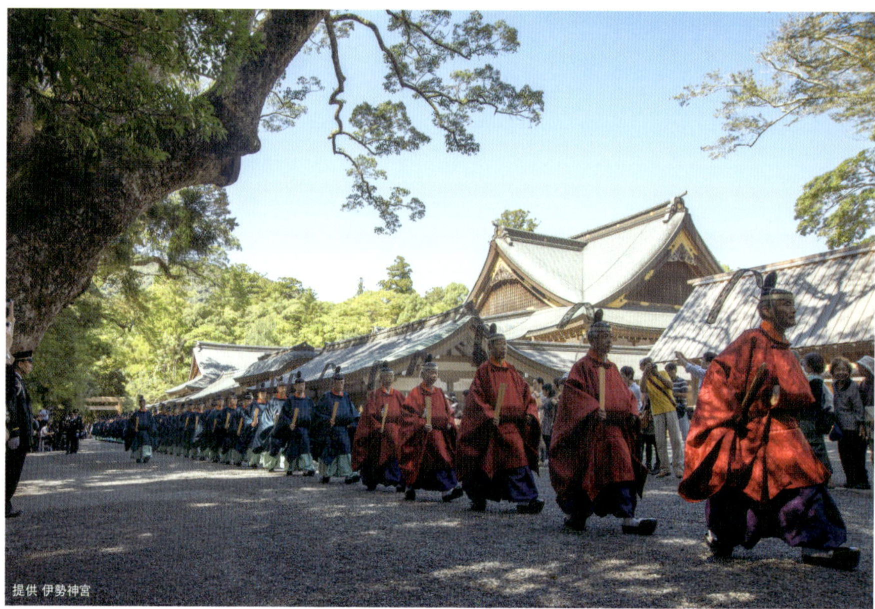

Ise-jingu's *Shikinen Sengu*

Ise-jingu's Shikinen Sengu is a great festivity celebrated every 20 years, during which the main shrine and other structures are rebuilt. According to legend, the first Shikinen Sengu took place in 690, during the reign of Emperor Jito. The most recent (62nd) round took place in the autumn of 2013. This cycle was temporary broken only in the medieval era of Warring States and has otherwise been sustained, according to the ancient rite, for 1,300 years.

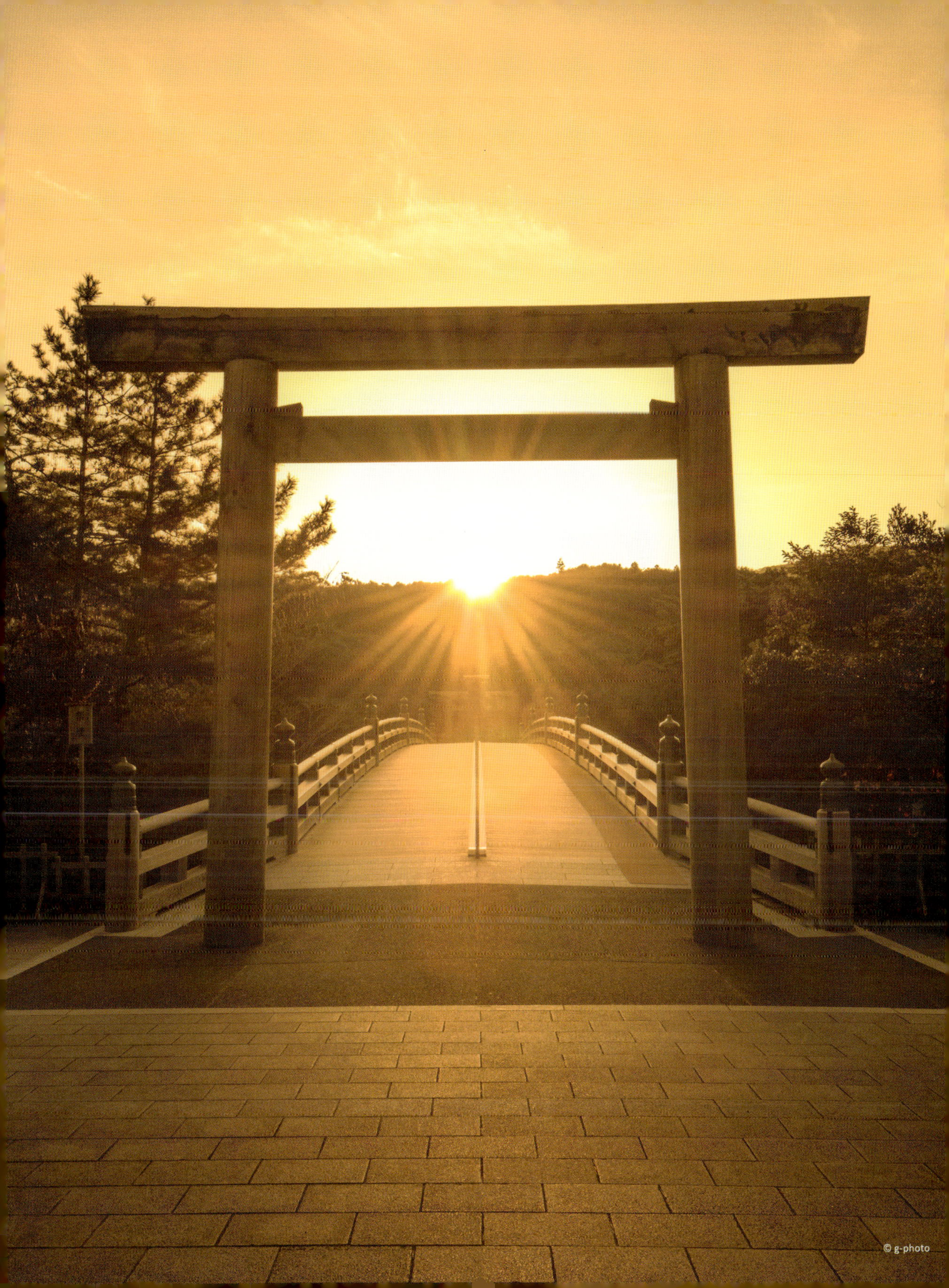
© g-photo

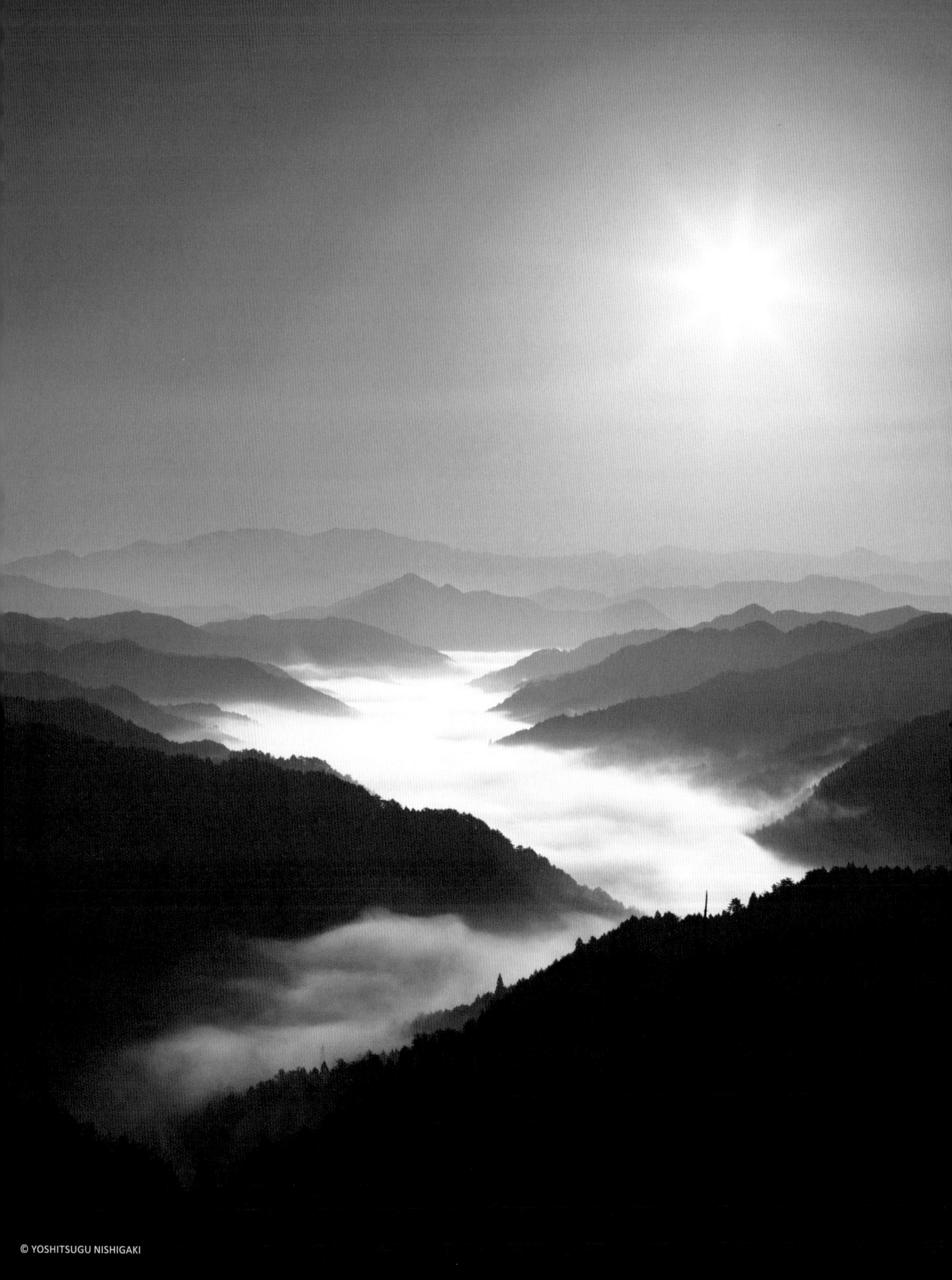

Koyasan (Mount Koya) ■ WAKAYAMA

Kongobu-ji, the head temple of the Koyasan school of Shingon Buddhism, is situated on Koyasan. The temple was founded in the early 9th century by Kukai. After Kukai's death, in the 10th century Emperor Daigo named him, Grand Master Kobo Daishi, and pilgrimages to Koyosan became popular.

Women were forbidden to enter Koyasan until 1872, after which many female pilgrims started to visit the temple. The places of pilgrimages that run in a strip between Koyasan and Wakayama's Kumano, and Nara Prefecture's Yoshino was registered as Sacred Sites and Pilgrimage Routes in the Kii Mountain Range, a World Heritage site in the year 2004.

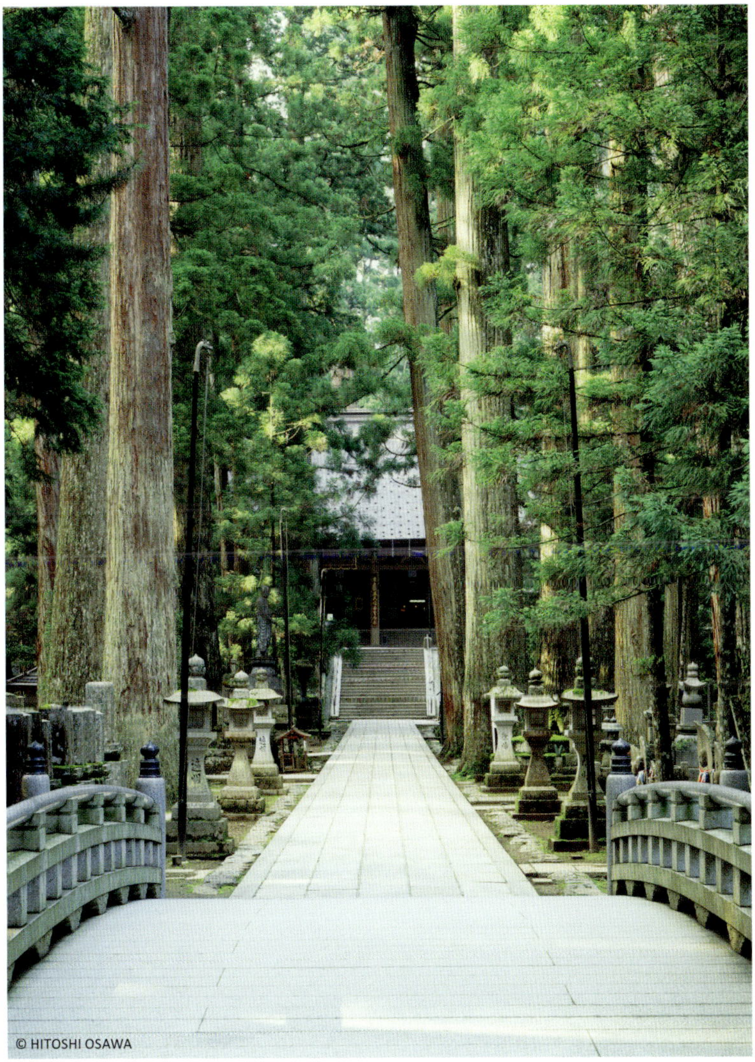

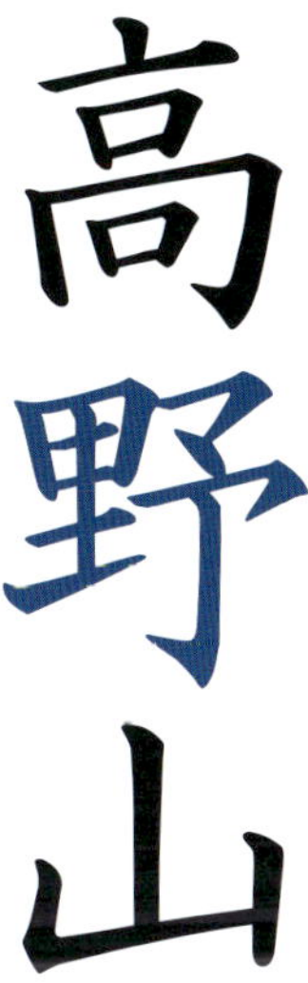

Pilgrim's route to Koyasan

The pilgrimage route of Koyasan is a cultural asset, which is unusual even among the World Heritage sites. It links the three major sacred sites of Yoshino and Omine, Kumano *San-zan* (three mountains of Kumano), and Koyasan, and has been walked by many ascetics as a part of their training. It is a place that symbolizes the Japanese spiritual culture of reverence for the gods that dwell in mountains and forests.

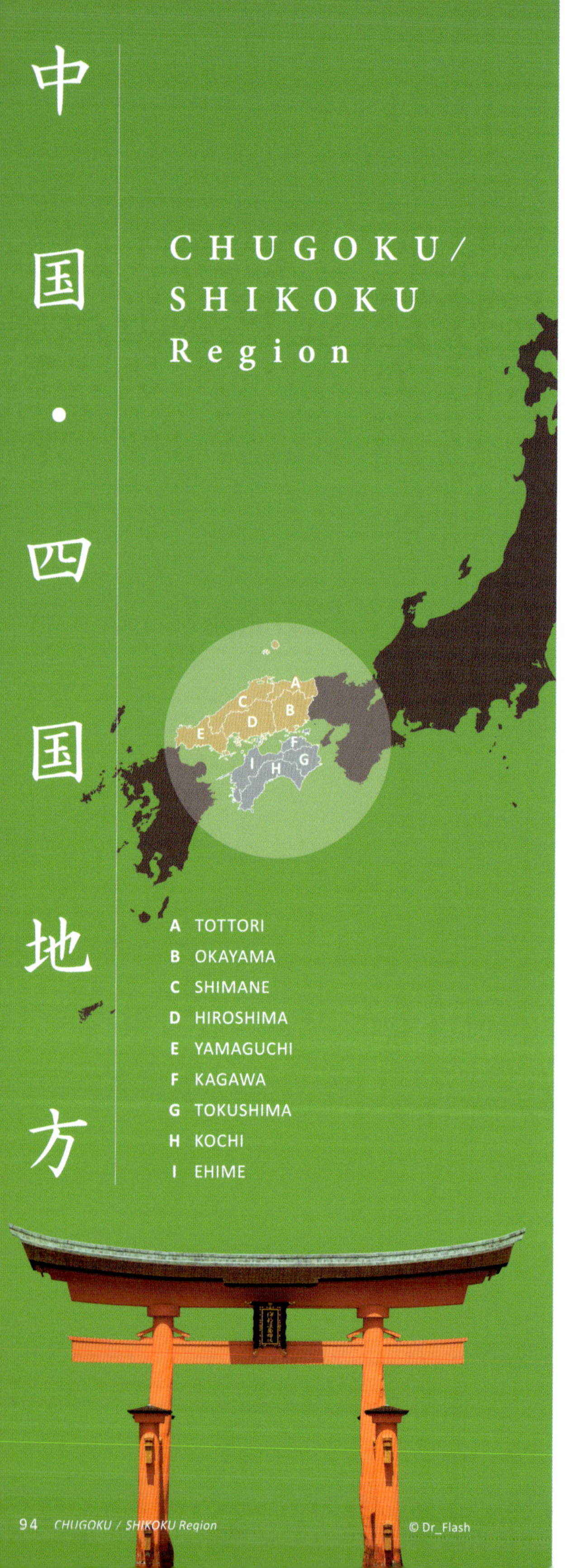

© Dr_Flash

At places like the Atom Bomb Dome, and Izumo Taisha Shrine, where the gods gather together, the past and the present day intersect.

Located in the western part of the island of Honshu, the Chugoku region is made up of the five prefectures of Tottori, Okayama, Shimane, Hiroshima, and Yamaguchi. Shikoku is one of the four main islands that make up the Japanese archipelago, and is made up of the four prefectures of Kagawa, Tokushima, Kochi, and Ehime.

Hiroshima Prefecture is a part of the Chubu region that is very well-known internationally because it contains the city of Hiroshima, the first place in the world to be hit by an atomic bomb.

In addition to the World Heritage sites of Miyajima and the Atomic Bomb Dome in Hiroshima, the region as a whole is distinguished by the peaceful rural village landscapes that are still to be found there.

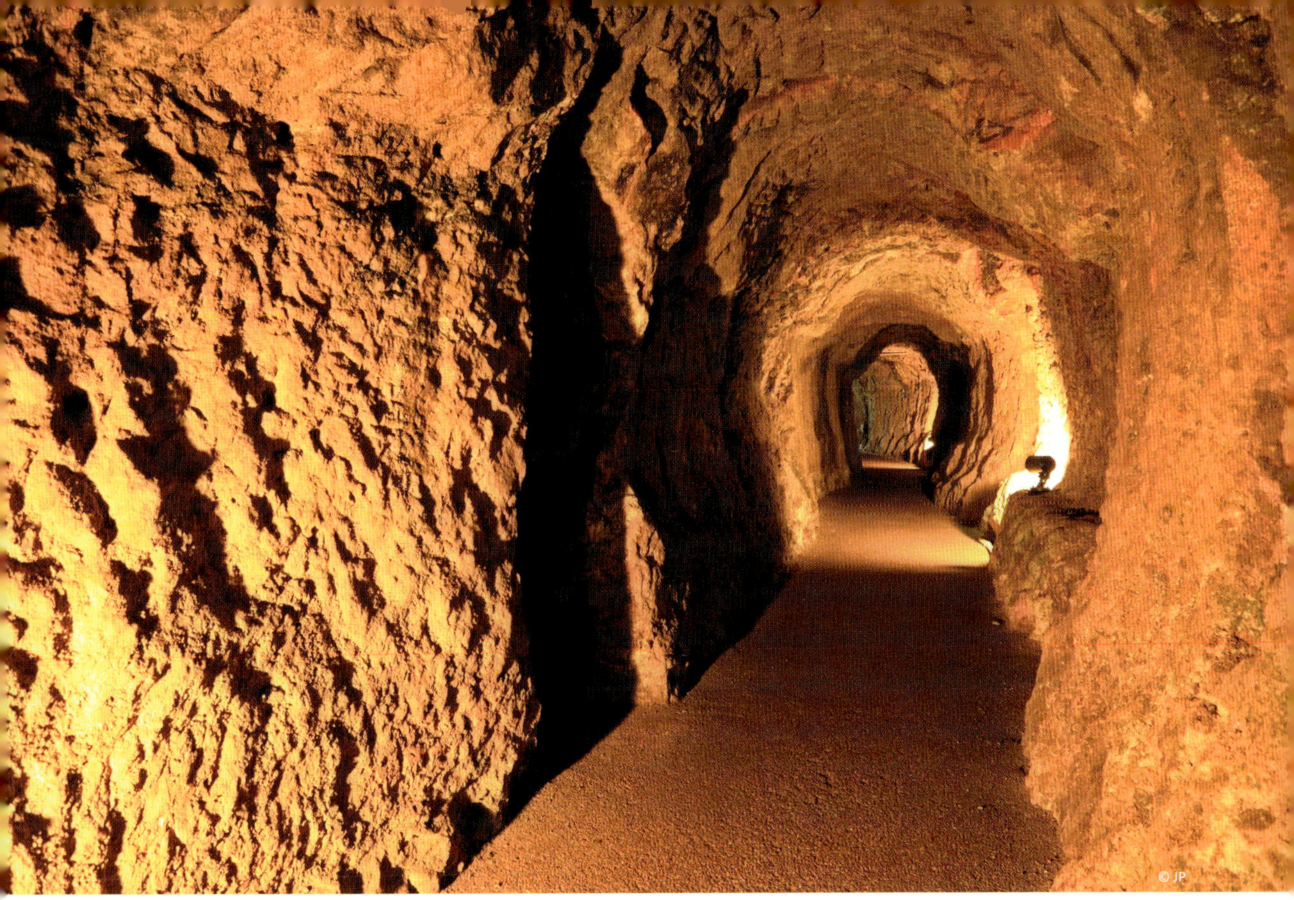

© JP

Iwami Ginzan Silver Mine

▪ SHIMANE

During the Age of Discovery in the 16th century, around one third of the silver that was distributed across the globe through trade originated in Japan. It is said that nearly all of this silver was produced at the Iwami Ginzan silver mine in present day Shimane Prefecture. In 1533 silver was successfully refined at the mine, leading to a tug-of-war over the mountain among the eminent figures of the district, the mine eventually being placed under the direct jurisdiction of the Tokugawa shogunate in the Edo Period (1603-1868). Silver production reached its peak in the 17th century, but subsequently declined and work stopped in 1923, and the mine was completely closed in 1943. The silver mine was listed as a World Heritage site in 2007, drawing special praise for the way that it had avoided damaging the natural environment while representing an environmentally considerate industrial ruin that existed in symbiosis with the natural environment.

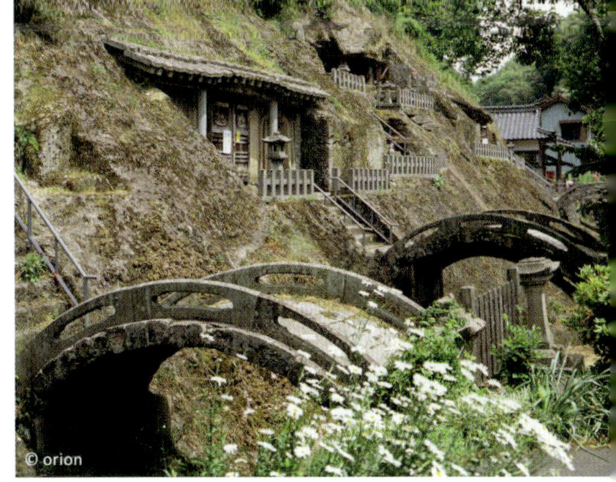
© orion

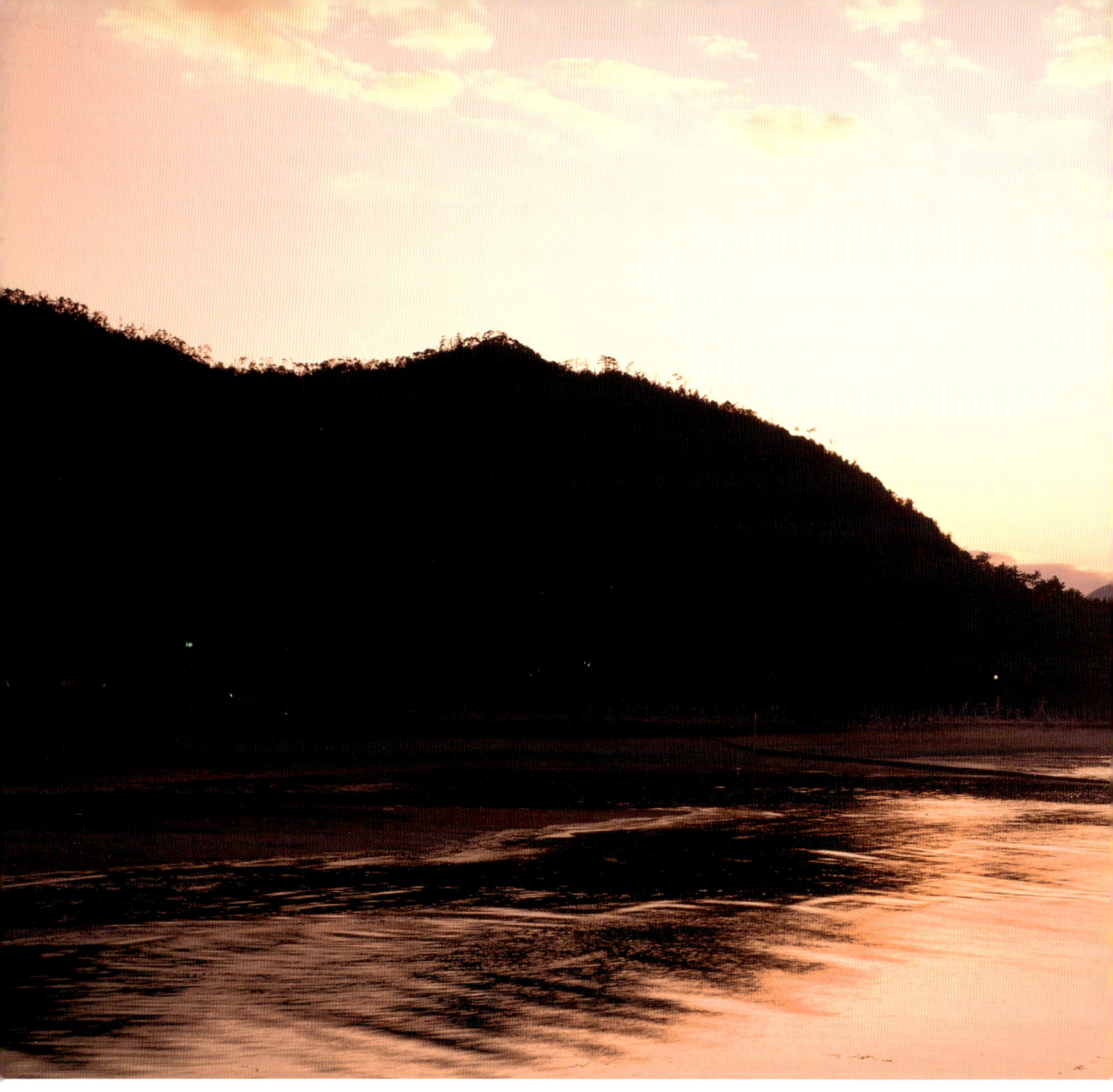

Miyajima ("Shrine Island") ▪ HIROSHIMA

Miyajima is an island in the western part of Hiroshima Bay with a circumference of 31 kilometers. It has been regarded as a sacred site since ancient days. It is also sometimes called *Aki no Miyajima*, in reference to the old name for the district, and is famed as being one of the three views of Japan, along with Matsushima in Miyagi Prefecture and Amanohashidate in Kyoto Prefecture. The island is covered with an ancient forest, and its highest point is Mount Misen, at 535 meter above sea level. To the northeast of Misen is the symbol of Miyajima, Itsukushima Shrine. The vermillion torii gate that seems to float in the sea, the main building and cloisters are designated as national treasures and were listed as World Heritage sites in 1996.

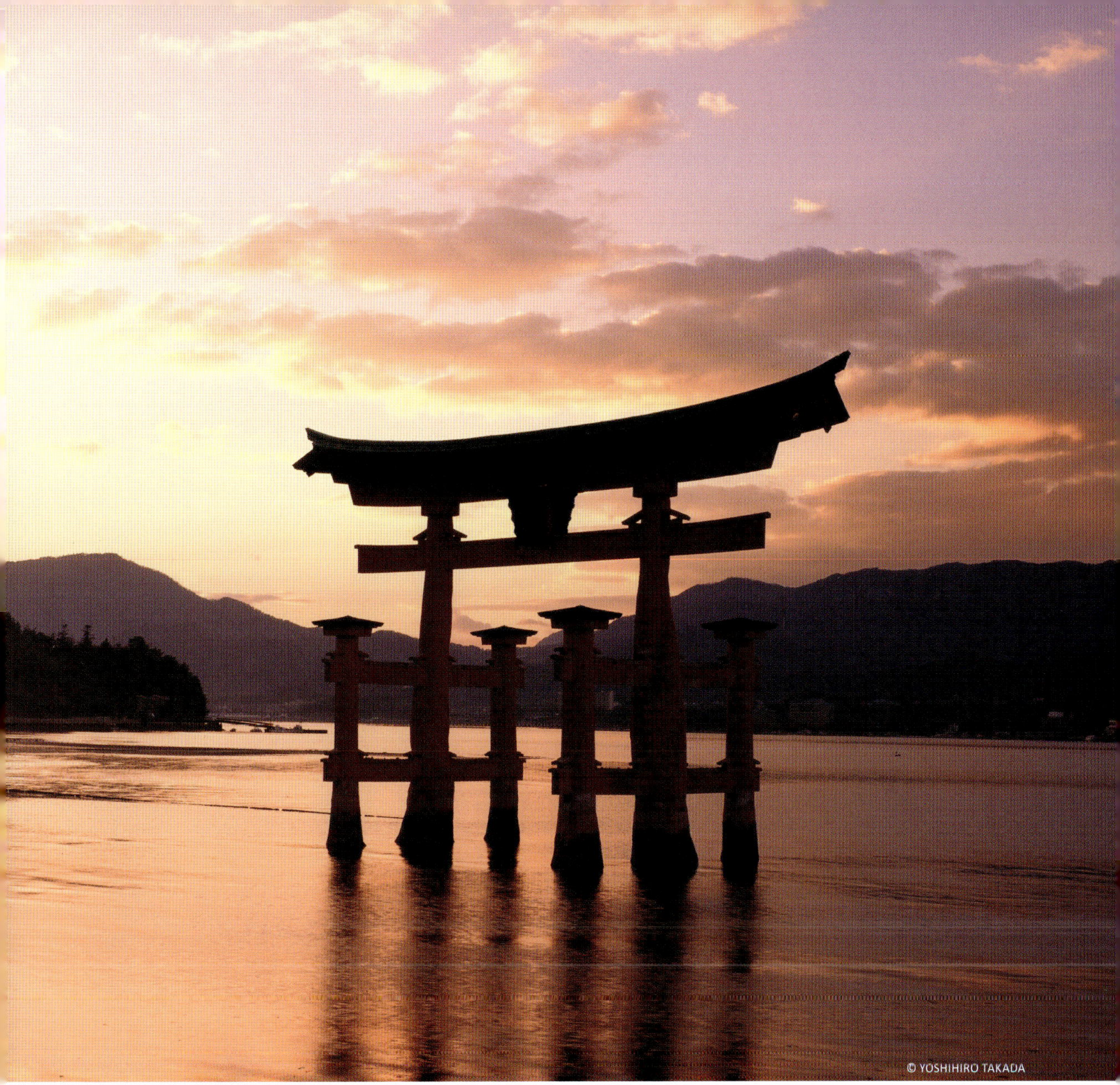

© YOSHIHIRO TAKADA

Island of the gods

There were a great many rules surrounding Miyajima as a sacred island. It was forbidden to farm, weave, or bury the dead on the island. It was not until after the Warring States Period (1467-1573) that people other than those serving at Itsukushima Shrine were allowed to live on the island.

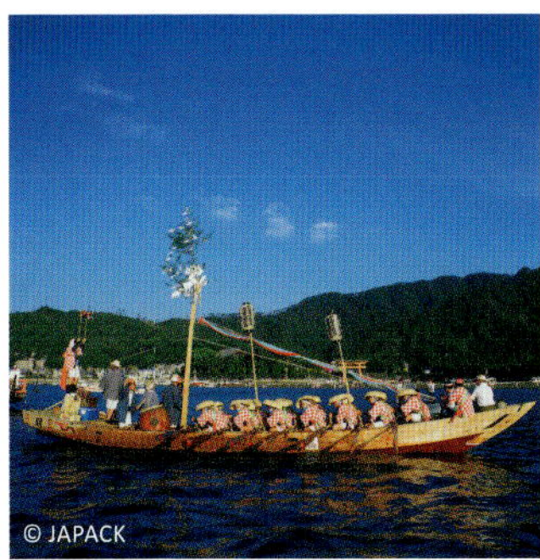

© JAPACK

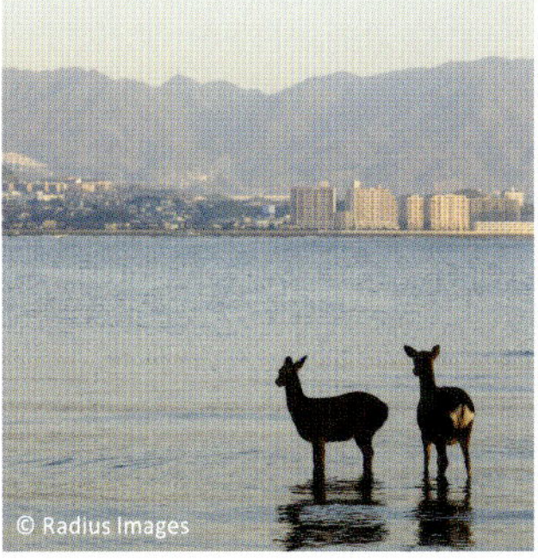

© Radius Images

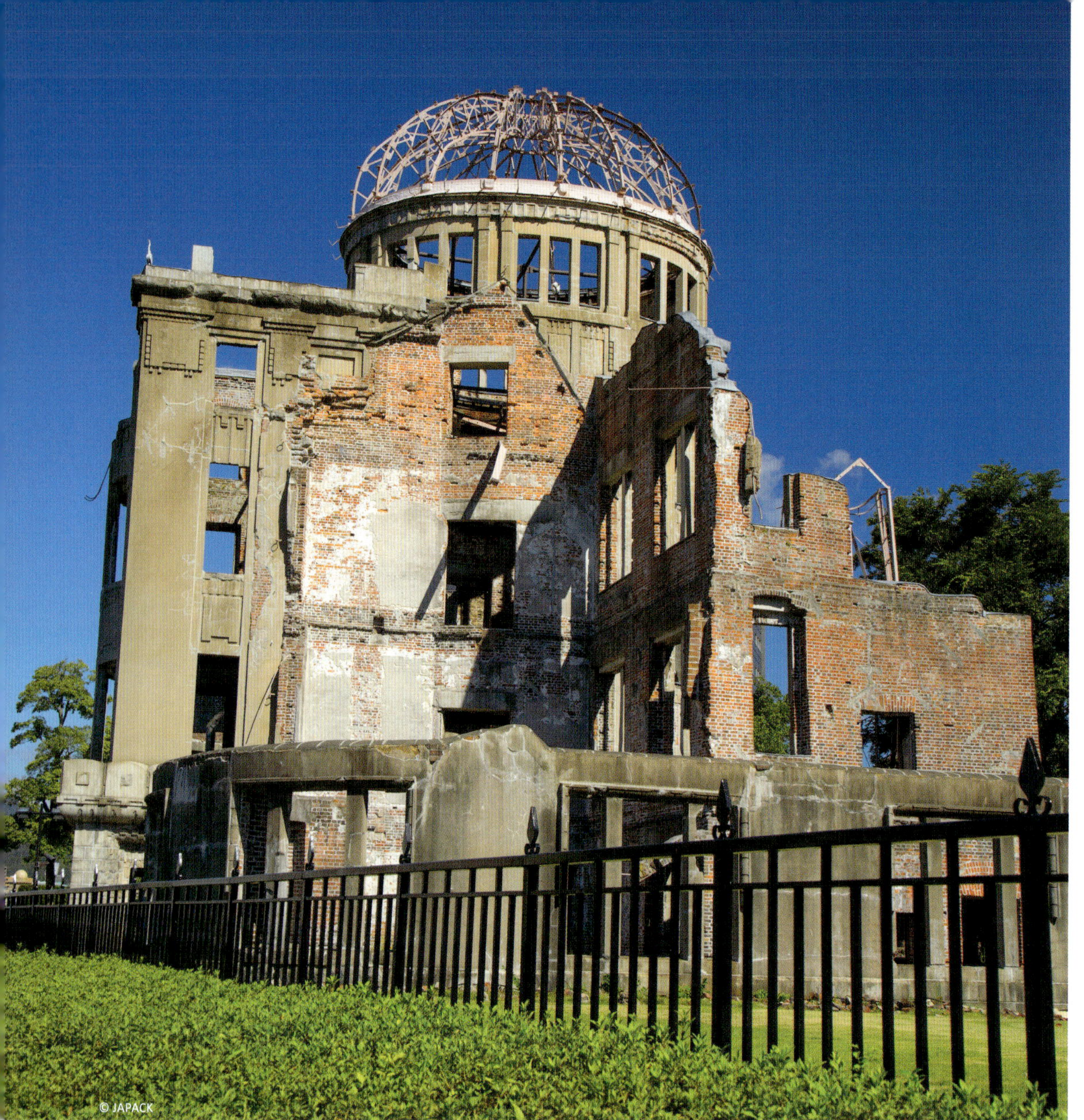
© JAPACK

Atomic Bomb Dome ▪ HIROSHIMA

On August 6, 1945, towards the end of World War II, the first atomic bomb in human history was dropped on the city of Hiroshima. The buildings in the city center were destroyed in an instant, leaving nothing but burnt ground. The oval-shaped Hiroshima Prefectural Commercial Exhibition Hall was completely destroyed by fire, but somehow the skeleton of the center of the building miraculously remained standing. Eventually the remains of the building became known as the "Atomic Bomb Dome" and it grew into the symbol of the bombed city. Conservation work was carried out in 1967 after donations from the public were solicited. In 1996 the dome, now part of the Hiroshima Peace Memorial, became a the World Heritage site as a structure that expresses the horrors of atomic bombs and war to future generations.

Tottori sand dunes ▪ TOTTORI

The sand dunes that stretch along the Sea of Japan coast in Tottori City are the largest in Japan, spreading over two kilometers from north to south and 16 kilometers from east to west. The sand dunes on the eastern side of the Sendai River are particularly high, reaching 90 meters in places; their deeply conical shape has been likened to the bowl of a pestle and mortar, and are 40 meters high in places. The sand dunes are shaped mainly in the autumn and winter by the seasonal northwesterly wind, and are famed for the patterns left in the sand by the wind that blows at a speed of five to six meters per second. The wind at a speed of more than 10 meters per second causes a sandstorm and the shape of sand dunes changes.

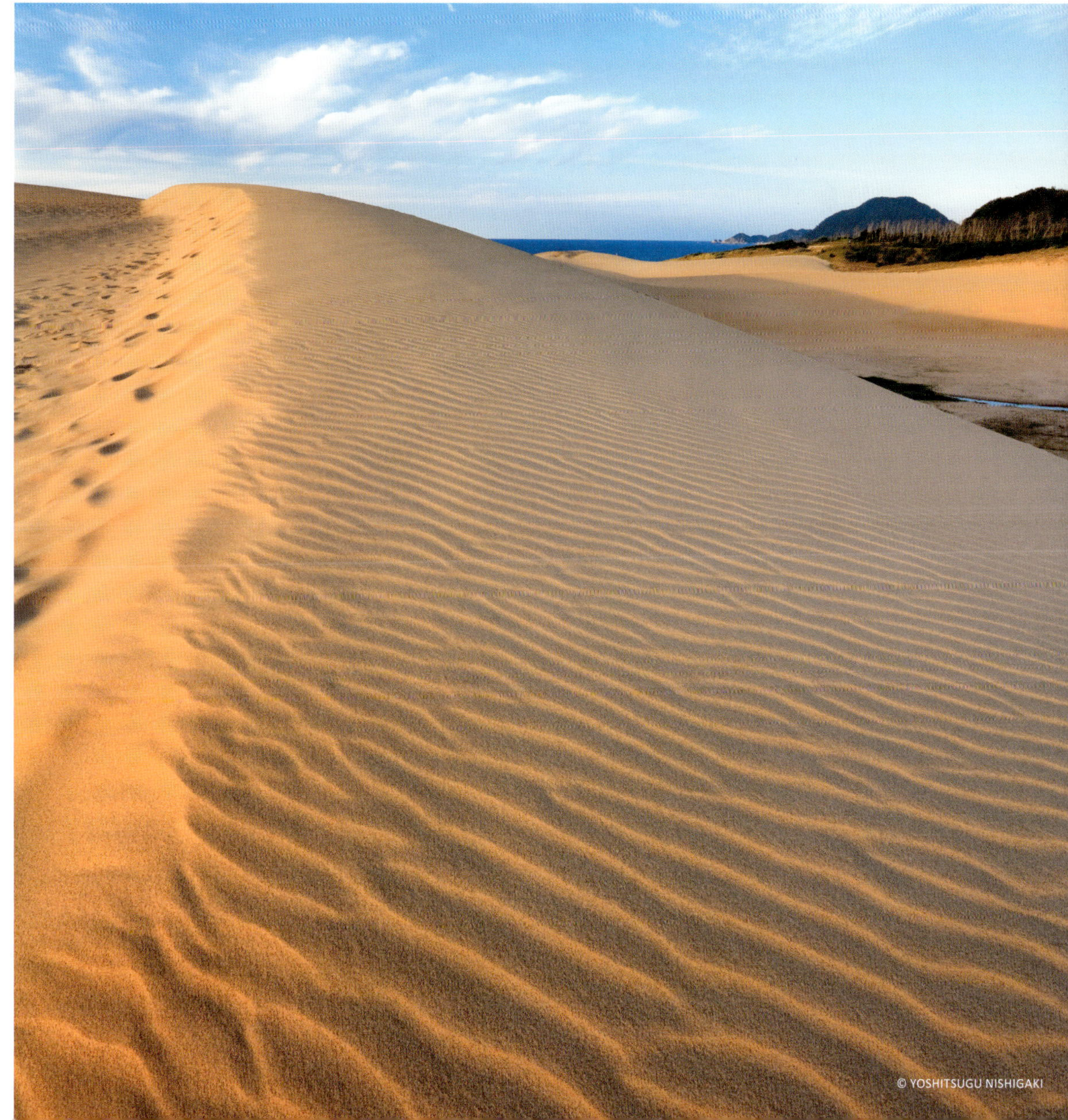

Land of gods

Izumo is called the land of gods and every year a seven-day festival is held between October 11 and 17 of the old calendar, a period known as the month of gods. It is said to receive eight million gods and deities that come to Izumo from all over Japan. As these divinities congregate, they are said to discuss various affairs, from marriage arrangements to next year's harvest, in proceedings called *kamuhakari* (divine discussion).

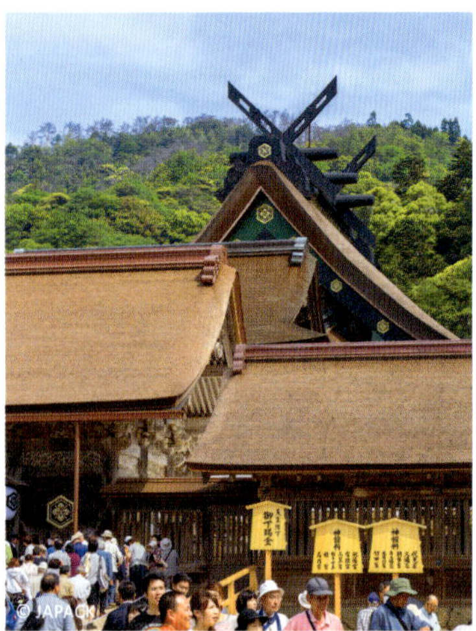

© JAPACK

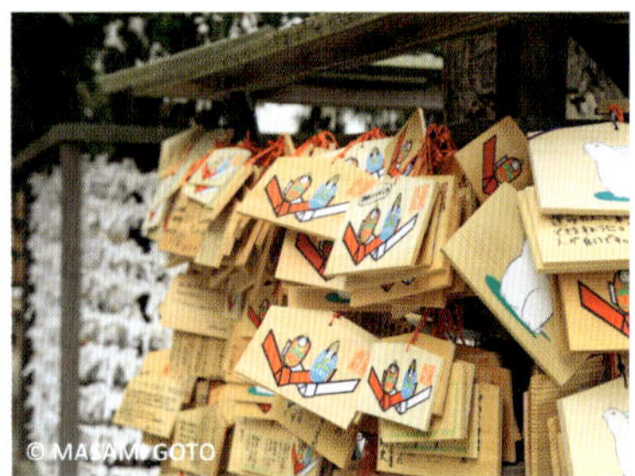

© MASAMI GOTO

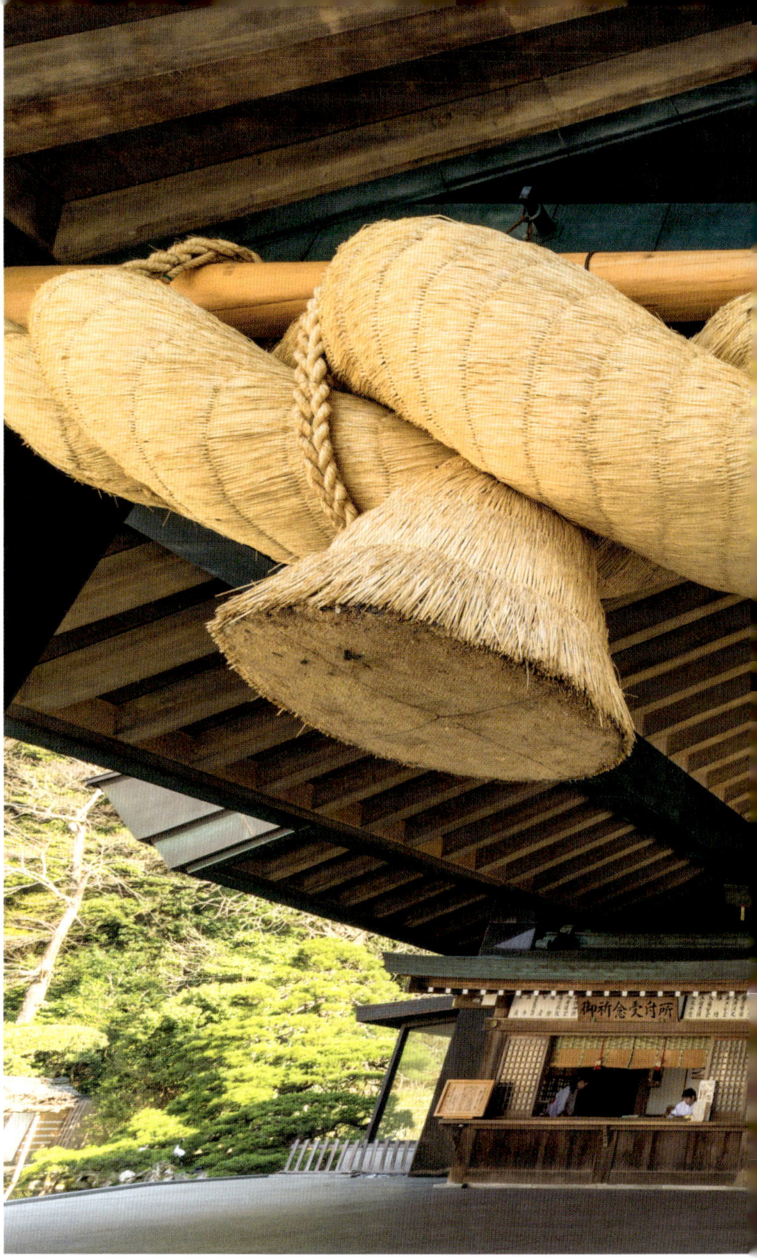

出雲大社

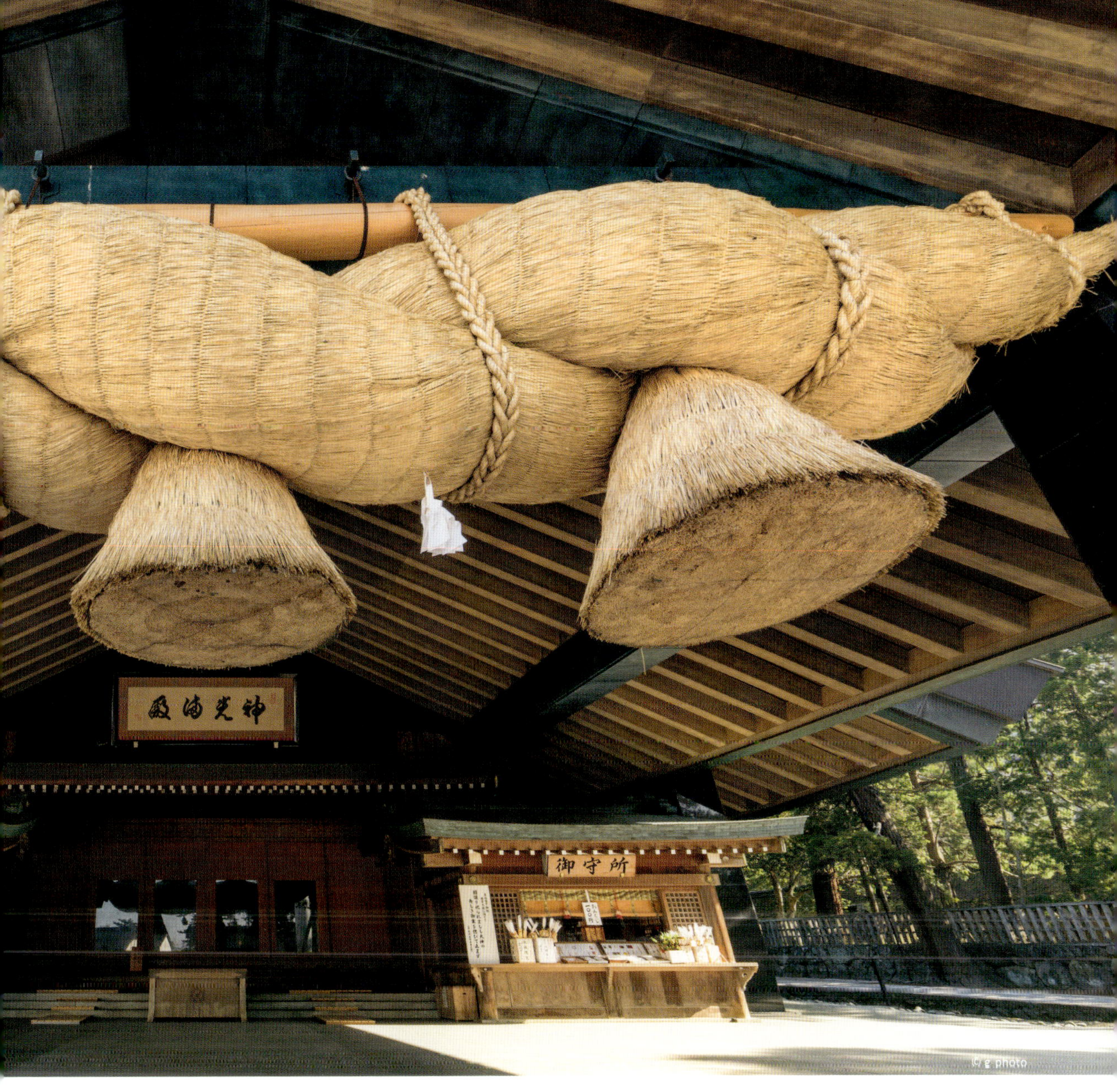

Izumo Taisha (Izumo Shrine) ■ SHIMANE

Ancient shrines are found everywhere in the prefecture and Izumo Taisha is their hub. Fervently worshipped by citizens, it is known as the god of marriage and good fortune. The main shrine or sanctuary, of the *taisha-zukuri* or "big shrine" style architecture, is 24 meters tall and is characterized by gently sloped roofs. The main shrine undergoes periodic reconstruction every 60 years, when the deity is removed and then restored after completion. The last reconstruction was finished in May 2013, after a five-year process, with the god returning from its temporary residence to the main shrine. The sacred *ohshime-nawa* rope in the Grand Shrine's Kagura hall—13.5 meters long, 8 meters in diameter, and weighing as much as 4.4 tons—is one of the largest of its kind. The rope is renewed every six to seven years.

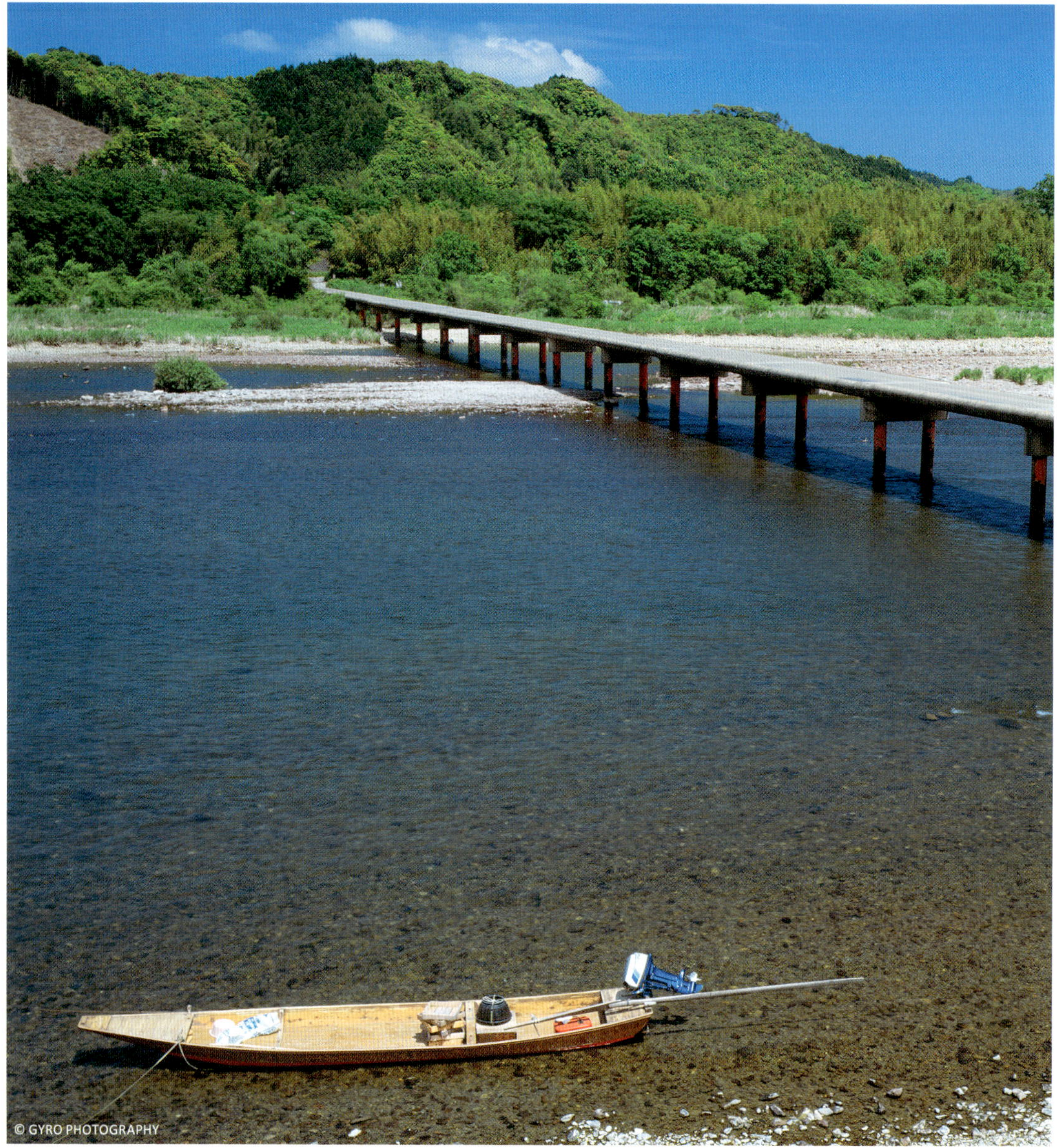
© GYRO PHOTOGRAPHY

Shimanto River ▪ KOCHI

The Shimanto river flows through the western part of Kochi Prefecture, emptying into the Pacific Ocean at Nakamura City. With a length of 196 kilometers, it is the longest river in Shikoku district. Including the tributaries of the river it has 47 bridges designed to be submerged under water during floods, so they do not become damaged by floating logs and other debris. Since there are no dams upstream the river is famed for the preservation of its natural ecology, scenery and clear water. There are still fishermen carrying out traditional fishing methods on the river, where ayu fish, eels, freshwater prawns and mitten crabs can be caught. Another well-known product of the river is green laver, a relative of the type of seaweed used to wrap sushi.

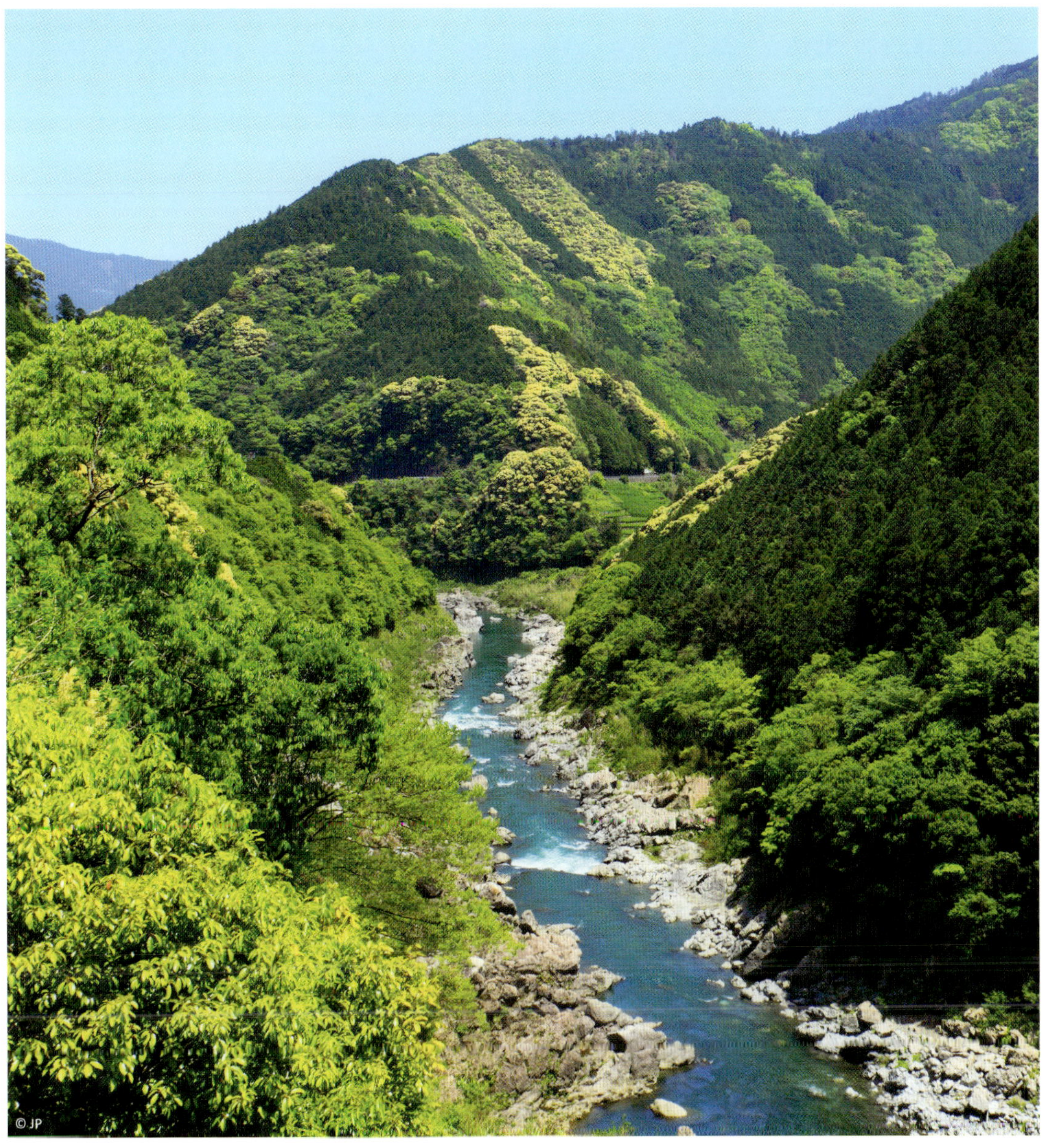

Niyodo River ▪ KOCHI

The Niyodo river is the third largest river in Shikoku in terms of length and basin area. In 2010, among Japan's first-grade rivers, the Niyodo River was named the best in terms of water quality. Its water, called the *Niyodo blue*, has a cerulean hue due to its excellent purity and transparency. The river travels across Shikoku's mountain range and the Niyodo Valley at its midpoint towers several hundred meters above the river stream. *Washi* (Japanese paper) production has been a common industry along the Niyodo River.

In a popular event, *koi-nobori*, carp-shaped banners made of Niyodo River paper and painted in bright colors, swim en masse in the river.

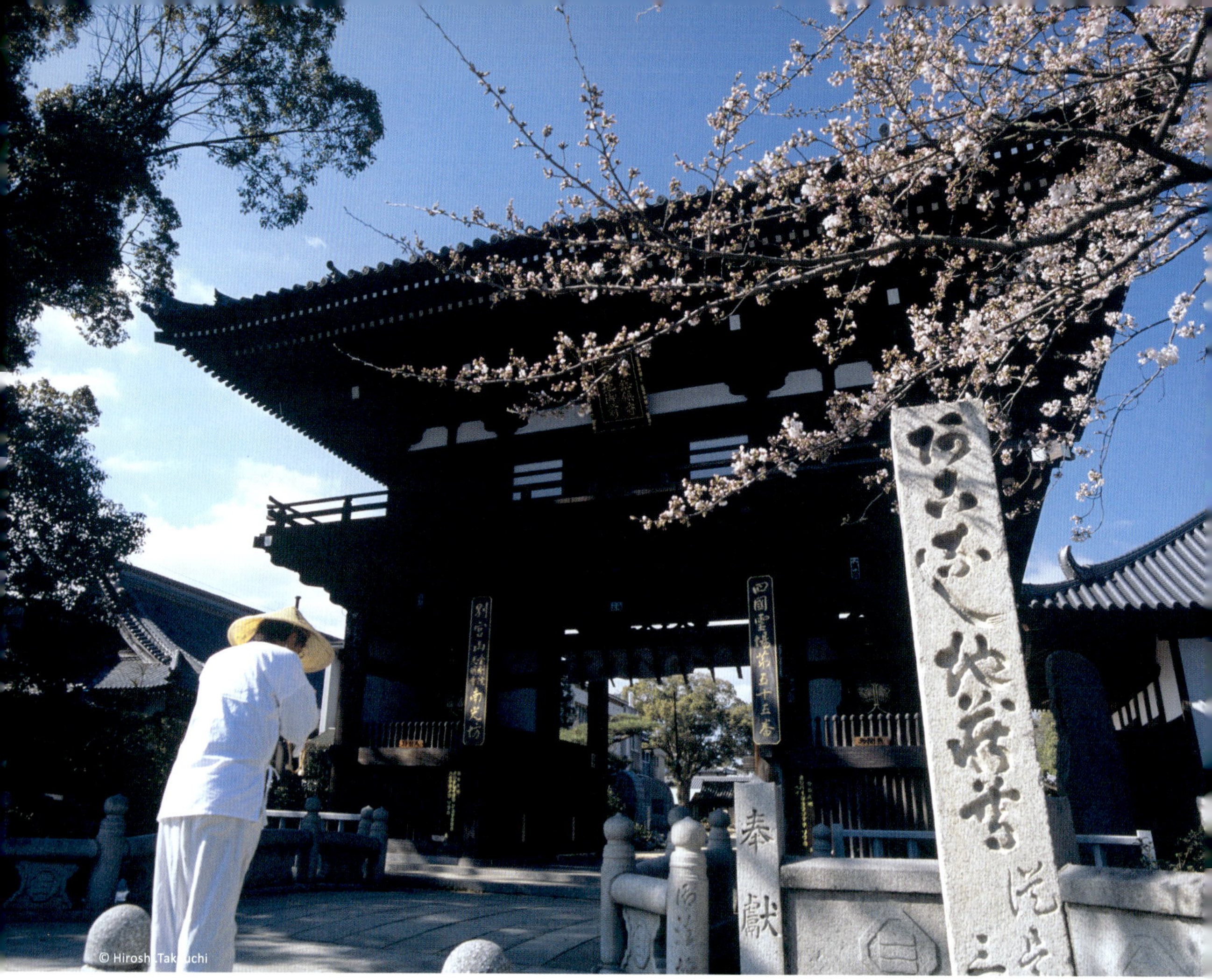

© Hiroshi Takeuchi

Shikoku Pilgrimage ▪ TOKUSHIMA

The Shikoku Henro is the name for a pilgrimage that consists of visiting all the 88 sacred sites on Shikoku associated with the Grand Master Kobo Daishi Kukai. The pilgrimage around all 88 sites covers a distance of between 1,000 and 1,400 kilometers, depending on which route is taken, and takes about 40 days on foot.

In recent years increasing numbers of pilgrims from overseas are taking part in the pilgrimage, many of them spending a long time completing the circuit. There are guidebooks available in English, so foreign visitors can enjoy the experience even if it's their first time.

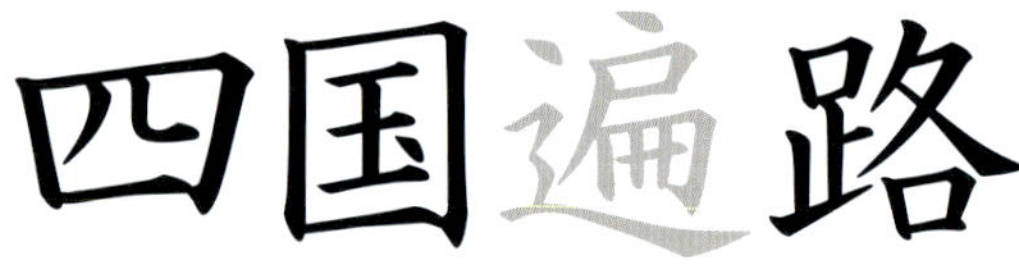

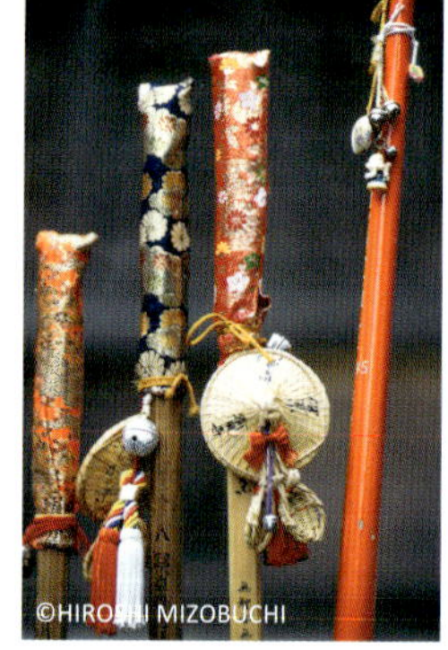
©HIROSHI MIZOBUCHI

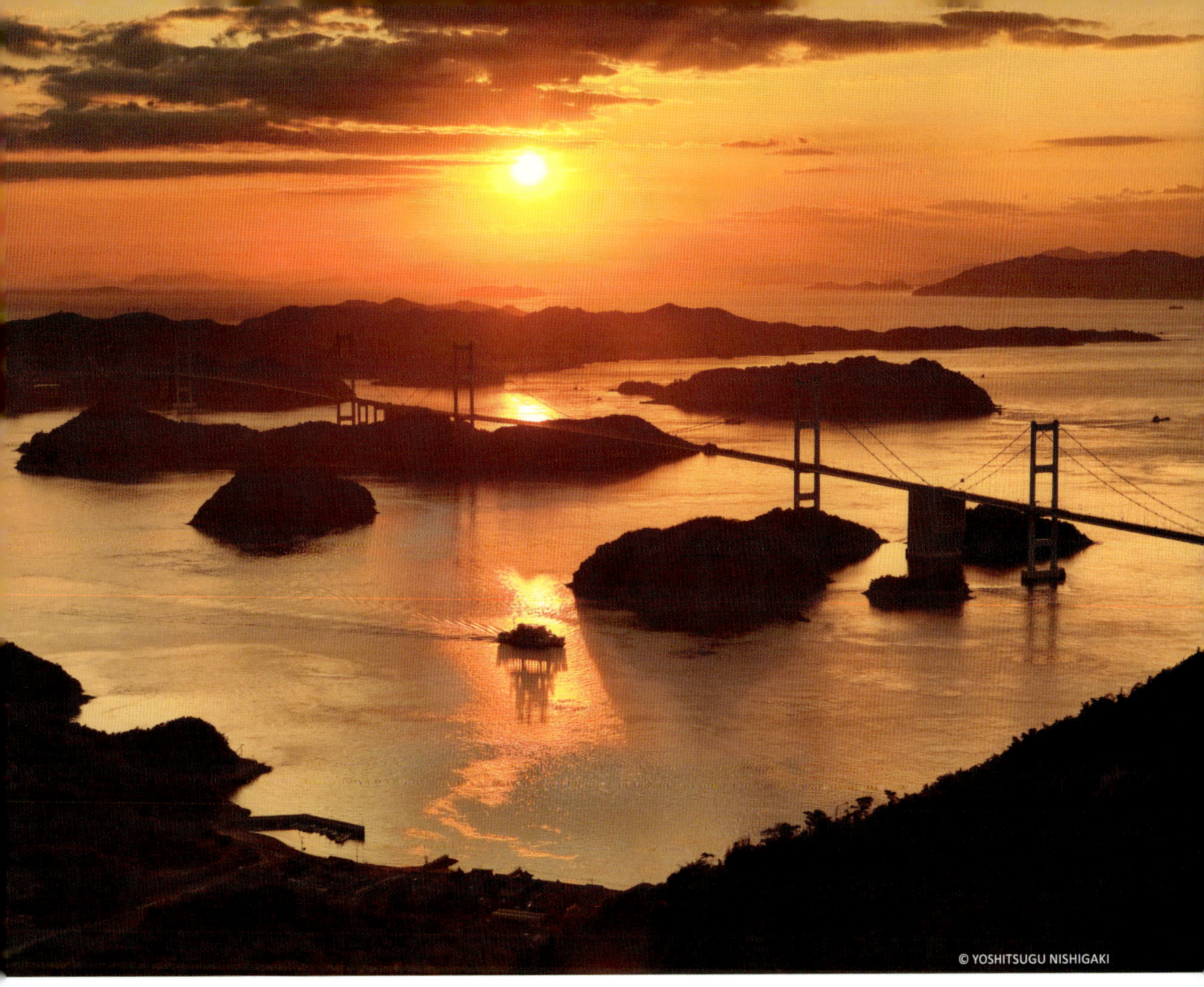
© YOSHITSUGU NISHIGAKI

しまなみ海道

Shimanami Kaido (Shimanami Expressway)

■ HIROSHIMA-EHIME

The Shimanami Kaido is a toll-paying road of 59.4 kilometers in length, which takes visitors through various islands of the Seto Inland Sea and Ehime Prefecture, and connects Onomichi City in Hiroshima Prefecture with Imabari City in Ehime Prefecture. A total of eleven large bridges join island to island, such as Shin Onomichi Bridge, Tatara Bridge and Kurushima Kaikyo Bridge. The road is a motorway that links the picturesque islands of the Seto Inland Sea together, but it is also equipped with dedicated paths for cyclists and pedestrians, making it a very popular route with cycling enthusiasts. The cycling road can be completed at a leisurely pace in around 10 hours, or four or five hours at faster speed.

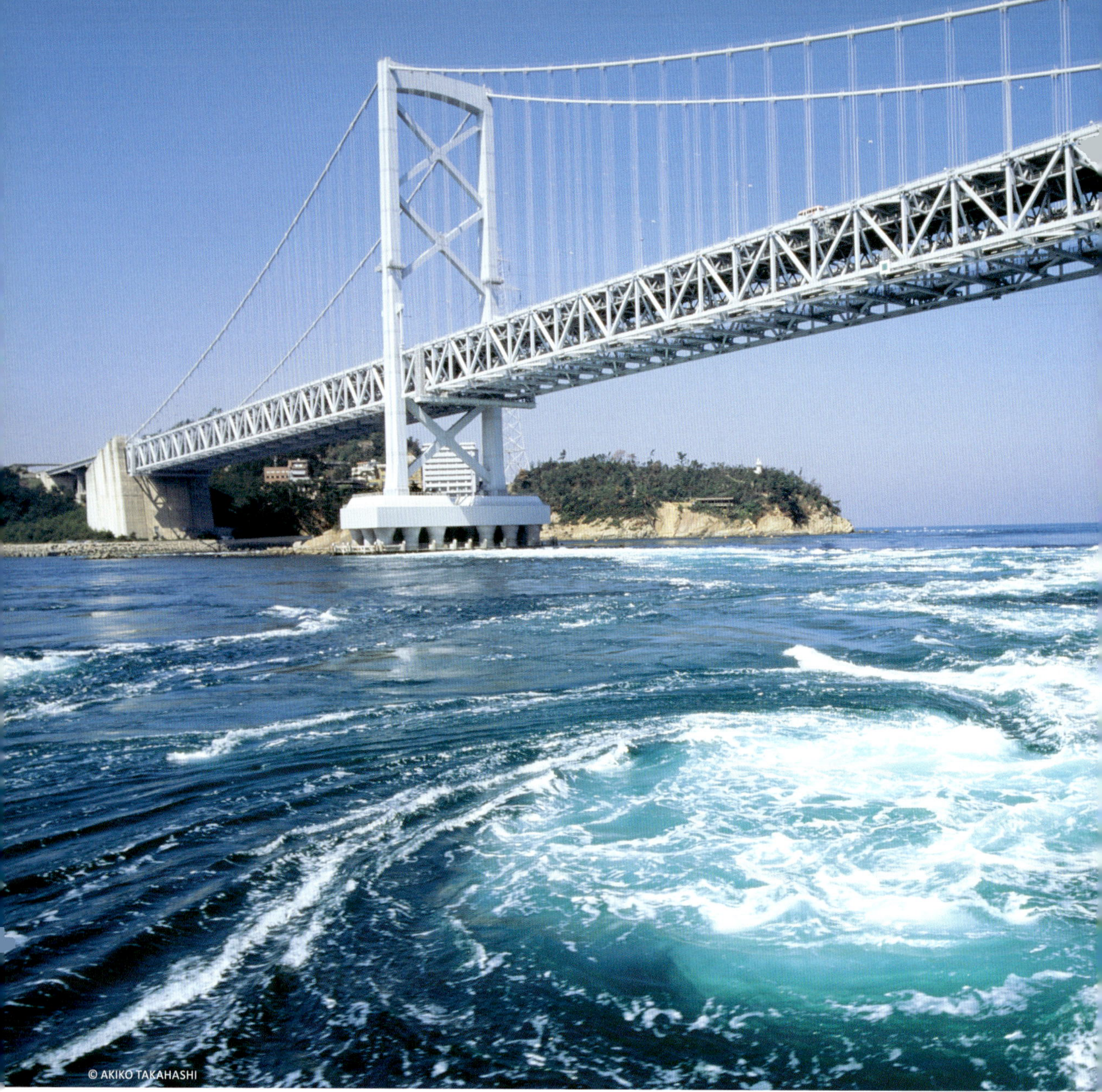
© AKIKO TAKAHASHI

Naruto Straits ▪ TOKUSHIMA

The Naruto Straits that are located between Tokushima Prefecture's Naruto City and Awaji Island are about 1.4 kilometers wide and the deepest central part around 90 meters deep; the water is shallow on either bank. The current at the center is fast and catches the gentle currents towards the banks, creating whirlpools. The Naruto Straits are one of the world's three famous whirlpool currents, moving at a maximum speed of up to 10 knots/hour. Large sightseeing boats and underwater observation craft operate in the Naruto Straits, enabling visitors to get up close to the amazing power of the tides.

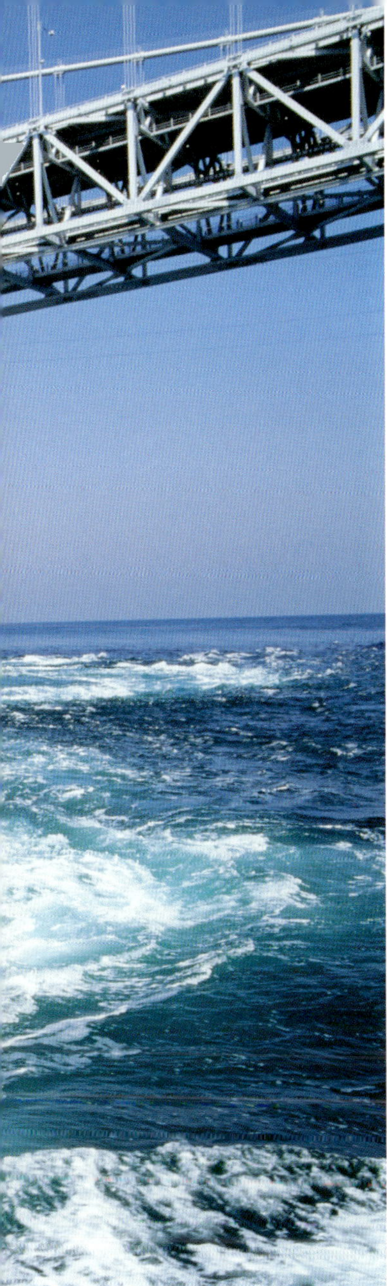

Naoshima Island ■ KAGAWA

Benesse Art Site Naoshima, spread across the three islands of Naoshima, Teshima and Inujima in the Seto Inland Sea, has drawn attention from both within Japan and abroad. It is a series of art projects and exhibitions organized by Benesse Holdings, Inc. and Fukutake Foundation. The art is everywhere on the islands, and visitors can enjoy contemporary art, architecture and nature.

Among the works, Yayoi Kusama's "Pumpkin" is especially popular. Against the backdrop of blue sky and ocean, the large, yellow pumpkin creates unusual space extraordinary with its peculiar presence surrounded by a natural. There are plenty to see on the island, including Chichu Art Museum, which was built underground in order not to spoil the beautiful views of the Seto Inland Sea, as well as Art House Project, in which empty houses have been restored by artists.

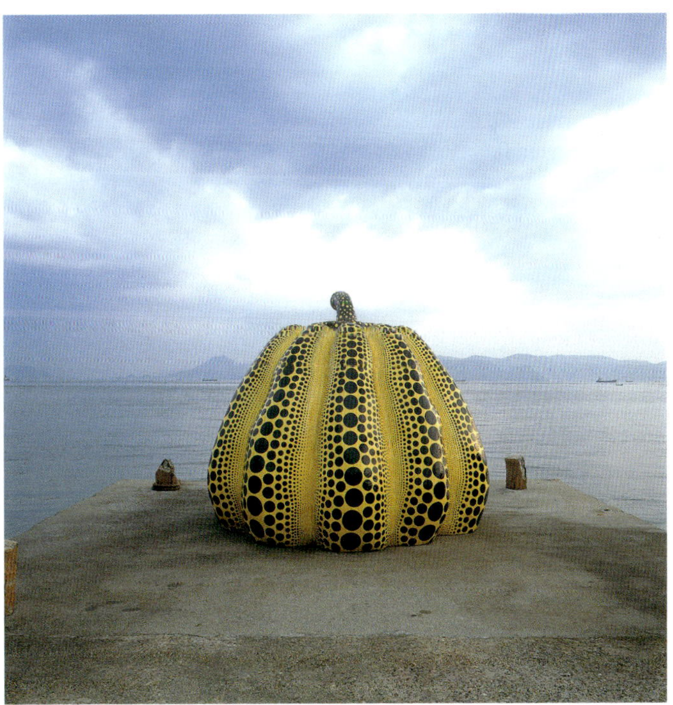

Yayoi Kusama "Pumpkin"
Photo : Shigeo Anzai

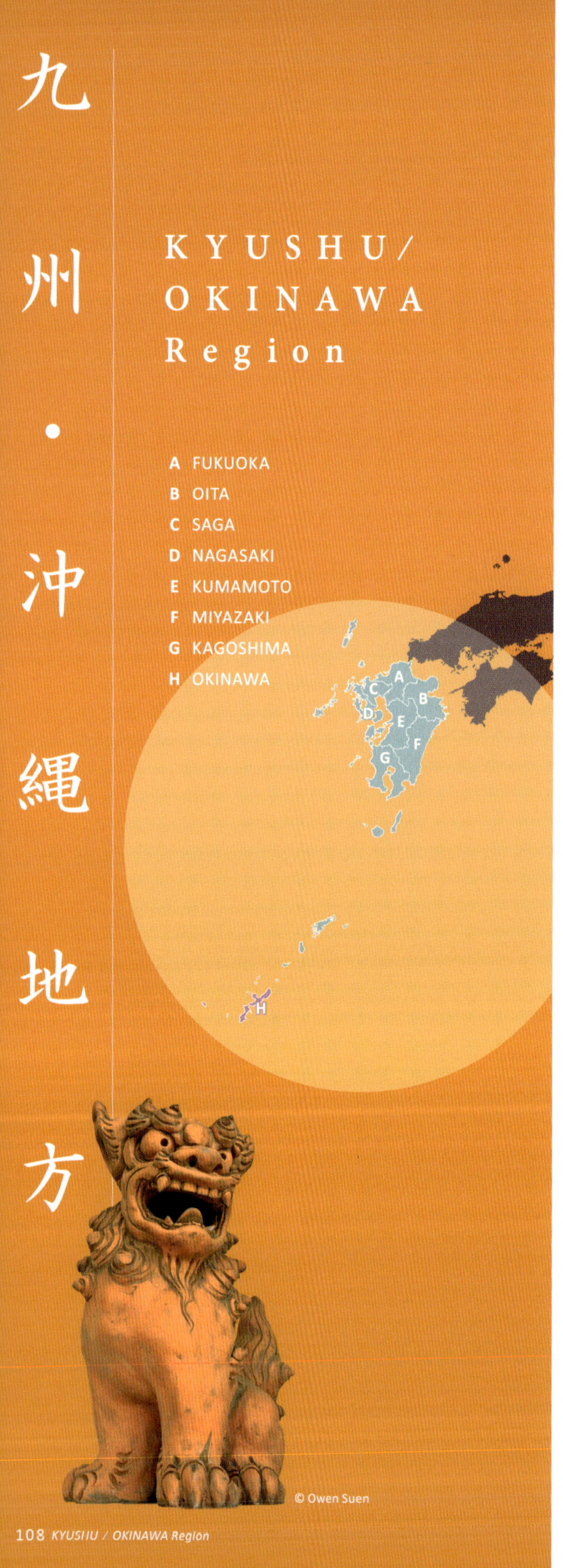

Kyushu and Okinawa Regions, home to unique, still-living cultures, have magnificent expanses of natural beauty.

The Kyushu region has Fukuoka, Oita, Saga, Nagasaki, Kumamoto, Miyazaki, and Kagoshima Prefectures, while the island of Okinawa is located for to the southwest of Japan's main islands. This area is notable in Japan for its mild climate and is situated close to the Korean Peninsula, China, and Southeast Asia, and has therefore been characterized in particular by flourishing trade and close contact with the rest of Asia.

Okinawa Prefecture was formerly home to a national entity called the Ryukyu Kingdom, and it has a deeply-rooted culture, customs, and manners that are different from those found in Japan's other prefectures.

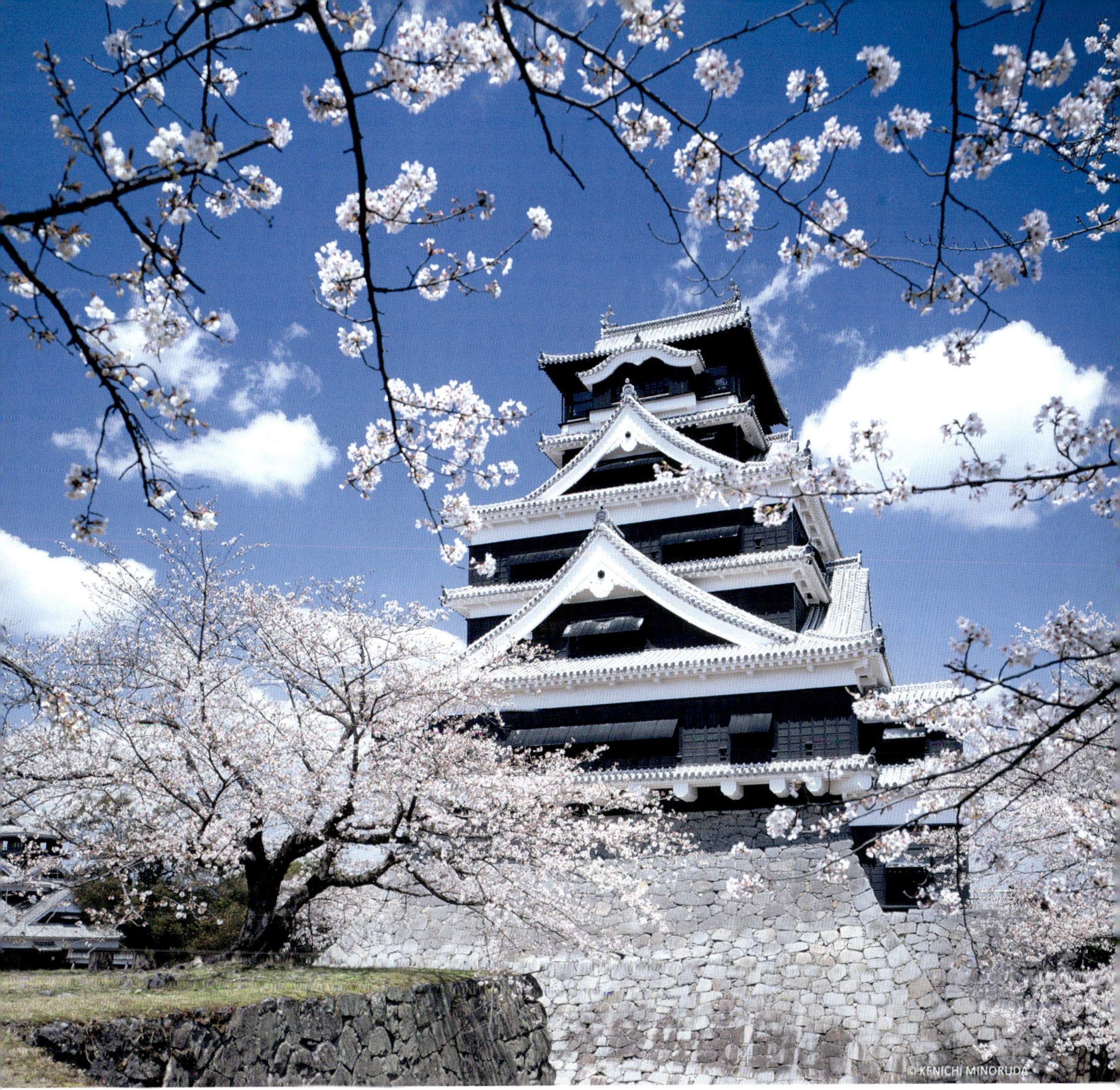
© KENICHI MINORUDA

Kumamoto Castle ▪ KUMAMOTO

Kumamoto Castle is the symbol of the city and as a famous castle. Its stone-lined walls with their graceful curves, designed to keep enemies out, are said to be the most beautiful in Japan. The present day keep is a reconstruction of the original that was destroyed by fire, but the *Uto Yagura* tower that survived the flames is designated as a national important cultural property. The builder of the castle, Kato Kiyomasa, was a military commander famed for his tiger hunting escapades, and was well-loved by the people for his innovations in erosion and flood control, as well as the development of new rice fields that brought wealth to the district. The present day castle is also renowned as a good site for viewing cherry blossoms in the spring.

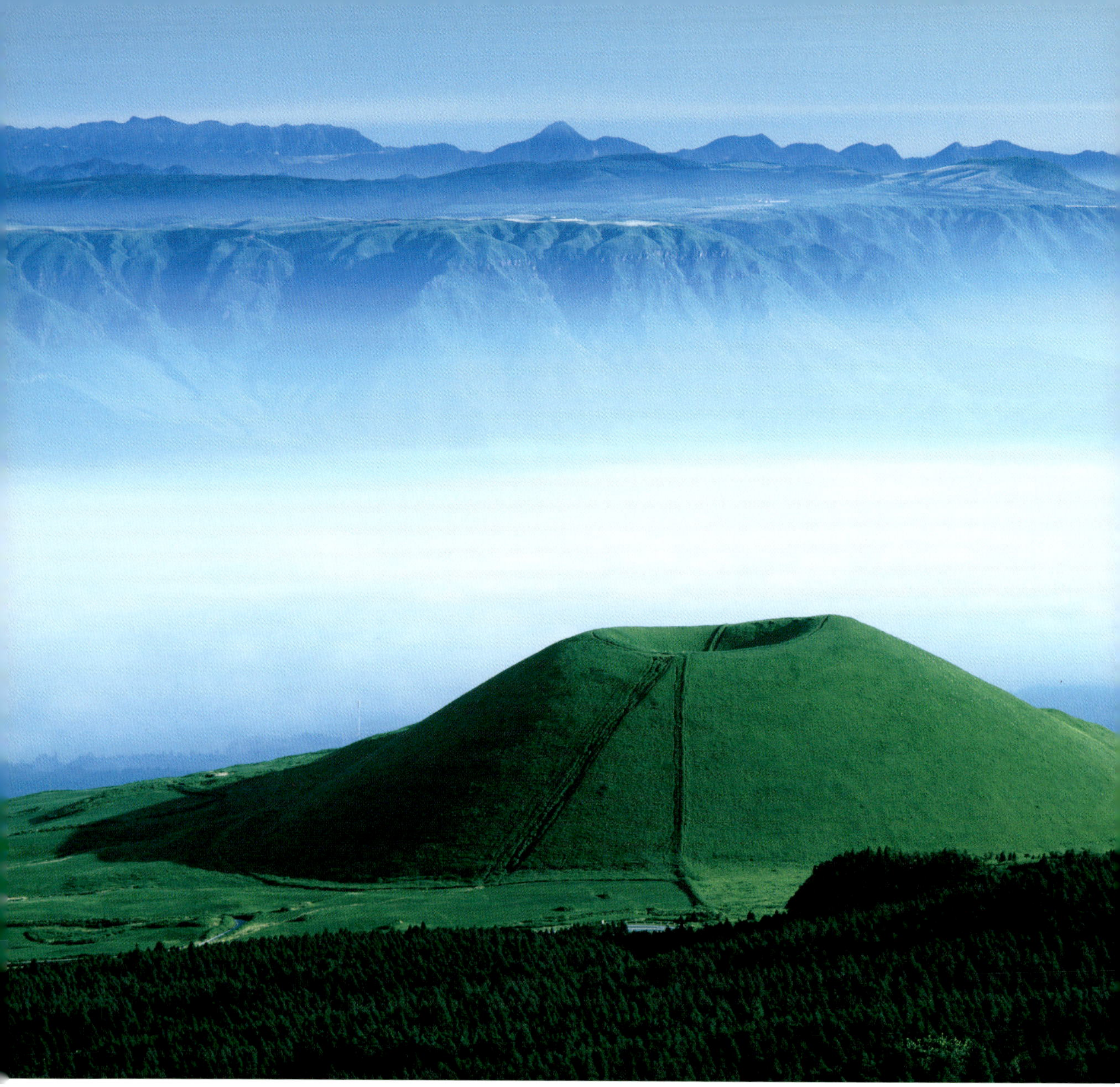

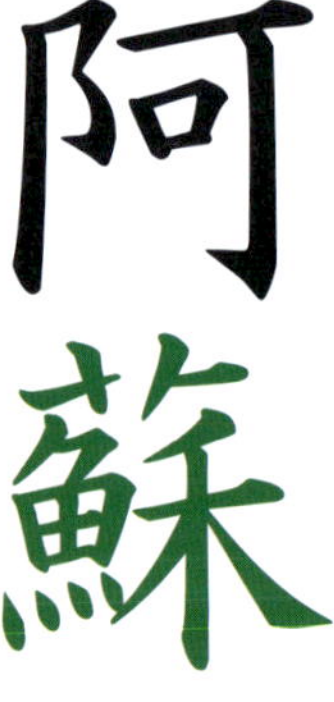

Mount Aso ▪ KUMAMOTO

Volcanic activity has left a basin-like shape on the top of Mount Aso, and the rounded and elevated area around the peak is called a *caldera*. The still active mountain is famed for the great size of its caldera and its outer rim crater. Wonderful views of the mighty caldera can be enjoyed from the ropeway that operates on the mountain.

Another representative view of Mount Aso is *Kusasenrigahama* or *Kusasenri*, which spreads with a radius of one kilometer. There are large ponds in the middle of it and bucolic views of the horses released there munching on grass. It is also possible to ride the horses here.

© GYRO PHOTOGRAPHY

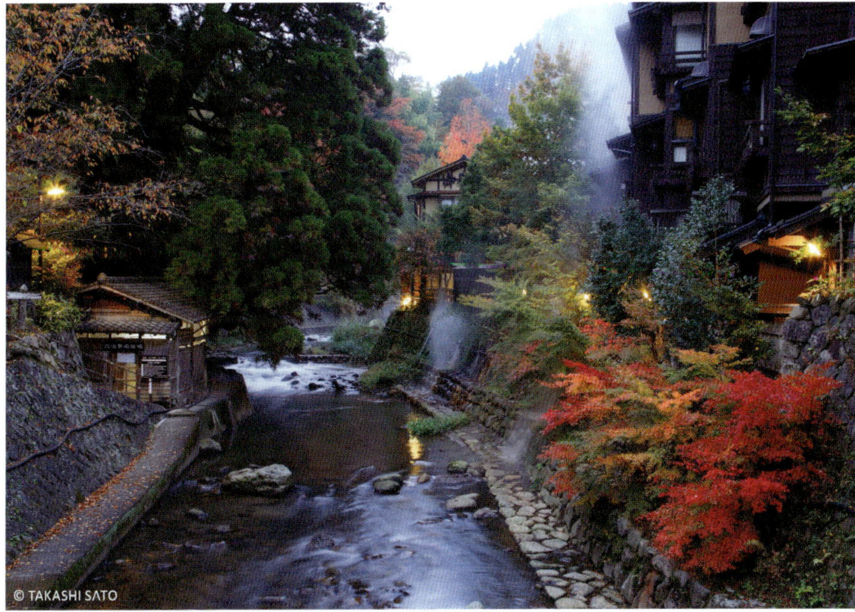
© TAKASHI SATO

Kurokawa Onsen (hot spring)

KUMAMOTO

Kurokawa Onsen is a popular hot spa to the north of Mount Aso, where welcoming Japanese-style inns line the narrow valley of the Tanoharu River. All the inns boast unique outdoor baths such as cave baths and rock pool baths. Many tourists visit the spa with the intention of trying out several of the different types of baths.
The sight of people in bathing clothes, towel in hand as their clogs clatter along the road is perfectly suited to this place, where time seems to have stood still.

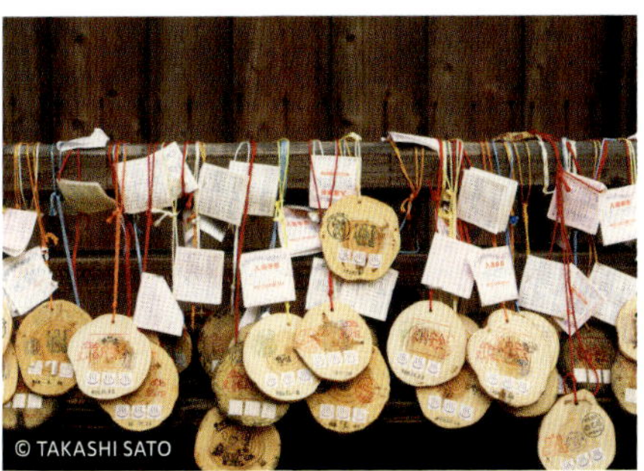
© TAKASHI SATO

Bath tickets

On sale at the hot spa are "bath tickets" which are made from small pieces of cedar wood that have been stamped with a hot iron, and allow entry to any of the hot spas you like. The 'tickets' can also be taken home, so they make a nice souvenir.

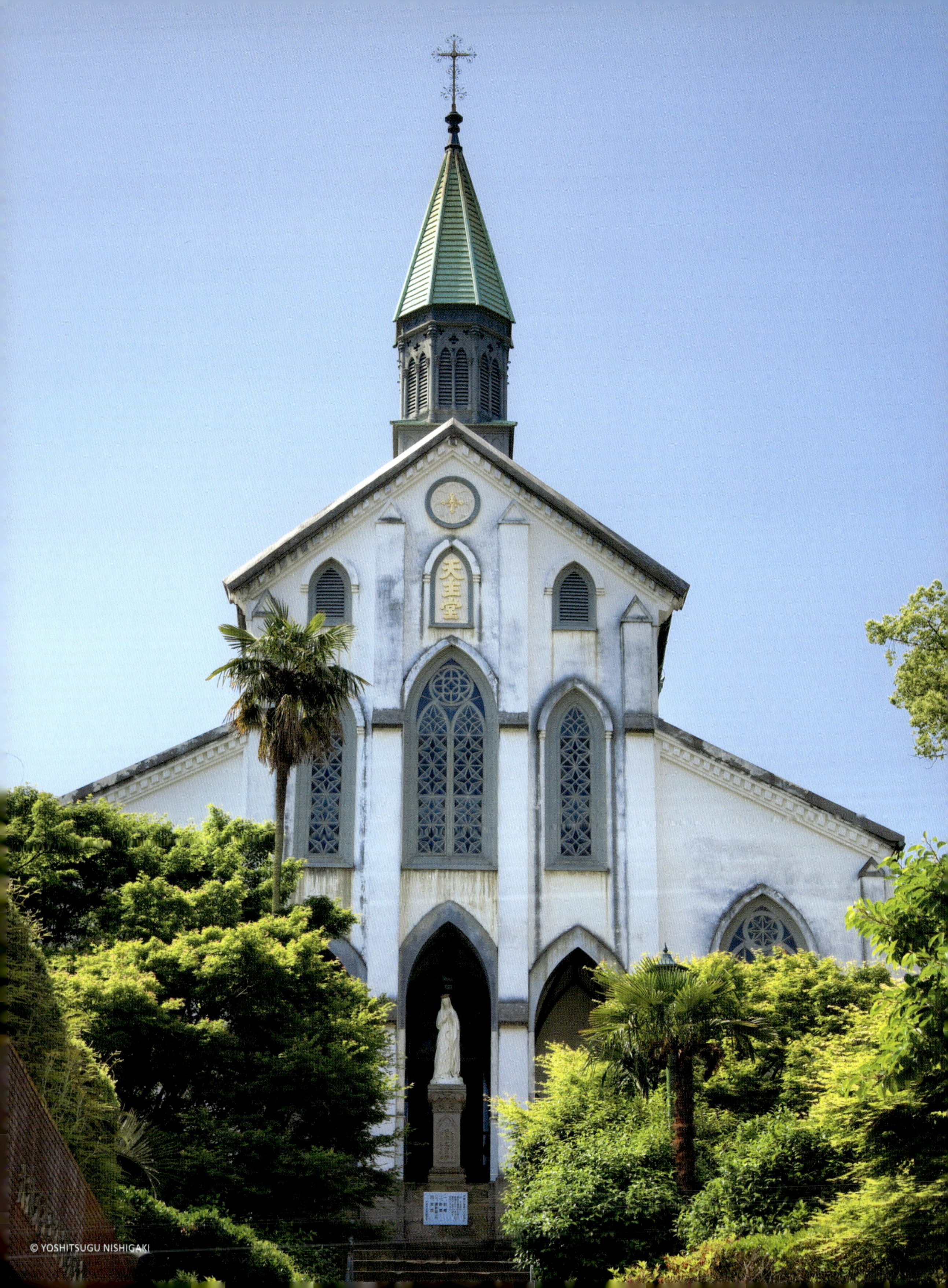
天主堂

Oura Tenshudo
(Oura Church)
▪ NAGASAKI

Oura Tenshudo was built for the foreigners staying in Japan when the Edo shogunate opened Japan to the outside world, and is the oldest church building in the country. Designed in the Gothic style that typifies medieval European architecture, the stained glass windows that decorate the interior are over a century old.

The church is built on a site that faces the hill where 26 foreign and Japanese martyrs were crucified during a period when Christianity was forbidden. Oura Church is designated as a national treasure, and efforts are underway to have the entire collection of Nagasaki churches and Christian relics listed as World Heritage sites.

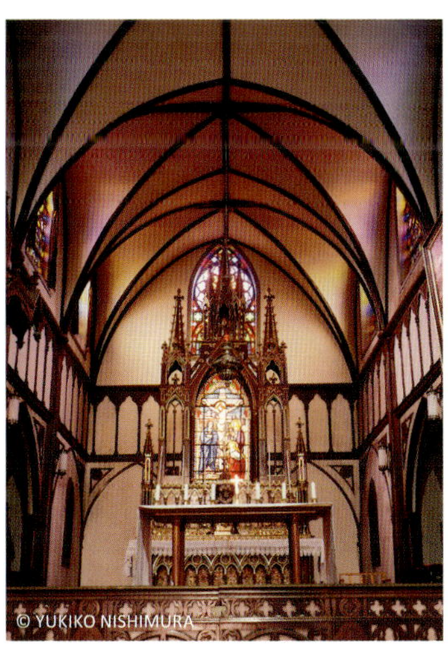
© YUKIKO NISHIMURA

Stained glass in the church

The statue of Jesus Christ on the Cross erected behind the front altar was donated to the church upon its establishment in 1865 by a Carmelite Monastery in France. It was badly damaged by the atomic blast, and the present day statue is a restored version made after the war by Rogé of Paris.

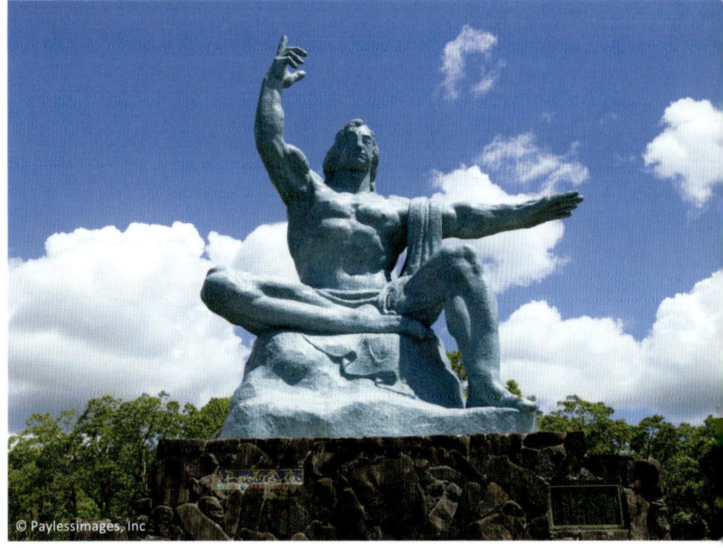
© Paylessimages, Inc

Peace Park ▪ NAGASAKI

Nagasaki Peace Park is located in an area running from the site where the atomic bomb was dropped on August 9th 1945 to the hills on the northern side. It was built with the wish that people would promise to never repeat the horrors of war and that world peace will prevail.

The Peace Statue that stands in the park is 9.7 meters high. The figure's right hand points to the sky indicating the threat of atomic bombs, while its left hand is outstretched horizontally in a gesture of peace. Its gently closed eyelids represent a never ending prayer for the souls of all those killed in the attack. Each year a peace ceremony is held in the park on August 9th, and a declaration for the sake of peace is broadcast to the world.

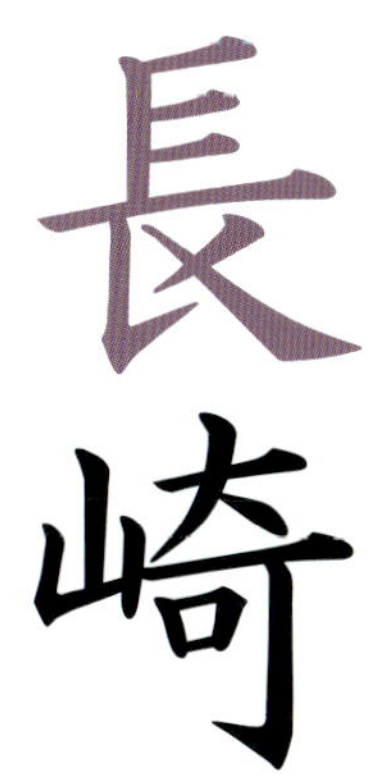

Yakushima Island
▪ KAGOSHIMA

Registered as a World Natural Heritage Site, Yakushima is the seventh largest island in Japan. It takes around two hours to circumnavigate the island by car. Around 90% of the island is covered by mysterious forests, and it also boasts pristine streams, several mountains over 1,000 meters in height and roaring waterfalls. The island is home to unusual plants and has its own indigenous ecosystem, which has led to it being called "the Galapagos of the east." Many people join eco-tourism tours in order to experience trekking through the primeval woods, but there are also other attractions to enjoy such as kayaking and diving.

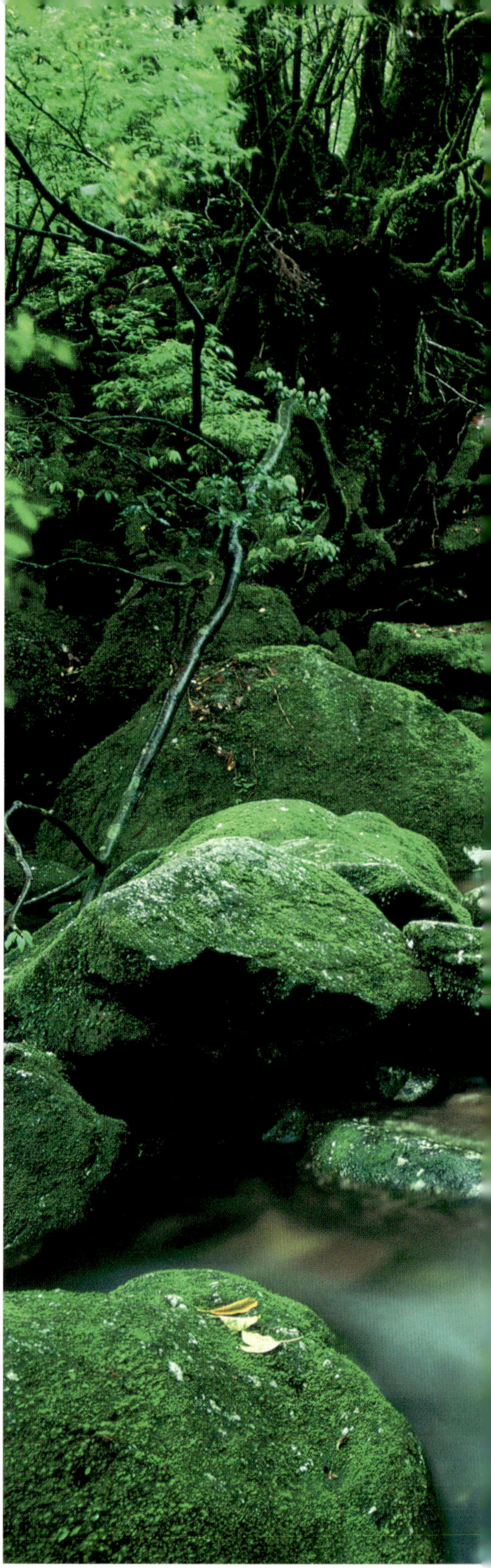

屋久島

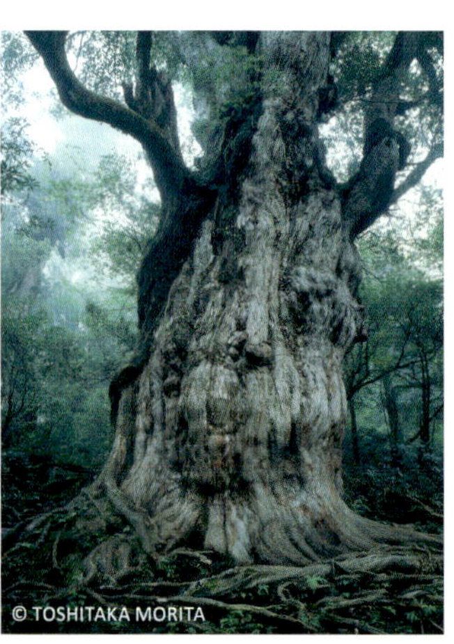
© TOSHITAKA MORITA

Yaku-sugi

The cedar trees that grow on the island above 500 meters are called *Yaku-sugi* (strictly speaking, those specimens that are believed to be one thousand years old or more). The cedar that is the symbol of the island is the *Jomon-sugi*, which is thought to be as old as anything between 2,000 and 7,000 years. The large tree is 25.3 meters in tall, with a circumference of 16.4 meters, and though the 10-hour mountain route leading to it is hard work, it is worth a visit for its overwhelming presence.

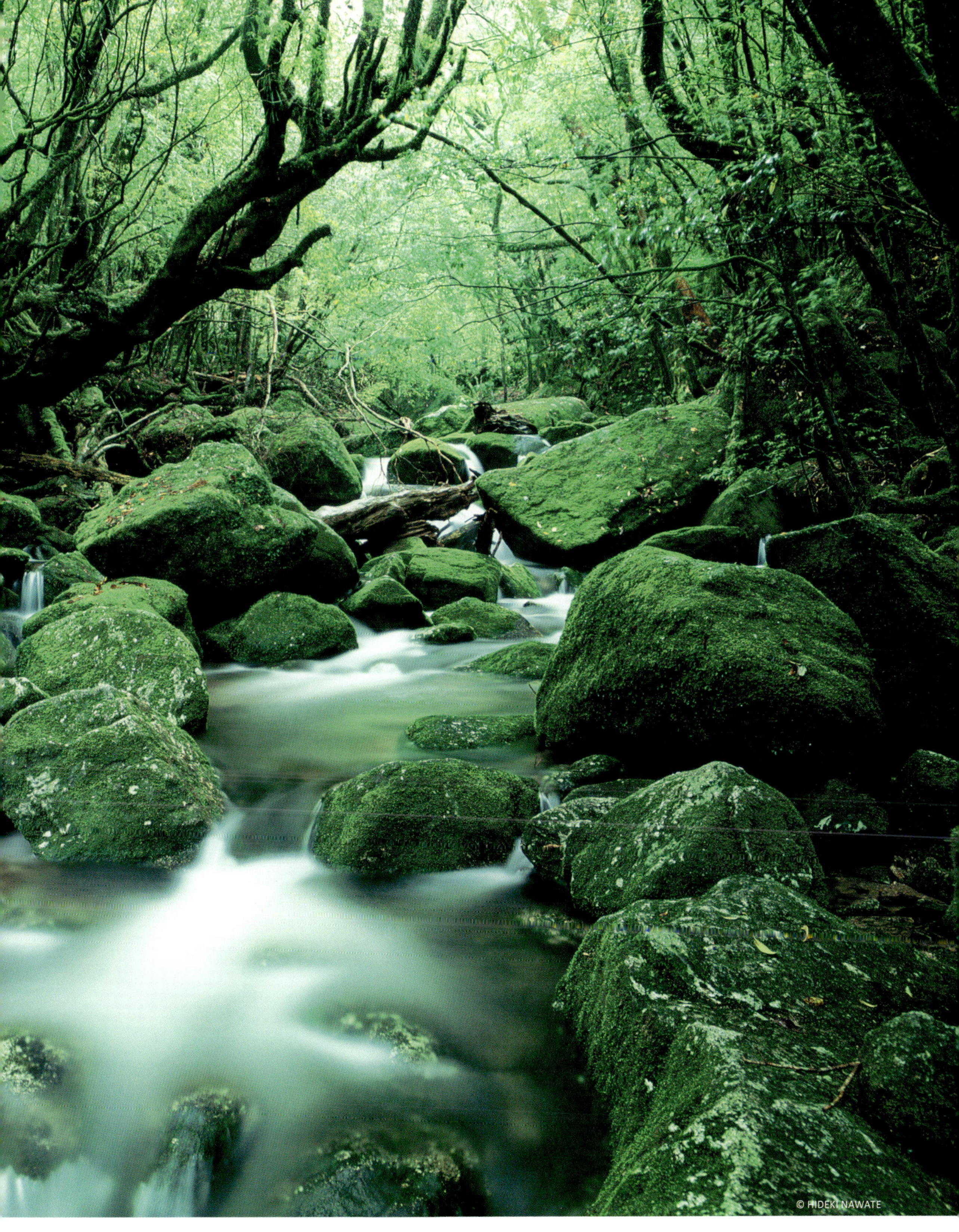
© HIDEKI NAWATE

Dazaifu Tenmangu Shrine
FUKUOKA

太宰府天満宮

Sugawara Michizane, who is enshrined in Fukuoka Prefecture's Dazaifu Tenmangu Shrine, was a brilliant scholar and politician, known as the "God of Learning" during the Heian Period. Each year seven million pilgrims praying for success in examinations and employment visit the shrine.

Legend has it that when Sugawara was demoted from Kyoto and sent to Fukuoka a particular plum tree yearned so much for Sugawara that it uprooted itself and flew to him at the shrine, where it now known as the "flying plum tree." More than one thousand years on, the tree still blossoms in the spring. In many of the shops around the shrine can be found *umegae mochi* (literally "plum branch rice cakes"), filled with azuki beans and served hot. They are a famous snack for pilgrims to the shrine.

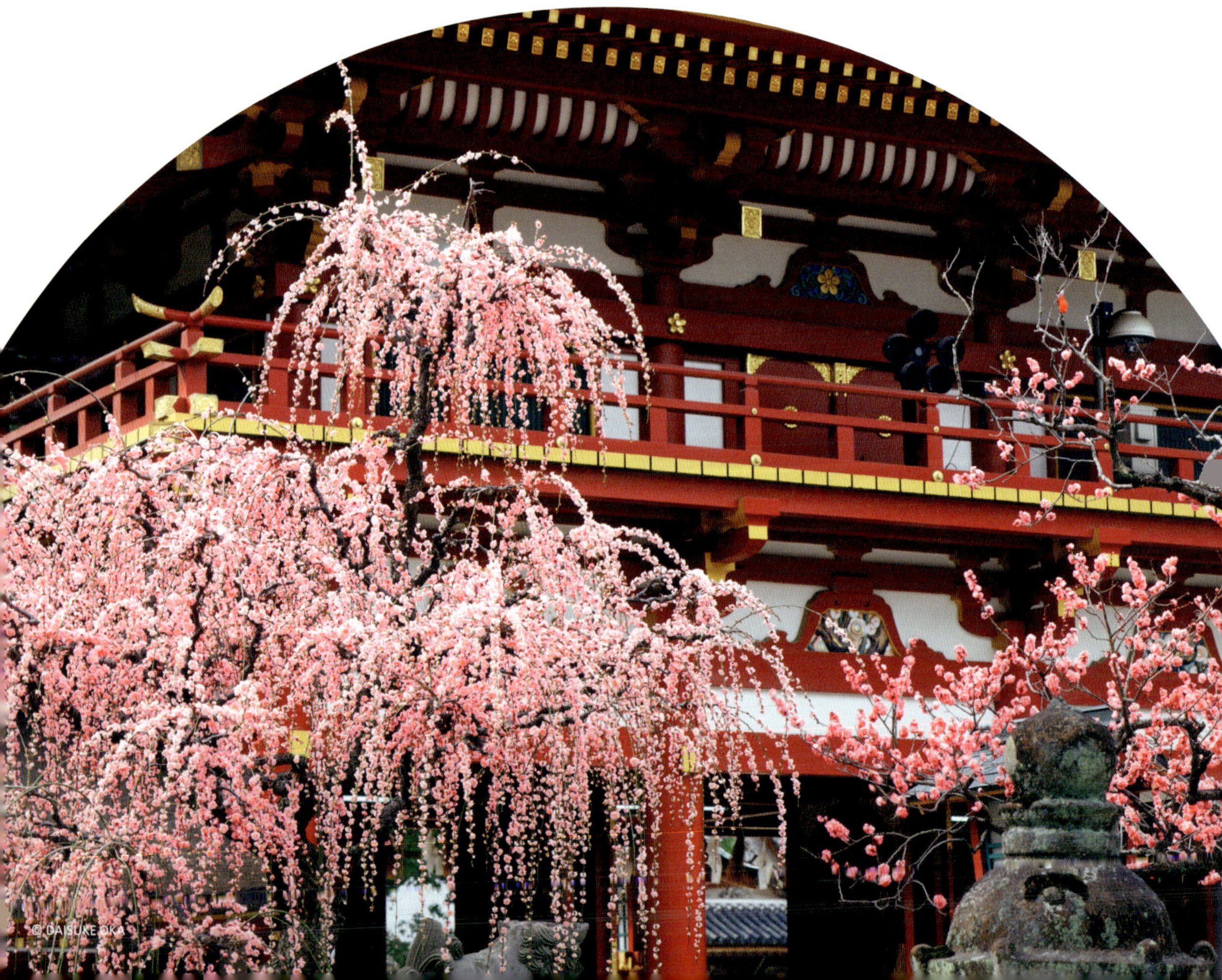

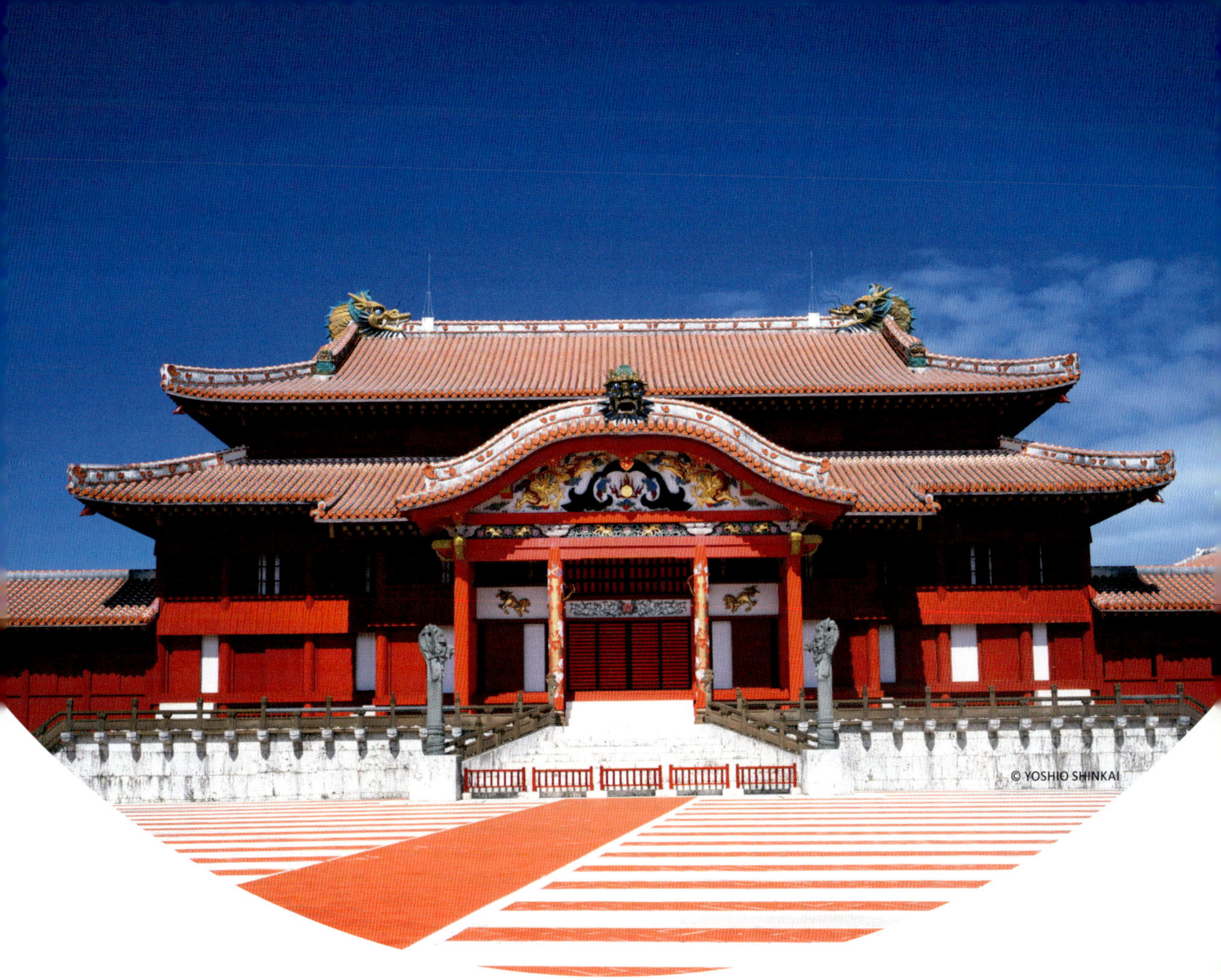

© YOSHIO SHINKAI

首里城

Shuri Castle ■ OKINAWA

Shuri Castle was the political, diplomatic and cultural hub of the Ryukyu Kingdom that existed in Okinawa for around 450 years from 1429, and which absorbed a mixture of cultures through its position as a place of trade, forming a unique culture of its own. The castle was listed as a World Heritage site in recognition of its invaluable and unique fusion of Chinese and Japanese castle architecture.

The bold figure of the castle, decorated in a dazzling vermillion, gives a flavor of the Ryukyu Kingdom's history and culture and can be described as the symbol of Okinawa.

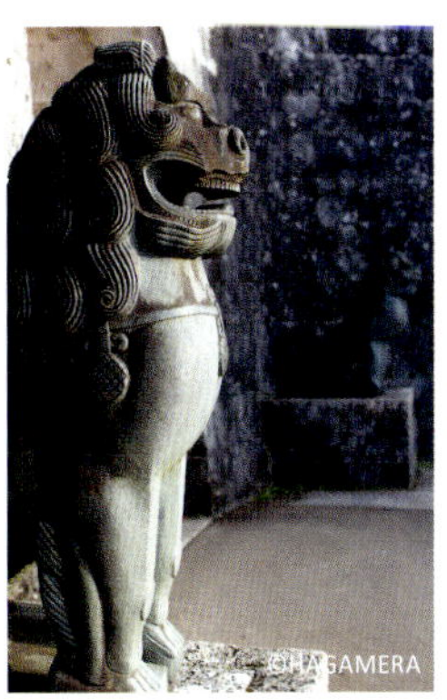

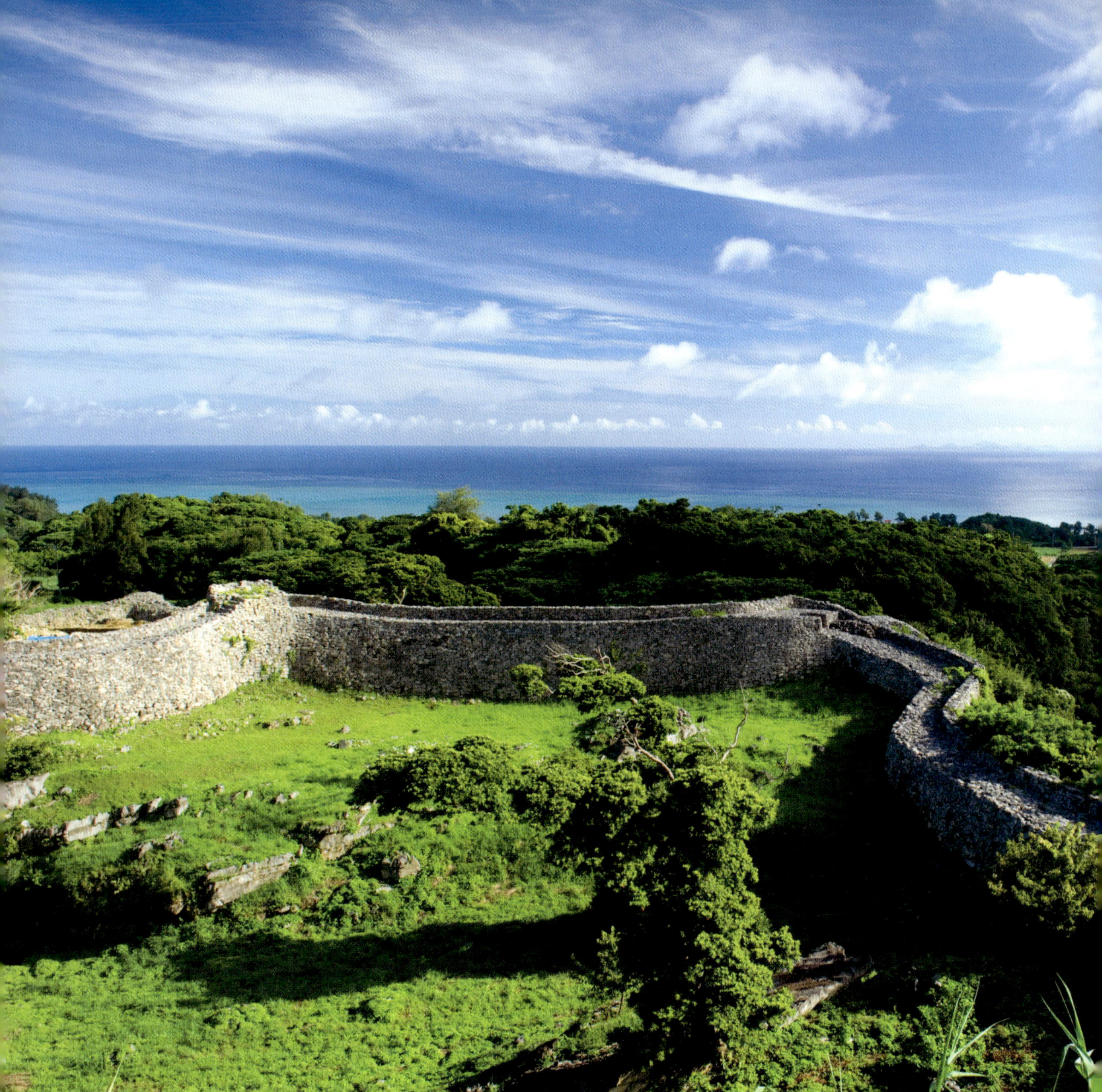

Nakijin Castle Ruins ▪ OKINAWA

In the 14th century three kings who split it into the northern mountain, the central mountain and southern mountain kingdoms ruled the main island of Okinawa, and Nakijin Castle was the seat of the ruler of the northern mountain kingdom. In later years the castle became a spiritual focal point for the local people as a place where rituals were conducted in *utaki* (sacred places). The castle is still regarded as a sacred place today. The traditional noro wedding ceremonies are conducted by a priestess (known as a *noro* in Okinawa). Along with Shuri Castle, it was registered as part of a World Heritage site called the Gusuku Sites and Related Properties of the Ryukyu Kingdom.

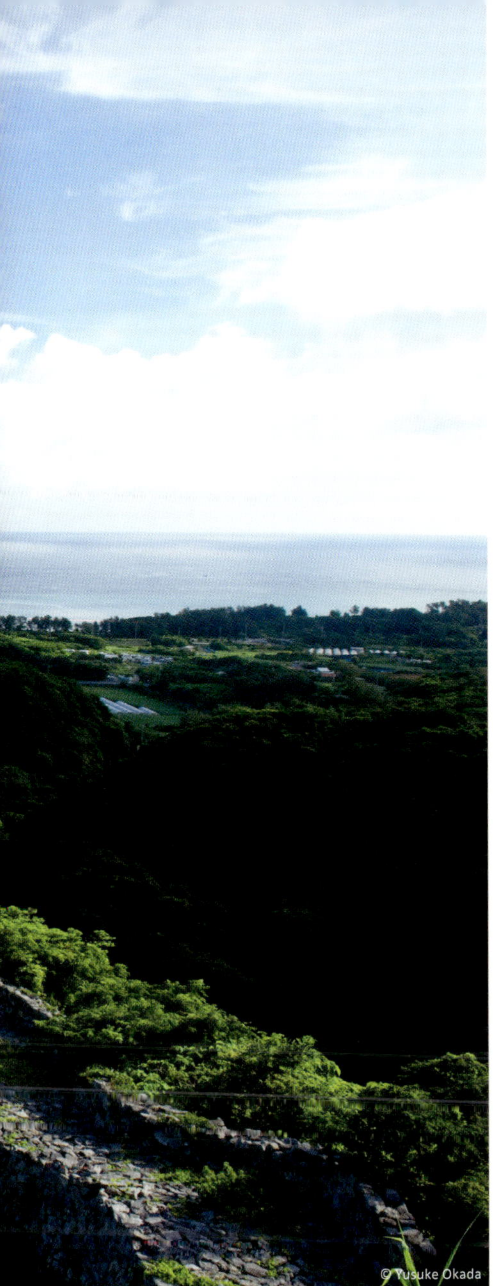
© Yusuke Okada

Seifa Utaki ▪ OKINAWA

In Okinawa an *utaki* is a sacred place where a god who descends from the heavens is enshrined, and the Seifa Utaki is the most revered of these places on the islands. It appears in the legends about the beginnings of Okinawa, and is the spiritual symbol of the Ryukyu Kingdom period (1429-1879). The photo shows a place called Sangui, which consists of places of worship formed by two stalactites and the protruding part of a triangular space.

Because Seifa Utaki was a sacred place where ceremonies took place it was a location that men were forbidden from entering. It is now a World Heritage site visited by many tourists.

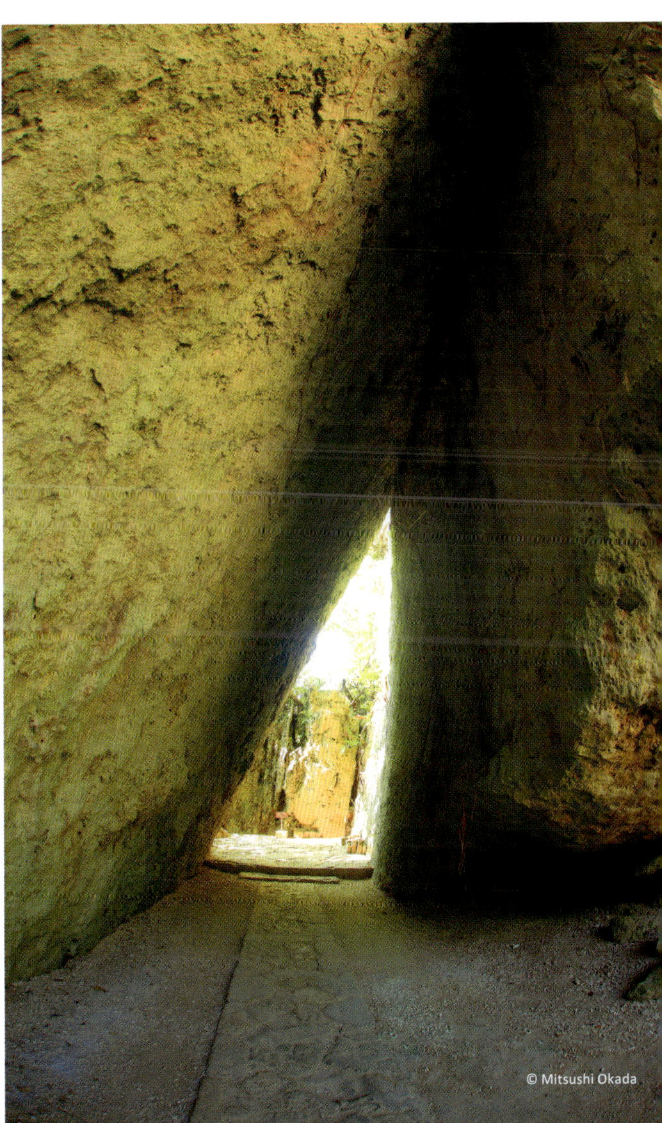
© Mitsushi Okada

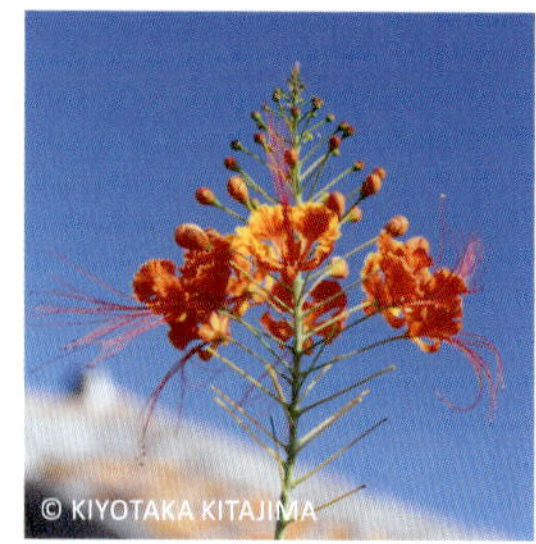

Taketomi Island ▪ OKINAWA

Red-tiled roofs and walls made of Ryukyu limestone. Roads sprinkled with white sand. A water buffalo carriage for tourists slowly meanders around the hamlets of the island, providing views of blooming hibiscus and bougainvillea. On the tiny island of Taketomi situated in the Yaeyama Islands not far from Taiwan this sort of scenery, redolent of old Okinawa, still remains today.

The island is also famed for its traditional textiles and the Tanadui harvest festival, designated as a national property of intangible folk-cultural importance, involves the participants dancing to pray that the seeds they have planted will grow well.

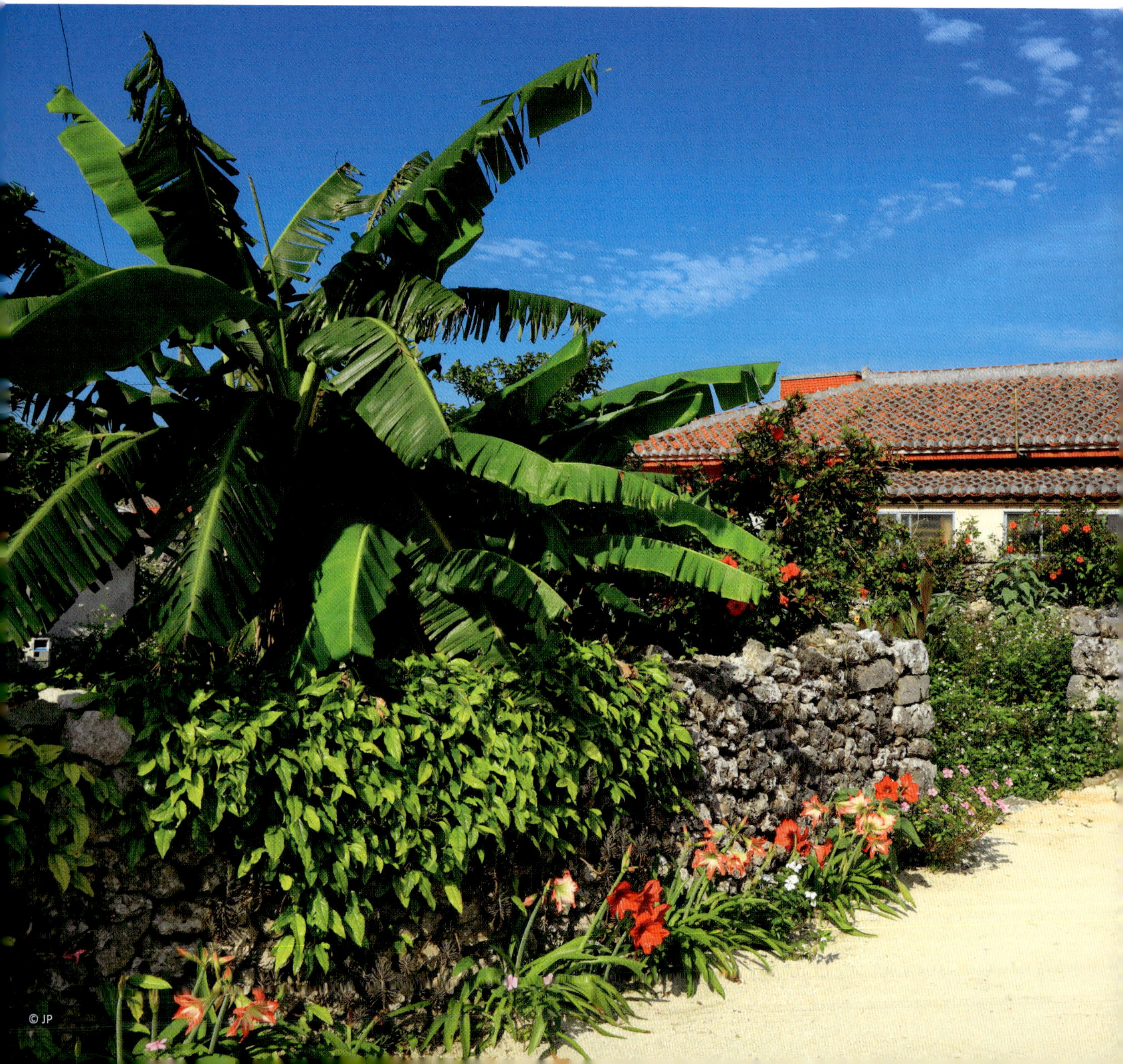

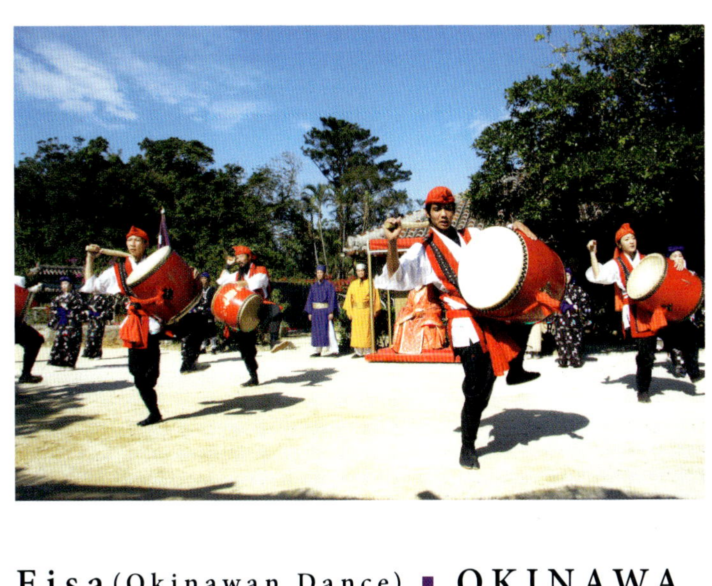

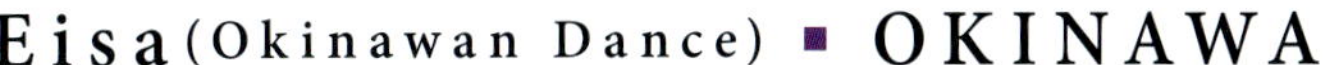

Eisa (Okinawan Dance) ■ OKINAWA

In Japan, there is a period called *Obon* during the middle of July and August in which it is thought that one's ancestors return to the real world. The *bon-odori* is a dance performed at these times to greet the returning ancestors. In Okinawa, with its own unique history and culture the dance that takes place is called *eisa* instead of *bon-odori*. Young people wear costumes characteristic of Okinawa, and parade around the streets banging on a large drum and dancing.

The local songs, *sansin* (Okinawan musical instrument), drumming and hand dances are all performed in perfect unison and are a sight not to be missed.

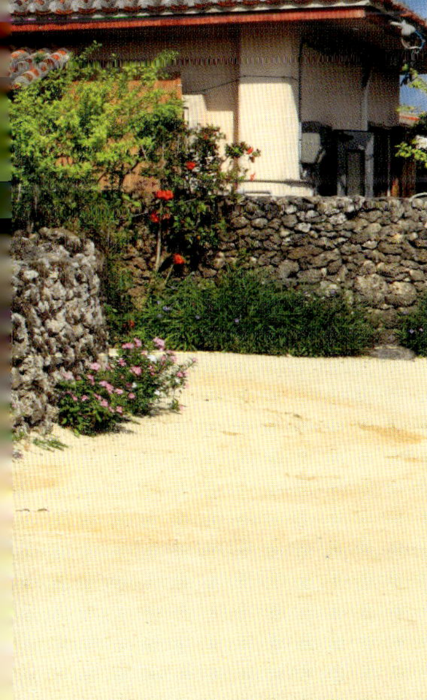

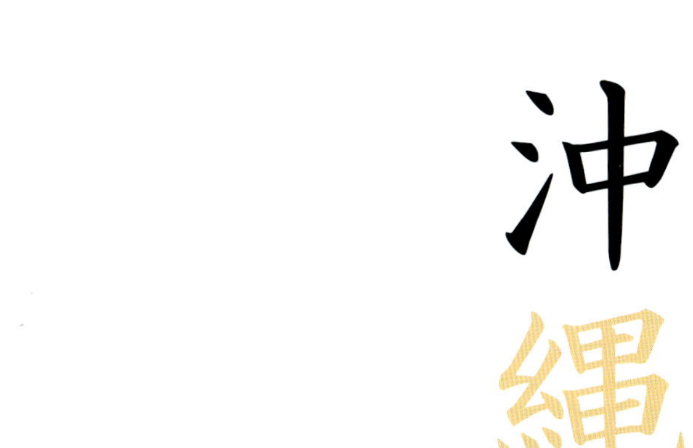

Tradition and Soul of Japan

Chapter2

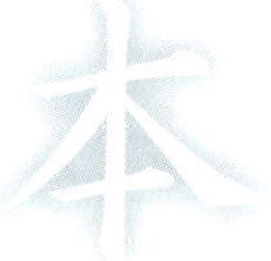

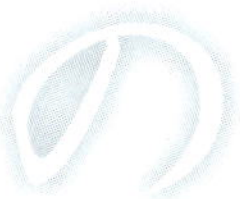

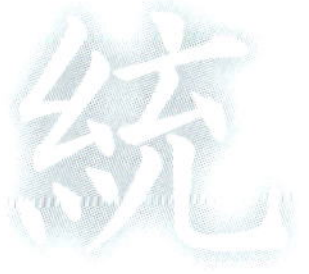

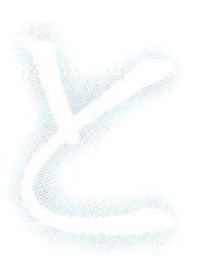

Festival of Japan

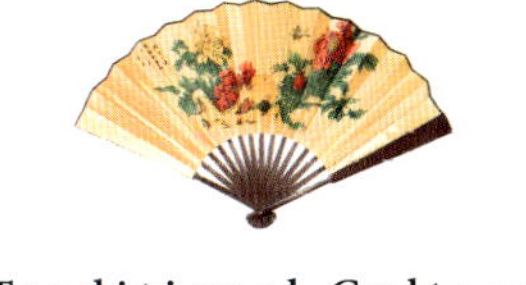

Traditional Culture

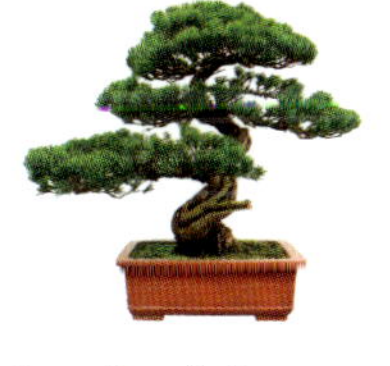

Soul of Japan

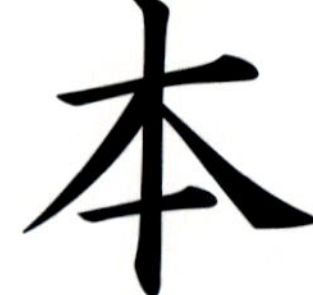
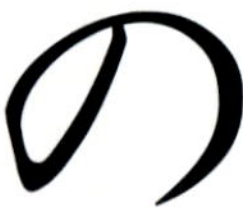
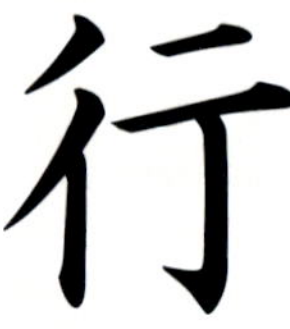
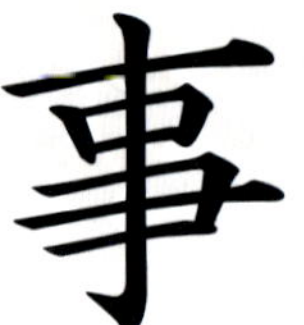

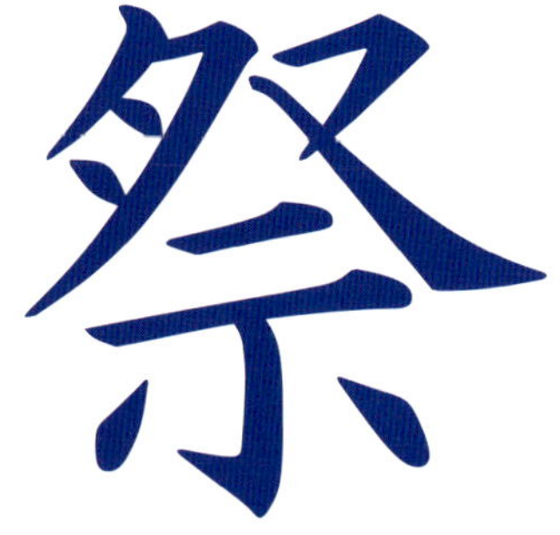

Following the changing of the four seasons, enjoy the ceremonies and observances of each time of year.

Since ancient times, Japanese customs have placed importance on season-specific observances and events associated with the time of year. The seasonal festivals that take place in every part of Japan are of course instances of this, and there are also events and observances such as *Shogatsu* (New Year's), *Obon* (a Buddhist festival of the Dead in the summer), and *O-misoka* (New Year's Eve), that have long been a familiar part of Japanese people's lives.

It is also interesting to note that even the very same events may be associated with various different traditions or have distinctive characteristics in Japan's different regions. We recommend you sample of some beautiful traditional customs that are so distinctively Japanese.

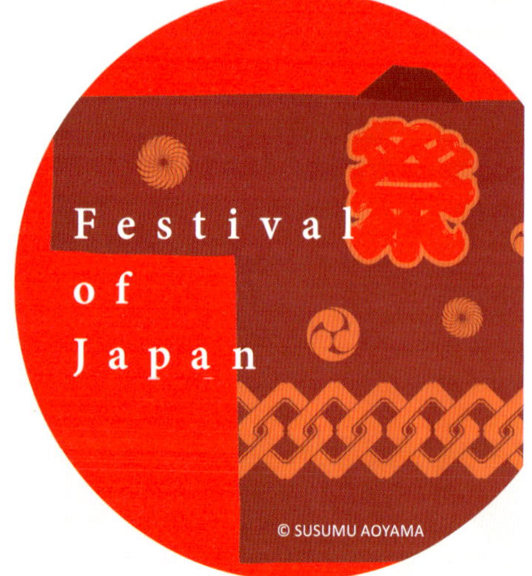

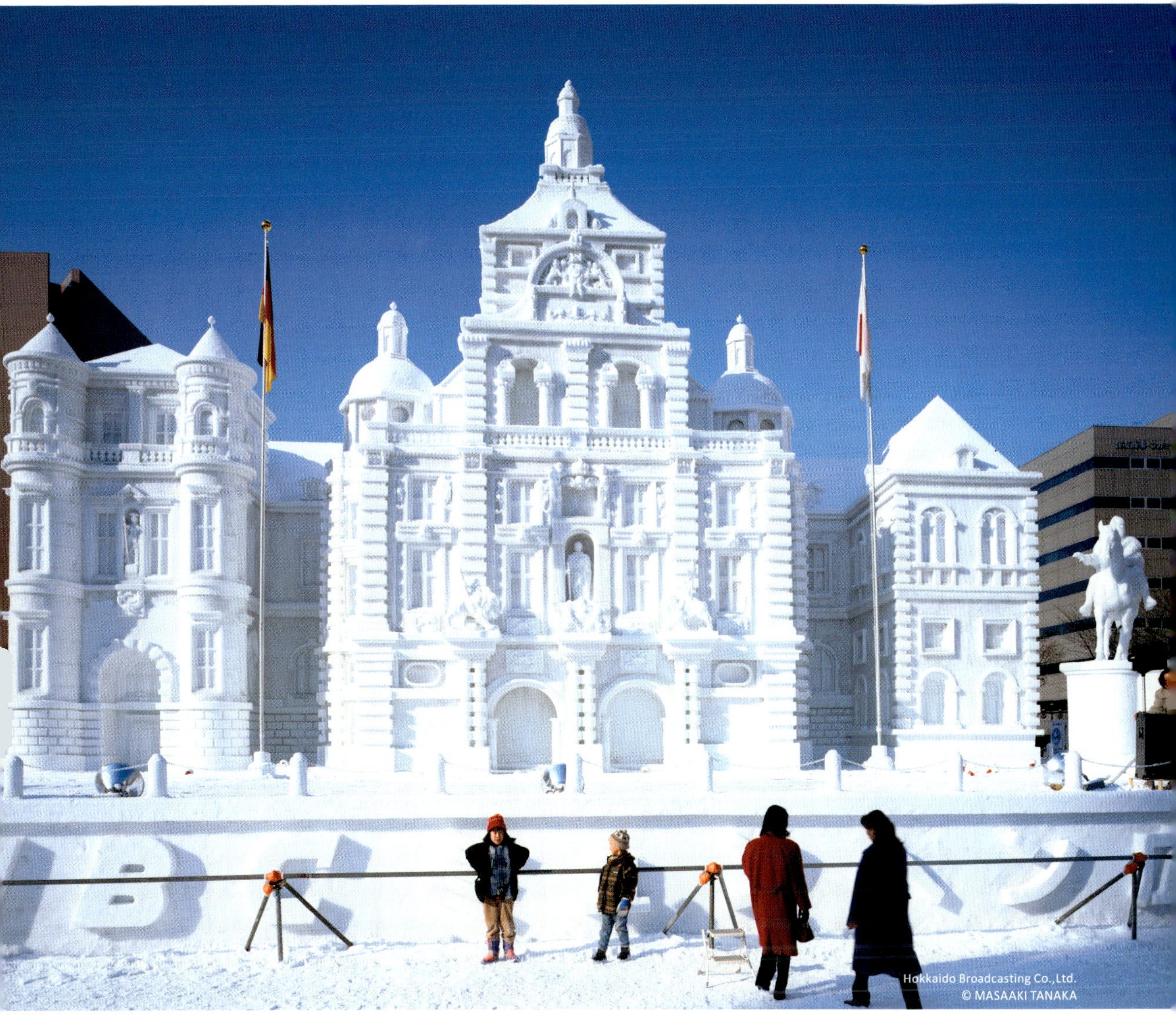
Hokkaido Broadcasting Co.,Ltd.
© MASAAKI TANAKA

Sapporo Snow Festival

Every year, from early February, Sapporo hosts a seven-day Snow Festival, showcasing snow and ice. It is the city's signature event for winter, with more than two million visitors from all over Japan as well as abroad.

The event, to which Japan's Self Defense Forces also contribute, showcases large-scale snow sculptures. In addition to some 200 of these sculptures in snow and ice, there will also be a skating rink and snowboard jumps.

There is also an International Snow Sculpture Contest, in which teams from various countries and regions compete. Snow cosmopolitan statutes are fun to watch.

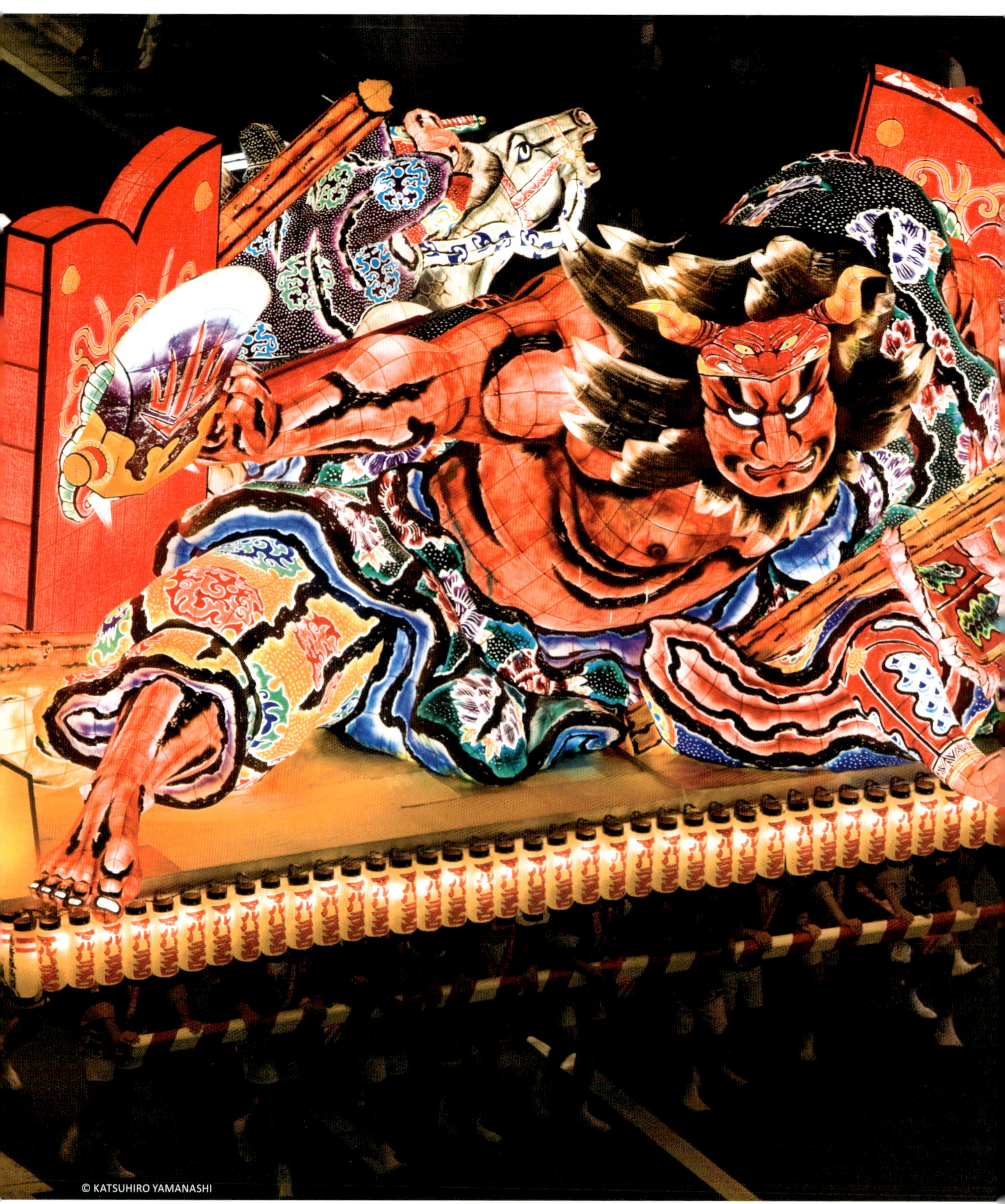

© KATSUHIRO YAMANASHI

© 2008 hiroo takenami

「黒旋風李逵」竹浪比呂央 2008年
マルハニチロ侫武多会

Aomori Nebuta Festival

Aomori City's Nebuta, held every year from August 2 over seven days, is one of the three greatest festivals in Japan's northeast region, know as Tohoku. Japanese *washi* paper is pasted onto wireframes and these structures are then painted to depict legendary warriors from ancient Japanese and Chinese history, or famous scenes from *kabuki*. Lit from the inside, they are placed on floats and parade across the city. These are limited in size to 9 meters in width, 7 meters in length and 5 meters in height, including the float and wheeled platform. Each is accompanied in its procession by between 500 and 1,000 people, although as many as 2,000 people can join. They are called *haneto* because they dance as if they're jumping, or *haneru* in Japanese.

Throughout Aomori Prefecture, there will be about 30 Nebuta festivals, large and small. Some, as in Hirosaki, are pronounced Neputa.

ねぶた祭

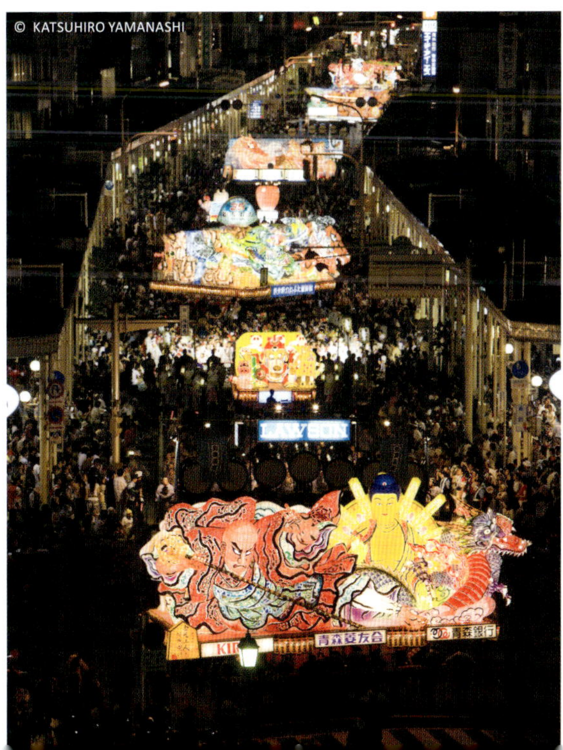

© KATSUHIRO YAMANASHI

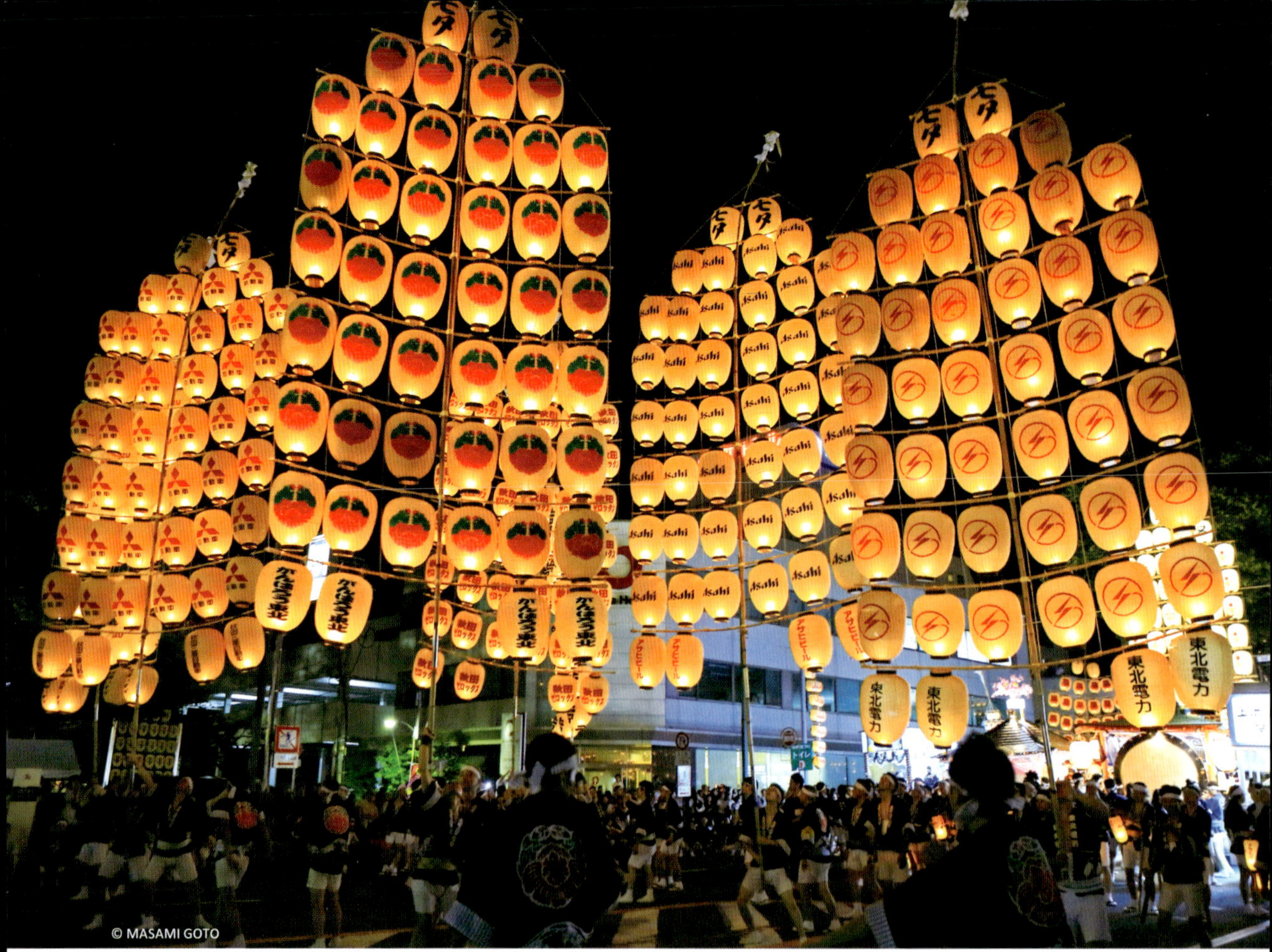

© MASAMI GOTO

Akita Kanto Festival

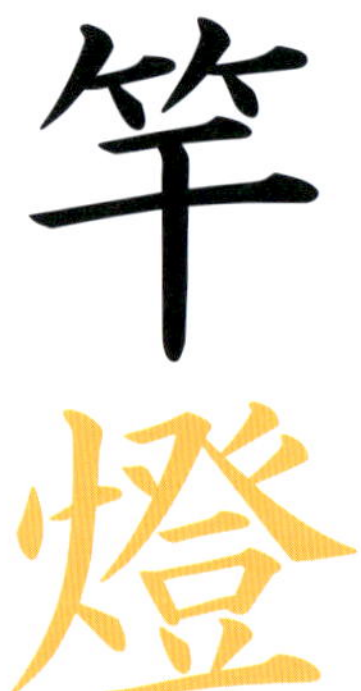

Akita City's Kanto Festival, which graces the city's summer evenings annually for four days in early August, is also one of the three greatest festivals in Japan's northeast. A large Kanto pole, carrying as many as 46 lanterns, can be 12 meters in height and weigh 50kg. Each Kanto pole is held by one man, on his shoulder, waist, forehead, in a dazzling display of techniques.

Each township in the city contributes some 270 Kanto poles to the Festival. The thousands of swaying lanterns symbolize bales of rice. The Kanto Festival's origin is said to derive from the ancient *Neburi-nagashi* festivity, in which people wished for a great harvest and tried to ward off diseases and evil spirits. The Kanto Festival seems to have been established in the current form by the middle of the 18th century. *Neburi-nagashi* used to be held around July 7 of the old lunar calendar.

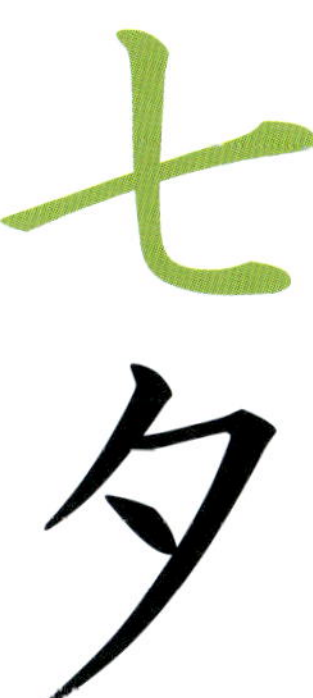

Sendai Tanabata Festival

Tanabata is a very popular festivity in Japan. During *Tanabata* people write wishes on small pieces of paper *tanzaku* and pray to stars. Sendai's *Tanabata*, the largest of its kind, is one of the three greatest festivals in Japan's northeast. It has a tradition of 400 years and Sendai City's shopping arcades are each adorned with some 3,000 *Tanabata* decorations of varying size called *fukinagashi*. Each summer the Festival draws two million visitors.

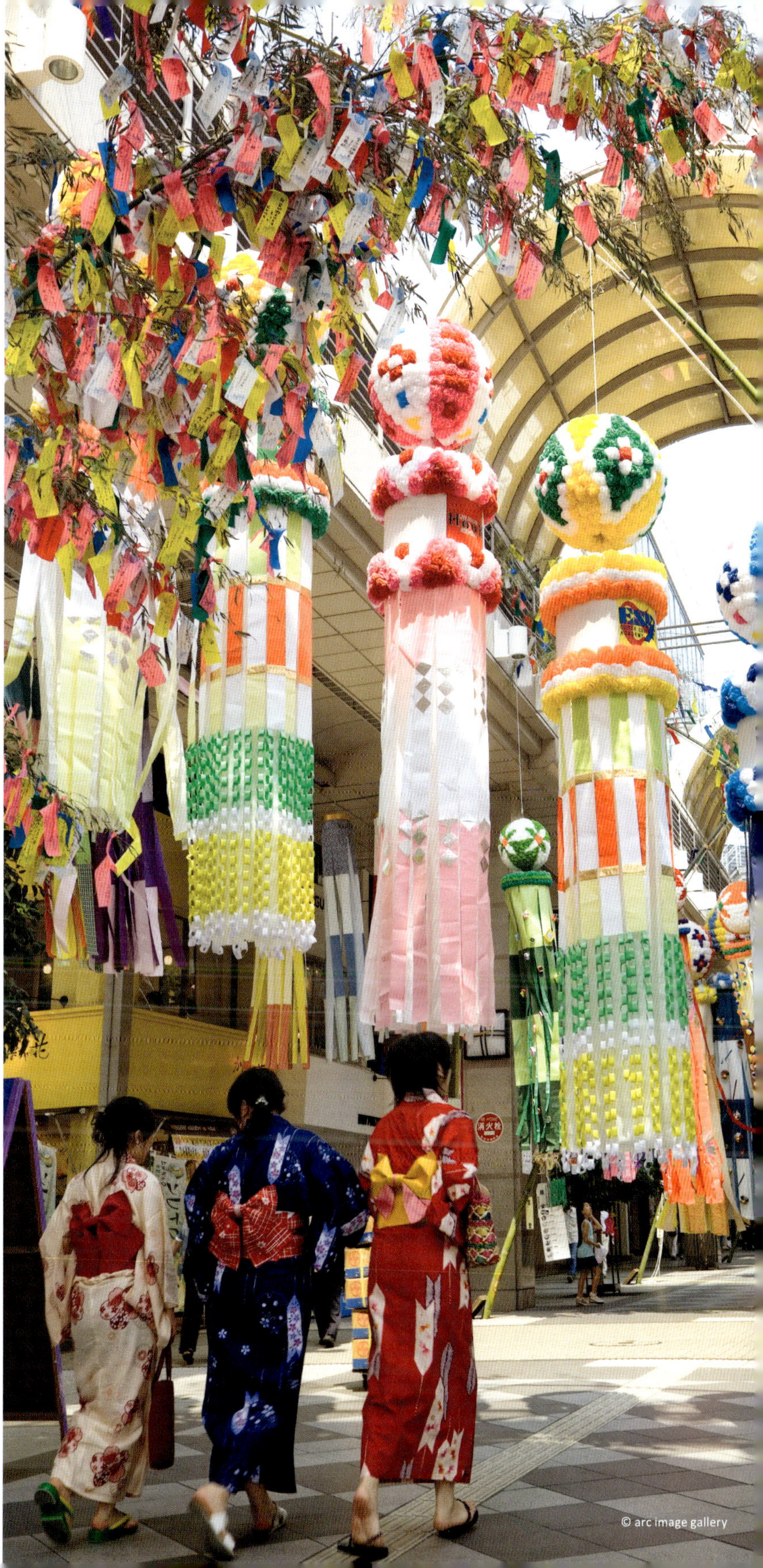

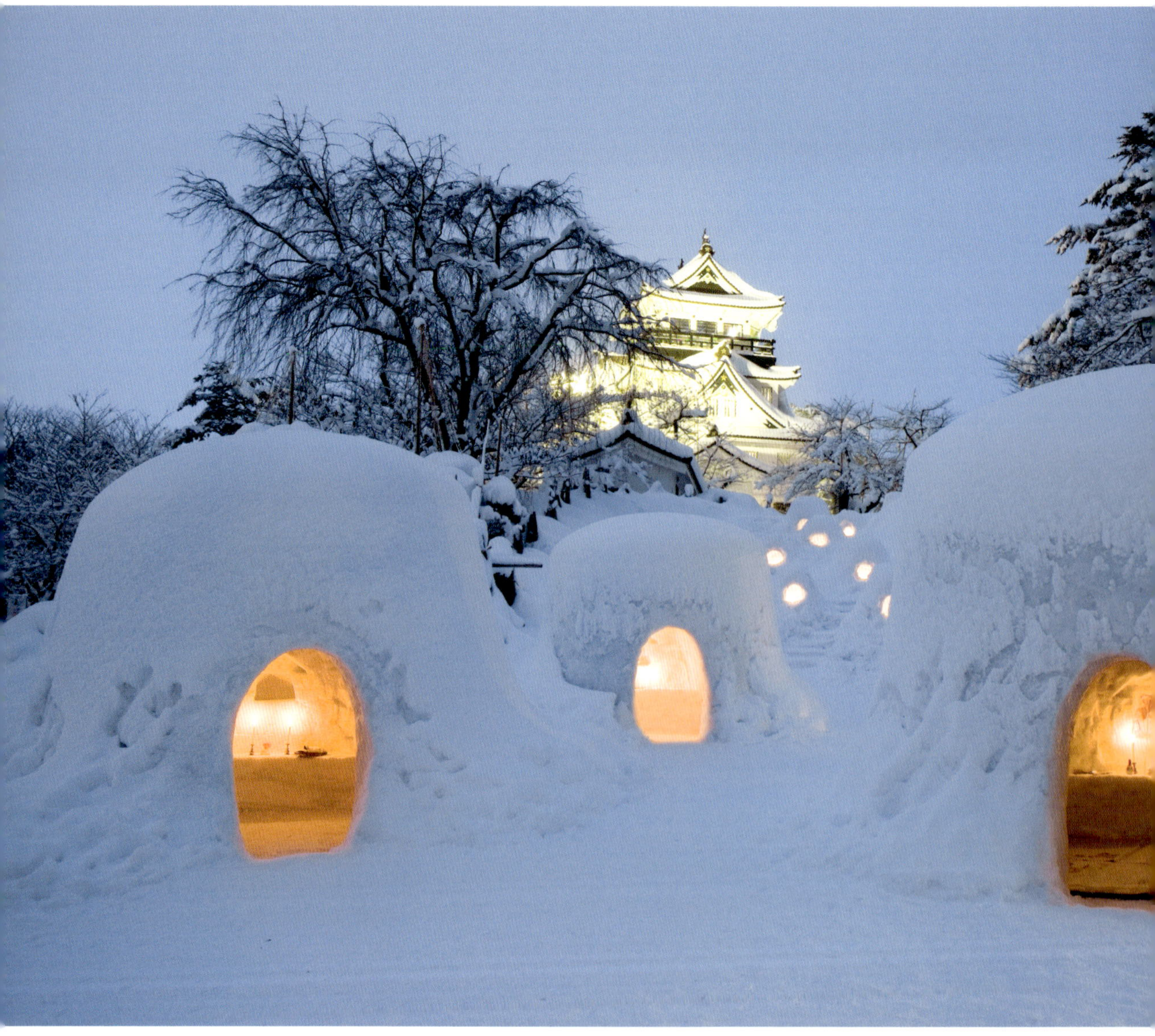

Yokote Kamakura Festival

The Yokote Basin, situated in Akita Prefecture's southeast, is one of the most snowy areas in the prefecture. Every winter people there build houses called *kamakura* with packed snow, light candles and worship a deity on an altar in the *kamakura*.

It is customary for children to treat passersby to *amazake* (a sweet drink made of fermented rice) and rice cakes. This way people befriend each other and relax despite the hardship of winter.

Yokote's Kamakura Festival is held from February 15 to 16. During the festival, the city is dotted with about a hundred of *kamakura* houses and transformed into a fairy-tale scene.

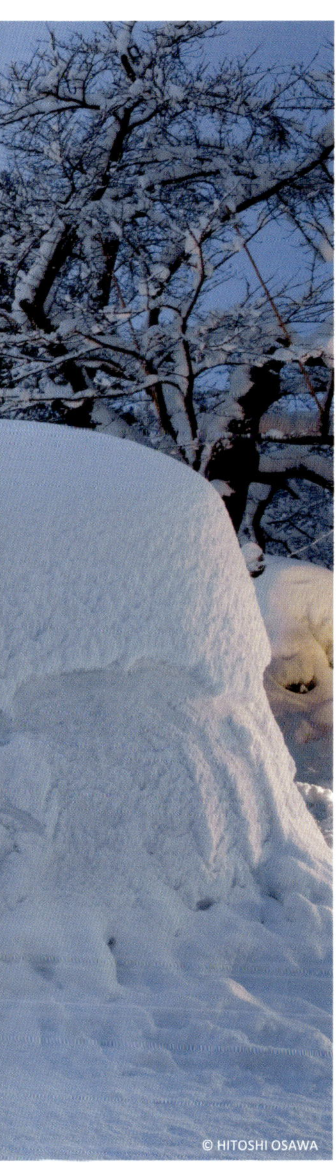
© HITOSHI OSAWA

Sanja Festival

Asakusa is one of the oldest parts of Tokyo and the Sanja Festival is the annual festival of the Asakusa Shrine. Today it ends on the third Sunday of May. In Sanja Festival, more than a hundred townships in Asakusa each contribute a portable shrine to the festival. By sheer size and its vibrancy it is one of Tokyo's representative festivals and annually attracts more than 1.5 million visitors, creating a major bustle there.

Ever since the Edo Period, Sanja Festival has been famed as a "wild" festival. Men and women carrying portable shrines, as they promenade through Asakusa, exciting spectators with their gallantry and shouts and cheers.

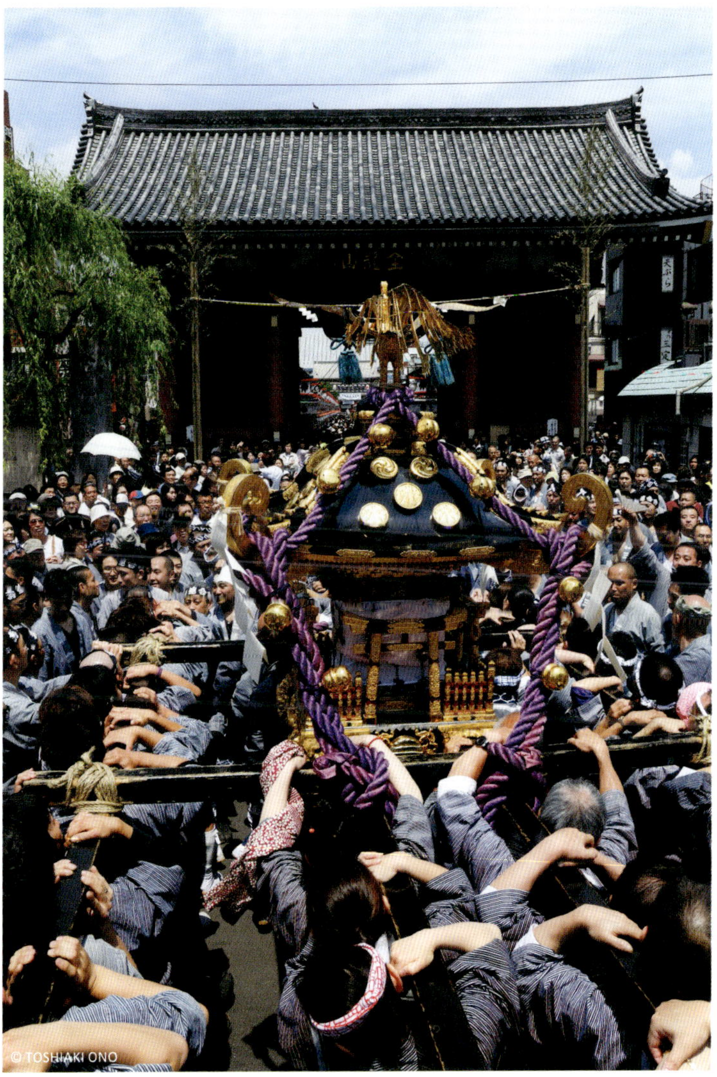
© TOSHIAKI ONO

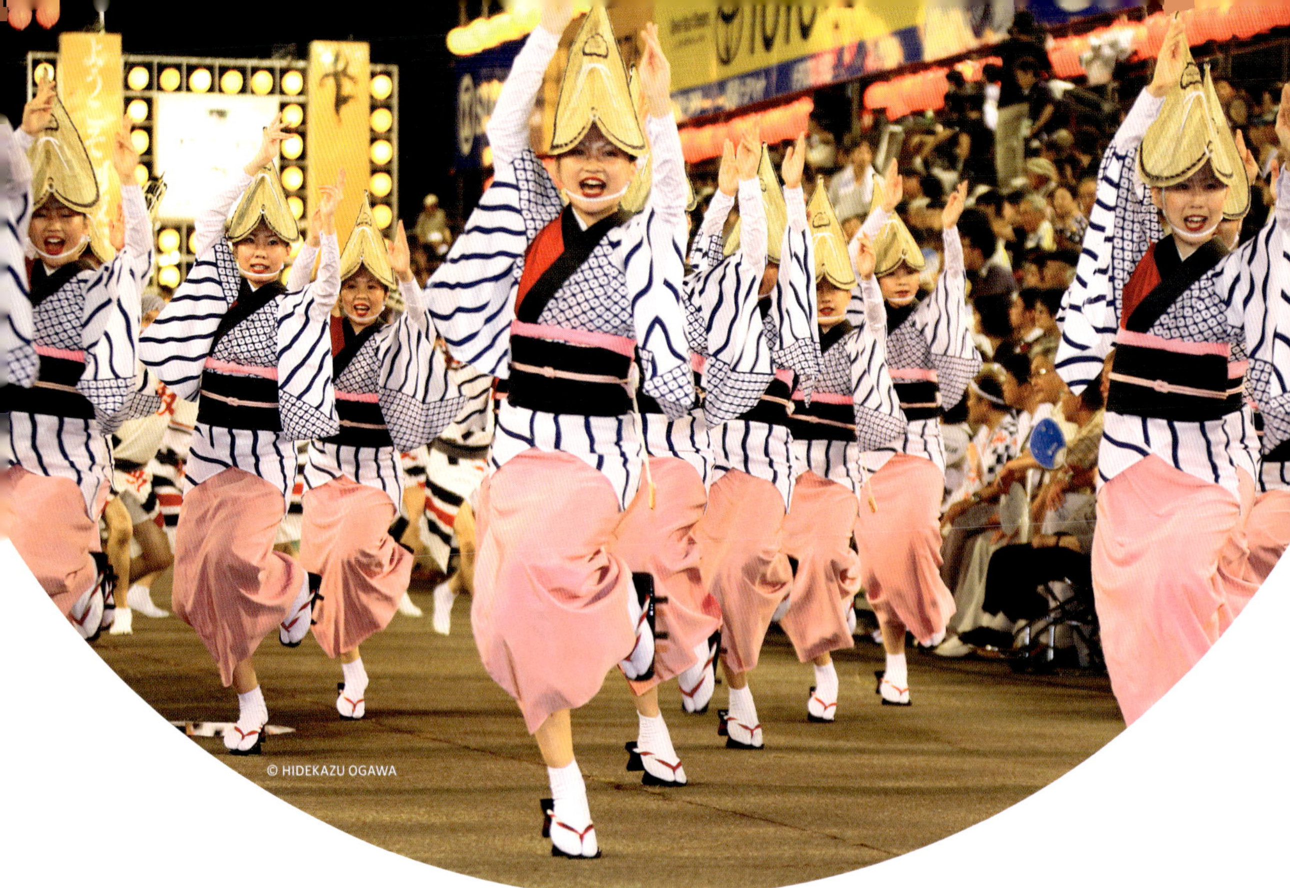

阿波踊り

Awa Odori (Awa Dance)

Awa Odori, used to be just another summer dance festival in the old country of Awa (today's Tokushima Prefecture), the only difference being that Awa dancers marched instead of dancing in a circle. This grew and developed into *Awa Odori*.

Scores of dancers and musicians form teams called *ren* and march as they dance to tunes played by *shamisen* lutes, flutes, bells, and *taiko* drums. Awa Odori choreography is rambunctious and comical. A line from a well-known song has it, *Some fools dance, some fools watch / If you're going to be a fool anyway, you might as well dance!* If you want to dance, come on and join the throng, is the spirit of the festival. The Awa Odori Festival is held for four days from August 12, pulling in tourists from Tokushima Prefecture and the rest of Japan.

Yosakoi Festival

The Kochi City hosts the Yosakoi Festival from the evening of August 9 (pre-festival event) through 12. Multiple stages built across Kochi City show case elaborate team dances. The festival was begun in 1954 as a challenge to the Awa Odori Festival of Tokushima, a neighboring city. The festival is in parade form and dancers holding *naruko* (originally wooden instrument to chase birds away from crops), are led by trucks called *jikatasha*. There is no restriction on dance and all kinds—whether samba, rock, hip-hop, or flamenco—are acceptable. In 1992, the Sapporo City in Hokkaido also held a Yosakoi Soran Festival of its own and now different cities around Japan have followed suit.

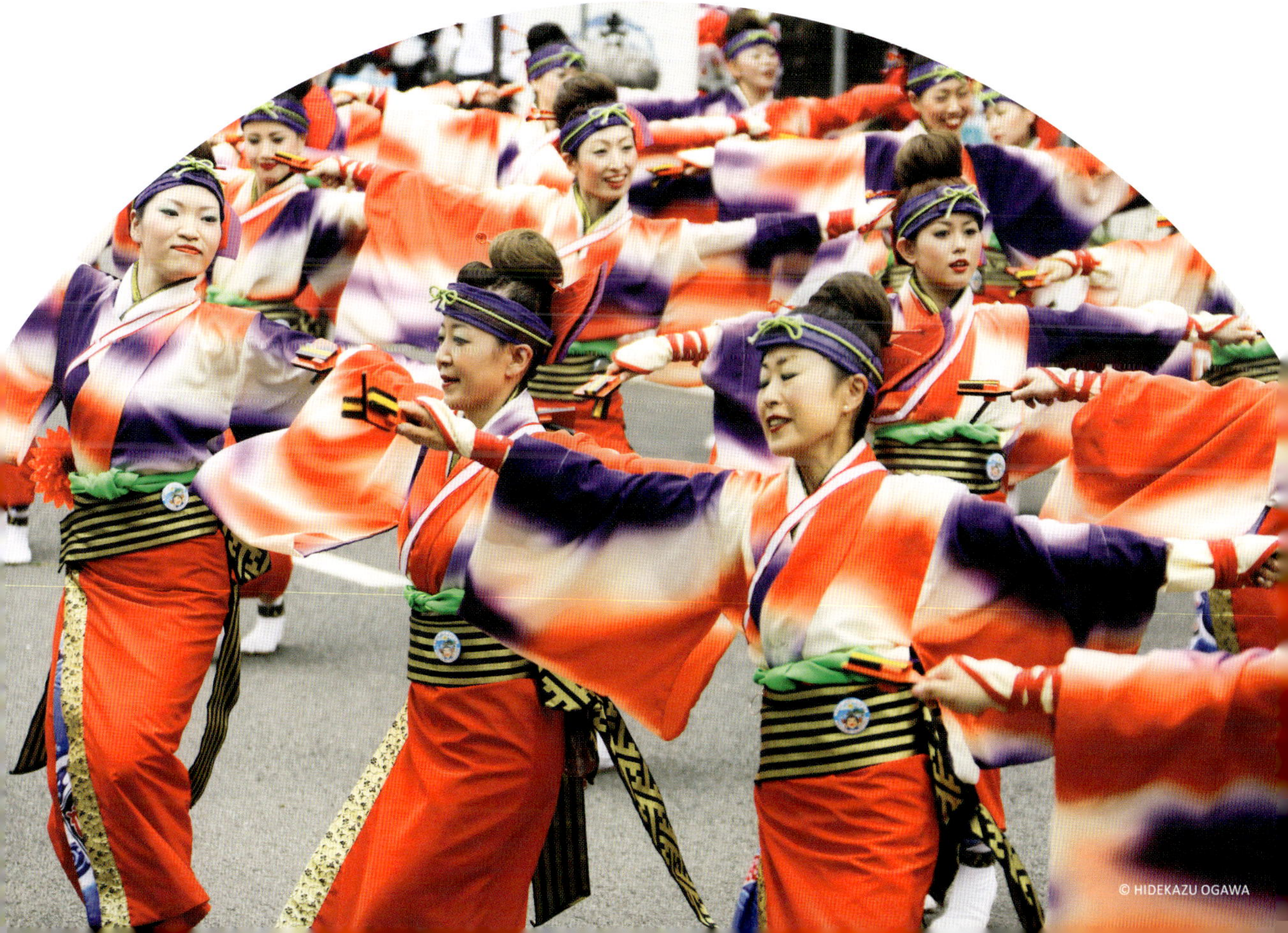

Shogatsu (New Year)

Shogatsu (New Year) originally connoted the whole first month of the year. Today, however, it usually means *sanganichi,* the first three of January, or *matsunouchi,* the first seven (or, depending on the region, first 15-20) days. Japanese celebrate *Shogatsu* by putting on new year's decorations and eating special dishes for the occasion.

Of *Shogatsu*, the very first day is called *gantan,* on which people welcome *toshigami* (new year's deity). *Toshigami* is the god of abundant crops and flourishing prosperity and also the spirit of ancestors. By welcoming and celebrating the *toshigami* you pray for good fortune in a new year. *Shogatsu* is the practice of entertaining this deity/spirit.

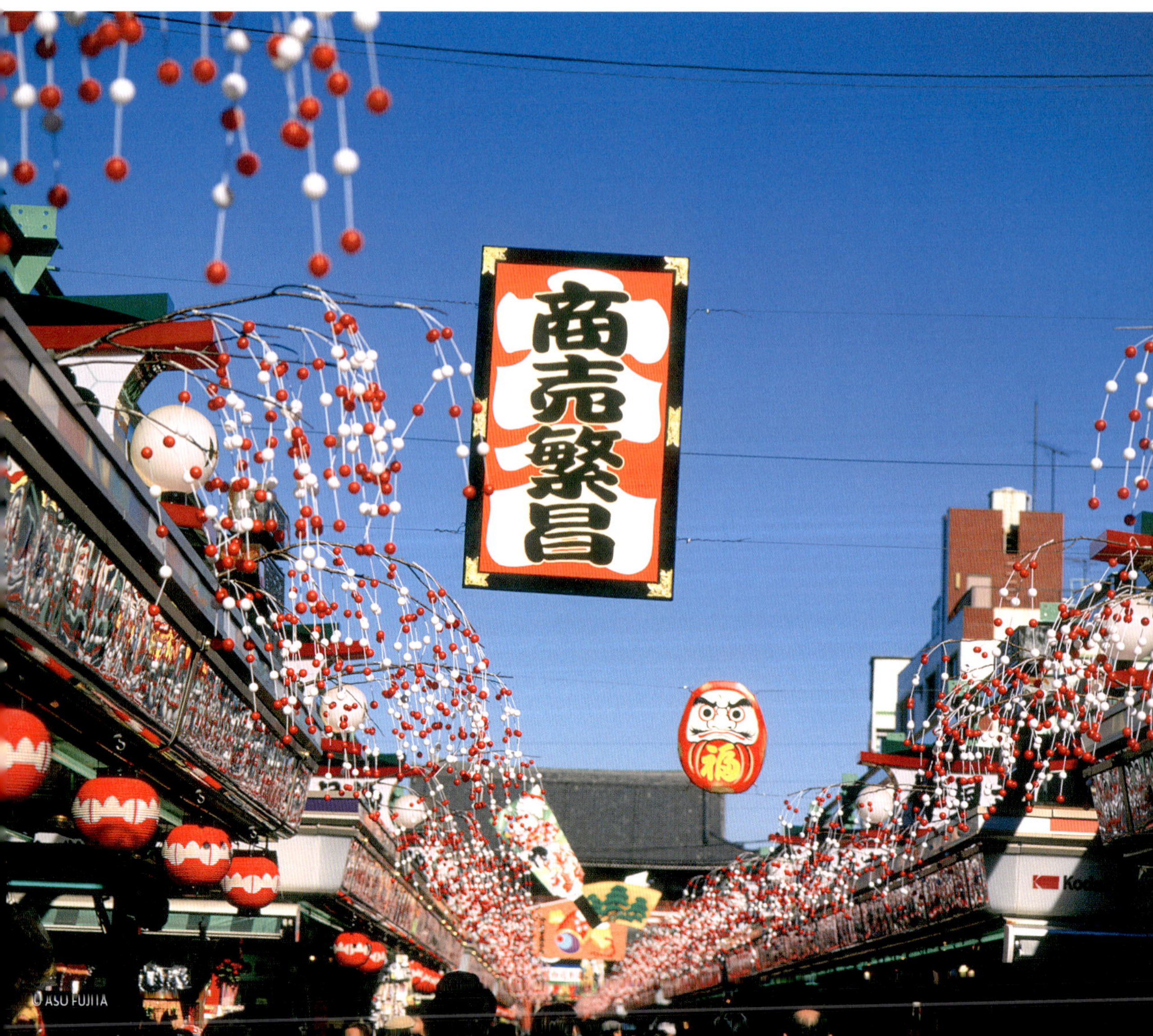

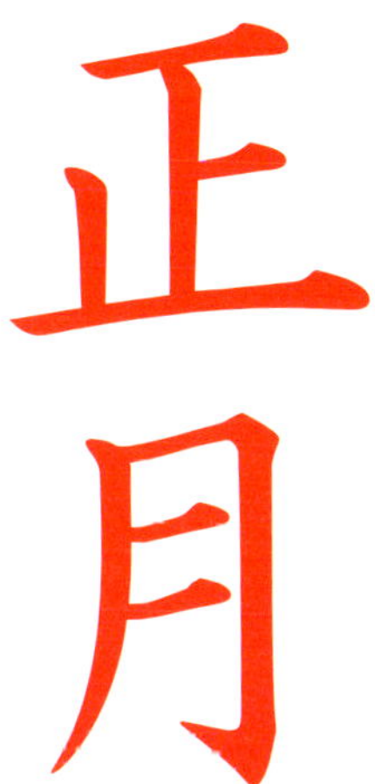

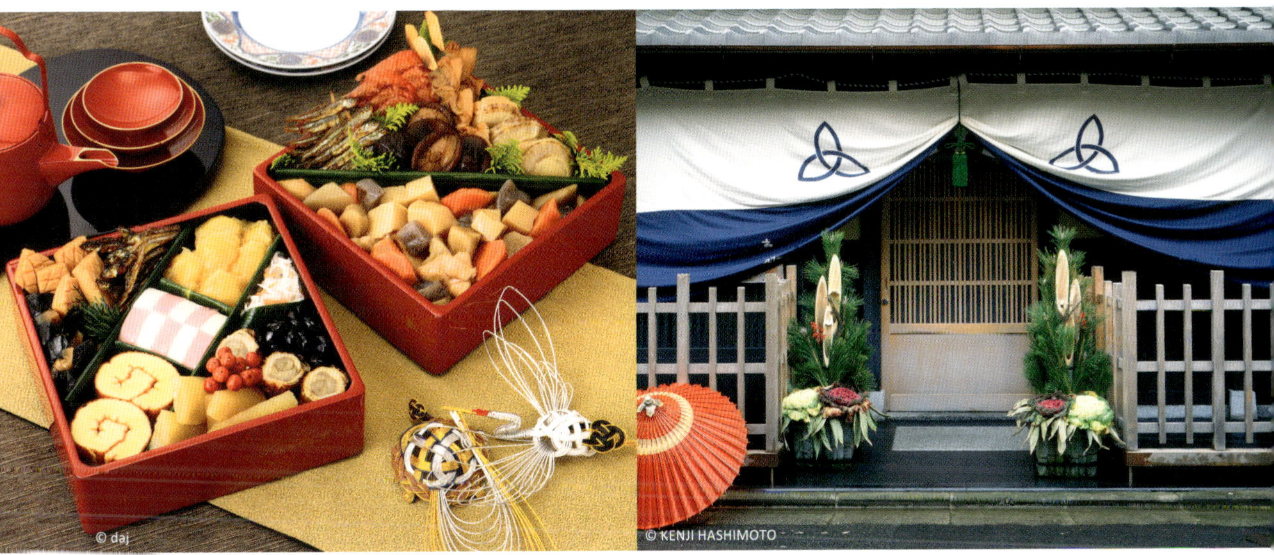
© daj
© KENJI HASHIMOTO

Osechi
(Specially prepared New Year's dish)

When you welcome the *toshigami,* you pack lucky dishes in a box and make an offering called *osechi*. Japanese used to prepare *osechi* at the beginning of each new season but today *osechi* refers to the special cuisine for *Shogatsu*, the beginning of a signally important season. Each *osechi* dish has unique significance. For example, *kuromame* or black beans signify prayers for good health and long life, without evil spirits, so you may be able to strong enough work in the field so long your skin gets brown.

Kadomatsu
(New Year's pine and bamboo decorations)

Shogatsu (New Year) decorations, such as *Kadomatsu*, a pair of male and female pines placed in front of the gate, are said to provide the visiting *toshigami* with a platform to dwell on. Because evergreen trees were believed to host deities in ancient Japan, people began decorating their house gates with such trees. Pines, which are pronounced matsu and alliterate with the verb *matsuru* (worship), are considered particularly auspicious.

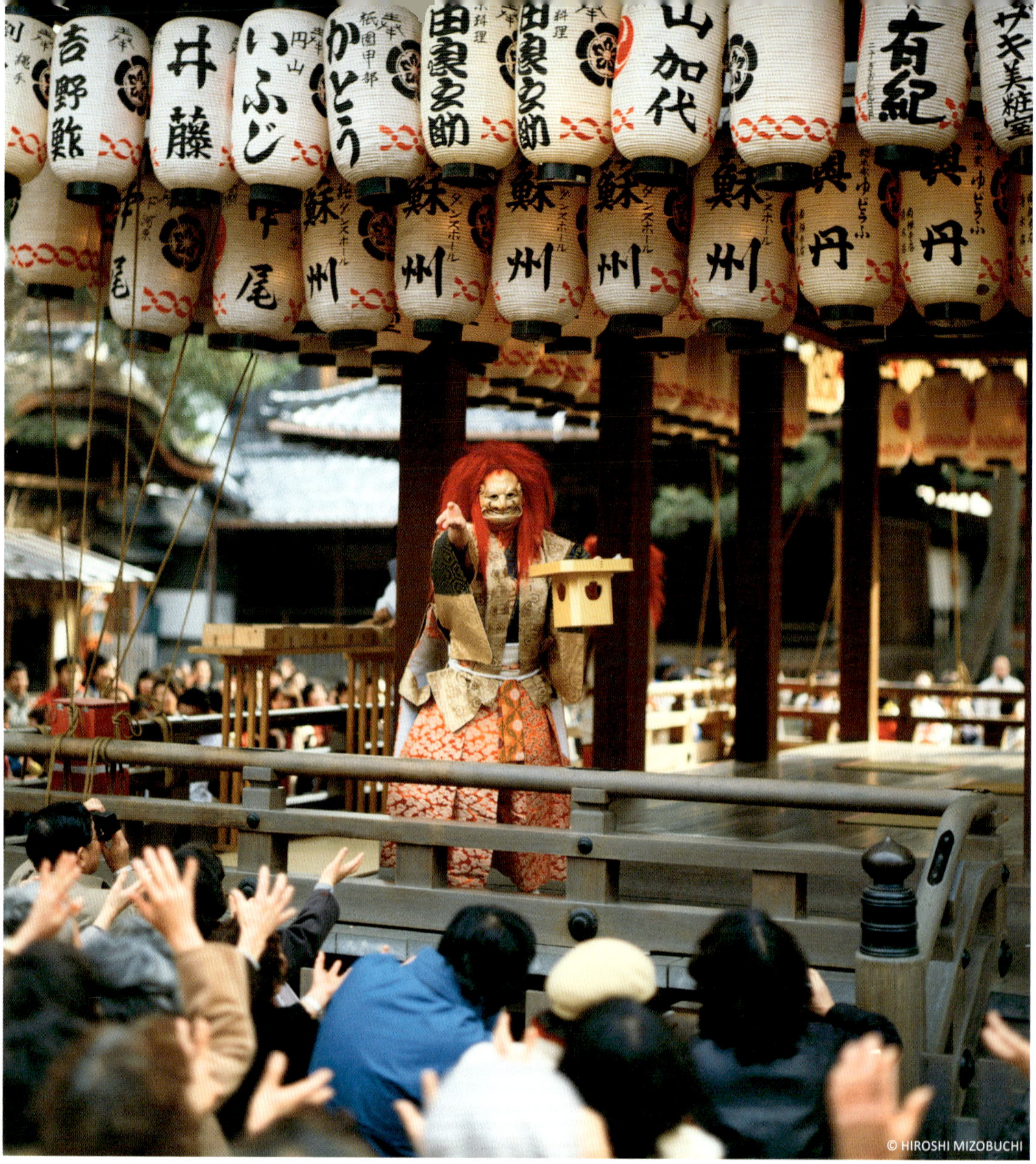

© HIROSHI MIZOBUCHI

Setsubun

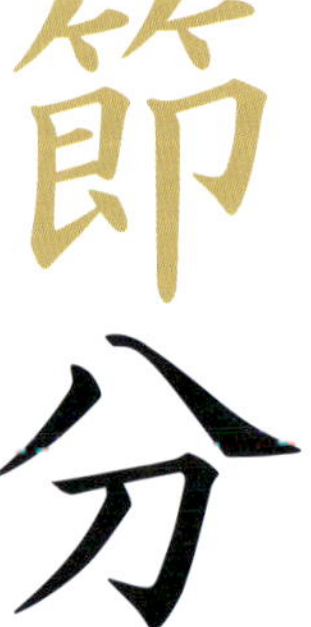

Setsubun is generally the day before the beginning of four seasons (spring, summer, autumn, and winter), but today it refers specifically to the day before the first day of spring in the traditional Japanese calendar (around February 3).

It was long believed that, when seasons change from one to another, evil spirits or devils were liable to emerge, so people began organizing events to ward off troubles and pray for good fortune. One such event was *mamemaki* (scattering of beans). You scatter roasted beans, chanting *Devils, out, good fortune, in!* This tradition remains alive today with many Japanese, in Shinto shrines all over the country as well as at home.

雛祭り

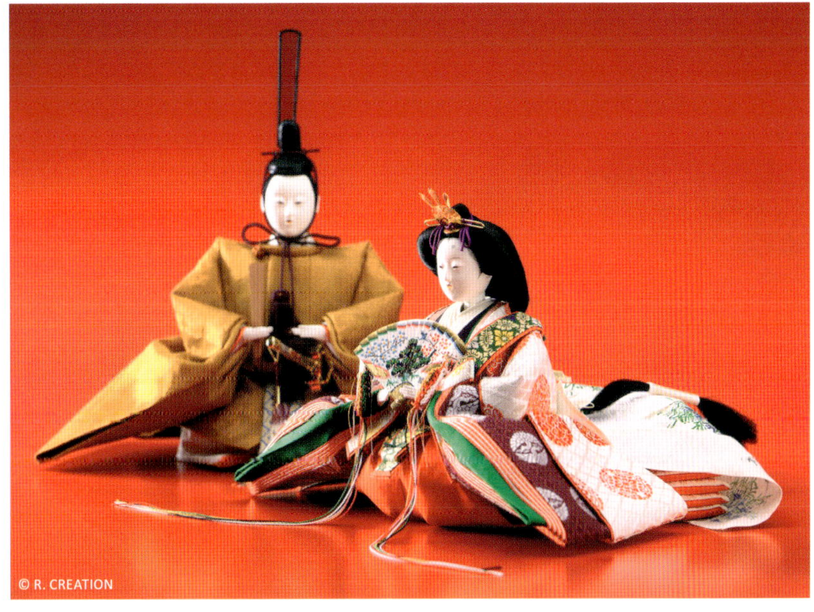
© R. CREATION

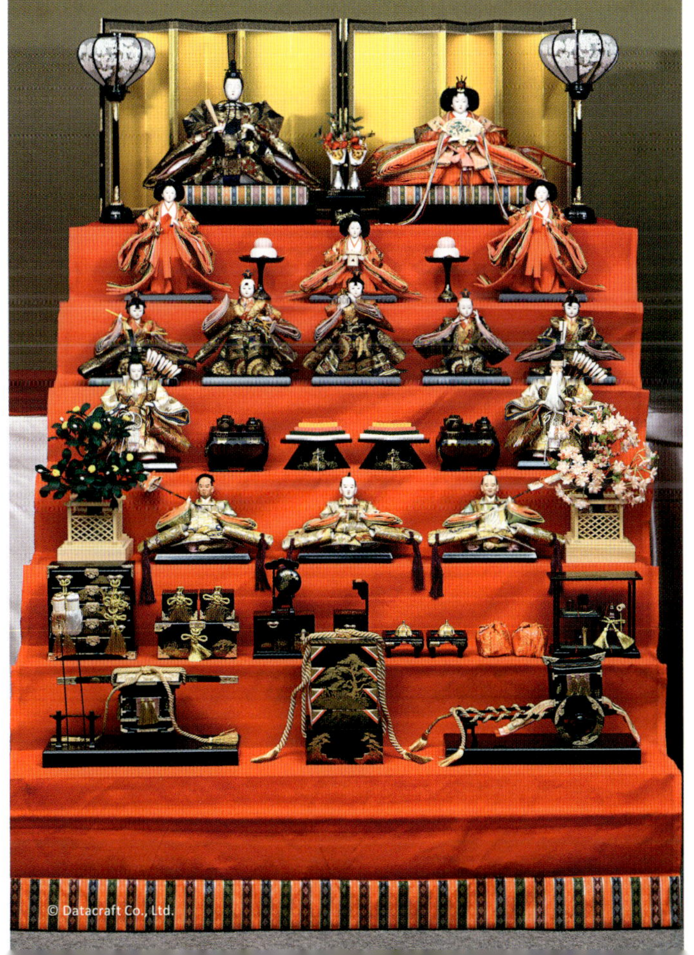
© Datacraft Co., Ltd.

Hinamatsuri
(Girls' Festival)

Hinamatsuri (Girl's Festival) is a familiar occasion celebrated annually on March 3, in which figurines imitating the Heian-period nobility are displayed to wish for healthy growth of girls. Since spring is the season of peach blossoms, and because peach trees are used as decorations to ward off evil spirits, the day is also known as the Seasonal Peach Festival.

In *Hinamatsuri*, offerings are made of *hishi-mochi*, rectangular rice cakes colored in red (pink), white and green and *hina-arare* (rice crackers). While opinions vary, some maintain that the colors symbolize peach blossoms (red), snow (white), and green (fresh verdure), all in prayer for healthy growth.

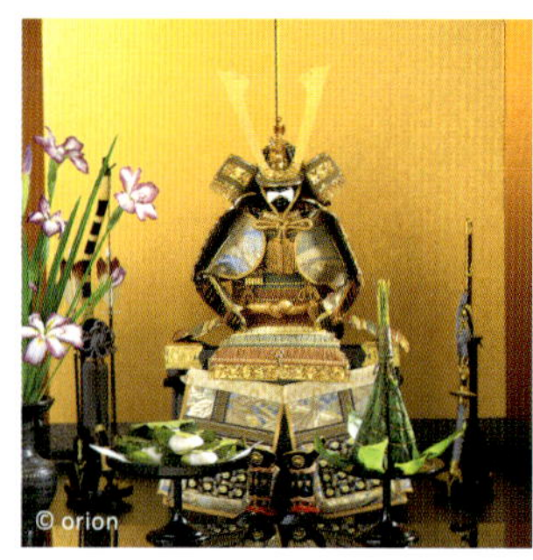

Tango Seasonal Festival
(Children's Day)

Also known as Children's Day, this is an annual festivity held on May 5 to pray for boys' healthy growth. People would hang sweet flags or Japanese mugwort plants, which emit strong scents and are thought to purge evil. Because it is customary to take a hot bath sprinkled with sweet flag leaves, for good health, it is also known as the Seasonal Festival of the Sweet Flag.

On this day, people display sumurai armor and helmets, *Gogatsu* (May) dolls of legendary heroes, and *Koinobori* (carp-shaped streamers) are displayed. Whereas the armor and helmet are meant to protect the boys' bodies, the dolls are supposed to be avatars to receive any misfortune instead of the boy. *Koinobori* streamers stand for the boy's future success and are said to derive from ancient China.

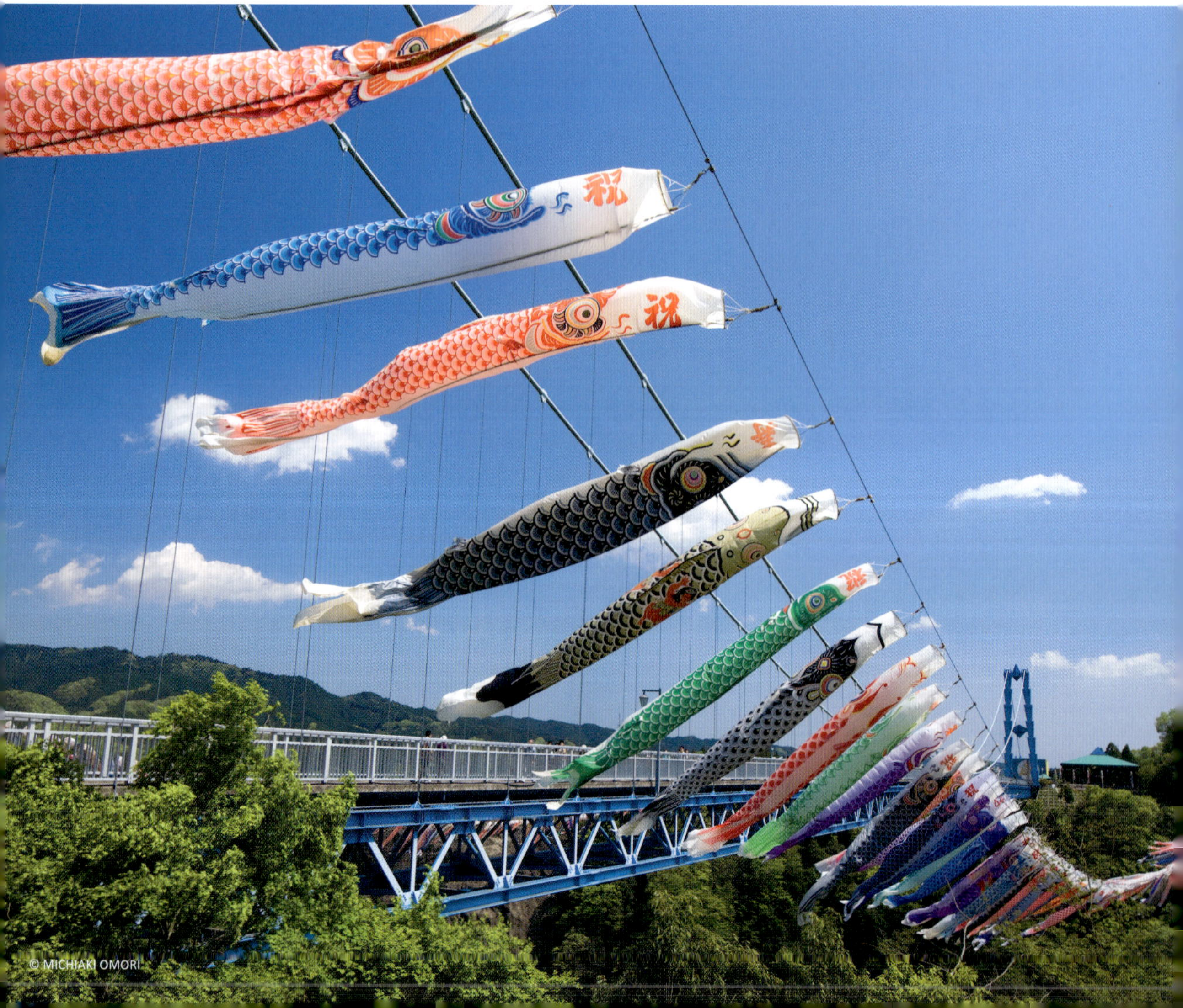

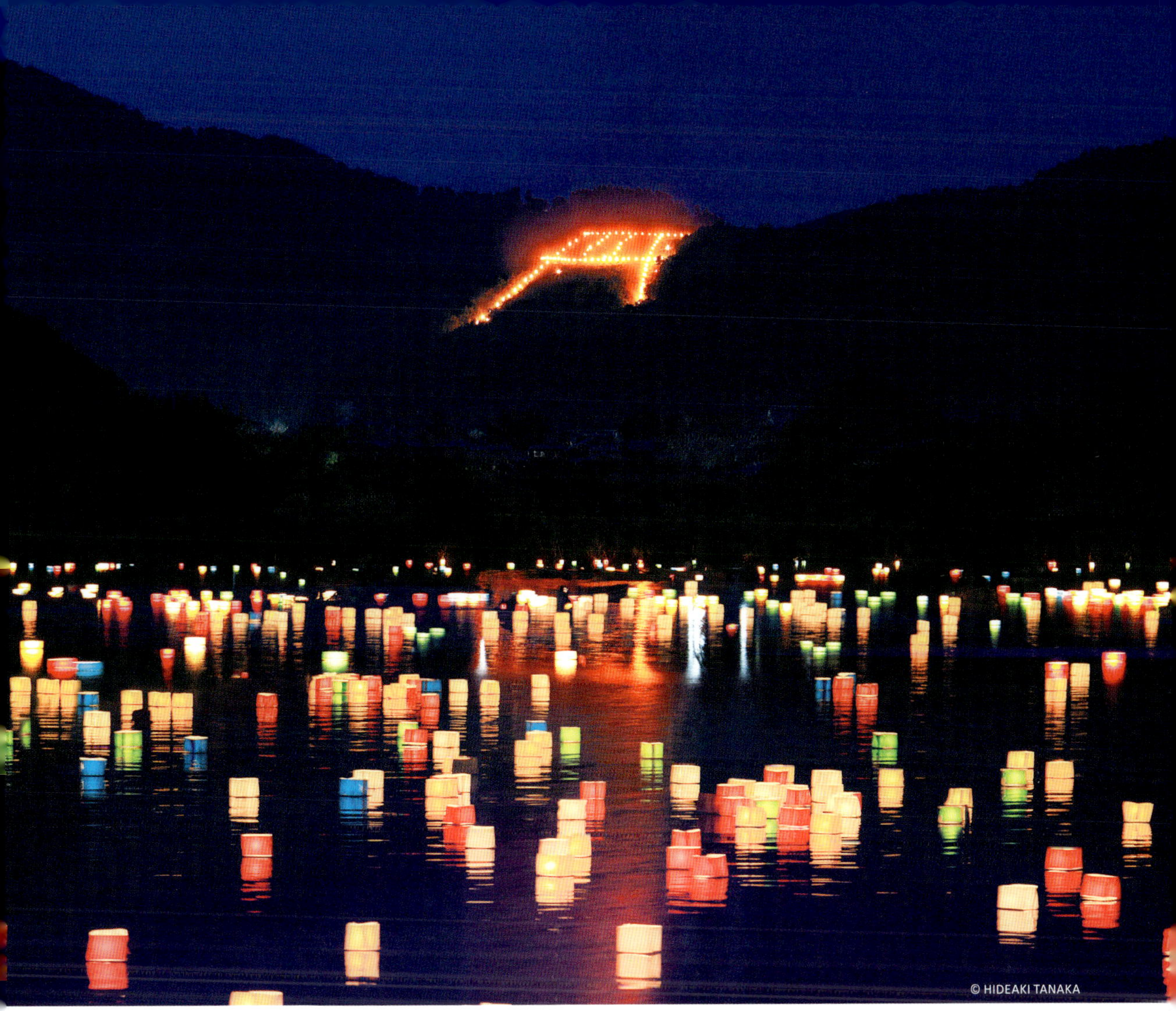

Obon

Obon is an occasion, usually held in August, to welcome back, worship and then send off ancestors' spirits. On the evening of 13th of the month, a welcoming fire (to receive spirits and visitors) is kindled for ancestors' spirits; on the following 14th and 15th, offerings are placed on family alters to worship them; and on the 16th another fire is kindled to send the spirits back to the spiritual world.

In Kyoto and Nara, it is traditional to build large-scale fires, respectively called *Gozan-no-okuribi* and *Daimonji-yaki*. In these events large letters are formed by fires on a mountainside to see off the departing spirits. In some other regions, in a festivity called *toro-nagashi* (lantern floating), lanterns are floated in the sea or river to commemorate the dead.

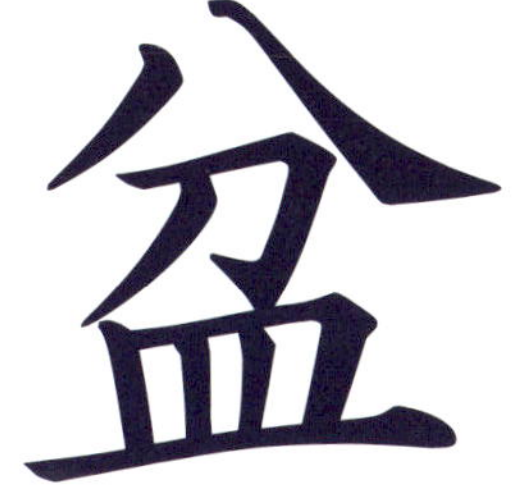

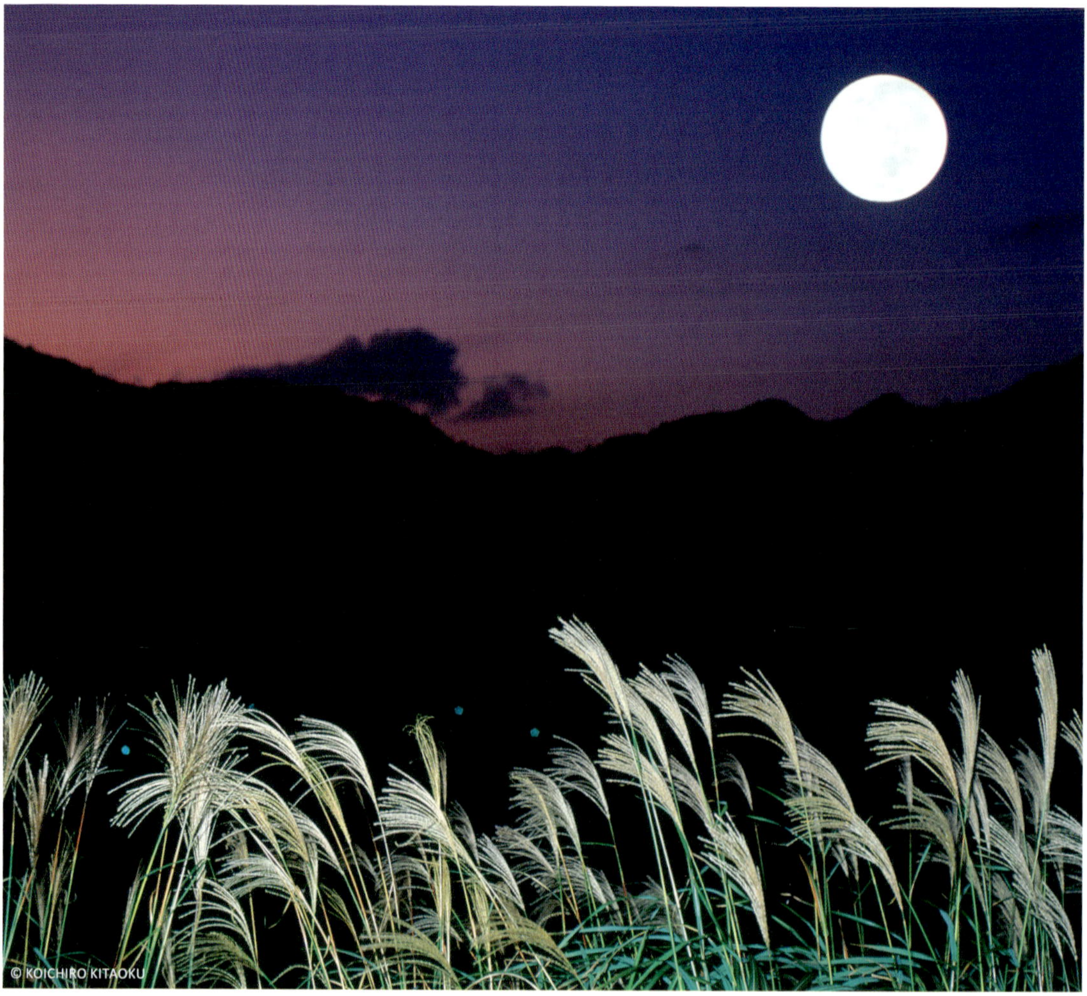

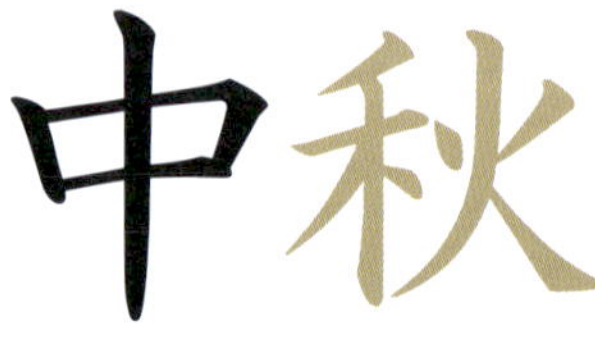

Harvest moon

August 15 of the old lunar calendar is called *Jugoya* or *Chushu-no-meigetsu* (Harvest Moon). Originally it meant a full moon and corresponds to the full moon between mid-September and early October in the modern calendar. Because August 15 is the midpoint in autumn, the moon on this night is called *Chushu-no-meigetsu.*

Nobility in the Heian-period used to hold *otsukimi* (a festivity to gaze at the mid-autumn full moon) and this custom is said to have turned into an occasion to give thanks for the season's harvest. Today, people make offerings of harvested taros, Japanese pampas grass and *tsukimi-dango* (rice dumplings), which are round like a full moon, for warding off evil spirits and praying for health.

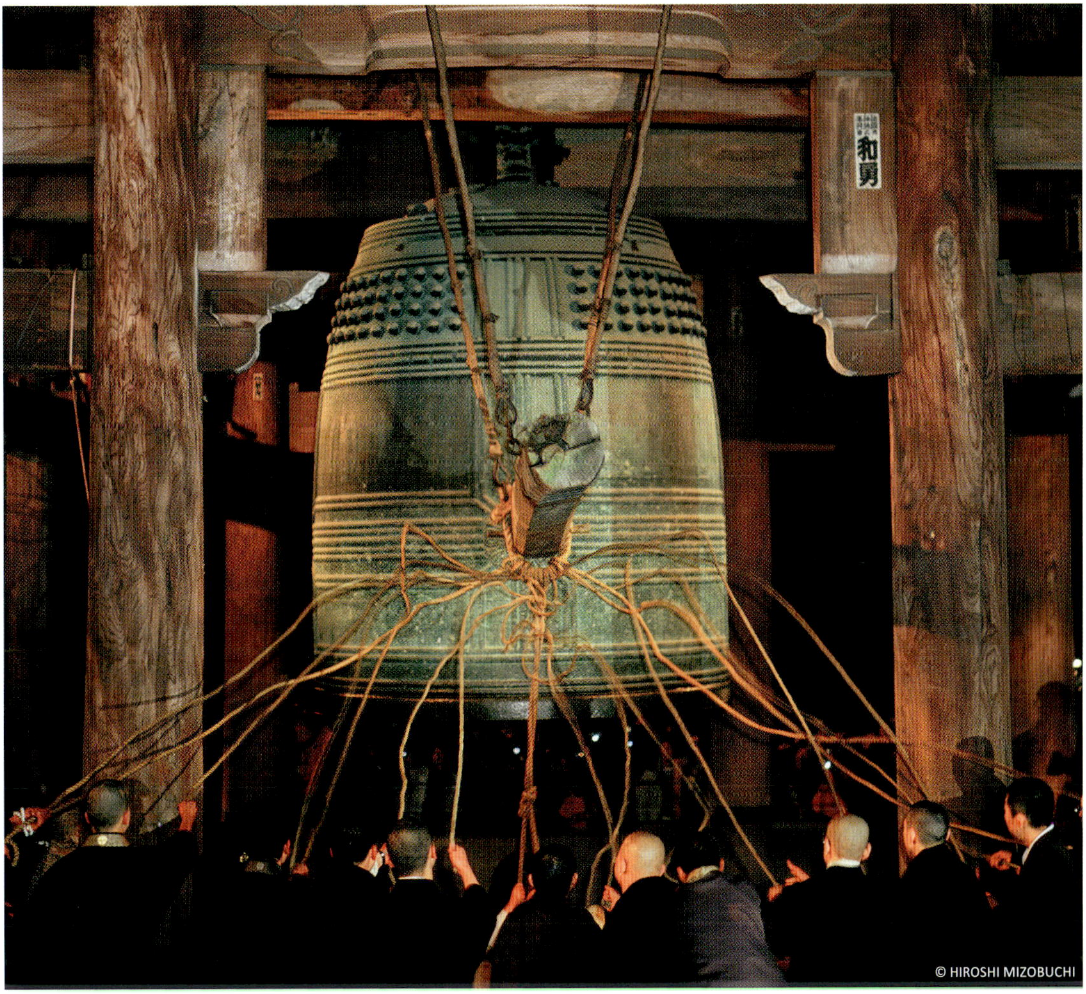

© HIROSHI MIZOBUCHI

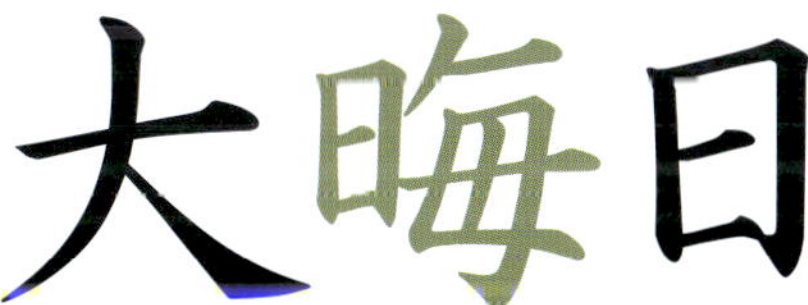

New Year's Eve

The last day of any month is called *misoka* and that of the year, December 31, is called *o-misoka* or *Otsugomori*. On *o-misoka*, it is customary to strike a bell at a Buddhist temple and pray there as you cross between the two years (*ninen-mairi*), or eat soba noodles called *toshikoshi soba*.

At a temple, the bell tolls for a total 108 times. Called *Joya-no-kane*, it corresponds to 108 sins in Buddhist philosophy and each strike is said to remove one sin. *Ninen-mairi* is a prayer at a Buddhist temple offered at 24:00 of the New Year's eve and continued into the New Year. It is believed to cleanse you of your sins and enable you to welcome the New Year in cleanliness.

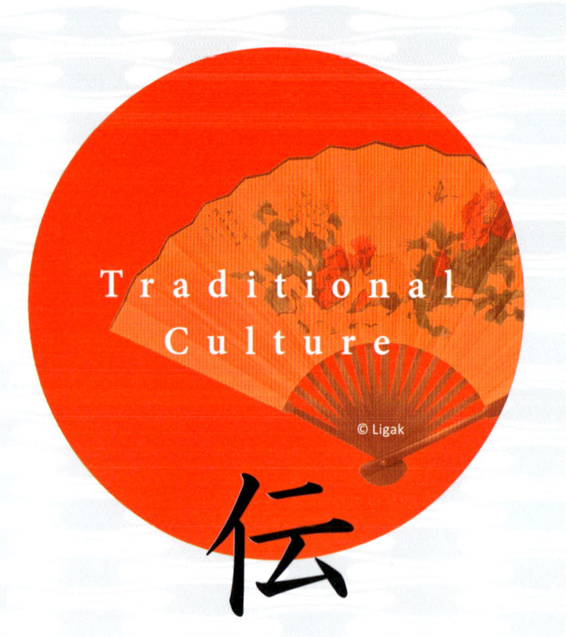

伝統

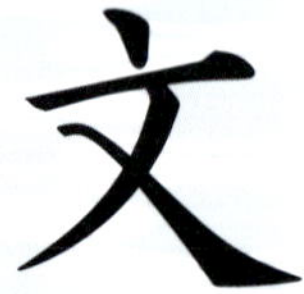

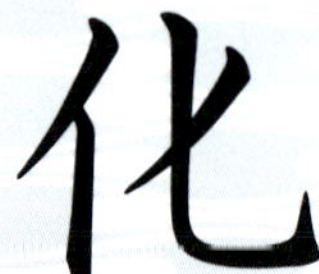

Traditional culture expresses the Japanese people's hearts and minds. Sense the heart and mind of Wa (harmony).

The traditional culture of Japan is now well-known even in other countries. Elements of traditional Japanese culture such as *Sado* (the Way of Tea), *Kado* (flower arrangement),and *Budo* (martial arts), express the *kokoro* (heart and mind) of the Japanese people. By knowing the unbroken continuity of Japan's history and the depth of its culture, you will no doubt be able to glimpse the kokoro on which the people of Japan place such importance.

The words "traditional culture" may give the impression of something distant and unapproachable. However, there are aspects that people from other countries can easily experience, and their beauty can be sensed by simply seeing them.

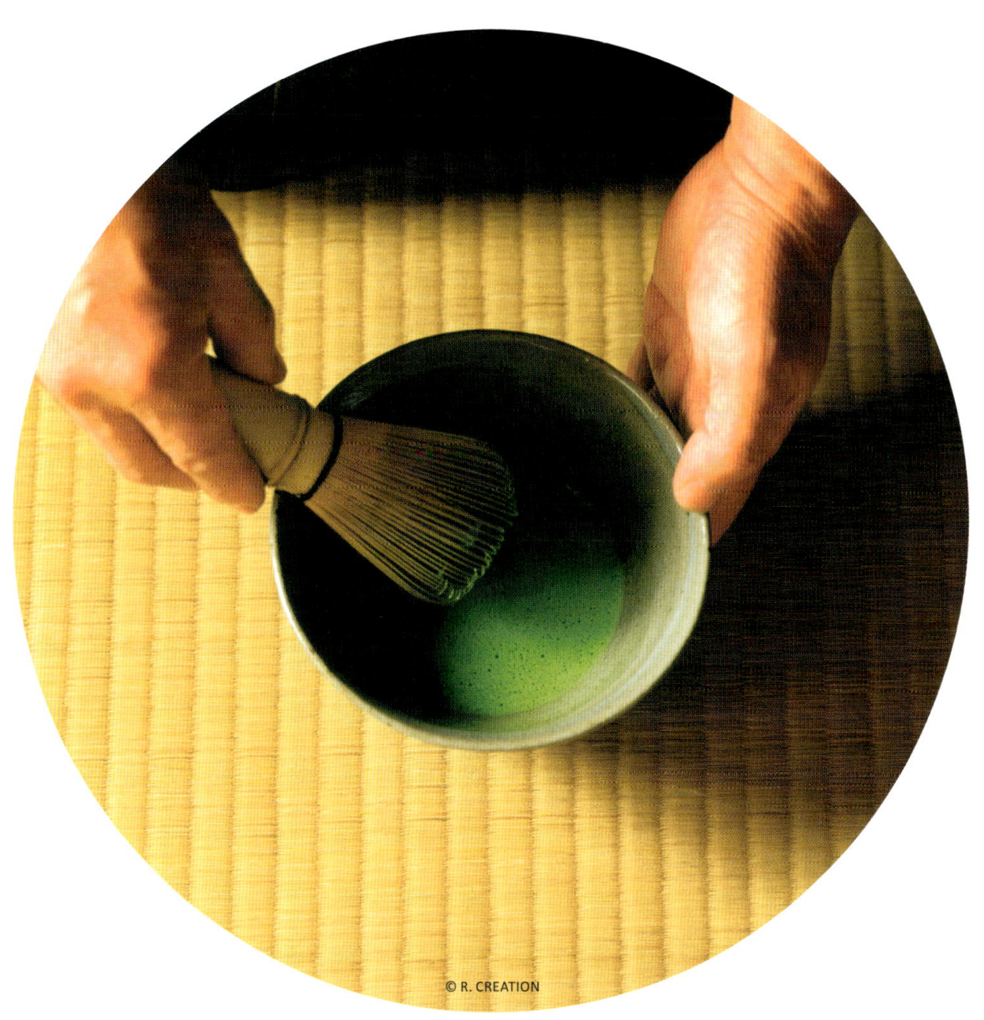
© R. CREATION

茶道

Sado (tea ceremony)

Sado, or the Way of Tea, refers to the Japanese tea ceremony involving from boiling water to making and serving tea, as well as etiquette and a mindset. Sado's basic procedures were formed by the middle of the 14th century but it was Sen no Rikyu in the 16th century who elaborated a new style called *wabi-cha* emphasizing spirituality and the exchange between host and guest. *Sado* procedures are so precisely defined that people tend to see it as something esoteric and forbidding, but it is basically a ceremony to care for and entertain guests. The spiritual beauty of people welcoming people is said to be sado's purpose. Recently, sado ceremonies are made available to foreign tourists, too. You may experience the Japanese culture of *omotenashi* (welcoming visitors) with tea.

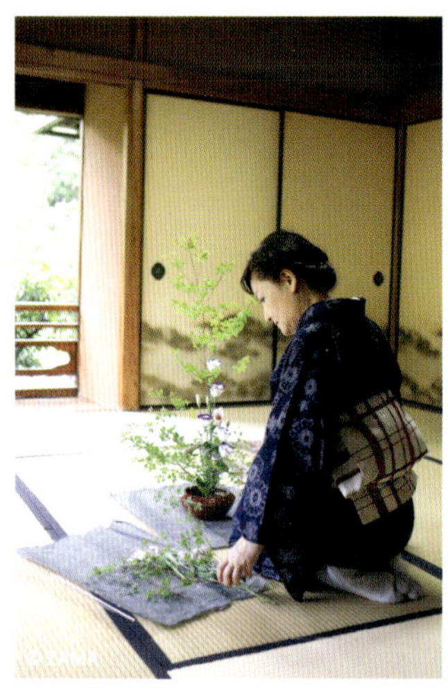

Kado (flower arrangement)

Kado, also known as *ikebana*, is the traditional Japanese art of flower arrangement. By cutting seasonal plants and arranging them in a container, *kado* seeks to present and enjoy beauty and nobility. There are many different schools in *kado* and techniques and styles vary considerably. *Kado* maintains that "flowers represent people's hearts and minds." By arranging flowers, one explores ideal aesthetics in them while expressing one's emotions.

As is the case with sado and other disciplines, *kado* also values etiquette and decorum. It is believed that, through flower arrangement, one faces one's inner self and gains a peace of mind.

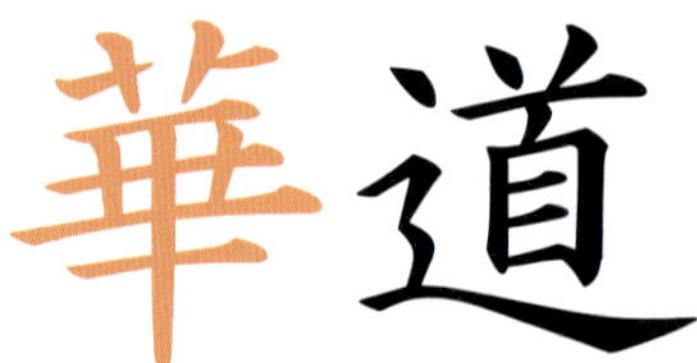

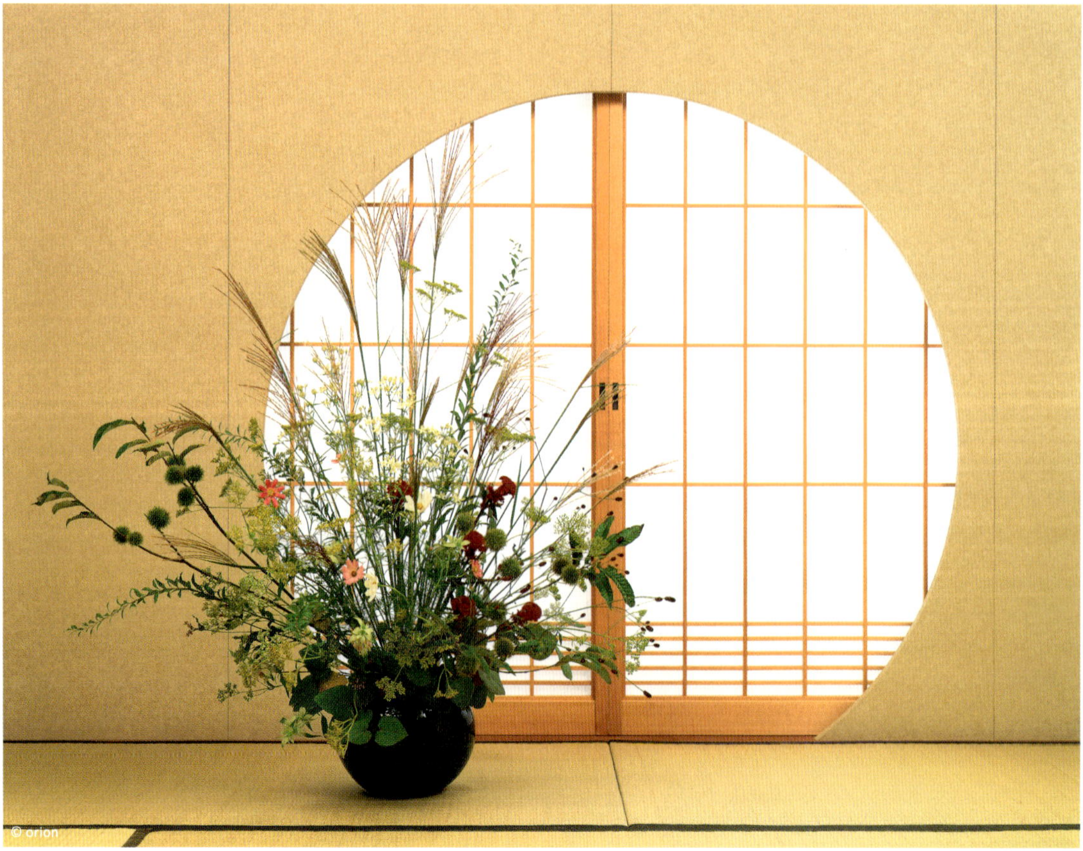

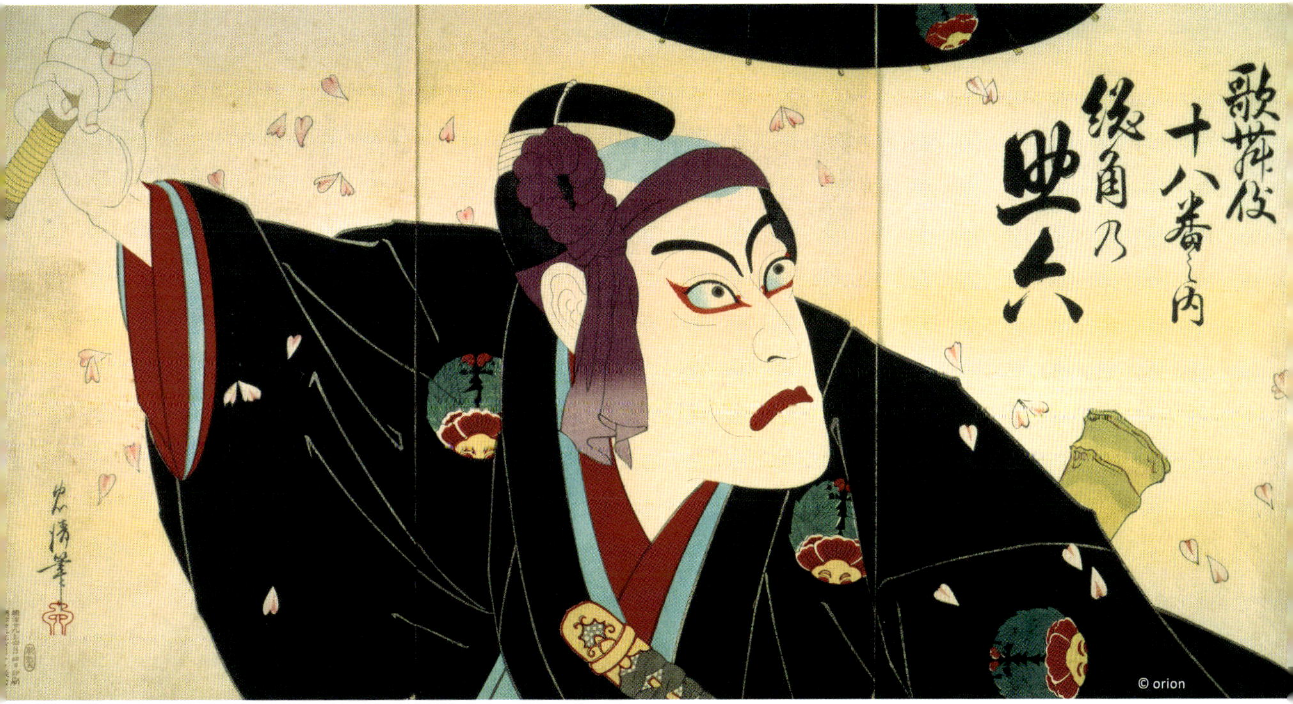

Kabuki

The three characters for *kabuki* refer to song (music), dance and performing skills. Its etymology is derived from the old verb *kabuku*, which meant to appear or behave in outlandish or avant-garde manner. In the Edo period, *kabuki* developed as a theater entertainment for ordinary town people, always absorbing new elements to keep up with the changing times. That is one reason why it has managed to sustain its popularity to date.

Kabuki drama is performed by male actors. Because some plays have female characters, male actors known as *onnagata* were used to perform these roles. Kabuki's theatrics encompass a wide spectrum of elements, from music to stage design. This is a very lively world of popular entertainment, with a whole repertoire depicting samurai warriors and town people.

歌舞伎

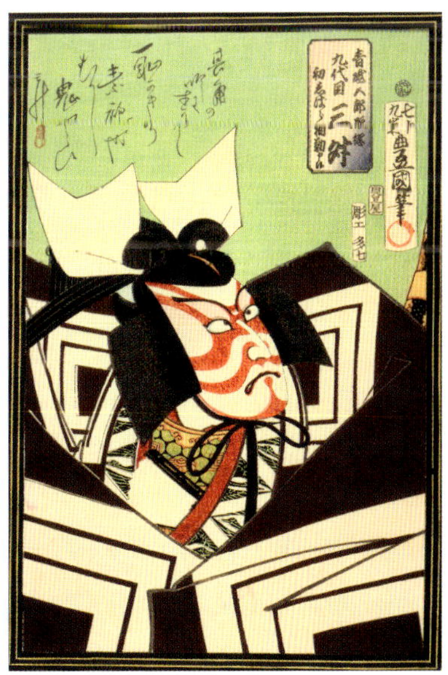

大相撲

Sumo

Considered Japan's national sport, *sumo* traces its history to the country's mythic past. Ancient forms of *sumo* were ceremonial and associated with Shinto rituals, as in *hono-zumo* performed in festivities and *shinji-zumo* in shrines. In the Edo Period professional sumo wrestlers emerged and *sumo* matches became an entertainment business as popular as *kabuki* performances.

Gradually *sumo* became the modern sport that it is today, establishing such standard practices as entry into the ring (*dohyo*), the league table, and the wrestler's characteristic *mawashi* belt and *mage* hairstyle. Professional sumo tournaments are held six times a year: three times in Tokyo and once each in Osaka, Nagoya and Fukuoka.

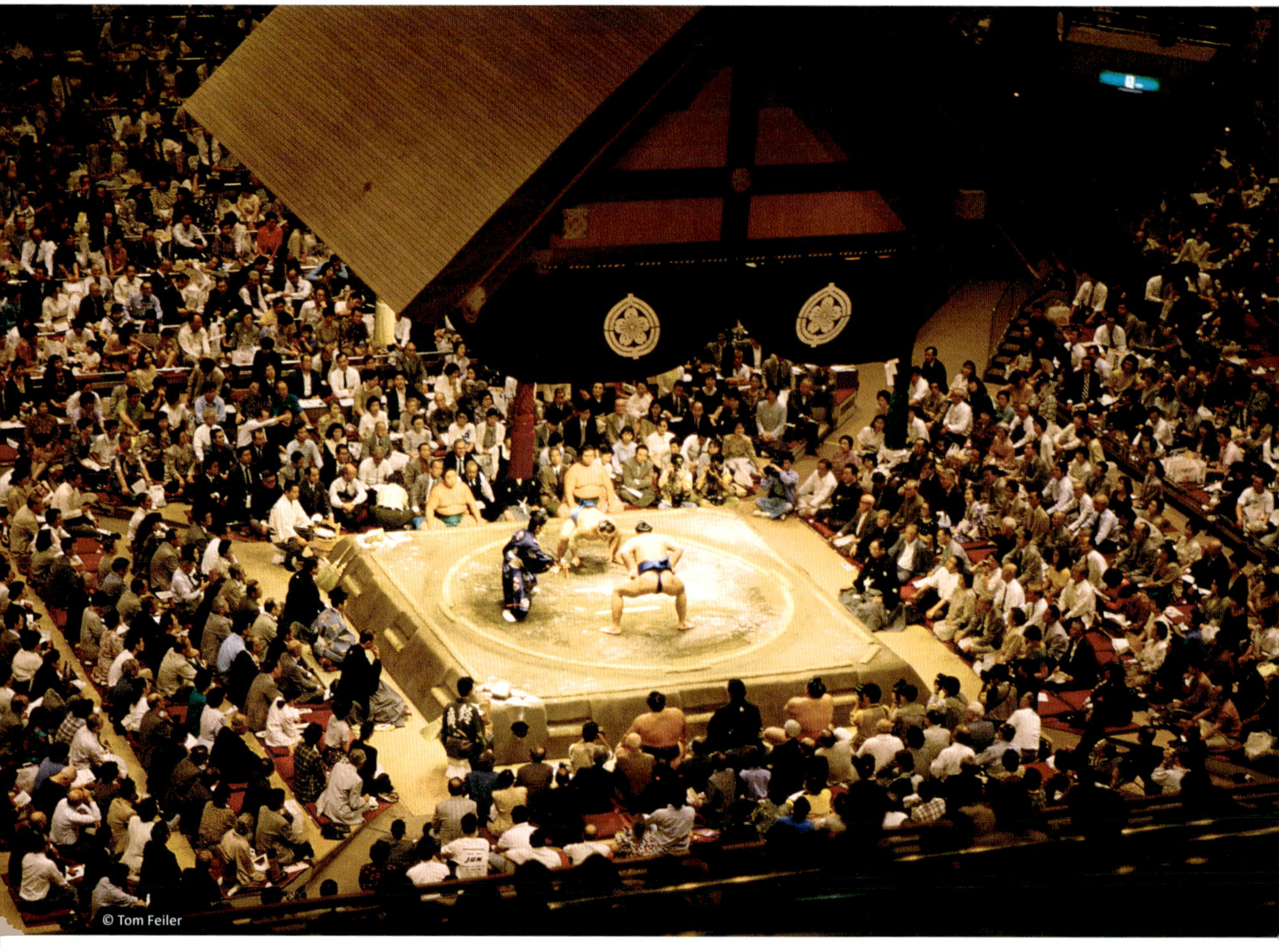

© Tom Feiler

Kendo

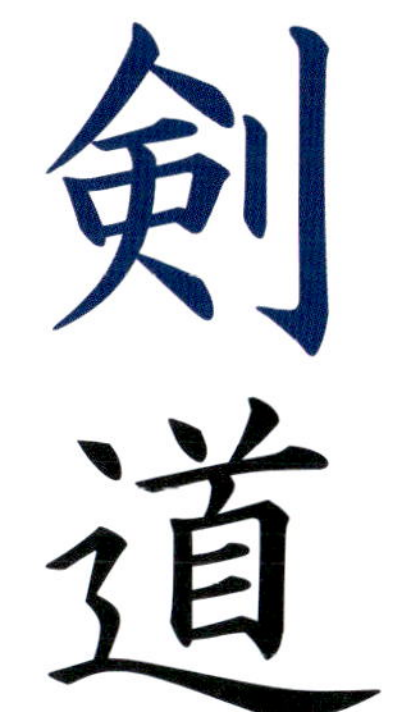

Kendo, or the Way of the Sword, is a Japanese martial art derived from traditional *kenjutsu* (swordsmanship) of the feudal times. In *kendo*, real steel swords are replaced by *shinai* (bamboo swords). Before, fighters would practice *kendo* to become better swordsmen and prepare for actual combat. Today's *kendo*, however, is, like fencing, in and of itself a modern sport. *Kendo* matches are fought one on one and players compete in attack and defense skills. In principle, the player who has delivered three hits on the opponent is the match winner.

Kendo—following tradition in *bushido* or the Way of the *Samurai*—values discipline and decorum and, through training, requires practitioners to master their mind, skills and body, develop character, and cultivate a sense of ethics.

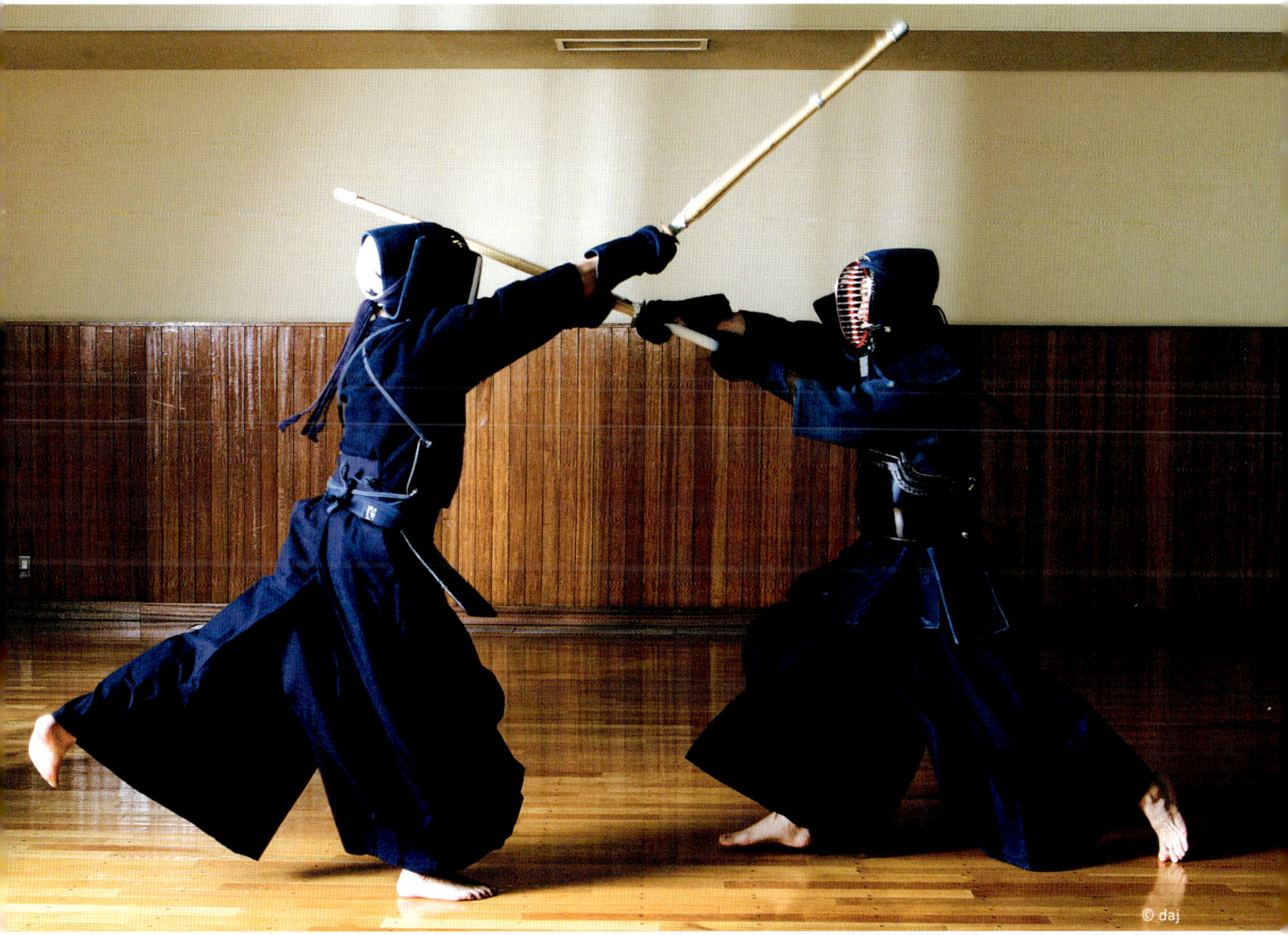

着物

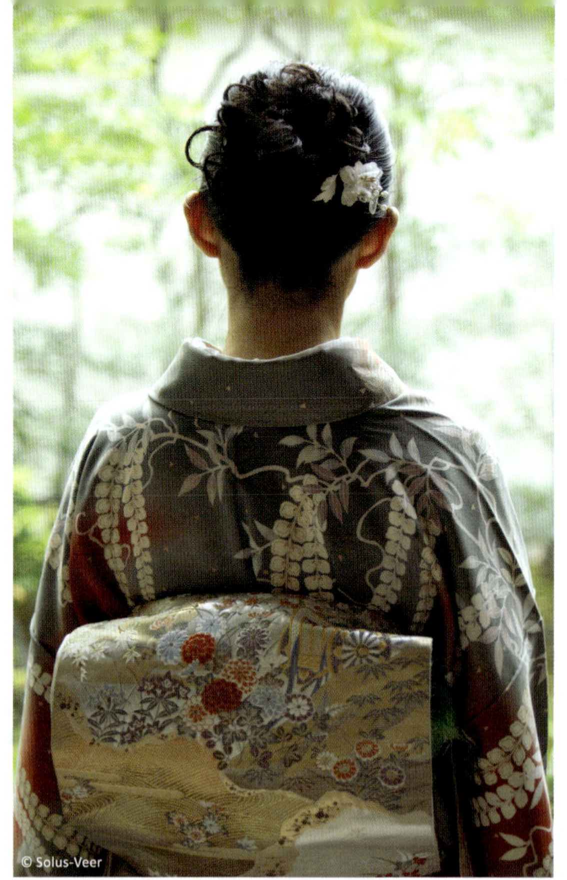
© Solus-Veer

白無垢

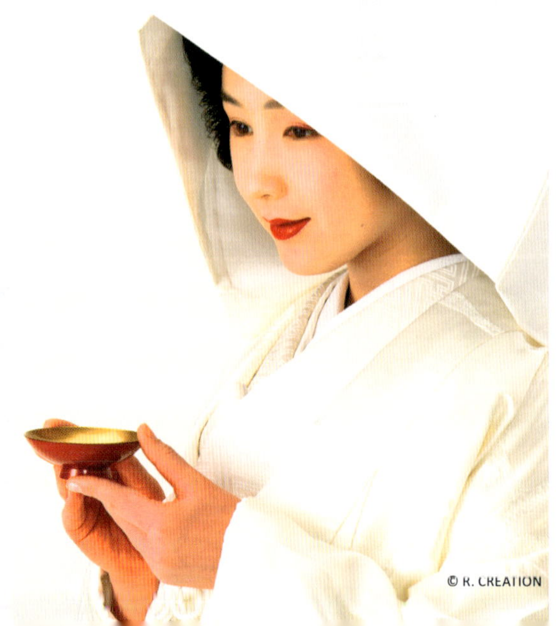
© R. CREATION

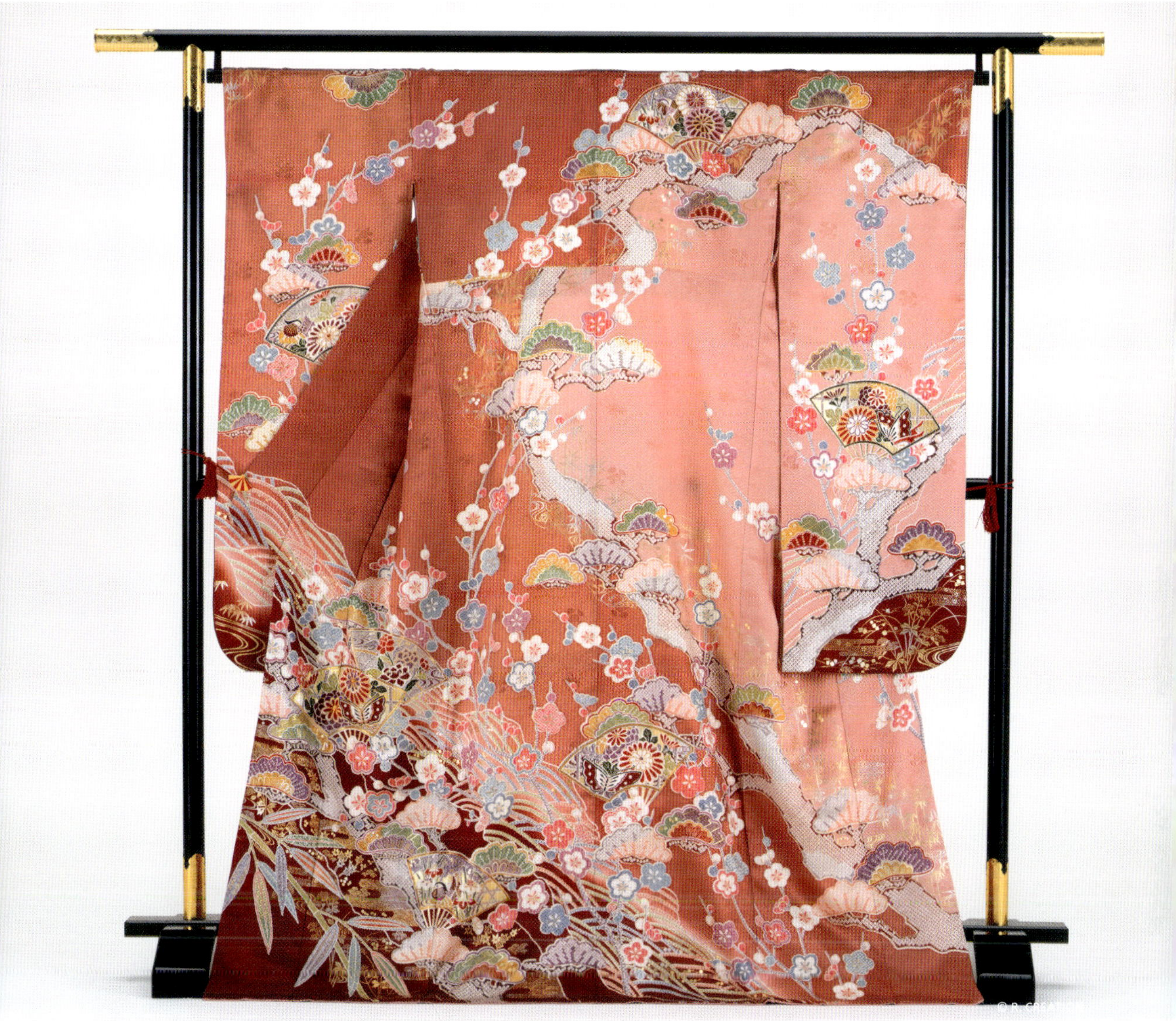

Kimono

Wafuku (Japanese clothes) means traditional Japanese garment or, in the broadest sense, anything worn by Japanese in olden times. *Wafuku* may include *kimono, haori*, and *hakama*. *Kimono*, because it consists of pieces cut along straight lines, may be shared and worn fairly comfortably by people of varying physiques. Few wear *kimono* today regularly but they remain common in such formal occasions as weddings and funerals.
Shiromuku (the bride's traditional wedding kimono) is pure white throughout, down to the obi belt and accessories. Worn only for sacred occasions, it symbolizes purity or chastity.

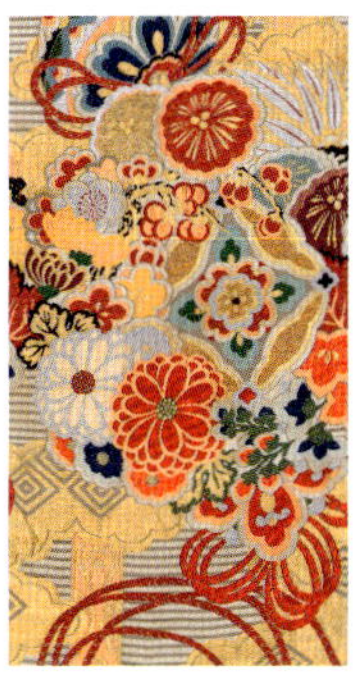

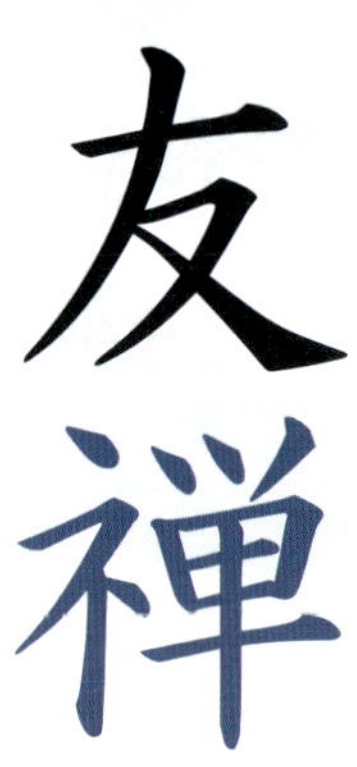

Kaga Yuzen

Kaga Yuzen is a traditional art in Ishikawa Prefecture. Its history is traced back to the late 17th century in the Edo Period, when the Tokugawa Shogunate frowned upon and was eager to suppress luxurious lifestyles. It was Kyoto's master artisan *Miyazaki Yuzensai* who began multi-colored patterned dyeing. Earlier it flourished in Kyoto, its place of origin, but later it developed in Ishikawa's Kanazawa City into the *Kaga Yuzen* school.

One unique process in *Kaga Yuzen* dyeing is *Yuzen Nagashi* (washing), which involves rinsing *kimono* textiles of glue and dyes in clean river water. The colder the river water is, the more firmly the fabric is said to tighten. While the practice used to be a common sight around Kanazawa City, today most dyers use artificial streams. But if you are lucky, you may still get to see *Yuzen Nagashi* in the Asano river.

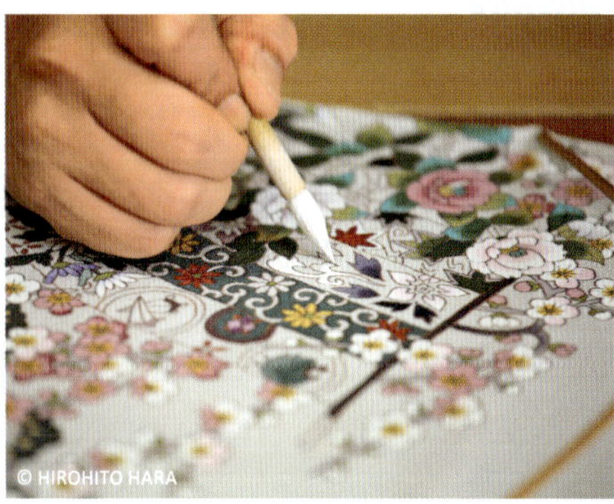

Hand-drawn

Kaga Yuzen is characteristically hand-drawn. This has enabled dyers to develop and refine multi-colored pictorial patterns, a landmark achievement in the history of Japanese dyeing craftsmanship. Typically represented themes, which have enchanted both the general public and the upper nobility, include landscapes; birds with flowers; plants and flowers; pine, bamboo, and plum; and cranes and tortoise.

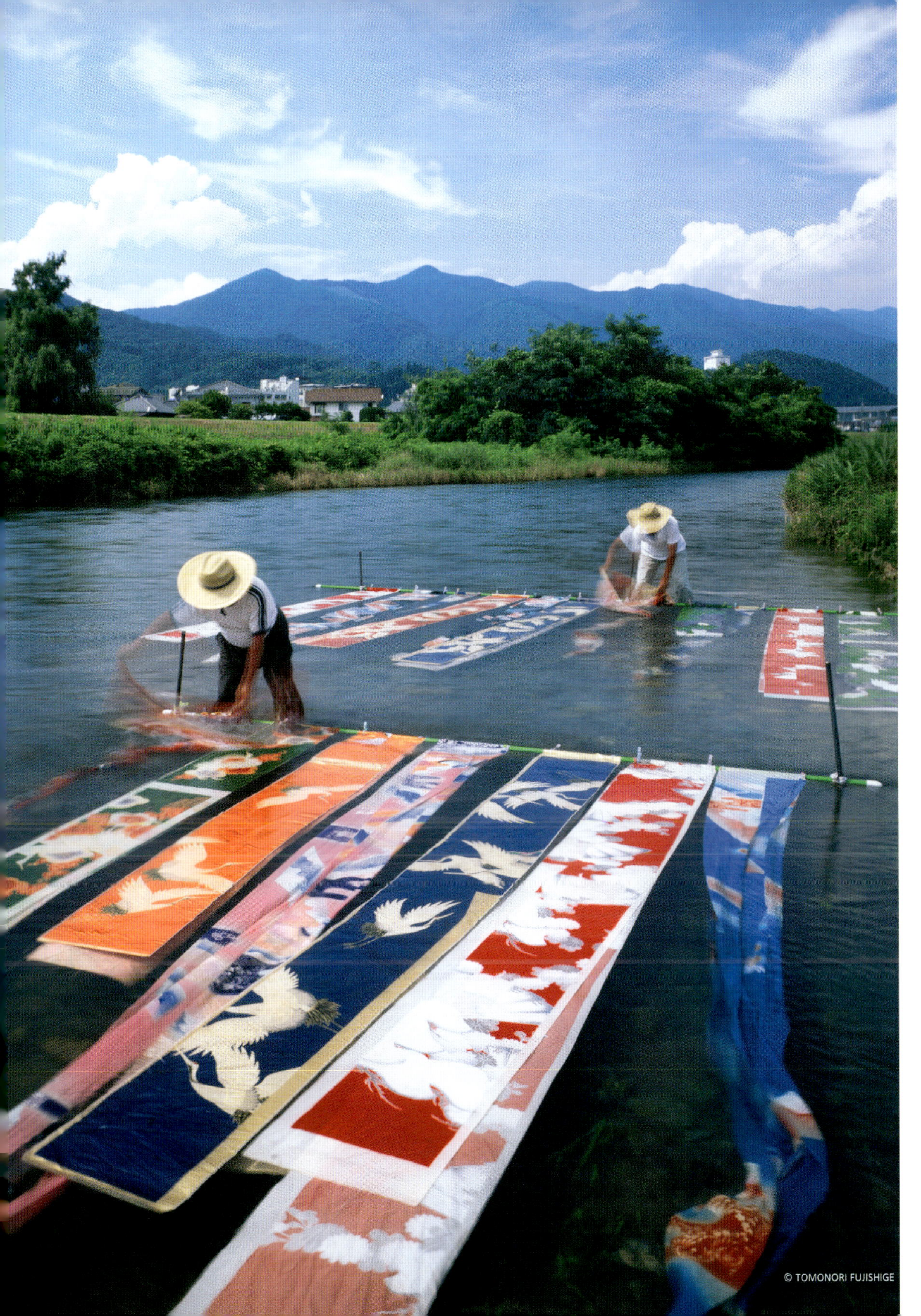

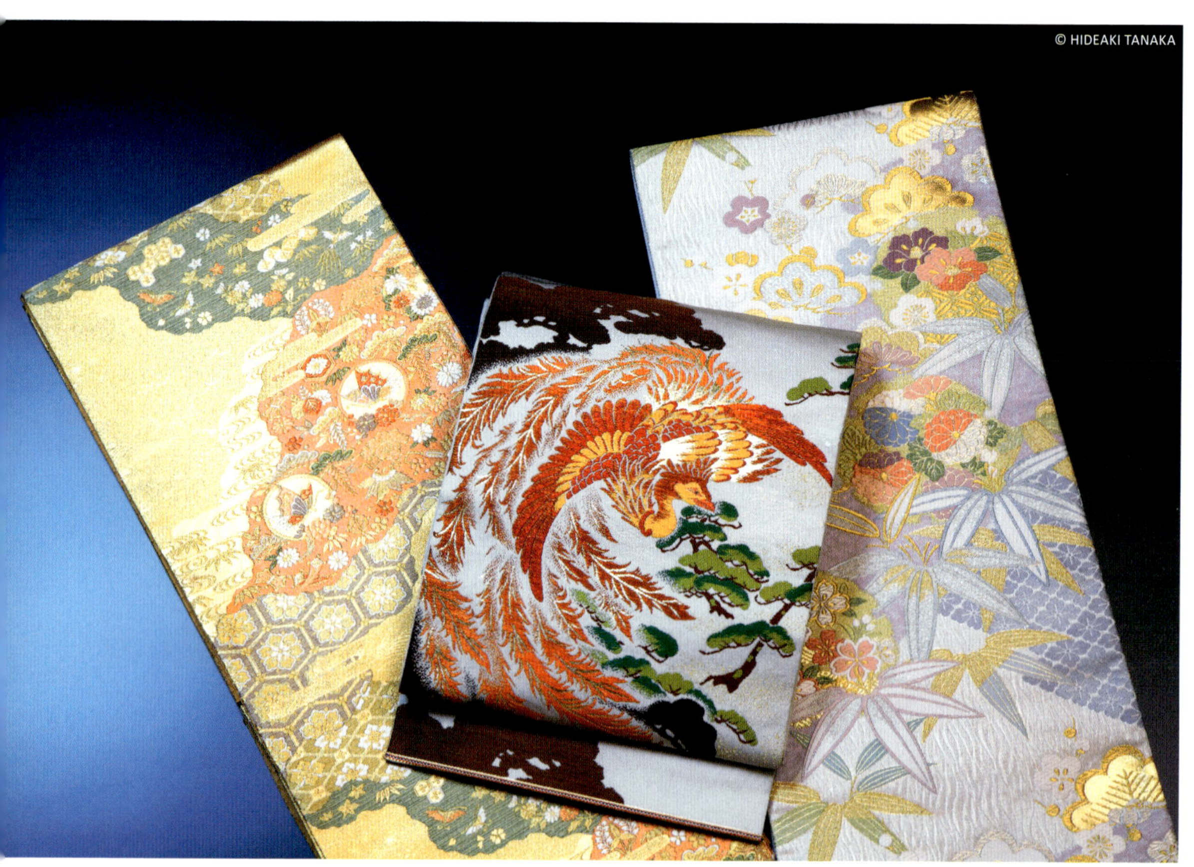

西陣織

Nishijin-ori

Nishijin is a Kyoto locality, famed for its textile industry, sprawling in the west and northwest of the Kyoto Imperial Palace. Textile produced in this area is known as *Nishijin-ori*. Slits on old wooden windows and the sound of looms echoing through narrow lanes are typical of *Nishijin*, which has been weaving exquisite textiles for more than a millennium. *Nishijin-ori* are considered luxury art works for their colored yarns (*nishiki*), gorgeous *kinran* patterns, and *donsu* (damask).

Nishijin-ori's attractions are its rich color palette made possible by yarns of numerous hues and intricately elaborate patterns.

Edo Kiriko

Edo Kiriko is said to have originated in 1834 in Edo, when glass cutters started using emery sand to cut patterns on a transparent glass surface. In the Meiji Period, cutters learned from Englishman Emanuel Hauptmann and *Edo Kiriko* techniques evolved, soon establishing Edo Kiriko's traditional methodology.
There are more than a dozen *Edo Kiriko* patterns, such as *Nanako* based on fish eggs. They all share simple but sophisticated aesthetics.

江戸切子

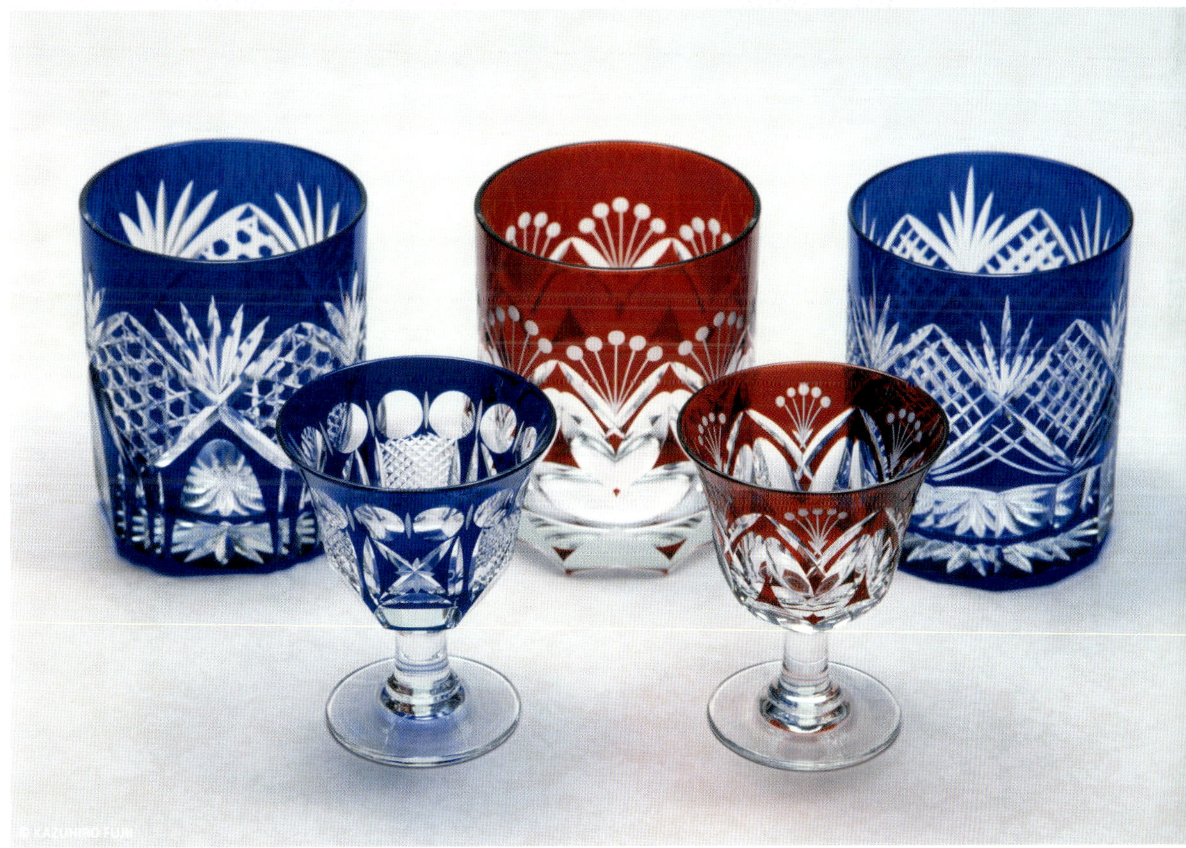

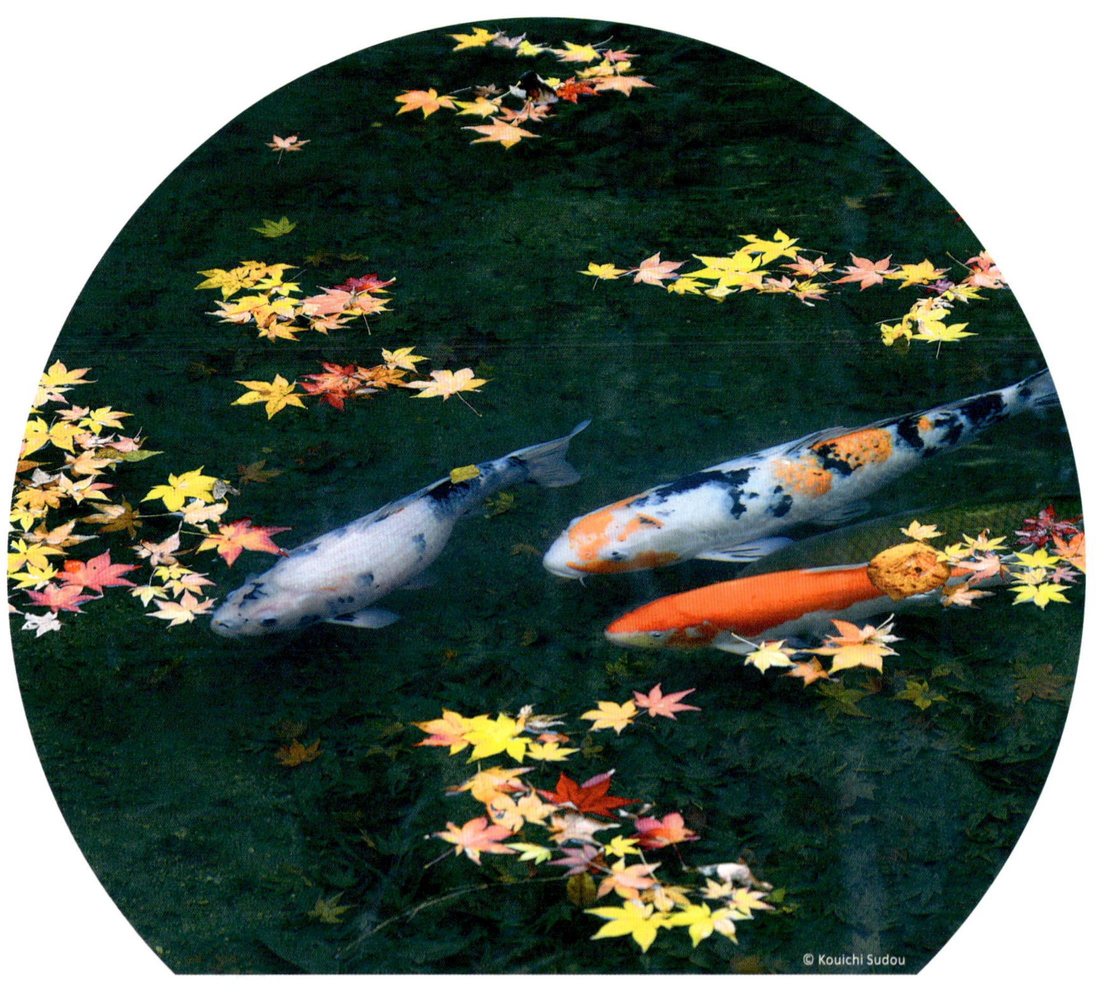
© Kouichi Sudou

錦鯉

Nishikigoi (Japanese colored carp)

Nishikigoi are breeds developed from natural carp selected for their superior hues, spot patterns and sheen. They are meant to be displayed in ponds in gardens. They are Japan's national fish.

Nishikigoi were developed originally in today's Niigata Prefecture during the Edo Period. In 1914, the *Kohaku* (red and white) breed was presented in the Tokyo Taisho Exhibition and *nishikigoi* became a popular sensation.

There are many different breeds with distinct color and spot patterns.

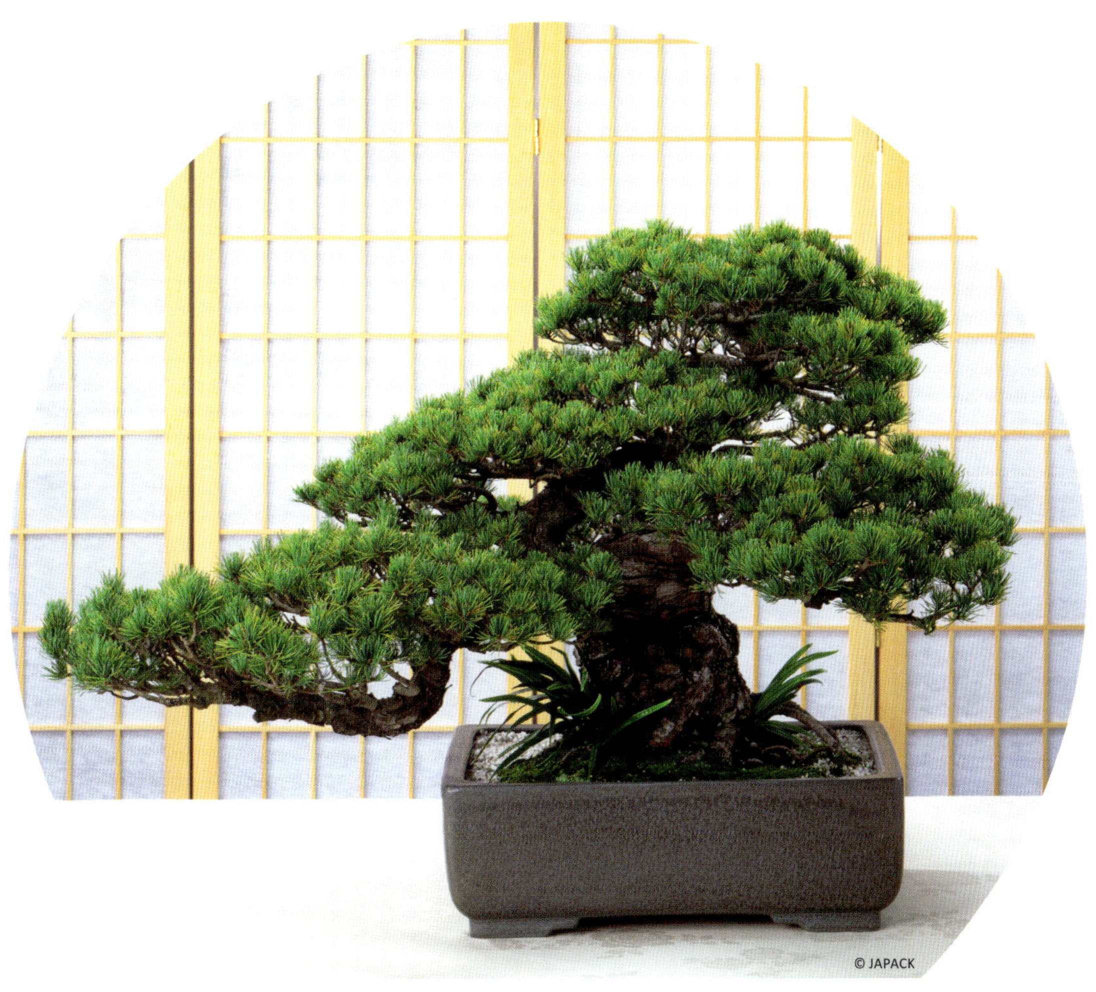
© JAPACK

盆栽

Bonsai

Bonsai is a highly artistic form of horticulture. It started in the Heian period (794-1185) and came from china's "penjing". Plant are placed in containers and viewed and enjoyed in their entirety for aesthetic appeal, including the form and style of their branches and leaves. *Bonsai* imitates natural landscapes by manipulating plants within a pot. It involves various techniques, such as pruning or trying up branches to fix them in place. *Bonsai*, which show seasonal change, is also acclaimed overseas. In the recent years, small-scale *bonsai* 20cm tall or mini-scale ones measuring 10cm are particularly popular among young Japanese people.

浮世絵

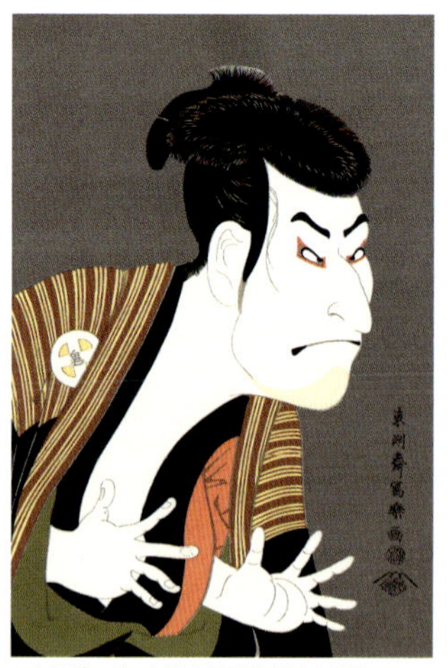

© (公財)アダチ伝統木版画技術保存財団

Ukiyo-e

Ukiyo-e was a popular fine art among people during the Edo Period (1603-1868). Because it flourished in Edo, which is now Tokyo, it is also called *Edo-e*, with "e" meaning picture. Its representative masters are *Katsushika Hokusai* and *Utagawa Hiroshige*. *Ukiyo-e* pictures are *Ukiyo*, or the floating world, represented reality and the secular world. Typical works were portraits of popular actors and beauties. *Ukiyo-e* was exported overseas after the end of the Tokugawa Shogunate and greatly influenced such impressionists as van Gogh and Monet. *Ukiyo-e* is more critically acclaimed outside Japan than at home.

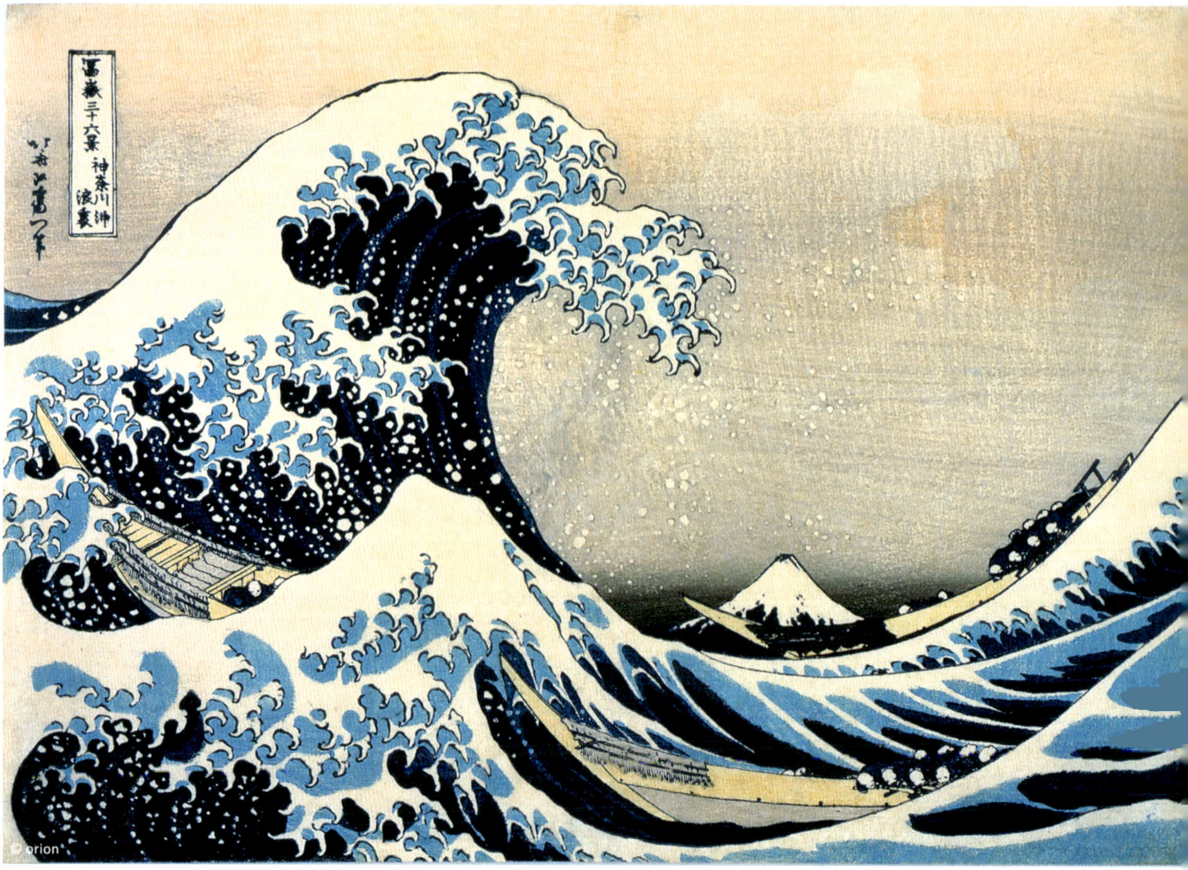

© orion

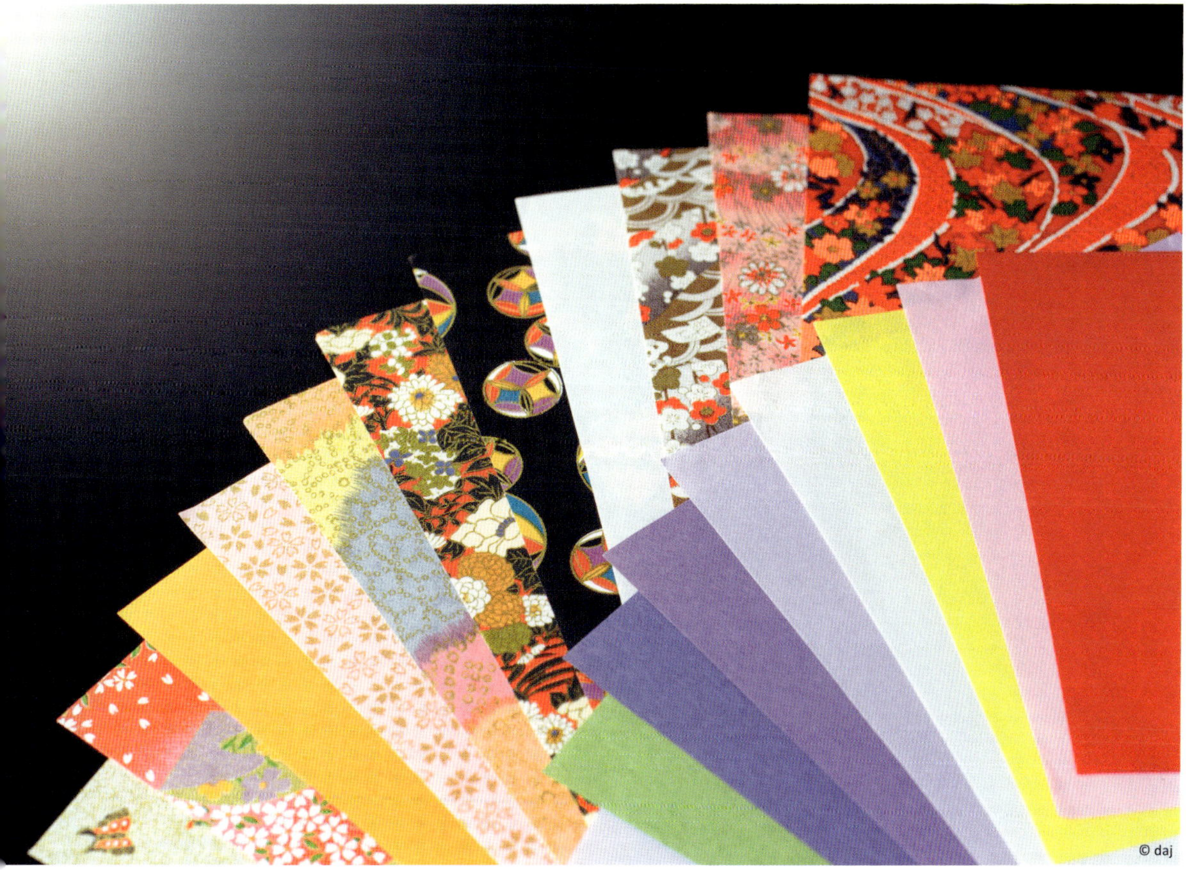

© daj

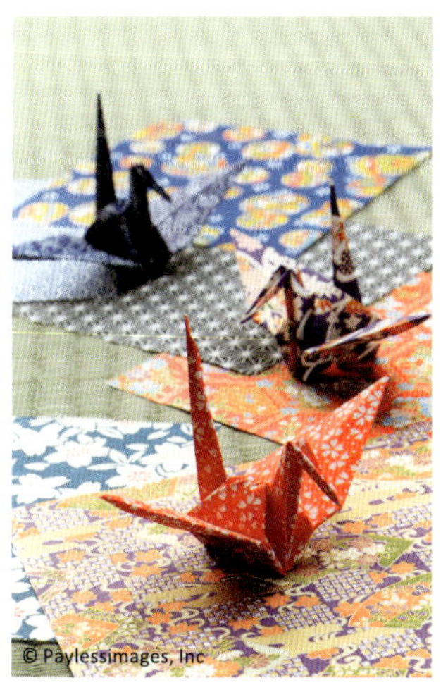

Origami

Origami is a traditional art which involves folding a single piece of paper into various shapes, such as a crane or a warrior's helmet. *Origami* is also used to mean the wrapping of a gift. While its origin is obscure, it is considered a unique Japanese art form. In origami, a square piece of paper is folded into a shape, usually without any cutting or pasting. However, some people make slits or draw on the paper. *Origam*i paper made of Japanese *washi* paper with colorful patterns of flowers and other seasonal themes is called *chiyogami*.

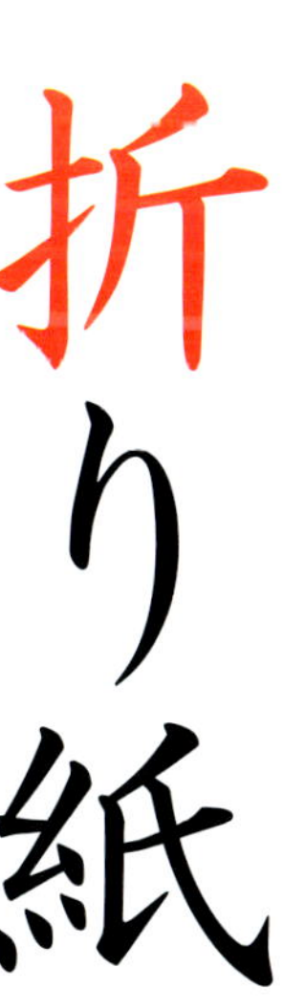

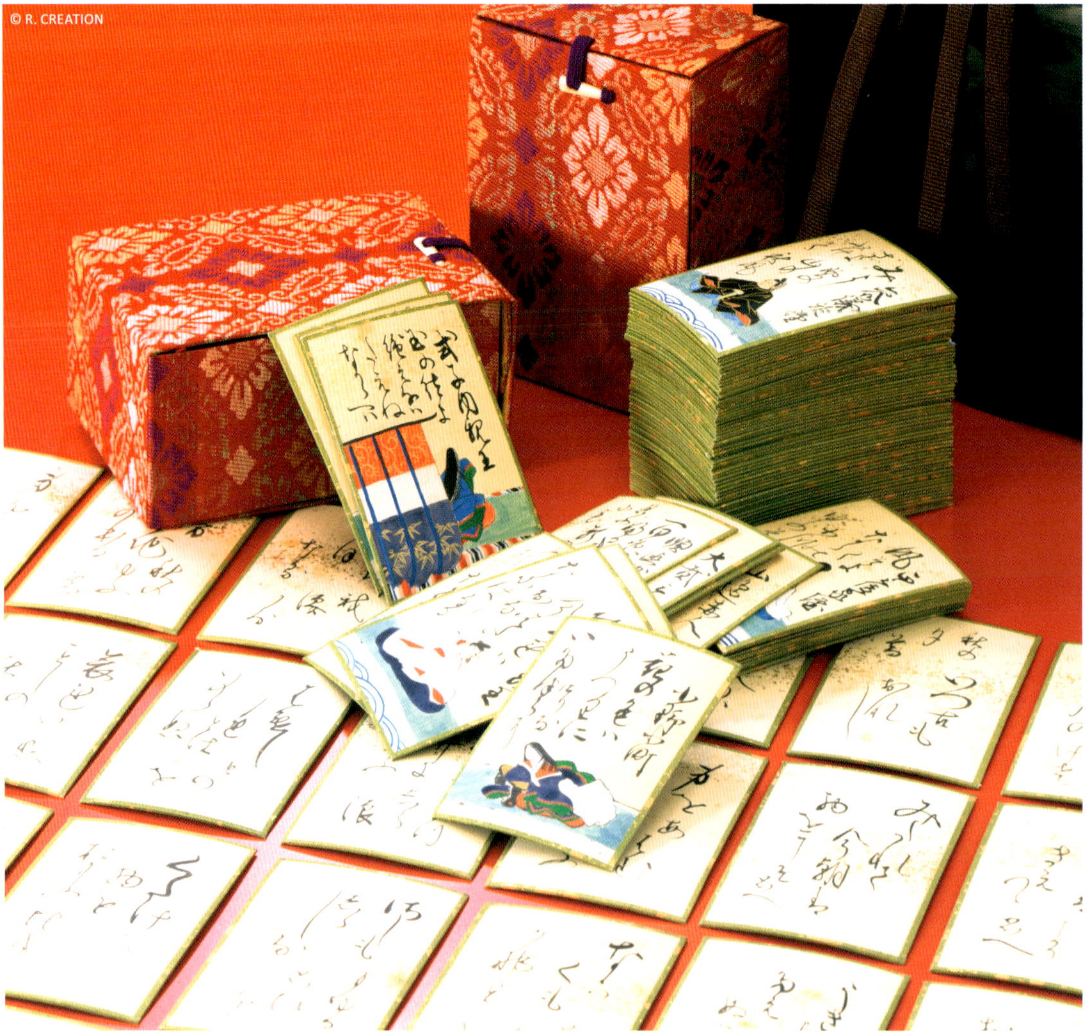

KARUTA

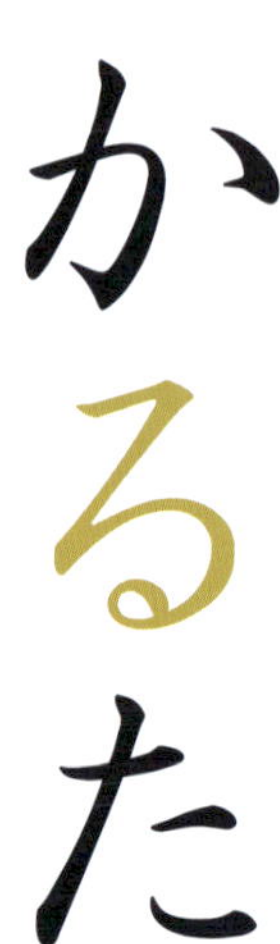

Karuta is an indoor card game played by two or more people. The classic *karuta* uses 47 hiragana characters. The reader reads from the 47 text cards and the players compete to win the corresponding picture cards. *Uta karuta* involves *waka*(a Japanese short poem), with the reader reading the opening stanza of a short poem and the players fighting for the concluding stanza. It is a traditional family game played in the New Year holidays.

There is also *karuta* that is played as a competitive sport. Sometimes called martial arts on *tatami* mats, competitive *karuta* requires determination and physical prowess. The top championships in competitive *karuta* are masters' and queens' games held at Omi Shrine. In recent years, non-Japanese players, too, are seen competing.

Washoku
(traditional Japanese cuisine)

Washoku (Japanese cuisine) is a culinary culture that reflects Japan's climate and was developed and passed down over centuries. Its basic menu consists of *ichiju sansai* (one soup, three dishes), meaning rice as the staple food, miso soup, and one main dish plus two side dishes. *Washoku* emphasizes seasonal ingredients and uses *miso*, *dashi* soup stock, and soy sauce for flavors. It is said to have a superior nutritional balance. Presentation, again emphasizing seasonal themes, and interior design of the dining space are considered integral factors in washoku reflects the Japanese spirit of *omotenashi* (welcoming visitors).

In 2013 Japanese cuisine or washoku was registered as a UNESCO Intangible Cultural Heritage, prompting renewed attention in Japan on the traditional food culture.

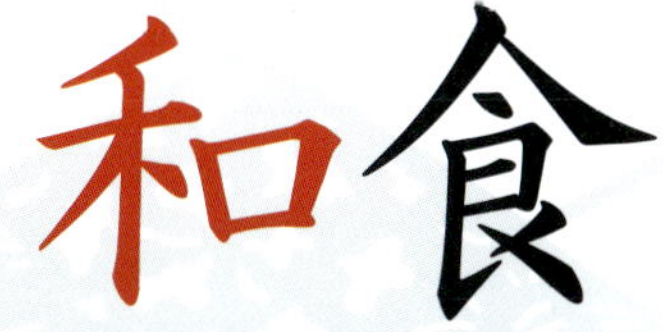

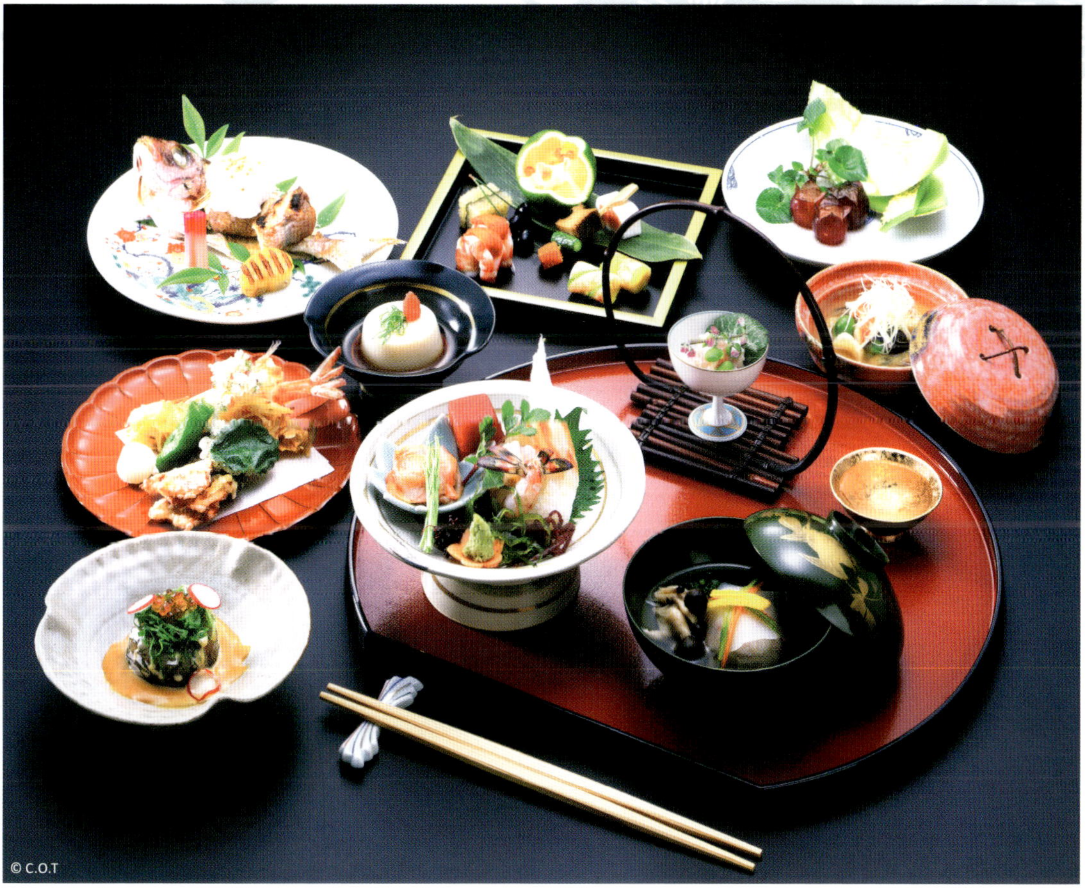

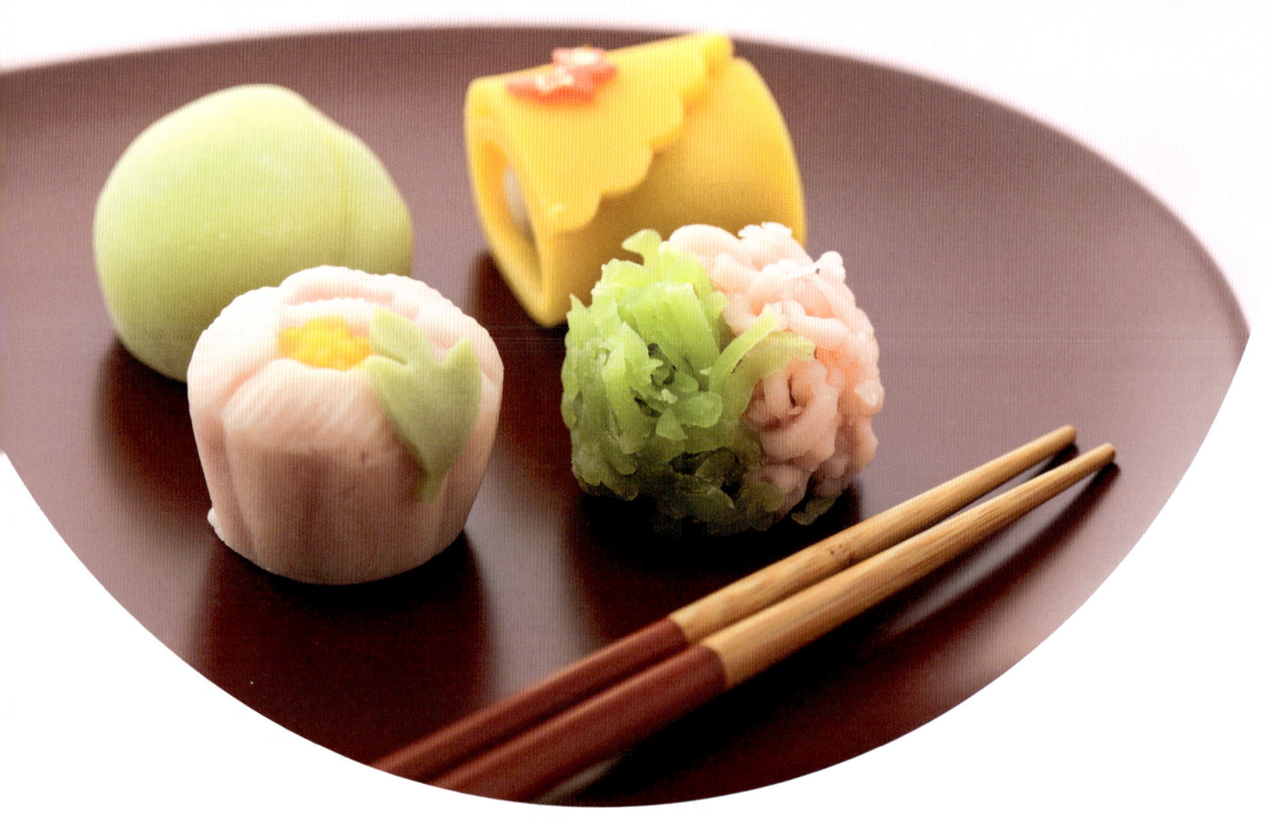

和菓子

Wagashi
(Japanese-style confectionery)

Wagashi are traditional Japanese confectionaries. Most derive from Chinese recipes imported prior to the Edo Period, which were subsequently refined by Japanese innovations. Main ingredients are such grains as rice and *kudzuko* (powdered arrowroot), beans like *azuki*, sugar and fruits. *Wagashi* rarely uses oil. *Wagashi* is roughly grouped into three: *namagashi* (raw) like steamed *manju* and *nerikiri*; *han-namagashi* (semi-raw) like *monaka*; and *higashi* (dried) like *rakugan*. *Wagashi*, which developed along with the art of the Japanese tea ceremony, are known for their beauty as well as their tastes. Particularly in *jo-namagashi* such as *nerikiri*, *wagashi* chefs are required superior skills to sculpt seasonal themes.

日本酒

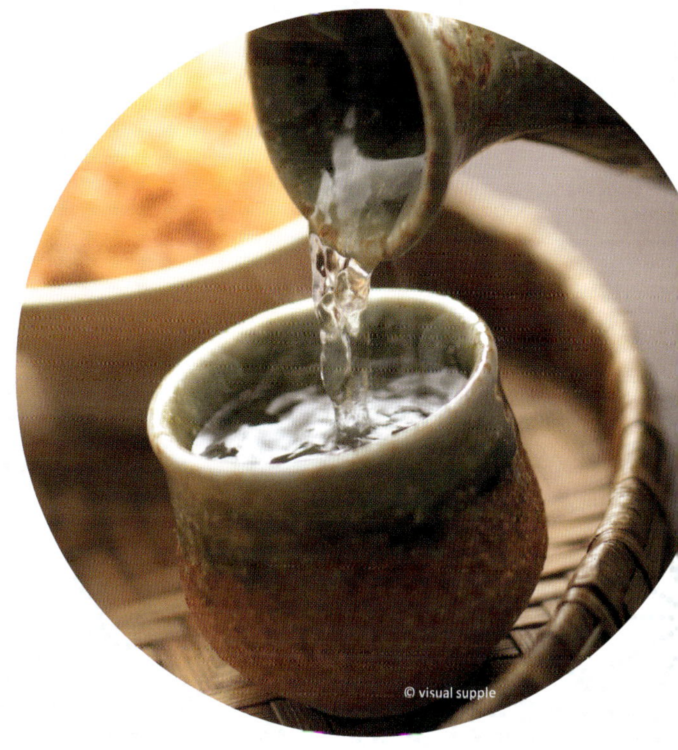

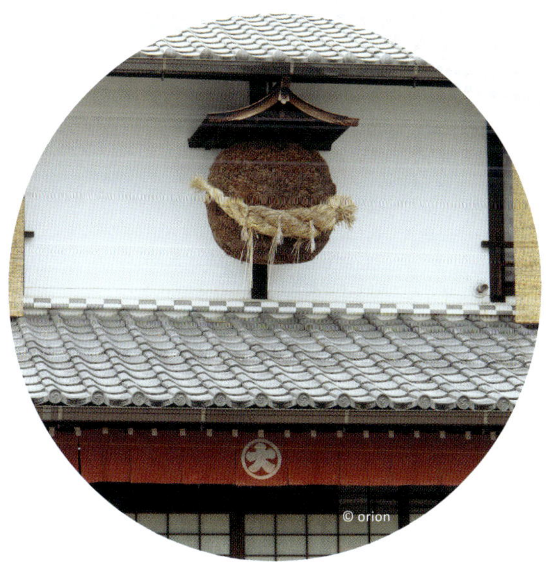

Sake (Rice wine)

Sake is fermented from a mixture from rice, *koji* (malted rice), and water and is then filtered. It is also called *seishu*. Because *sake* is 80% water, good *sake* is generally found where water quality is superior.

Sake is categorized into *honjozo*, *junmaishu*, and *ginjoshu*, depending on the degree of rice milling (amount of surface ground off brown rice grains) and the materials used. It is further categorized minutely according to the way it is produced and other factors. *Sake* may be served over a wide range of temperatures, from 5 to 55 degrees Celsius, and enjoyed chilled or warm. In this sense, it is unique among alcoholic beverages. For Japanese, *sake* is a familiar taste and a standard fixture in joyous occasions.

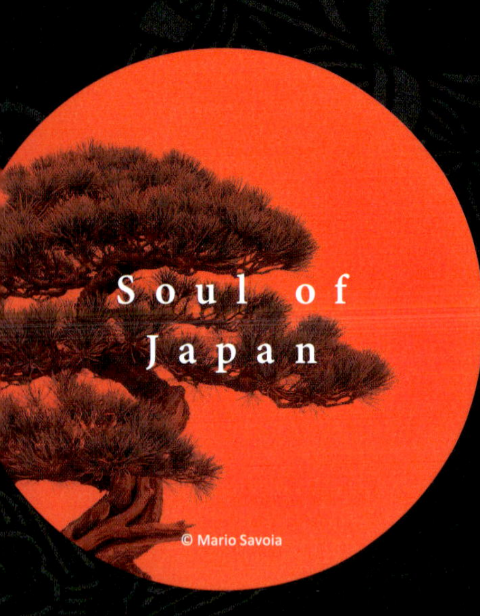

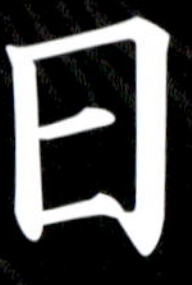
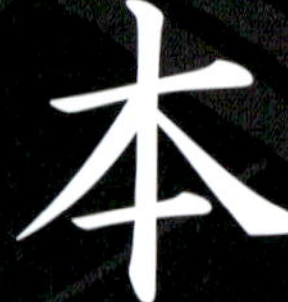
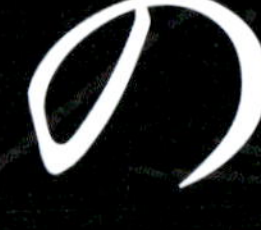
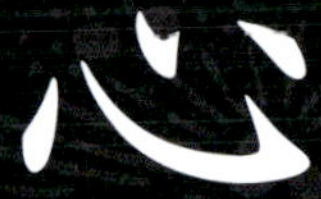

日本の心

The unique sensibility of the Japanese people A beautiful significance in words

The Japanese language contains many words with subtle nuances that cannot be translated into other languages. Such words embody feelings and thoughts that cannot readily be understood by people from other countries, while at the same time those words refer to things that the people of Japan take very much as a matter of course, and do not pay any special attention to, which makes them even more difficult to explain.

Someone who is able to understand the various shades of meaning in a single Japanese word might be able to sense the quality of Japaneseness that is so important to the Japanese people.

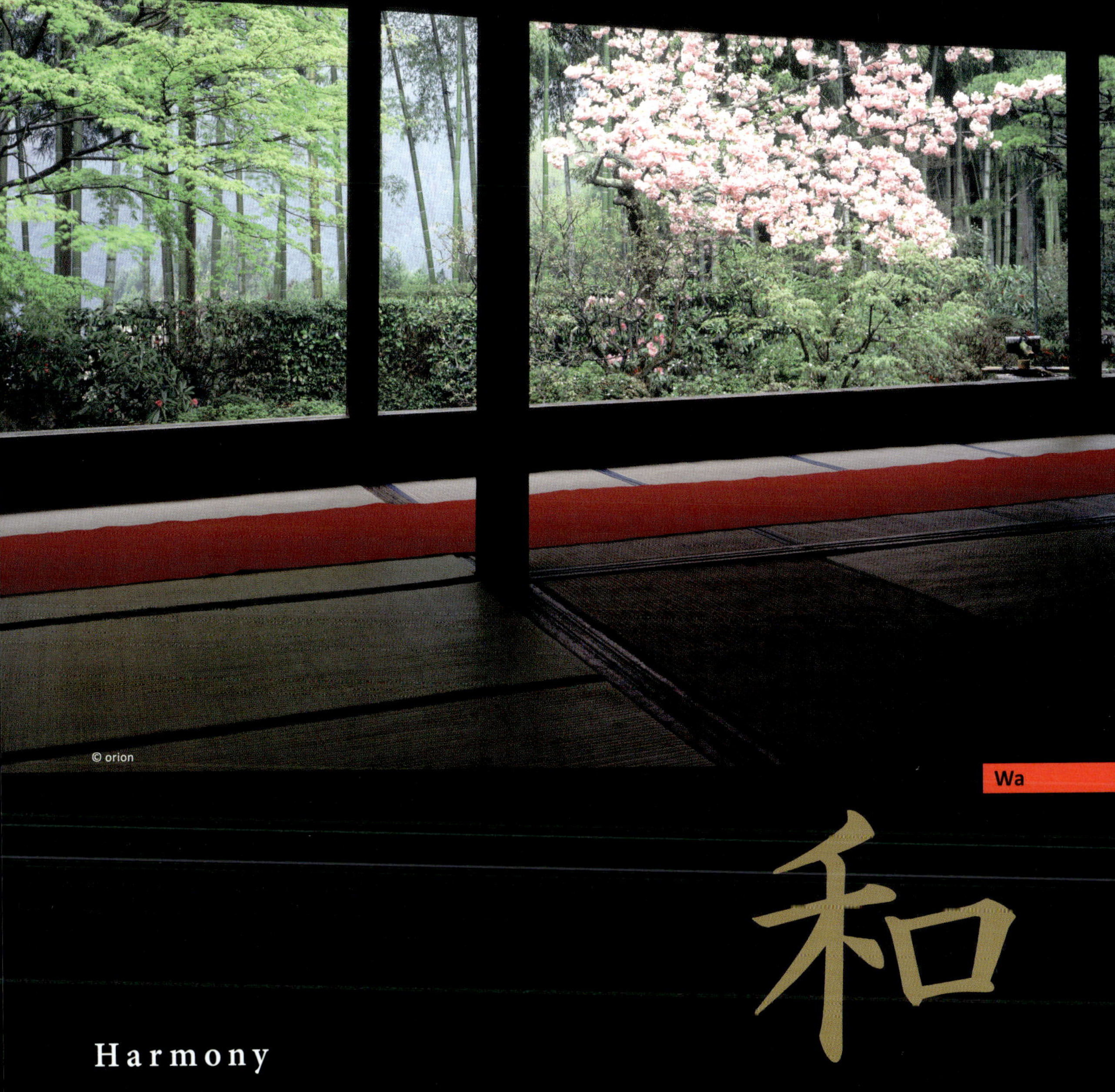
© orion

Wa

和

Harmony

The character for *wa* is used to identify something as Japanese, for example the 'wa' in 'washoku', or Japanese food. It also connotes harmonious relationships with mutual respect or an equilibrium consisting of diverse elements. The word thus sums up the Japanese character.

This word appears at the beginning of Japan's first legal code from some 1,400 years ago, *Junana-jo-kenpo* (the Constitution of Seventeen Articles, which reads), *Harmony is of utmost value*, meaning that it is most important that people should get along with each other harmoniously. Such acceptance of plurality and peaceful coexistence has forged Japan's unique cultural outlook.

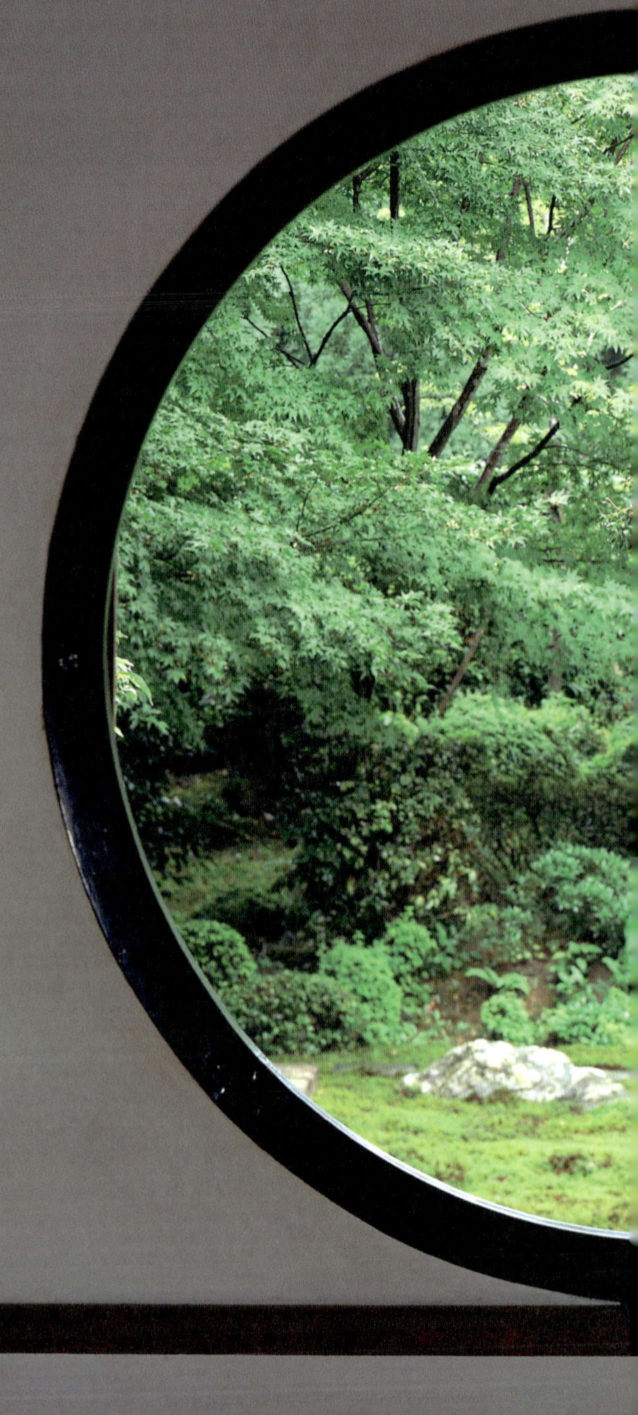

Enlightenment

Generally, *satori* means an understanding of essential things. As a Buddhist term, however, it carries a more profound meaning. In this sense, it means freedom from all attachments, including life and death, and acquisition of eternal truths. A person who has gained *satori* is able to live the way nature has intended.

Dogen, a renowned priest in 13th century Japan who founded a *Zen* school called *Sotoshu*, wrote in a poem, *Flowers in spring, cuckoos in summer, the moon in autumn / The cold snow in winter, all feel pleasing.* A person who has attained *satori* is thus moved by seasonal changes and pleased even by snow and cold.

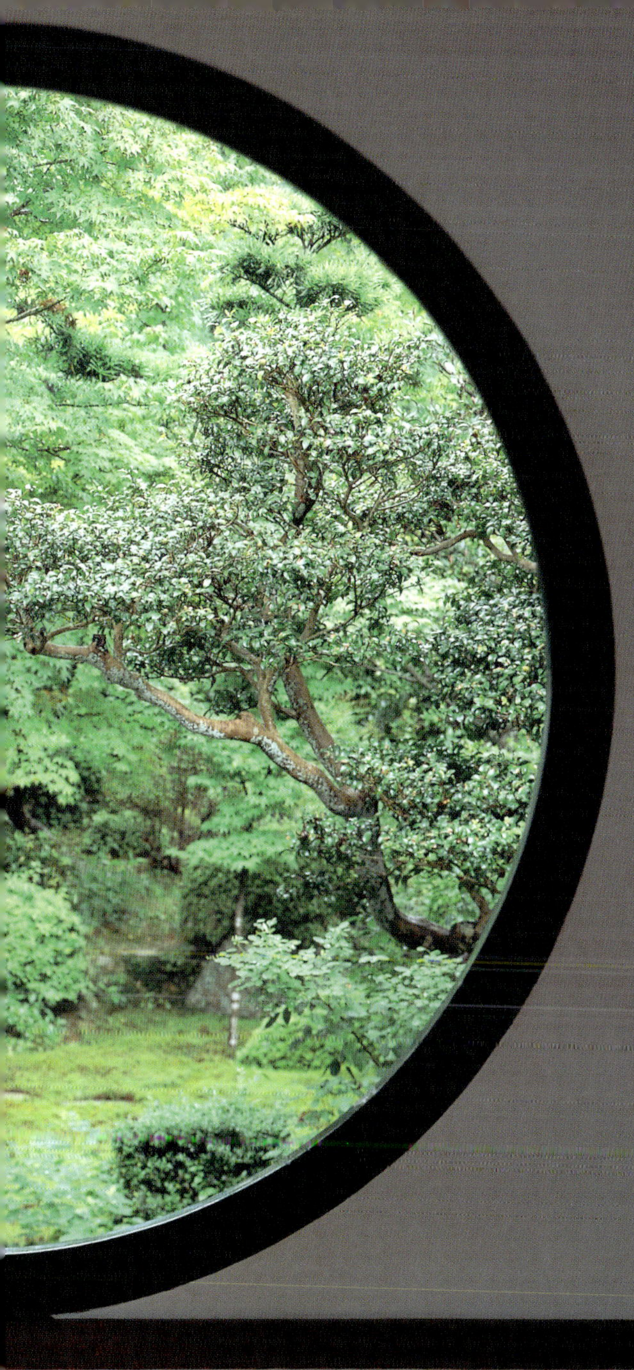

悟り

Satori

Wabi-Sabi

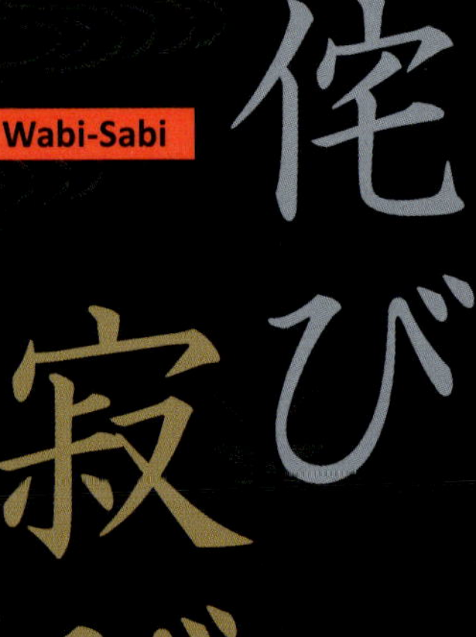

austere refinement and quiet simplicity

Wabi-sabi is often invoked to explain Japanese aesthetics. It connotes simplicity and quietude, or a withered state devoid of color.

Originally, *wabi* meant disappointment, despair or frustration at the lack of control, and *sabi*, the loss of vitality or original state through aging over the years.

Traditionally, Japanese frown upon fame or personal greed and find themselves attracted qualities that may appear negative but actually evoke humbleness and a down-to-earth quality.

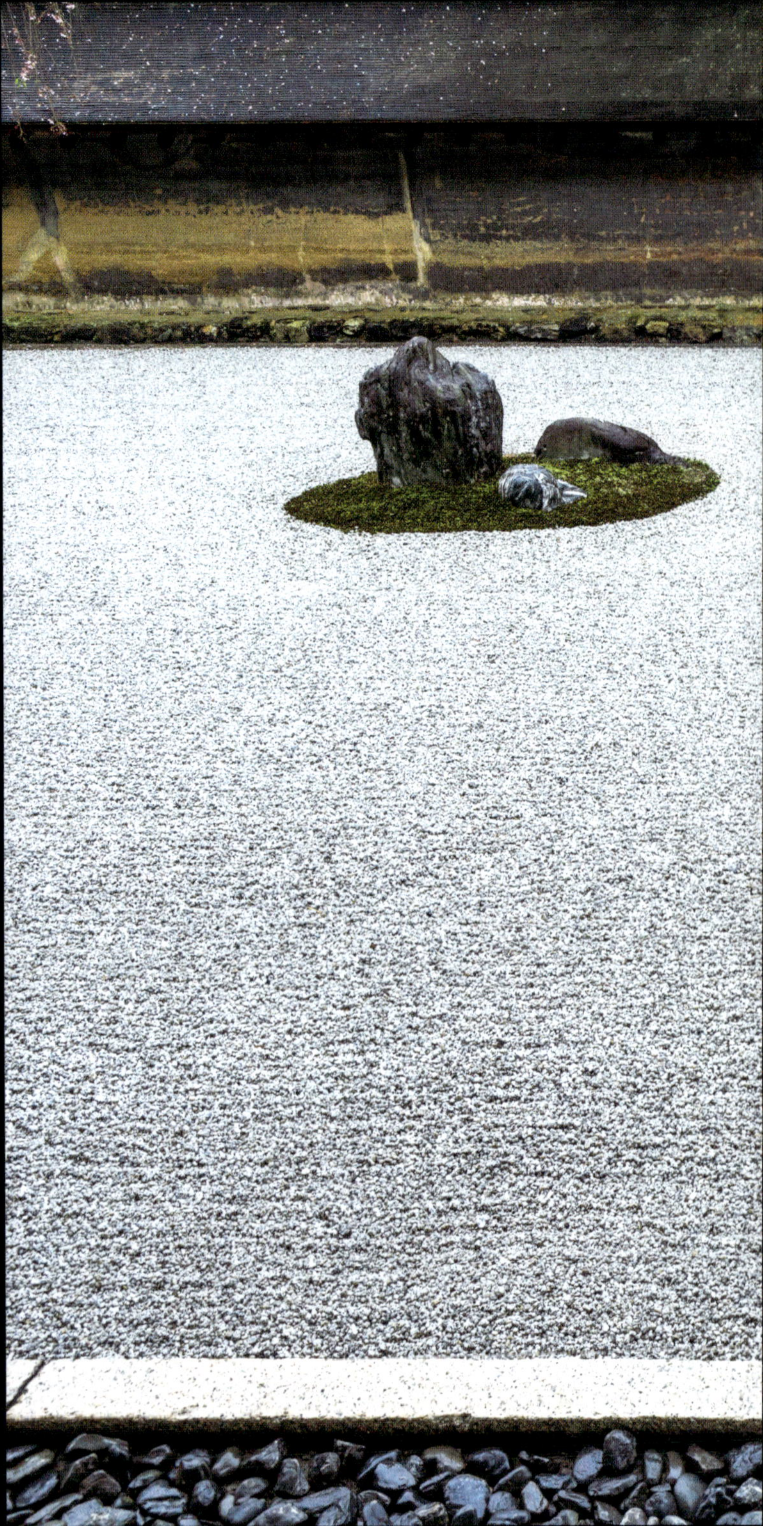

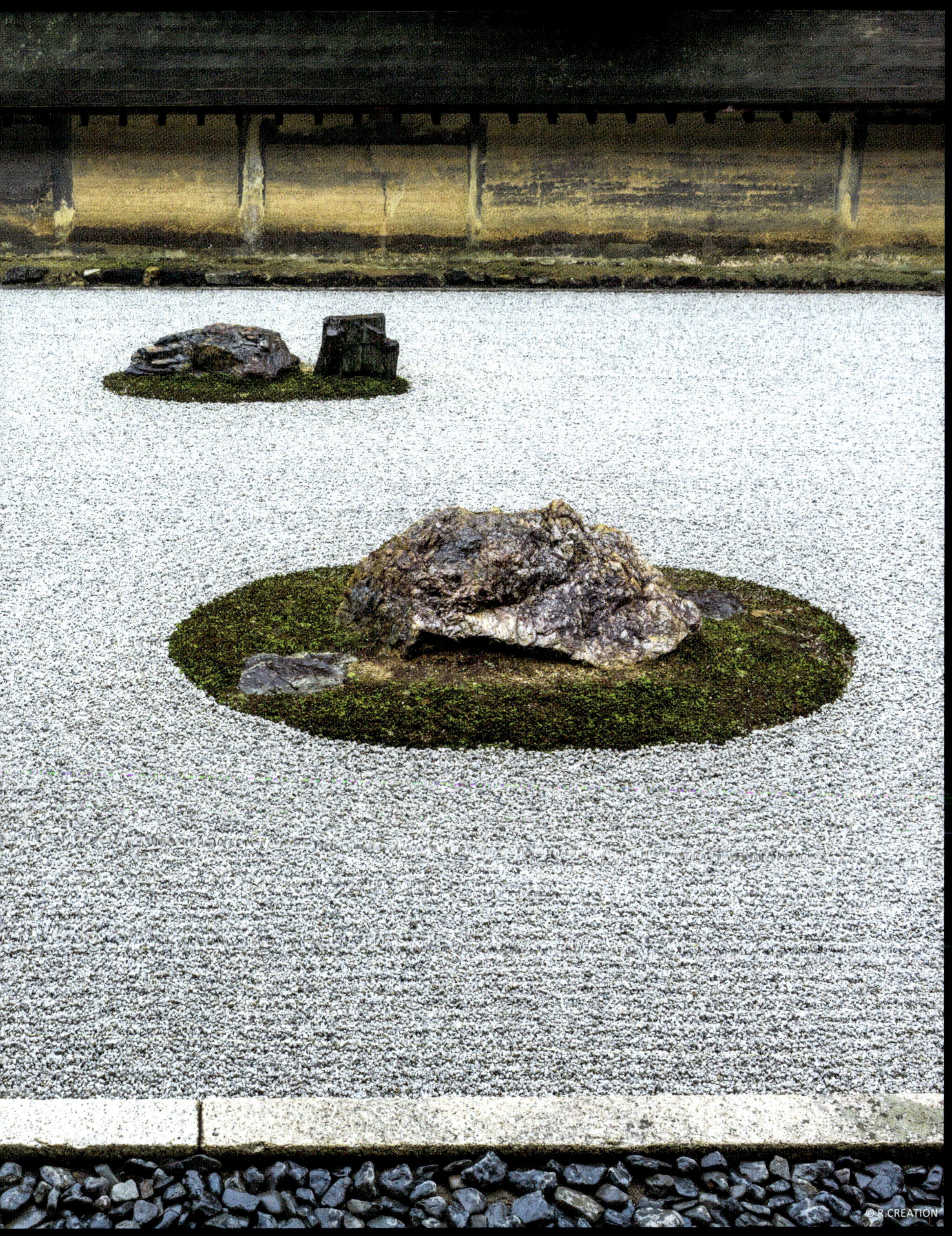
© R.CREATION

Buddhism

Japan is generally thought of as a Buddhist country. When Buddhism arrived via the Korean Peninsula in the middle of the 6th century, it transformed into something uniquely Japanese and different from the original form of the religion. This was because, prior to the advent of Buddhism, the population used to believe in *yaorozu-no-kami* (eight million gods and deities in Japan). Japanese, as they received Buddhism, understood their native deities as Buddha's tentative manifestations and equated them with Buddha. Accordingly, for Japanese, Shinto shrines for the mythic deities and Buddhist temples are equally beneficent.

Hotoke

仏

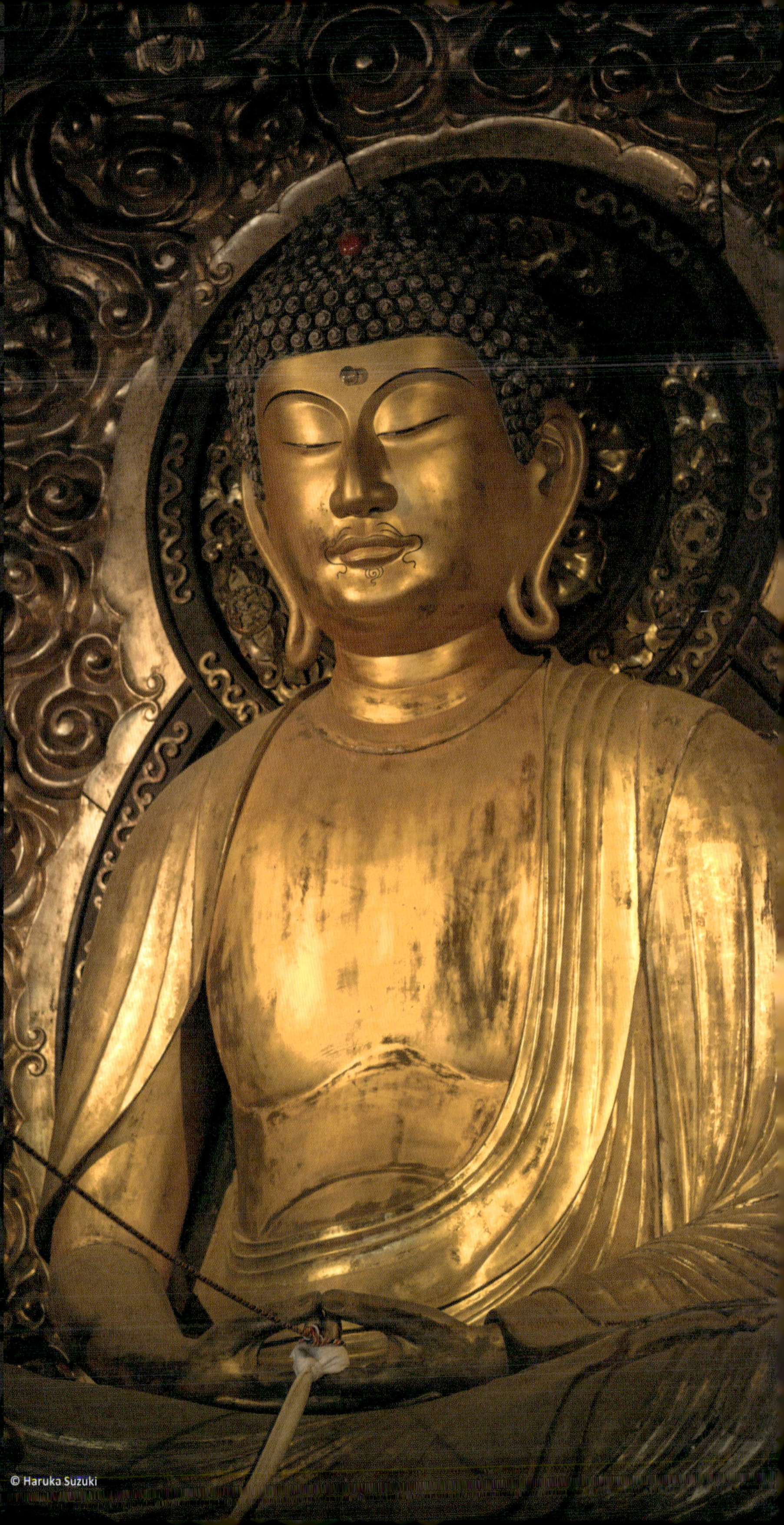

© Haruka Suzuki

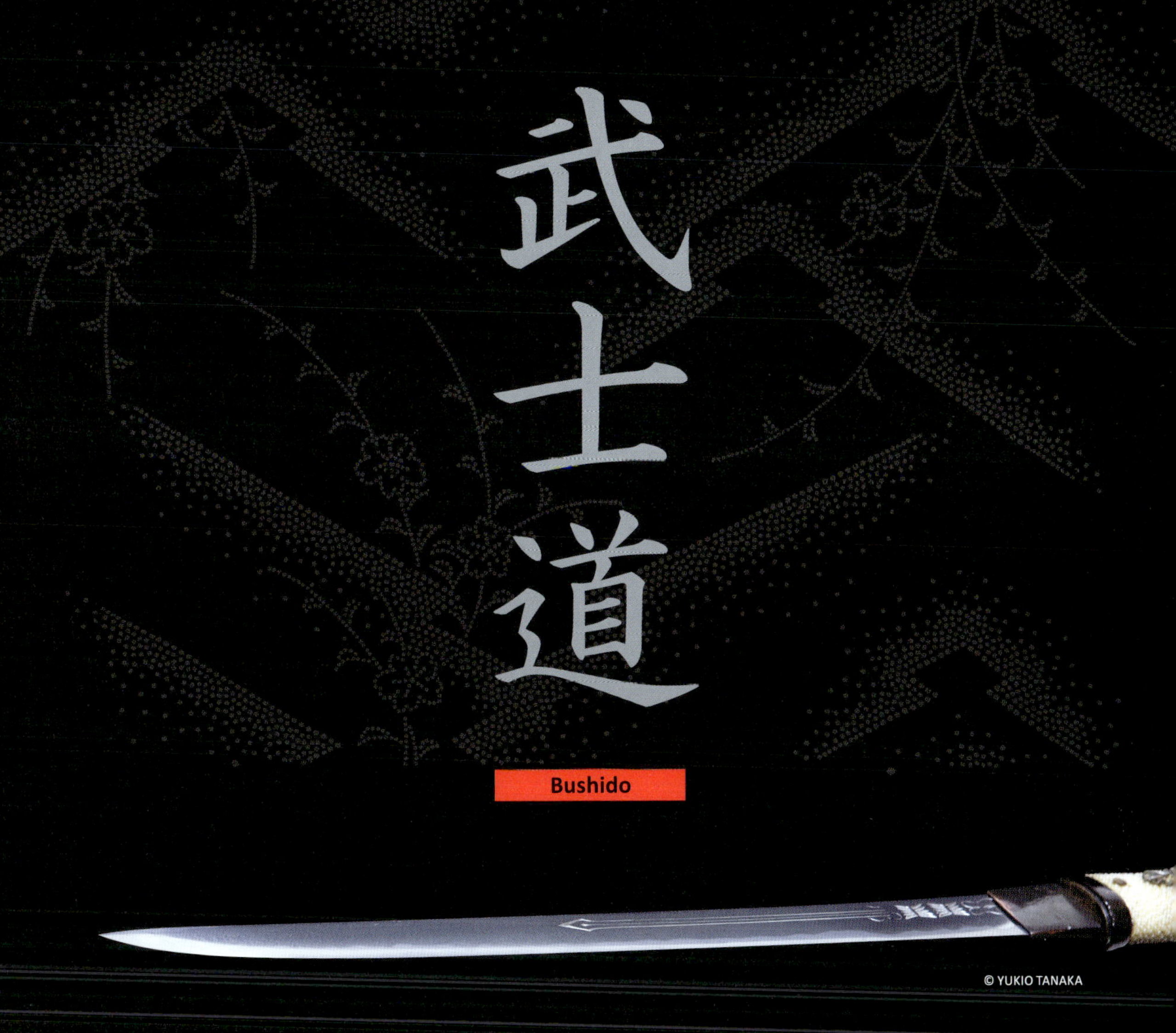

© YUKIO TANAKA

The spirit of the Samurai

Bushido is the philosophy underlying the Way of the *Samurai* and upholds such virtues as rectitude, courage, benevolence, respect, honesty, honor, and loyalty. It resembles but is distinct of the Western code of chivalry, since the knight swears loyalty to the Christian God, whereas the *samurai* is bound by loyalty to his lord.

In this modern age, we no longer have samurai warriors and *Bushido* is rarely spoken of outside martial arts, but many of Japan's ethical concepts and social ideals have originated from *Bushido*.

礼儀・礼節

Courtesy and decorum

The starting point of Japan's courtesy and etiquette lies in the way that they respect relationships between person and person, and deeply value a sense of respect. Quite apart of course from daily life, a sense of courtesy and decorum towards other people is an essential part of the fabric of Japanese traditions such as *budo* (martial arts) and *sado* (tea ceremony). Most famous among the behavior of the reputedly courteous Japanese is the custom of *ojigi* (bowing). The practice of bowing is an everyday action for Japanese people, but it appears to be something that leaves a deep impression on foreigners.

Reigi / Reisetu

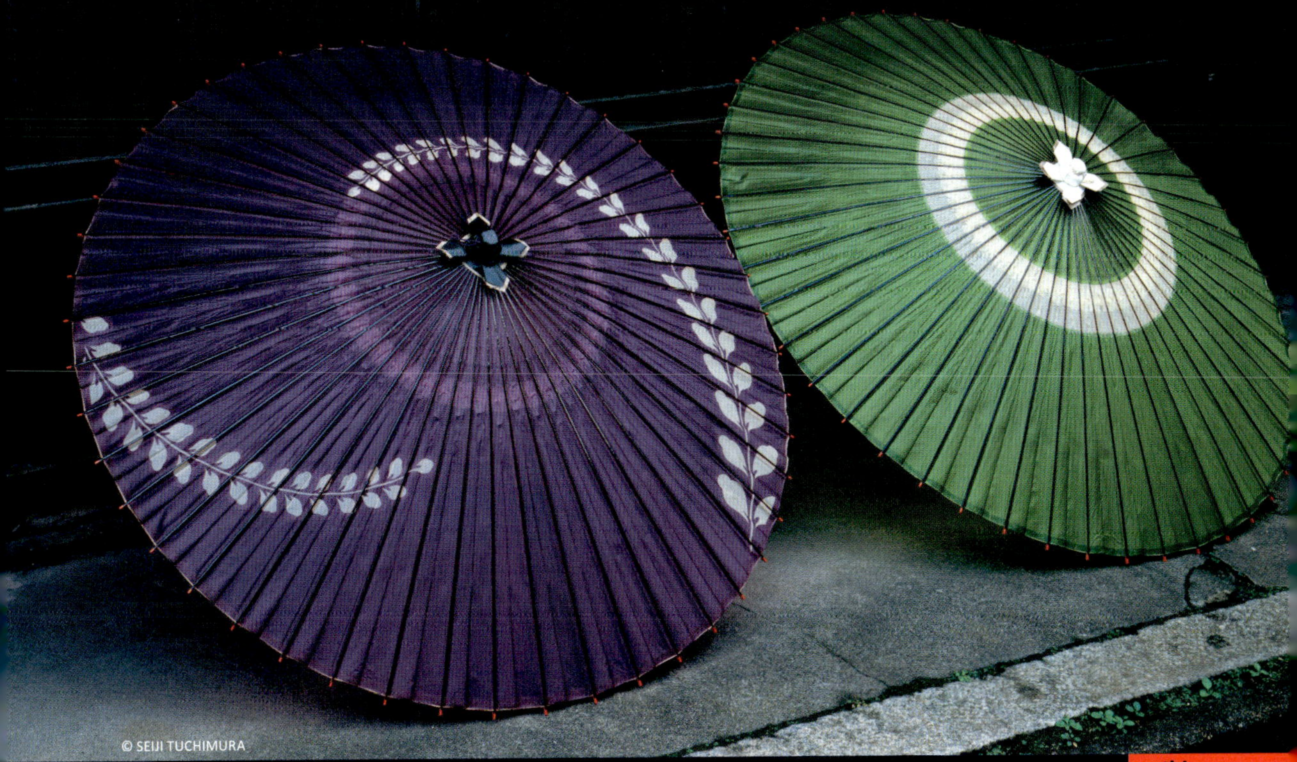

© SEIJI TUCHIMURA

Iki

Chicness

The set of values that was fashionable among the courtesans of the Edo Period, and spread to their clientele, was *iki* (chicness); the term described the cool attitude of men who were well aware of the ways and games of men and women, but who didn't show off their worldliness. Men who were not overly attached to the opposite sex and whose appearance was refined were lionized as being *iki*, and the term eventually became used to describe people who did not exude a sense of attachment and displayed a stylishly fun-loving temperament. At the other end of the spectrum, those who were unsophisticated in their speech and interests were called *yabo* (the uncouth).

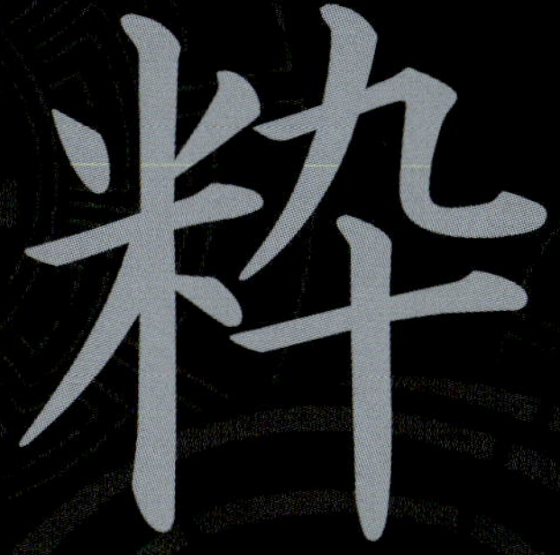

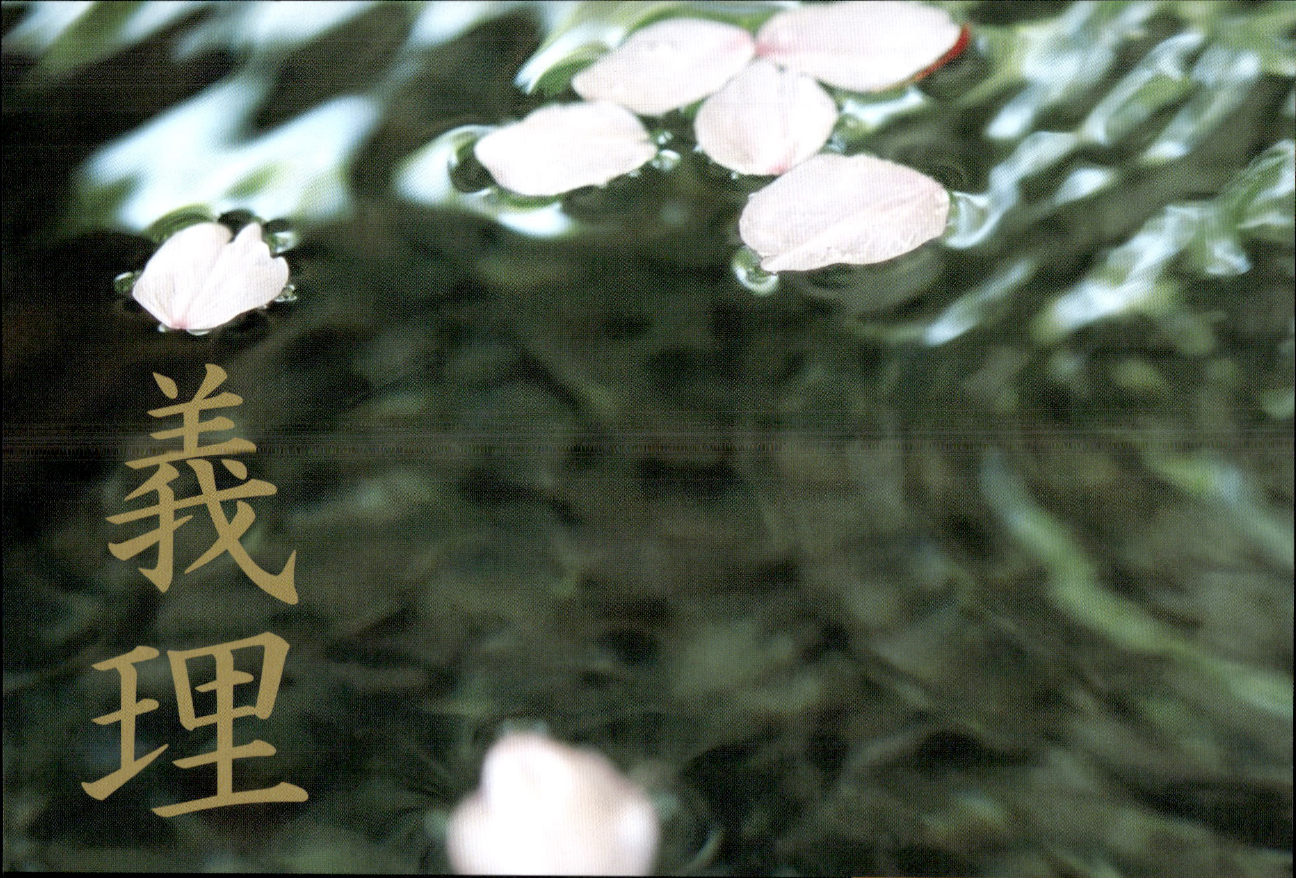

義理

Ninjo

Sentiment

Ninjo (human warmth) is a phrase indicating the feeling of consideration towards others, and expresses the typically human feelings that are inherent in people. It is one of the sentiments that the Japanese place an emphasis upon. It is a feeling that arises when people come into contact with each other and as such is therefore not unique to Japanese people, but the Japanese are constantly aware in every aspect of their daily lives of obligation and human warmth.

In the traditional Japanese entertainment of *rakugo* (comical stories told by a single raconteur) there is a genre called *ninjo* stories. One of these stories tells of a man who, when he hears that another man he meets has had his money stolen and is trying to end his life, gives him the money that he has made from selling his own daughter.

© orion

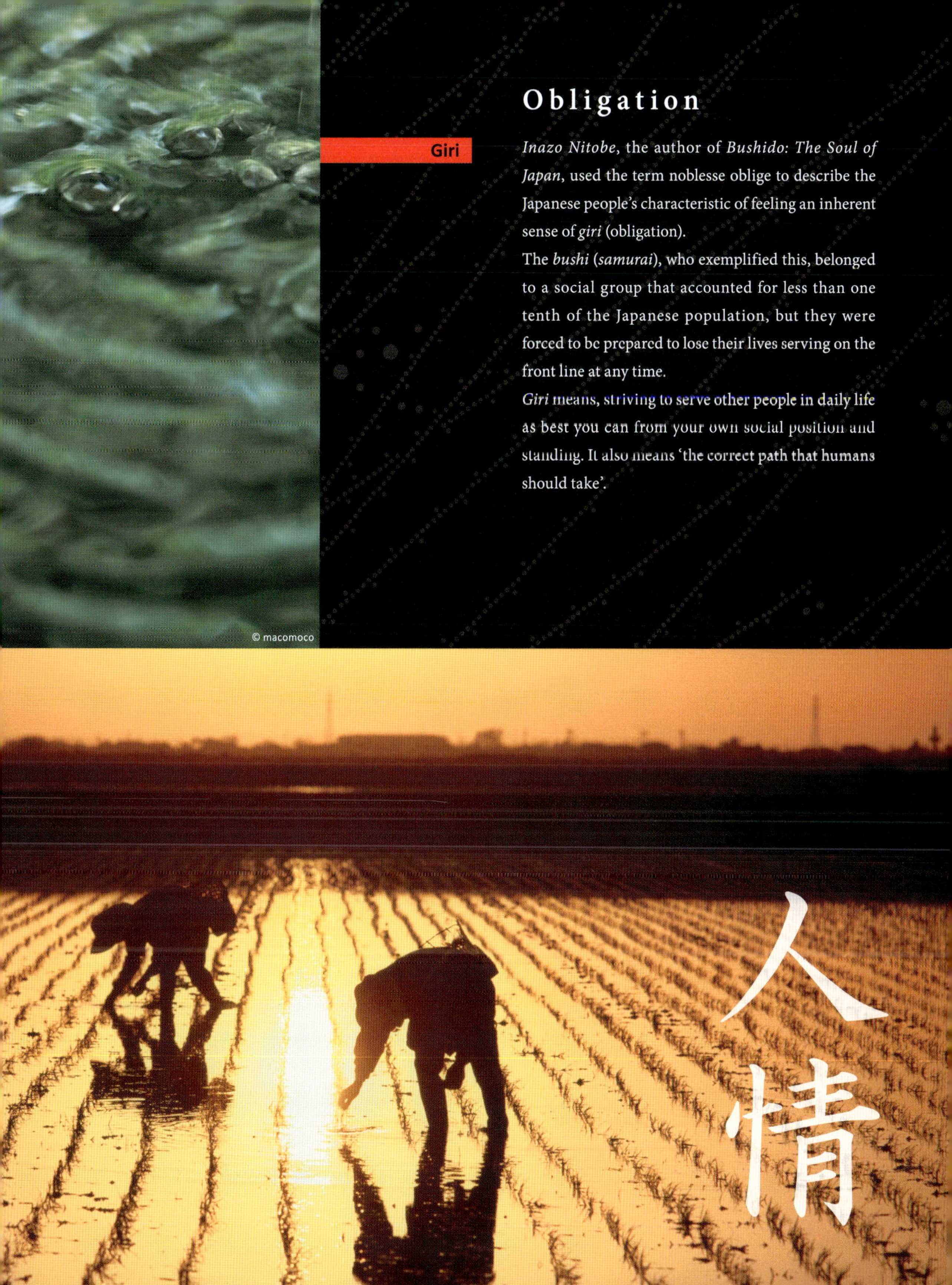

Obligation

Giri

Inazo Nitobe, the author of *Bushido: The Soul of Japan*, used the term noblesse oblige to describe the Japanese people's characteristic of feeling an inherent sense of *giri* (obligation).

The *bushi* (*samurai*), who exemplified this, belonged to a social group that accounted for less than one tenth of the Japanese population, but they were forced to be prepared to lose their lives serving on the front line at any time.

Giri means, striving to serve other people in daily life as best you can from your own social position and standing. It also means 'the correct path that humans should take'.

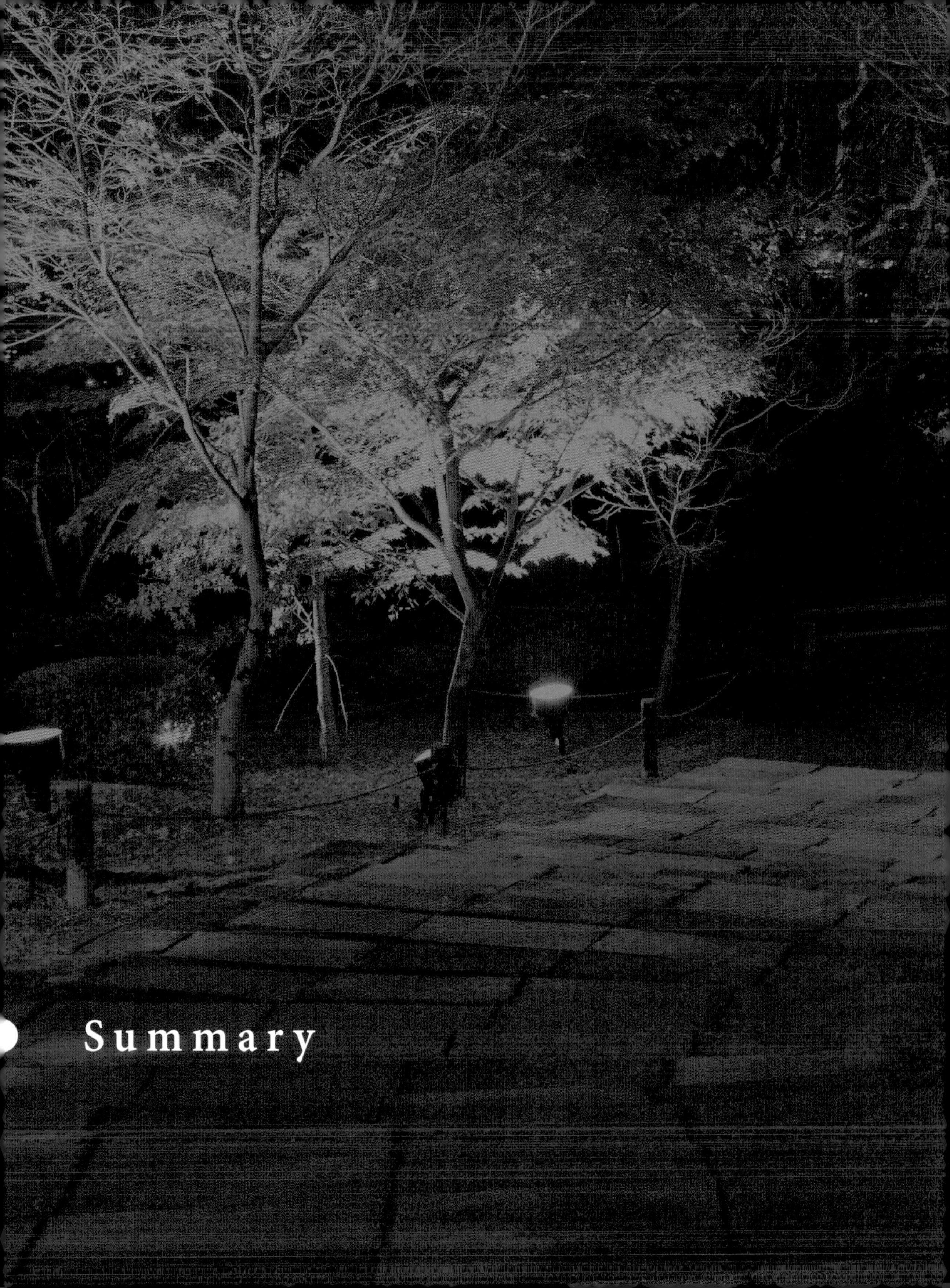

Summary

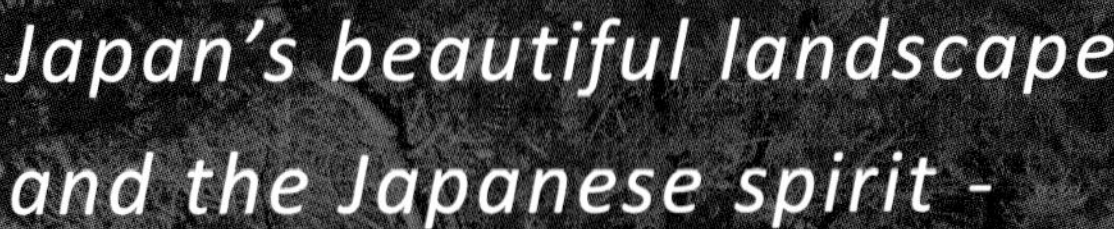

Japan's beautiful landscape and the Japanese spirit -

A Japan that displays different aspects of its beauty throughout the four seasons.

An explosion of pink-tinged cherry blossoms in the spring, blue skies and lush greenery in the summer, fiery autumn leaves in the fall, and a quiet, silvery snowscape in the winter...

It can be amazing how such a small island nation as Japan can have such breathtaking beauty and majestic structures.

The people who live in this beautiful nation – the Japanese – are well-known by foreigners for their politeness, kindness, punctuality, and for being inscrutable as to what they are thinking.

What makes the Japanese like that?

Of course, a tell-all explanation does not easily come forth.

However, a small glimpse can be gained into the kokoro (heart and mind) highly valued by the Japanese people through traditional Japanese arts such as sado (the Way of Tea), kado (flower arrangement) and budo (martial arts).

Nothing would please us more if this photography collection prompts even the slightest desire in you to want to visit Japan and to want to experience Japanese culture.

編者 ◎ 日本の美研究会
美しい風景や伝統文化など、日本の魅力を
海外に伝えるために活動しているグループ。

編集協力 ◎ 長谷部祐子（株式会社アーク・コミュニケーションズ）
写真 ◎ amanaimages　清水亮一（アーク・フォト・ワークス）（P.52-53）
写真提供 ◎ 中尊寺（P.31）　鹿苑寺（P.74）　慈照寺（P.75）　平等院（P.84）　株式会社ベネッセホールディングス（P.107）
装幀・本文デザイン ◎ 岡村大輔
執筆 ◎ 清野博　堀雅俊　大滝慶子　長谷部祐子
翻訳 ◎ Bilingual Group Ltd.
校正 ◎ Sophie Knight
DTP ◎ 明昌堂
編集担当 ◎ 齋藤友里（ナツメ出版企画株式会社）

JAPAN –Beautiful Landscapes ● Japan's Soul–
美しい日本 〜四季の美景と和のこころ〜

2014年10月30日　初版発行
2016年5月10日　第3刷発行
編　者　日本の美研究会　　Japan's Beautiful landscapes study group, 2014
発行者　田村正隆
発行所　株式会社ナツメ社
東京都千代田区神田神保町1-52　ナツメ社ビル1F（〒101-0051）
電話　03(3291)1257（代表）　FAX　03(3291)5761
振替　00130-1-58661
制　作　ナツメ出版企画株式会社
東京都千代田区神田神保町1-52　ナツメ社ビル3F（〒101-0051）
電話　03(3295)3921（代表）
印刷所　図書印刷株式会社

ISBN978-4-8163-5731-2　　Printed in Japan

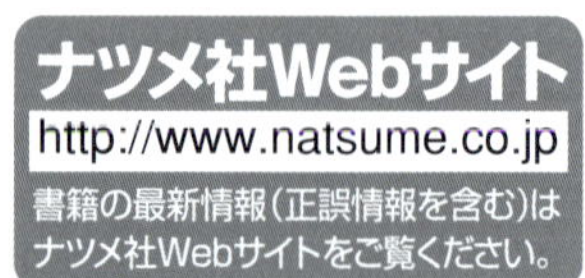